APOCALYPSE THEN

APOCALYPSE THEN

Prophecy and the Making of the Modern World

Arthur H. Williamson

Praeger Series on the Early Modern World
Raymond B. Waddington, Series Editor

Westport, Connecticut
London

Library of Congress Cataloging-in-Publication Data

Williamson, Arthur H.
  Apocalypse then : prophecy and the making of the modern world / Arthur
H. Williamson.
      p. cm. — (Praeger series on the early modern world, ISSN 1940-1523)
  Includes bibliographical references and index.
  ISBN-13: 978-0-275-98508-0 (alk. paper)
  1. End of the world. 2. Prophecies. 3. History—Prophecies. I. Title.
  BL503.W55 2008
  202'.3—dc22   2007044131

British Library Cataloguing in Publication Data is available.

Library of Congress Catalog Card Number: 2007044131
ISBN-13: 978-0-275-98508-0
ISSN: 1940-1523

First published in 2008

Praeger Publishers, 88 Post Road West, Westport, CT 06881
An imprint of Greenwood Publishing Group, Inc.
www.praeger.com

Printed in the United States of America

The paper used in this book complies with the
Permanent Paper Standard issued by the National
Information Standards Organization (Z39.48–1984).

10 9 8 7 6 5 4 3 2 1

To Liz and Vanessa,
and Paulina

CONTENTS

LIST OF
ILLUSTRATIONS

ACKNOWLEDGMENTS

This project has been assisted hugely and at moments decisively by a number of scholars, librarians, art specialists, and friends both here and abroad. Notable among them are Bernard McGinn, Ray Waddington, David Scott, Steve Buss, Allan Macinnes, Tom Lisanti, Christopher Wm. Linnane, Jenny Ramkalawon, Gary Kurutz, Joanna Snelling, Cathy Cherbosque, Sydney Moritz, Margarida Ramos, Jennifer Belt, Ken Krabbenhoft, Jack Smith, Donis Guilloton, and Duncan Campbell. The professionalism and solidarity of Heather Staines and Randy Baldini have proven heartening, insightful, and invaluable.

An unabridged version of this book—fully annotated and more expansively illustrated—is available for consultation at the California State University Library in Sacramento.

CHAPTER 1

ENCOUNTERING THE BEAST

Today few people accept the notion that the world is about to end through a prophesied supernatural act. Despite Tim LaHaye, Hal Lindsey, and even former president Ronald Reagan, the Judeo-Christian apocalypse, at least literally understood, is normally discounted as a creed for cranks.

And yet this has not always been the case. Between 1500 and 1800 many of Europe's and America's most creative minds (Catholic, Protestant, Orthodox, Jewish) believed that they were living in the latter days of the world and the culmination of human history. The apocalypse underwrote the Reformation in the sixteenth century, the British Revolution in the seventeenth century, and the American Revolution in the eighteenth century. Moreover, it proved a crucial catalyst in the emergence of liberal values, political democracy, and even modern science. There is nothing in the least liberal, democratic, or scientific about the apocalypse, but none of these developments would have occurred without it. The apocalypse could fuel philo-Semitism no less than anti-Semitism, toleration no less than religious persecution. It could inspire the program for modern science; it could activate the enemies of science. Even so, whether liberal or otherwise, apocalyptic ideas and expectations during the early modern period exercised the European social imagination quite literally from Moscow to Mexico City, from Scotland to the Yemen. They would shape the world in profound and enduring ways.

The early modern period was not the first time that the apocalypse penetrated the Western intellect and redefined it. That had happened once before during the Intertestamental years (*c.* 150 BCE–200 CE). In antiquity apocalyptic expectations permanently transformed the religious landscape and, eventually, the political landscape as well. Between 1500 and 1800 they created modernity. During that second great encounter with the apocalypse, such expectations played a central role in the emergence of secular culture—arguably the signal achievement of the postmedieval West. There exists no small irony here. A deeply religious set of ideas proved instrumental in enabling people to see their world through prisms other than those provided by religion. Secular categories, initially, arose less from the rejection of religion than through the dynamics and tensions within religion itself.

Accordingly, this study examines the prophetic, the apocalyptic, the eschatological within larger political and cultural patterns. Considered from this vantage point, these strains of thought will turn out to be far less "weird" and still less dangerous or "explosive" than commonly portrayed—and far closer to what we are as modern people. Before anything else, the apocalypse and its attendant complex of ideas comprise mechanisms for imagining time. That is, they created ways for making change meaningful and enabled people to make sense of a transforming world. The questions confronting us in this study concern less the advent of the Messiah or of Christ than the advent of time itself. When and why did a prophetic future become persuasive? How did history and concepts of change become articulate and acquire importance, providing intelligibility that other ways of thinking no longer seemed to offer?

Only within the last 300 years has it become possible for people to develop a coherent explanation of the world around them outside of a religious framework. Throughout the past, to dismiss religion— individuals have occasionally done so in all ages—was to dismiss coherence and despair cognition. Further, for most of its history European culture had visualized time and change as marginal, irrational, and emblematic of man's fallen state. The burden of the Western message has been atemporal and indeed anti-temporal. The apocalypse alone allowed people to conceptualize qualitative change. It alone has enabled people to say that today may be one way, but tomorrow will be both completely different and altogether explicable. The role of the apocalypse has almost always proven fecund rather than destructive, and never more so than in early modern Europe.

The study that follows concerns itself less with formal theology than with the broader intellectual questions that exercised contemporaries. The eschatological "systems" of such great exegetes of the apocalypse as Joachim of Fiore, Joseph Mede, and Johann Heinrich Alsted will not receive close analysis, but their cultural context will be of major interest. The Reformation will illustrate this approach. The millennium, the thousand-year reign of righteousness and justice at the "end of days," re-emerged within mainstream thinking during the course of the sixteenth and seventeenth centuries. Protestants in this period used the idea of the millennium to develop a coherent and, for the first time, a linear vision of the European past. The new past made events in the present meaningful and urgent on a cosmic level. But it also did more. At the same time, people during these centuries were hugely preoccupied with the future, anticipating the culmination of the human experience that lay, they believed, in the immediate offing. Increasingly, it seemed that there might be a moment of "latter-day glory" before the end of days and the conclusion of time. That expectation, shaped and reshaped by the course of political events and the prospects for the future, eventually grew into a full future millennium that complemented, refocused, but never supplanted the millennial interpretation of the past. What made the idea plausible, and then compelling, will concern us rather more than a full review of the varied readings it was given. Major intellectual fissures rather than narrow doctrinal disputes comprise our subject. Confrontations about time and its meanings shape the discussion. Because the apocalypse takes place literally within the saeculum, it has served, overwhelmingly, to validate the physical world. Further, because the apocalypse described the story of a community, the community of the redeemed, it inherently spoke about common interest and developed concepts of public culture.

This sort of inquiry will not fit comfortably within the well-wrought categories of nineteenth- and twentieth-century theologians. Modern theology all too often has been projected onto the past, and has long promoted anachronism and drastic misconceptions as a result. The quest for denominational pedigree and doctrinal legitimacy has removed the complexities of previous generations and impoverished our understanding of the dynamics that drove earlier ages. The categories of pre- and postmillennialism provide an example. On the face of it these terms are quite clear and carry drastically conflicting implications: Christ will inaugurate the millennium (pre-), or Christ will turn up at the end of that prophesied period and draw it to a close (post-). Theoretically the latter should point to activism, the former to quietist "ready waiting." In practice, they have consistently proven highly unstable frameworks of distinctly limited usefulness. Even in recent centuries people often can elide from one to the other without significantly altering their outlook or expectations. Further, they comprise nineteenth-century terminology that earlier generations would have found puzzling or tangential to their concerns. Resort to such anachronism seriously distorts the world before 1800.

No less does apocalyptic thinking defy easy functional analyses. The apocalypse does not "stand" for something other than itself, but comprises an intellectual structure of great importance that needs to be understood within its own terms rather than made over into something more familiar. It simply will not do to see modern political movements as warmed-over Judeo-Christian messianism.[1] Nor can apocalyptic preoccupations be dismissed as a piece of residual belief tucked away in the corner of otherwise significant minds. Isaac Newton's apocalyptic was by no means incidental to his most serious reflection. Similar distortion results from treating the apocalypse as a self-contained stream of thought, largely disconnected from the cultural environment of which it formed an integral part. Our understanding of this axial period will find itself ill-served by neat religious formulations, reassuring reduction, or casual dismissal.

The central concern of this study is to understand the foundations of modernity. Why is the apocalypse—so alien to us today—yet so pivotal to the creation of our culture and to what we are? Only by seeing the apocalypse's central—and often highly creative—role historically within Western civilization can we meaningfully assess its significance to the current world. Only by grasping "Apocalypse Then" can we ever truly comprehend "Apocalypse Now."

ANCIENT JUDAISM: FROM PROPHECY TO ESCHATOLOGY

The civilizations of both the ancient Mediterranean and the ancient Near East were awash with prophecy. We will recall Thucydides' wry comments about prophetic sayings that forecast the coming of the plague to Athens at the outset of the Peloponnesian War. The pagan sibyls produced volumes of prophecies that played a vital role in the cultural life of antique Rome. Virgil became Rome's most famous prophet with his vision of the city's imperial destiny. But the Near East simply seethed with mythologies, stories, and visions that found their way into inspired statements about the future. Overwhelming, prophecy came out of Asia, as Westerners long recognized.

Among the peoples of the Near East none absorbed, developed, and identified with these lines of thought more thoroughly than did the ancient Jews. The idea of the promise, arguably, proved more telling and more defining than any other doctrine or belief, more significant than even monotheism. Yahweh, the God of Israel, might well be a jealous god, but that did not preclude the existence of other deities. By accepting the Lord God and then by following his instructions, good things would happen (and bad ones would be avoided). One's seed would be multiplied: there could be no greater triumph than living to see three, even four generations of offspring (and no greater calamity than an untimely death). The success of the individual was bound up immediately and inextricably with the peoplehood that was Israel. The Lord God meant the promise of success in battle, liberation in moments of defeat, and, in time, literally the promised land. Only later still did ethical notions become integrated into the prophetic. Prophecy implied human agency, in a sense free will. Both the individual and Israel might choose not to obey, and the (normally dire) prophetic consequences would ensue.

Prophecy also validated this world and this life almost entirely to the exclusion of any alternative. In these matters, the early books of the Bible were unrelenting. "The dead do not praise the Lord, / nor do any that go down into silence" (Ps. 115:17). From She'ol, the subterranean region inhabited by "shades" of the dead, there was neither God, nor future, nor purpose. "For in death there is no remembrance of thee; / In She'ol who can give thee praise?" (Ps. 6:5). Not even the sufferings of Job could secure him any postdeath compensation. Ancient Judaism concerned itself with life, not death.

By the middle prophets the picture had become a great deal more complicated. Yahweh now unmistakably ruled the nations and the universe. He did much more as well. His activities went beyond simple prophecy, the future contingent upon divine promise and human response. In addition, God's revealed will manifested itself through an underlying program, as part of a narrative framework—an apocalypse. The Jewish apocalypse comprised a great sacred drama, possessing a beginning, a middle, and an end. That culmination, the eschaton— eschatology is the study of final things—would mean the realization of Israel's destiny and, increasingly, that of humankind as well. The earliest to speak of "the end" is the prophet Amos (c. 786–746 BCE). Although the end he had in mind was a local event, the destruction of the northern Jewish kingdom, he clearly saw the Lord God as a universal deity, and the event held universal significance. However, it was only with crushing Jewish defeat and then the Babylonian exile of the indigenous elites (587–538 BCE) that the apocalypse became highly articulated and a standard mode through which the divine word needed to be comprehended.

Many different eschatological scenarios emerged. The most prominent was the restoration of the great Davidic kingdom and the line of Jesse, a "latter-day" empire that would defeat contemporary powers and endure forever. The latter-day David would be the promised messiah, the "anointed one," who would inaugurate this last age, the messianic era. Alternatively, however, Yahweh's wrath might fall so heavily on a sinful world that only a saved remnant of Israel would survive. The messianic age might not require a messiah. In a still different variant Israel might find itself redeemed and restored as "a light to the nations" where the peoples of the world would come to learn its law, ethics, and wisdom. In time Jewish prophets imagined the redeemed as joining the divine itself and inhabiting or visiting the realm of the stars. Nature itself could undergo a transformation. The end of days had often been envisioned as involving natural upheaval, and, as part of the eschaton, the upheaval in nature expanded from a local event to a cosmic catastrophe. In the end, nature too might become "redeemed" in the sense of renewed and revitalized, augmented in its fecundity. One of the most consequential end-time expectations was the resurrection of the dead. Initially a prospect reserved for the social elite, the resurrection had become a universal event by the Hellenistic era after the fourth century BCE. As earlier, this world and this life remained decisive.

Whatever the expectation, the revealed program of the apocalypse entailed a linear time sequence running from the fall of man from the garden of Eden to the "end of days." As such its importance cannot be overstated. History provided the framework of meaning, the context of redemption. Such a divine plan limited, if it did not foreclose, the role of human agency. Unlike prophecy, eschatology was fully preordained. Nevertheless, despite these differences, the potential conflict between the two all but never arose. Instead, the divine scheme and human volition became interleaved with one another, reinforcing prophetic purpose and rarely posing a problem.

Moreover, the apocalypse and attendant eschatological projections arose as a courtly phenomenon and spoke to royal contexts. It was the work of an intellectual elite and a scribal culture altogether removed from the Jewish peasantry. Its message was primarily communicated through the written word to literate audiences and concerned the crisis of dynastic disruption. Jonathan Z. Smith was surely right to describe it as "a learned rather than a popular religious phenomenon," and to reject what he called the "lachrymose theory" of apocalypticism which claims that the apocalypse manifests deprivation and "reflects lowerclass interests."[2] For most of its history, from biblical times up to the early modern period, the apocalypse rarely fired social revolution. Even after 1500 messianic revolutions remained an occasional phenomenon, occurring most spectacularly (and most successfully) within the English-speaking world.[3]

If a veritable smorgasbord of end-time possibilities had appeared, an increasingly detailed apocalyptic trajectory also came into being. Succeeding symbols, succeeding names, places, and events fleshed out the narrative and located the present moment within what seemed an ever-sharper relief. No prophet did this more dramatically or with greater consequence than did Daniel (c. 150 BCE). The prophet envisioned a series of spectacular animals: a lion with eagle's wings that walked on two legs, a gigantic flesh-devouring bear, a winged leopard, and then, greatest of all, an enormous beast with ten horns. The last beast then developed a little horn with "eyes like the eyes of man" which plucked out three of the Beast's other horns. Eventually the great beast was slain, and in that moment arrived the "son of man" at the end of days. Each of these extraordinary creatures, the prophet indicated, depicted a political empire, and their succession described the political history of the world. Daniel thus offered a developed time-line through which to imagine not only the history of the Jews but the history of humankind. Daniel sought to address the contemporary Jewish struggle against the Seleucid successors to the empire of Alexander the Great, but the significance of his vision lies in its linear worldview.

Daniel went further, developing a similar idea through a quite different kind of vision. The text misled its readers in a way common to prophetic writing, for Daniel portrayed himself as an advisor to the powerful Babylonian king Nebuchadnezzar who had lived centuries earlier (605–562 BCE). Thereby the prophet made his writing seem hugely old, and its vision of the future became substantiated (after the fact) and compelling. As Nebuchadnezzar's advisor, Daniel was called upon to interpret the king's troubling dream: a great statue of a human figure comprised of a golden head, silver chest and arms, bronze belly and thighs, legs of iron, and feet of both iron and clay. A little stone "cut from a mountain by no human hand" subsequently struck and destroyed the great colossus, whereupon the little stone grew into a great mountain. Odd indeed, but Daniel's explication turned it into an emblem of human history and the apocalyptic program: the statue embodied a succession of empires, all ultimately overthrown by spiritual truth at the end of days. Both the vision of the great beasts and Nebuchadnezzar's dream had an extraordinary history before them, inspiring apostles, church fathers, sixteenth-century reformers, early modern revolutionaries, and even Martin Luther King Jr. in the later twentieth century. Daniel's immediate impact was in many ways no less impressive. He at once manifested and promoted a deepening preoccupation with eschatology that transformed the ancient world.

THE INTERTESTAMENTAL PERIOD: APOCALYPTIC CRESCENDO

Between about 150 BCE and about 200 CE religious revival and eschatological expectation challenged and ultimately convulsed antique civilization. What Daniel had initiated subsequently climaxed with the second letter attributed to Peter (c. 130–150 CE) and the contemporaneous Jewish revolt of Simon Bar Kochbah (d. 135 CE)—to be followed by aftershocks in their immediate aftermath. Apocalyptic movements proliferated, competed, and interacted, all variously anticipating the end of days and imminent judgment of the world. Sectarian groups and often their enemies as well adopted apocalyptic vocabularies. Expectations of the end now reached into all layers of society. The Jewish historian Flavius Josephus (*c.* 35–*c.* 100) was surely right when he noted the popularity of Daniel and its appeal to "the multitude" during the first century CE.[4] It can be no accident that this was one of the rare moments in the pre-modern past when the apocalypse inspired popular uprisings. Most remembered and best documented today among the intertestamental apocalyptic movements are that of John the Baptist, the Qumran community, and, above all of course, the Jesus movements.

There can be little doubt that Jesus' thought arose directly from Jewish eschatological expectations and, further, conformed fully to them. He looked to the restoration of Israel and the revitalization of Judaism. He anticipated the transformation and restoring of nature. He believed that the eschaton had already begun and that the boundary between the living and the dead had diminished in significance. His own sacrifice and resurrection became the prototype for the immediate future, the universal resurrection. The imminent messianic age would entail an "in-gathering" of the Jews (not Gentiles) living outside Palestine; because they were remote, they would not face the same moral standard as the locals who had heard the message of the new Judaism. Jesus certainly regarded himself as a prophet, possibly the figure described in Isaiah 61—though, it seems, not necessarily as the "son of man." He clearly did not anticipate a new faith, much less a church.[5] His message was utterly eschatological and completely focused on this world.

The apostles inevitably shared Jesus' expectation of an imminent end, even if they endowed him with greater divinity than he had apparently claimed. Paul's first letter to the Thessalonians (*c.* 50 CE), the earliest surviving New Testament text and the earliest Christian document, is alive with anticipation of the resurrection. The continued "presence" of the post-Easter Jesus similarly speaks to the sense of immediacy. Doubts may have been raised about Jesus' eschatological status, but these were decisively overborne. The transmutation of the Jesus movements into "Christianity" by Paul in no way qualified the faith's apocalyptic energies. Universalism and mission found themselves completely compatible with the expectation of a rapidly approaching terminus. What did emerge was an increasingly detailed timeline. There would appear a false prophet, an Antichrist, before the end—as Paul stated most tellingly in his second letter to the Thessalonians. There might even be more than one such figure. By the last decade of the first century John of Patmos on the coast of Asia Minor produced the most dramatic delineation of the Christian version of sacred time: the Book of Revelation. John spoke of seals being opened, trumpets sounding, and bowls being poured out as spectacular sequences of events. He spoke of various great beasts, false prophets, and satanic figures. He placed a "scarlet whore" drinking from "the cup of iniquity" atop the back of Daniel's ten-horned creature. Most notably of all, he transformed the messianic age into the "millennium," the thousand-year reign of right-eousness and justice under Jesus and his saints. We can now never know the full context that motivated John, but his commitments could hardly be more clear: the Roman Empire is the last great beast, the last great test for the faithful; its doom is imminent; its mighty capital city will be utterly destroyed. Collaboration with it will mean damnation. Only well into the second century do we encounter clear evidence of anxiety about the failure of the man-god to return. The second letter ascribed to Peter, and the latest document to enter the New Testament, suggests that Jesus may delay his coming in order to give more people an oppor-tunity to encounter the faith and to repent.

By the late second century apocalyptic prospects had clearly begun to wane both within Judaism and Christianity: the Lord God now mani-fested himself through his law, Jesus through his sacraments. Yet escha-tological interest, however imminent these events might be imagined as being, retained remarkable resilience. Papias, an elder in the Asian city of Hierapolis (c. 140), vigorously promoted the idea of the millennium and stressed the fecundity of nature during that era. The burden of labor would end along with the burden of sin. Similar doctrines were main-tained by Irenaeus, the third-century bishop of Lyons, the early fourth-century writer Lactantius, and a great many fathers of the early church. In this respect they remained very much in the Jesus tradition. Even when the parousia, the return of Christ, no longer seemed imminent, it remained the defining event, the focus of Christian expectations. Ori-gen alone seems to have given the millennium a spiritual interpretation. Images of the apostles during these centuries portray them as clasping the sacred word, awaiting the return of the savior (Figure 1.1). Images of Christ stress his power (and thereby, among other things, his capacity

Figure 1.1 Images of the apostles. This mid-fourth-century fresco of the apostles, Domitilla Catacomb, Rome, characterizes the attitude of all early Christians. They await the return of the Son of Man to judge the quick and the dead. A long wait, as it turned out. *(Hirmer Verlag, Münich)*

to defeat death and return to this world). At the same time messianic interest persisted within Judaism despite the Bar Kochbah catastrophe, even if Jewish apocalypses tended to die out in the early second century.

Nevertheless, after about 170 a new sensibility visibly began to emerge. People of all social classes experienced a deepening sense of disconnection between public life and their personhood. Politics became less meaningful, traditional communal worship less compelling, the civic less purposeful, the familiar social self less persuasive. To the extent that the apocalypse validated this world, it too became marginalized. The man-god had not returned. Nor did the course of human events point to the historical redemption and the resolution of humanity's destiny.

THE DECLINE OF THE APOCALYPSE

The new sensibility affected both Judaism and Christianity, and interest in the apocalypse within both faiths waned more or less together during later antiquity. By the late fourth century its grip on the spiritual imagination had become highly tenuous, and in the Christian West Augustine of Hippo (354–430) introduced a major intellectual reformulation that dispatched it all but completely. Probably no individual at any time more effectively terminated apocalyptic expectations than did this North African bishop, the greatest and by far the most influential of the Latin fathers. On a variety of fronts he struck tellingly and, for Westerners, convincingly, against the significance of the physical world. The city of God, the community of the saved, bore no connection with the earthly city of politics. The pursuit of the public good in no way led to the divine good that allowed for salvation; citizenship distracted fatally from redemption. Political organization in any form possessed no inherent value and could have legitimacy only in a negative way: providing peace that would allow the saved to experience divine grace. Otherwise, government did not differ from robber bands. So, too, the philosophic pursuit of final truth and ultimate good could never escape its earthly dimension. It was one thing to discover the good (if that were even possible simply within the realm of nature), quite another to desire the good that required a transformation of the self. Much the same applied to the apocalypse, and especially the millennium. It too validated this world, it too looked to the "material," it too directed people away from the transcendent.

What then did all these prophetic biblical statements actually mean? Augustine was emphatic. The millennium simply referred to the spreading of the gospel and Christian authority. It comprised nothing more than the everyday world we now inhabited. The apocalypse offered no road map to sacred history and human destiny, Augustine insisted, because the sequences of symbols could not be correlated to political experience or the course of events. Yes, there would occur a terminus, possibly in the year 1000, the number in scripture and, perhaps more significant, a "perfect" number in that it comprised ten cubed. The end was very far from imminent and did not link with certainty to any time or "times." Further, scripture indicated that the end-day events would occur quickly and precipitously. Human involvement was neither required nor of concern. Men's eyes needed to be cast elsewhere.

Augustine thereby disconnected both the classical and the Judaic traditions from the world of contemporary people. His views proved decisive. The Council of Ephesus (431) formally adopted his eschatological reading of scripture and made "amillennialism" canonical. Thereafter, millenarianism would not resurface before the twelfth century, and even then it failed to become mainstream. Moreover, apocalyptic reflection in any form, while far from unknown, emerged only on the margins of medieval civilization. Late antique and early medieval Europeans, especially in the West, ceased to seek the intervention of their "patronus" with the imperial hierarchy and instead appealed to their patron saint to intercede with the heavenly hierarchy. On earth, an ever more stratified church, a structure created by God's grace that existed outside the realm of nature, increasingly supplanted the functions of civil government. That ecclesiastical order mirrored, however imperfectly, the eternal order through which God ruled the universe. People of every social status found themselves living in a world populated with angelic and, far more prevalently, demonic forces, but these agencies were an atemporal phenomenon, quite outside any time frame.

Only in the Greek East, where imperial government continued to be effective (and where Augustine's influence was less authoritative), did the apocalypse persist as a significant mode of thought. Despite persecution, many Christians early on wanted to see the Roman Empire as their protector, the universal authority that allowed for the spread of the universal faith.[6] They took pains to proclaim that *Romanitas* was fully compatible with *Christianitas*. They dissented vigorously from John of Patmos. The conversion of the emperor Constantine (c. 274–335), his subsequent military victories, and the writings of Eusebius of Caesarea (c. 264–340) underscored the idea that the empire had arisen providentially to serve Christian purposes. Struggles between Roman civilization and its barbarian challengers were increasingly read as an ongoing struggle between Christianity and heathenism.

Then Constantine moved his capital to Constantinople in the East, both symbolizing and working the shifting political and cultural center of gravity. By the sixth century Constantine's capital had emerged as the new Jerusalem, and the Byzantine Roman Empire had now become the latter-day Israel. Imperial apologists succeeded in interweaving the triumphalist claims and prophecies of the classical era into the Judeo-Christian apocalypse. The Byzantines would create a synthesis of Daniel, Ezekiel, Paul, Sibylline prophecies, and pagan literature (notably absent was the violently anti-Roman Revelation). From Constantinople radiated nothing less than Daniel's fifth empire, the final world order before the return of King Jesus. The emperor stood in the "figure" of Christ, representing and anticipating the divine autocrat. The political disasters of the seventh century that occurred with the coming of the Slavs and the Arabs crystallized this eschatology around a vision of Roman restoration—a vision that would endure in centuries to come.

There would arise a great Last World Emperor who would overthrow the enemies of the faith and confront the Pauline Antichrist. Thereafter Christ would return and the Last Judgment would occur. The focus was on the awesome woes that faced Byzantium and, still more, the extraordinary figure of the prophesied ruler—the Last Judgment itself almost an afterthought. In what became typical medieval fashion, hope lay in an exceptional individual, not in the thrust of history or the logic of time. The preoccupation was restoration, a lost Roman past. In both respects its implications were conservative and attenuated. If it remained implicit within Byzantine ideology until the destruction of the empire in 1453, apocalyptic thought lost its vitality after the tenth century and end-time reflection declined. Survivalism, not triumphalism, became the manifest mode. Links with timeless heaven rather than sacred mission became the dominant discourse.

Apocalypticism revived at a number of junctures in the history of the medieval Latin West, especially during the fourteenth and fifteenth centuries. Moreover, people were generally aware that the end might come suddenly and at moments believed the great events were about to happen. But they did not see history or even daily life as going anywhere. Quite the contrary. The most deep-seated habit of mind encouraged a sense of timeless continuity. Even major transformations were instinctively characterized as affirmations of tradition. The defining intellectual constructs of the era reinforced this outlook by providing a deeply static view of society, nature, and the faith.

The human environment sought to replicate the immutable heavenly hierarchies. Again, as in heaven, all earthly potentates held their office as unworthy imitations of the divine ruler and judge. All political order was also of a piece with the hierarchies to be found everywhere in nature. Hierarchy and headship concurrently existed at every plane of being: whether in the body, family, society. Such hierarchies within hierarchies and heads above heads comprised universal principles that obtained among the fauna and the flora in exactly the same way. Each element within any hierarchy had its unique function or purpose—its "telos"—that identified it and made it what it was. All these "functions" fit together and were "logically" necessary. The human body provided the governing metaphor: even if each of its parts possessed a different dignity, a higher or lower "quality," each also served a necessary purpose. John of Salisbury (c. 1117–1180) described political society in these terms, terms that had long become commonplace. He found the place of the head to be filled by the prince; the heart had its counterpart in the king's council; the eyes, ears, and tongue served as the judges and governors of provinces. "Officials and soldiers correspond to the hands." Those who always attended upon the prince were "likened to the sides." Financial officers and keepers found their analogue with the stomach and intestines, increasingly concerned with physical matters and increasingly inferior as a result. At the bottom were the peasants who corresponded to the feet, who walked "upon the earth doing service with their bodies" and especially needed the foresight of the head.[7] Reciprocity reigned. Time did not. Function never changed.

At the local level each political jurisdiction operated with an allied set of assumptions. The "common custom of the realm" was instinctively thought of as "ancient" and as valid for that reason. In a world without historical analysis or social theory, tradition provided its own justification. Of course everyone knew that all things on earth constantly changed. But all such flux, mutation, transience, decay were irrational and thus marginal. They suffused the sublunar regions and had resulted from sin and the fall from Eden. Lady Fortune and her wheel symbolized just this irrationality and the limits of the human mind. Change and, above all, mortality did not invite explanation, but enjoined that men look to the enduring, the significant, the underlying atemporal patterns of the divine, and especially the glorious world of redemption beyond time.

This signal commonplace, the bedrock of the university and the law court, hallmarked the Middle Ages and was never successfully challenged. Quite the contrary. These lines of thought became systematized, integrated, elaborated, and made ever more articulate by figures such as Albert the Great and Ranulf de Glanvill, Thomas Aquinas and Henry Bracton, and the most powerful minds of the period. Roman legal categories and Greek metaphysical categories provided the foundations for the intellectual triumphs that defined the age.

Accordingly, the apocalypse never guided medieval civilization. It never organized medieval cultural achievement, never became the dominant mode of cognition. The formative events of the era—its turning points, its characteristic institutions, and its greatest upheavals—all attest to the marginal role of the apocalypse in the experience of the Middle Ages.

The crusades may have held vast consequences for Europe and have expressed unprecedented self-confidence, but they did not comprise the expression of an apocalyptic impulse. As Bernard McGinn has commented, "If apocalyptic motifs were used, they do not seem to have played a major role."[8] Joachim of Fiore, undoubtedly the most significant apocalyptic thinker of the medieval world, declined to make the Crusades a decisive event within what he saw as the deepening crisis of history. No amount of well-intended crusading could change the prophetic program. Joachim actually conferred with the leader of the third crusade, Richard I of England, and was far from encouraging.

The rise of the papacy and its ferocious struggle against royal authority failed to enjoin an apocalyptic vocabulary before the thirteenth century and even then the apocalypse did not supply the predominant voice. We will be hard put to find more than a whiff of the end of days and certainly no articulated apocalyptic vision with Pope Gregory VII (c. 1020–1085) and his "reforming" successors. The apocalypse did not frame the debate; it never even became a focus of dispute within the "investiture contest." The clericalization of the Latin West took place within an atemporal language. Innocent III (1160–1216), surely the most powerful and far-reaching of the medieval popes, at no point adopted any such vocabulary. In the fourteenth century we do encounter prophecies about a final angelic pope, the West's belated counterpart to Byzantium's Last World Emperor. But the formulators and promoters of this apocalyptic were critics of the papacy rather than occupants of the apostolic chair—outsiders attacking from the sidelines, papalist but not papal.

Even the fourteenth-century Black Death pandemic that carried off perhaps a quarter to a third of Europe's population, McGinn tells us, "had at best a minor effect upon the history of apocalypticism, at least in comparison with other less troubled times." A recent study of the plague that sought to "map" in detail its eschatological impact has found an ambivalent reaction to the catastrophe: naturalism competing with apocalypticism, "in no simple sense apocalyptic."[9] The "apocalyptic year" 1000, Marjorie Reeves observes, "passed with little dramatic demonstration." When apocalyptic reflection did occur during the medieval era, there rarely appeared a developed historical time-line, virtually never a millennial future. As Reeves has trenchantly argued, "it was only within the context of end-time that history since the incarnation had any significance for medieval people. There was no prospect of endless progressive change, only of a drama tightly bound to its final climax."[10] The regnant epistemologies—the so-called Gothic spirit— pointed away from time as a meaningful category.

THE JOACHITE CHALLENGE

By far the most complex and original apocalyptic thinker of the entire period was Joachim of Fiore (*c.* 1135–1202). He has had an enduring impact well beyond his own times, yet the marginalizing of his thought during the centuries following his death will illustrate the priorities (and limitations of the apocalypse) for his civilization.

The twelfth century had famously "naturalized" its universe in the sense that Aristotelian categories organized knowledge of the physical world and, no less, knowledge of the divine, of theology, of the revela- tory. As we have seen, all creation was imagined as a vast organism or body in which every element had its special "function"—the necessary activity that it alone performed. Joachim shared with his contemporary John of Salisbury this quite un-Augustinian understanding of society and the cosmos. But he transformed it from a grand scheme of organic integration into a vast vision of organic growth and development. The story of mankind involved three great periods, each one experiencing moments of "germination," "fructification," and "consummation." Every succeeding period led to a higher spiritual state of being on the road to redemption and manifested a different person in the godhead—the trinity comprising for Joachim temporaling aspects of the deity. The first—the age of the father, of the law, of the married elect—ran from Adam to Christ. It began its fruition in Abraham, Isaac, and Jacob, faced the great crisis of Antiochus Epiphanes, and culminated with Christianity. In the midst of this first age the second found its germination with Elijah and then King Uzziah (783–742 BCE). That succeeding age—of the son, of grace, of the priest—fructified with Jesus and continued into Joachim's time. Once again, in its midst had germinated the third age with Benedict and the rise of monasticism (*c.* 500 CE). This last age—the age of the holy spirit, the age of the monk—lay in the immediate offing. The prospect was at once exhilarating and terrifying. The reign of Antichrist, whom Joachim seems to have imagined as a false pope, was about to commence.

Christianity would be subverted; infidelity would reign. The faithful would experience the most determined persecution, as scripture had made abundantly clear. But the crisis would be met by two new forms of monasticism, a contemplative order and a preaching order. These new "spiritual men" would assist a preaching pope in guiding mankind through its greatest crisis. The latter would emerge not as a mighty potentate but as a "suffering servant." Joachim believed that this "novus dux" might well prove a pope who had experienced defeat at Rome. Only spiritual energy, not military force, could induce the new age.

That third age would entail world renewal and the triumph of the spirit. Mankind would be organized into the highest form of association, the monastery. Joachim envisioned them as five oratories, each one potentially enormous. They corresponded to Mary, John, Paul, Stephan, and Peter, and symbolically embodied the central features within the Christian church. These oratories would be in direct communication with the spirit of God. In addition, Joachim foresaw two suburbs, one of which would include married people who had off-spring and who, together with their children, lived "a common life." The other suburb provided education, tended the sick, and dealt with taxes and administration. All would be under the direction of "the Spiritual Father" who inhabited the first oratory, evidently a spiritualized, monastic pope. His authority, Joachim implied, derived from his charisma rather than his office.[11]

The most striking feature of Joachim's vision for a modern reader is its progressivist vision: each age improves upon the one before it, and each happens in history as the result of human endeavor. The third age would end eventually, and with it time itself, but the meliorist, even utopian character of his thought remains unmistakable. Joachim was a highly visual thinker whose ideas were explicated through *figurae* or pictorial diagrams, and the best illustration of the developmental and organic dimension of the Joachite apocalypse is provided by his "tree circles" (Figure 1.2). During the age of the father, figured by Moses, the Israelite progeny of Shem prove the most fruitful. In the succeeding age of the son, the gentile children of Japheth blossom. In the age of the spirit everyone flourishes to an unprecedented extent. Joachim offered a sweeping apocalypse that entailed far more than simple restoration or revitalization and went well beyond anything proposed in antiquity, whether by the Byzantines, Papias, Lactantius, or even John of Patmos.

Joachim's startling originality appears in still other ways. Almost uniquely in medieval Europe he projects the Antichrist as a false Christian rather than a renegade Jew. His time-scheme is driven in part by mystical numerical parallels in each age. This focus on the esoteric went still further. Bernard McGinn has noted Joachim's "proto-Kabbalist" use of names, drawn from the converted Spanish Jew Petrus Alphonsi. Moreover, Joachim envisioned an uncharacteristically positive role for the Jews in the apocalyptic narrative and the final age. "I think the time of forgiving them, the time of consolation and their conversion is here." Perhaps predictably he would be attacked as a false prophet of Jewish origin.[12]

It is important to stress that Joachim was close to the Roman curia and an advisor to several popes, most notably Lucius III (r. 1181–1185). At the same time, Joachim's apocalyptic altogether denied any spiritual significance to royal authority: there could be no Last World Emperor; the Crusades were hopeless; temporal princes proved persecutors, not liberators, divine scourges rather than redemptive agencies. The church alone provided the key. Nevertheless, Joachim's papalism was far from militant. His friends in the curia were consistently in the "peace party" and sought accommodation with the crowned heads of Europe, especially the German emperor. Joachim had no connection with the "reforming party" that sought to extract the church from society and establish clerical, indeed theocratic hegemony. The powerful popes we remember today were not his popes, and the intellectual dynamics that underwrote their triumph and created high medieval Europe were not his either.

In the years following Joachim's death, new "spiritual men" did indeed appear, in the form of the Dominican and Franciscan orders. But the world they constructed differed drastically from Joachite ideals and expectations. Only an increasingly isolated minority of Franciscans upheld and developed Joachim's vision of transformation. The severe contrast between the great Dominican doctor Thomas Aquinas (1225–1274) and Joachim is instructive: a face-off between the professor and the abbot. The rising institution in the years ahead would be Aquinas's university, not Joachim's monastery, a movement already in decline during the twelfth century. The new era looked to Aristotle and not, with Joachim, exclusively to scripture. The university doctors organized knowledge about timeless "scholastic" universals and "proof"

←——

Figure 1.2 Joachim of Fiore's "Tree Circles" from the twelfth-century *Liber Figurarum* illustrates both the organic and progressivist character of the abbot's thought. At the same time the diagram also shows the philo-Semitic dimension within Joachim's apocalyptic program. This relatively positive view of the Jews—like his progressivist vision—is uncharacteristic of the Middle Ages, both East and West. It was increasingly at odds with the development of attitudes in the West that became more violently anti-Semitic from the thirteenth century onward.

At the base of the tree is the Father who is the first person of the trinity and who is manifested through Noah, literally the father of postdeluvian humanity. Noah and his sons—Shem, the progenitor of the Jews, and Japheth, the progenitor of the Gentiles—comprise the "fructification" of the Age of the Father, the first age of humankind. They are directly comparable to the "fructification" with Abraham, Isaac, and Jacob. During this period the Jews flourish, represented by the branch on the left, while the Gentiles on the right are less fruitful (though the presence of buds seems to suggest their potential).

At the center is the failed and blasted branch of Noah's third son, Ham. Ham had seen his father's drunkenness and was cursed. He represents the reprobate and the damned. Joachim did not identify Ham with any particular people.

The Jewish and gentile branches draw together with the inauguration of the Age of the Son. During the second age the Gentiles flower with the greatest spirituality, while the Jews emerge less so—their positions literally reversed. The illustration suggests that the Jews in the Christian era remain far from barren. Nevertheless, the illustration also suggests that the Christian Gentiles have achieved a more robust spiritual state than that of their Jewish predecessors.

Once again the branches draw together at the outset of the third age, the Age of the Holy Spirit. At this point everyone becomes fruitful on a scale well beyond that of either previous period.

Following the apocalyptic wave that resurfaced with the sixteenth-century Reformation, both progressivist historical visions and philo-Semitism would emerge as part of mainstream European culture. The intellectual assumptions of the Reformation differed widely from those of Joachim, but highly developed versions of his conclusions came to hallmark major currents within Protestantism. Several of his works and works attributed to him saw print in the early sixteenth century. Anglophone reformers such as John Bale, John Knox, and James Maxwell were in varying degrees familiar with him and his expectations. *(Reproduced by permission of the President and Fellows of Corpus Christi College, Oxford MS 255a, f. 12v.)*

rather than about development and growth, Greek logic rather than Jewish history. Scholasticism now lay at the heart of cultural achievement; Joachim had protested against scholasticism and linked it with heresy. The doctors recognized that the idea of a prophetic terminus could not be abandoned. To do so could only mean atheism. But these spectacular end-time events remained as much in the remote future as they had for the Augustine they rejected. For Joachim, the apocalypse defined reality, and the final age lay within the lifetime of the present generation. Running counter to the entire thrust of Joachite thought, the thirteenth-century preoccupation became the sacraments, which underwrote a timeless present and, with them, clerical power. It is no accident that the thirteenth century witnessed the most fulsome sacramentalism in Aquinas's doctrine of "transubstantiation."

The contrast between Joachim and Aquinas runs deep and in many directions. Joachim had taken an unusually generous attitude toward the Jews; Aquinas and his age became ever more violently anti-Judaic. "Forgiving" the Jews was supplanted by expelling the Jews. Hierarchy and the "frame of order" validated lawyer-administrator papal theocrats—against a new heaven, new earth that validated charismatic papal hermits. Joachim thought through symbolic images, Aquinas through discursive language: it is hard to imagine an illustrated *Summa Theologica*. At heart, temporality had faced off against rationality: process, history, time against an unchanging framework of deduction, logic, necessity. McGinn spoke to the point when he observed that Joachim's thought "was diametrically opposed to the forces that triumphed in the thirteenth century" and in effect comprised "a radical critique of the thirteenth-century church."[13]

The radicalism potentially present in the Joachite apocalyptic occasionally surfaced in quite striking, even seemingly bizarre ways during the century following Joachim's death. In 1254 the Franciscan Gerald di Borgo San Donnino announced in Paris that if men entered into direct communication with the holy spirit in the imminent third age, then surely the scriptures became (or would become) superceded. The apocalypse so contextualized the sources of our understanding of history as to make even them time-bound and redundant. Although Gerald occupied a totally different cultural environment, one that had no sense of textual criticism, his view of scripture anticipated seventeenth-century radical Quakers. Joachim had systematically rejected any such idea, but the notion of transition to a new age of the spirit made

Gerald's proposal far from implausible. In 1282 one Manfreda in Milan and her advisors adopted the commonplace medieval notion of an inverted world, a world turned upside down, and applied it to gender relations in the Joachite third age. The final period of human history would be a gentler, "feminine" time with women in the curia and occupying the papal throne. Church authorities duly condemned Gerald, Manfreda, and their associates. Yet these "scandals" did not discredit Joachim's eschatology decisively. Nor did spiritual Franciscan radicals who urged apostolic poverty on the medieval church and wrote pseudo-Joachite apocalypses to support their struggle. Nor did the Fraticelli dissidents, their successors, in the fourteenth century. Nor did even the Taborite uprising in fifteenth-century central Europe, one of the exceptional instances where the apocalypse fueled pre-modern social upheaval. Well beyond any of this, at a far more basic and decisive level Joachim fell before the cultural thrust of the High Middle Ages, before scholasticism and the power of tradition.

The apocalypse had never played well in Rome, even at moments of greatest transition or greatest danger. Before anything else, the apocalypse articulated change, and thereby it qualified the present— potentially undermining contemporary institutions, contemporary authority. The intellectual foundations for that authority argued powerfully against any such vocabulary and sidelined all apocalyptic schemes. A deep sense of continuity and the inherent legitimacy of changeless custom at the local level combined with the schoolman's Aristotelian naturalism to create a environment where Taborite revolutionaries, Lollard reformers, angelic popes, Last World Emperors (or some combination of the last two) would necessarily prove marginal. In the end the apocalypse turned out to be a modern or proto-modern phenomenon, not a medieval one.

Perhaps surprisingly, the medieval outlook became unhinged before a combination of revived Augustinian piety and a much deepened understanding of the apocalypse. Signs of both appear with the English intellectual John Wycliffe (c. 1329–1384). The first element rejected scholastic "naturalism" in favor of grace, direct contact with divine power and agency. The second temporalized all aspects of the physical and political world by imagining the divine as operating immanently within it. To sacralize the physical was also to validate it, to endow it with the utmost importance, the highest relevance. God's grace now penetrated his creation and gave immediate experience unprecedented stature and compelling significance. Simultaneously, it blurred the hitherto severe distinction between the church and other forms of human association. This Augustinian-motivated validation—politics and time, public culture and the material universe—could only have astounded and appalled the repressed North African.

REPUBLICAN REDEMPTION: FROM MEDIEVAL COMMUNE TO ESCHATOLOGICAL CITY

A further temporalizing dynamic proved decisive in achieving this massive reorienting of the Western intellect, one that found its origins in the city-states of Renaissance Italy. To live in a city was to inhabit a far more time-bound environment than elsewhere. The medieval commune was a notoriously unstable place where political upheaval and bloody social revolutions occurred regularly. Everything below the moon comprised the empire of Lady Fortune, but the commune seemed her special province. Urban politics bore a far less evident parallel to the hierarchies in heaven and the hierarchies that university men perceived in nature. People who lived in cities found themselves subject to radical contingency and thus to time: omnipresent contingency meant omnipresent temporality. As Niccolò Machiavelli later put it in his verses on Fortune, individuals were forever tied to fortune's wheel, never able to "leap from" it.[14] Time proved inescapable, and never more so than when interacting with our similarly placed fellows.

In these circumstances of direct action and face-to-face confrontation, politics—indeed justice—became less a matter of applying the law than harmonizing wills, less upholding custom than securing agreement. The communal environment demanded eloquence, and education in the models of eloquence that antiquity had provided. Eloquence meant a major shift in focus: not formal logic, but compelling rhetoric, not rigorous proof, but uplifting persuasion, not dry deduction, but cunning seduction. There need be nothing in the least cynical about such undertaking. It might easily become just the reverse, highly moralistic.

City-states and even leagues of cities long existed in many parts of Europe—along the Baltic littoral, along the Rhine and Scheldt estuaries, and elsewhere. But what would make the Italian cities so precocious to moderns and so wicked to northern contemporaries came with their achieving unduplicated political, juridical, and moral autonomy. During the fifteenth century Italian cities became self-legitimating, self-creating polities largely disconnected from any external authority. The step proved a momentous departure, one often not fully recognized today. Within its walls the medieval commune might prove fortune's unbridled domain, but from without it remained a polity contained inside larger legal frameworks and overarching political structures. By the 1490s something quite different, quite unprecedented, and hugely portentous had emerged.

The city of Florence may never have had a more loyal or committed citizen than Dante Alighieri (1265–1321). The city's interests and ideals, however, found their achievement within the prophesied Last World Empire. Florence, like all medieval communes, emerged as a protected enclave within this higher order and, for Dante, as part of the universal government that realized man's earthly destiny. As he put it in his *De monarchia* (c. 1310–1313), providence had endowed mankind with a twofold destiny: "bliss in this life which consists in the functioning of his own powers and which is symbolized by the earthly paradise [Eden]; and the bliss of eternal life, that consists in the enjoyment of the divine vision which he cannot attain by his own powers."[15] Brutus and Cassius, as the murderers of Caesar, become the great betrayers of empire and thereby of human destiny. Accordingly in his great spiritual epic, the *Comedia*, Dante located them at the lowest place in Hell, where they joined Judas Iscariot, the betrayer of man's divine destiny, in Satan's mouth. All three would be munched forever by evil incarnate.

Dante looked to Germany's Henry VII to create the new order, and when the emperor's expedition into Italy (1312–1313) failed to achieve this purpose, he began work on the great epic. We should not understand Dante either as a naive visionary or as a practical man who briefly seized on the emperor as Florence's best hope. Rather, despite his remarkably radical separation of humankind's earthly and heavenly goals, Dante's attitudes never escaped the mainstream cognitive boundaries of the later Middle Ages. To be sure, Dante greatly admired Joachim and celebrated him in the *Paradiso*. He adopted elements from Joachim's imagery and that of the Revelation, lambasted the worldly papal monarchy, may even have intimated that the entire structure of Hell, Purgatory, and Paradise remained contingent on the Last Judgment. Surely, humanity's double destiny could converge only within a Joachite third age or within a Johannine millennium. But Dante also celebrated Thomas Aquinas, and in the end Aquinas triumphed:

teleology trumped time, the medieval ratio overcame the sacred drama, and the *Comedia* resolved itself more into personal pilgrimage than political history. Within such a circumscribed mental world, urban invocations of classical antiquity, the public good, civil liberty, or even popular sovereignty, could only carry constricted meanings quite removed from modern politics.

Within just a couple of decades much of this might appear to have changed. In the 1340s Cola di Rienzo (1313–1354) proclaimed himself tribune of the Roman people and led a revolution that overthrew the city's clan-based baronial oligarchy. Armed with Livy's histories of the Roman republic, Cola seemed to derive the authority of both emperor and pope from the sovereignty of the people of Rome—and through some unspecified imputation more generally from the people of "sacred" Italy. His friend and promoter, the poet and early humanist Francesco Petrarch (1304–1374), inverted Dantean assumptions when he transvalued the figure of Brutus from the betrayer of mankind into an archetypal republican hero—and in whose tradition Cola nobly and outstandingly participated. Most telling of all, Rienzo identified the emerging communal government, which would administer justice and pursue the public good, with the redemptive regime of Joachim's third age. Rienzo's new *buono stato* converged with the Joachite final *status*, literally the good state with ultimate state of being. The heavenly city and popular sovereignty became conterminous, the restoration of the classical republic at one with the restoration of post-Edenic man. Here indeed arose a challenge to the medieval order—intellectually, politically, spiritually.

Or did it? Despite the fulsome eloquence of the "Lord Tribune," Rienzo did not distinguish sharply between popular, imperial, and papal apocalyptic, and the three easily elided into one another. Rienzo eagerly adopted Constantinian coronation styles and in highly medieval fashion propagated myths about his own imperial genealogy. Claims for universal empire, far more than populist posturing, troubled Pope Clement VI. The prospect of the German emperor, Charles IV, establishing himself at the new Rome with the popes away at Avignon posed an exceedingly serious challenge—prompting the pontiff to turn on his former protégé and identify Rienzo with the emergence of Antichrist. The sovereignty of the Roman people did not prove incompatible with larger authorities, and Rienzo's latest biographer has portrayed him as far more a papal creature than previously recognized.[16]

In the end the Last World Emperor–Angelic Pope dualism was not supplanted. The *buono stato* seems to have embraced medieval notions of justice and peace rather more than social activism and civic involvement. Rienzo's eschatological republic failed to serve as an antonym to monarchy, whether papal or royal.

The earliest sign of a plausible transition from the privileged commune to the independent republic occurred at the outset of the fifteenth century. The city of Florence confronted the aggressive Visconti tyrants of Milan, and that precipitated what Hans Baron famously described as a "crisis of liberty."[17] According to Baron, civic-minded Florentines saw themselves facing their direct opposite, and this moment of acute danger precipitated a radically new ideology about the city, its purposes, its significance. Florence now appeared as an independent republic much like the great republics of antiquity. Accordingly, the city shared the politics, learning, and language of the antique world. It was also a civic society, again as in antiquity, where citizens contained fortune through open participation in defining and pursuing the public good. Citizenship became at once the manifestation of liberty and the realization of the personality: being an articulate and socially effective individual inherently made possible the achievement of the public good. These values stood in the starkest contrast to monarchy and any form of empire. The rise of the Roman Empire thus emerged as the greatest catastrophe of the antique world. The Florentine chancellor Leonardo Bruni (1361–1444) portrayed this event in dramatic terms, for eloquence, culture, and politics were integral to one another and perforce declined together. The end of the republic meant the end of civilization.

Accordingly, Florentine intellectuals and politicians such as Coluccio Salutati (1331–1406) and Bruni developed a new history of their city that placed its foundation and identity squarely within the republican, pre-imperial era. Florence achieved stability against the flux of time through a continuous act of self-creation. It would be a world vastly different from that of John of Salisbury. The Florentines along with most city-state Italians did not refute John's categories or discover them to be "wrong"; they simply and increasingly found them irrelevant.

Baron's thesis, however, has been variously criticized. Most recently, David Wooton has shown that the step into the realm of autonomy and time was taken fitfully and hesitantly. Efforts to stabilize the republic within a civic framework, integrating individual wills into common causes through public debate, normally proved short-lived. Bursts of patriotic enthusiasm, as in the Visconti crisis of 1400–1402, faded and became replaced by stability achieved through authoritarian styles of government. Local princes, not self-constructed republics, characterized the era. This experience took place in all Italian city-states, even occurring in Bruni's Florence with the rise of the Medici family. Further, republican rhetoric itself, however stirring, did not prove unqualified and broke incompletely with earlier patterns of thought. As Wooton has observed, intellectual and political leaders such as Bruni did not see the republic as a total contrast to monarchy, one founded on radically different assumptions and capable of achieving a moral order decisively at odds with traditional society. Bruni went no further than to suggest that monarchies and aristocracies comprised forms of *res publica* that were not fully realized.[18]

Only during the 1490s did civic values triumph in unqualified and thoroughly republican form—launching a political movement that lasted some fifty years and generating many of the central elements in modern political thought. They did so because they became intensely spiritualized with apocalyptic and specifically millennial expectations. Quite unlike Rienzo's Rome a century and a half earlier, revolutionary Florence identified the Joachite "spiritual man" with the classical citizen. The virtuous political decision-taker merged with the illumined saint. The "true republic" became inseparable from the "true faith," and the distinction between heavenly and earthly felicity began to disappear. The preoccupation no longer aimed to stabilize society and escape time. Instead, it sought to transform society and fulfill time. Historical process and apocalyptic progression supplanted Fortune's wheel, the recurring cycles that one might hope to stop. Competing types of government ceased to be morally neutral forms which might or might not achieve the public good and social justice, as the antique classical theory itself had always maintained. Rather, they now comprised conflicting moral alternatives of the starkest sort. To chose monarchy could only mean spiritual failure.

The decisive figure in these extraordinary events was the Dominican friar from Ferrara, Girolamo Savonarola (1452–1498). An intellectual of significant stature as well as a prophet, Savonarola effectively began his career at Florence in 1490 announcing the end of days and preaching repentance and reform. God's wrath lay in the immediate offing; Italy (and notably Florence) could expect to experience the *flagellum dei*, all part of the upheavals leading up to the Last Judgment. In 1494 the divine scourge duly appeared in the form of the impetuous young French king Charles VIII who crossed into Italy with a huge force seeking to make good his claim to Naples. All powers along his route faced attack, and catastrophe loomed for Florence. Medici rule disintegrated before the crisis, revolution occurred, and then, against all expectations, the city won over the king. His armies passed through Florence without incident, and in the heady months that followed the city adopted a succession of republican constitutions. The end result was a broad-based polity—not democratic certainly, but still one involving unusually wide levels of public participation.

Savonarola played an instrumental role in each of these develop-ments, from the agreement with Charles to the new political order, and emerged the city's leading political and spiritual figure. During this time his eschatology visibly shifted. The success of Florentine ref-ormation indicated that the great crisis did not presage a terminus, but a transition. Old Florence had become New Jerusalem, the latter-day Israel of the messianic age. The harbinger of the final era took form as the new *governo popolare*, the *vera politica*.

The young king and his publicists had also promoted an apocalyptic perception of the French expedition into Italy. The French would take Naples and from there conquer Jerusalem. At that point Charles would convert and reunite the world—the familiar, if not shopworn, medieval imperial vision. But to Savonarola and Florence he appeared a far more modest figure. Charles might prove a Cyrus, even a second Charlemagne, but he was no Last World Emperor. He might be an enabler, but never a model. The future was the Florentine republic. His empire served larger purposes and would prosper only if it did serve those purposes. He might assist world reformation, but he would never embody it. The Florentine triumph was assured: prophecies about the city would undoubtedly happen, for the Virgin had granted them "in an absolute and certain way." Not so the French. "The promises and graces granted to the King of France are conditional, not absolute like the prophecy of the reformation of the Church and the graces promised the Florentines."[19]

Savonarola was surely right in the sense that eschatological expec-tation and politico-religious reform had penetrated the textures of his city's culture in ways quite unlike the French court, much less the French kingdom. The Florentine mission became persuasive as a result. Florence, as he variously put it, was the head, the heart, the navel of Italy and consequently the spiritual center of the world. That future meant human liberation, the exportation of the republic as a moral imperative. David Wooton has convincingly portrayed Savonarolan Florence as "the key moment in the transition of the modern language of republicanism"; that is, the origin of the modern concept of the republic as radically distinct from any other form of rule.[20] With the city now appearing in so many ways as an altogether novel society, and thus uniquely existing in a state of grace, its normative status became unavoidable. Accordingly, Savonarola and his followers expected their city to attract preachers from around the world, including the infidel Turks, who would propagate and replicate the Florentine experience. Failure to do so, perhaps inevitably, could only mean coercion and conquest.[21] Still, the emphasis lay elsewhere, for the future promised nothing less than a new (and final) era of *vera libertà*. Political life did not end with salvation but meant salvation.

More radical still, even scholasticism itself need not obtain. Savonarola defended his status as a prophet who spoke directly with God, we now know, by drawing on newly discovered skeptical doctrines preserved in the writings of Sextus Empiricus (*c.* 200 CE).[22] All human knowledge turned out to be vulnerable, as reason itself and pagan philosophy amply demonstrated. Consequently, the only secure knowledge arose from immediate revelation. The only certain authority became the authority of the inspired. Improbable as it may seem, for Savonarola, eschatology and skepticism became mutually reinforcing allies. At the same time, a cosmos permeated by timeless hierarchies within hierarchies could no longer carry reflexive conviction. The radical republic, newly minted at Savonarolan Florence, entered the realm of grace in total autonomy. Contemporary observers found it startling no less for its exhilarating innovations than for its terrifying implications.

Florence now became the spiritual capital of Christendom, effectively the new Rome, and inherently posed an enormous challenge to old Rome, both city and church. The contrast could only be patent and sharp: the reformed city stood out against the corrupt one; the saintly Savonarola against the conniving Borgia, Alexander VI; the community of the elect against its opposite. Savonarola made clear that he did not seek to supplant the papacy or to overthrow sacramental authority. The prophet would submit himself willingly to a legitimate pope. But such a pope needed to be Joachim's suffering servant, "angelic" in that he bore no connection to Italian politics (not even Savonarola's powerful imagination could envision a civic pope). The contrast and then the conflict reached further still. At issue were two competing ideas of governance (republican and hierarchical), two visions of the city of God—accompanied by two different concepts of spirituality and two types of eschatology.

We encounter a landscape quite removed from that of Rienzo and his papal contemporary Clement VI. A new language of politics arose to describe the unprecedented, spiritualized republicanism that was Florence in the 1490s. Niccolò Machiavelli emerged not merely as a commentator on the revolution brought about by the transforming Savonarolan moment, but as an expression of it. Far more than simply a bystander viewing events with detachment and bemused disbelief, he fully embraced Savonarola's central distinction between *governo civile* and monarchy, shared his intense moralism, and in many respects became his follower. Moreover, Machiavelli's subsequent stature as a political theorist ought not to inflate retrospectively his impact on Florence. Savonarola, not Machiavelli, ignited a political movement that lasted more than a generation. Savonarola, not Machiavelli, was first "prepared to rebel against" scholastic claims for the superiority of monarchy.[23] In time Machiavelli would excite scandalized horror among northern Europeans, but only Savonarola cut such a figure with contemporaries as to be called, alternatively, the herald of the millennium or the precursor to Antichrist.

That dispute may even have played out in the fine art of the period. Donald Weinstein has argued that in the early years of the sixteenth century Sandro Botticelli did several allegorical paintings, all intended to promote the Savonarolan movement and its eschatological vision. The most direct commentary about Florence (Figure 1.3) portrays an angel flaying the heraldic Florentine lion / fox in the vineyard (literally the *flagellum dei*), then Mary Magdalene / Florence repenting at the base of the crucifixion, and finally the city triumphant in the divine light. Weinstein has further suggested that the painting contrasts redeemed Florence with accursed Rome, the city of God and the city of the damned.[24] At just this juncture, fine art also appears to have served the

Figure 1.3 Sandro Botticelli (1444–1510) became a *piagone* or hard-core follower of Savonarola. His *Mystic Crucifixion*, executed *c.* 1500, comprises one of a number of early sixteenth-century paintings that promote the late prophet's vision of Florence. The painting, as Donald Weinstein has analyzed it, shows at center right an angel flaying a fox-like creature, at once the Florentine lion and the fox in the vineyard. Here is the prophesied *flagellum dei*, the punishment and purging of the sinful city. At the center Mary Magdalene/Florence seeks forgiveness at the foot of the cross. To the left a city, recognizably Florence, basks in the divine light. To the right of the cross above the angel, the wrath of God descends on the earth. Apparently another city is in that part of the painting, although deterioration makes it hard to see. That city, Weinstein suggests, is not prepenitential Florence, but the city of darkness, Rome. The two cities both symbolize and embody the prophetic future. (*Fogg Art Museum, Harvard University, Friends of the Fogg Art Museum Fund, 1924.27. Photo: Rick Stafford © President and Fellows of Harvard College.*)

enemies of Savonarola's movement. A number of critics have identified Luca Signorelli's massive fresco of the Antichrist in the Orvieto cathedral as referencing Savonarola (Figure 1.4).[25] There the Antichrist preaches the words whispered into his ear by Satan, while Dominican friars dispute and seem to conspire in the background. If the critics are right, two major Renaissance artists participated in contesting the meaning of the Florentine revolution. They did so not only contemporaneously, but in the shared vocabulary of the apocalypse.

The upheaval in Florence had challenged profoundly traditional European notions of politics, spirituality, and eschatology. With it we stand on the cusp of the sixteenth century's redefining revolutions. In the new century there occurred not the apocalyptic mood that had intermittently seized parts of Europe, but apocalyptic programs that shifted Europe's cultural foundations. The concern became less to identify authority than to transform society. From the 1490s onward we witness a deepening sense of expectation and with it a sharpening focus not on underlying structure but on the meaning of time. In the eleventh century Henry of Germany advanced his claims on the basis of the unchanging, god-like office he held ("though unworthy"); in the sixteenth century Henry of England advanced his claims on the basis of "sundry old histories and chronicles." Apocalyptic moments were supplanted by an ongoing and expanding apocalyptic vision: one that looked not to individuals who might anticipate the coming Antichrist or even embody that prophesied figure, but instead took up the history of institutions. The point was not reallocating labels to shifting dramatis personae but reflecting on cultural development. That is, a growing set of ideas and values that might be termed prophetic and "anti-Christian"—dark yet coherent; terrifying but completely intelligible. For the first time in some ten centuries the apocalypse re-entered the mainstream.

Still, why in the world should northern Europeans have taken up eschatology on so massive a scale? North of the Alps lay great territorial kingdoms. There radically autonomous city-states were nonexistent. In the north society took the form of well-defined legal orders and intricate hierarchies. In the north the cosmic order made sense and spoke to everyday reality. There too governance truly consisted of applying the law and doing justice. Advisors to royal, baronial, and ecclesiastical potentates might adopt the new civic vocabularies, but they inhabited highly circumscribed environments. Only the most

←————————————————————————————

Figure 1.4 Luca Signorelli (c. 1441–1523) executed the massive fresco, *The Reign and Deeds of Antichrist*, as part of a series for the San Brizio chapel of the Orvieto cathedral (1499–1504). Pictured here is a detail of the central figures.

Orvieto, a papal territory and stronghold, sponsored a strongly clerical statement that repudiated earthly government and, specifically, apocalyptic preachers who promoted such government and denounced papacy—that is, Savonarola. It is a measure of the Florentine crisis and its eschatological claims that the curia and its supporters felt the need to adopt a highly articulated apocalyptic vocabulary in response. For this reason, among others, the work is at once highly innovative and utterly reactionary.

At the center, the Antichrist preaches through the inspiration of Satan. About him are figures associated with earthly rule and the anti-Christian order. The key is the seduction of false prophecy. There among the listening crowd is the "bad" Dante of the *De monarchia* (we will remember that it remained on the papal Index until 1908)—not the "good" Dante of the *Comedia*, whose language shapes many of Signorelli's images at Orvieto. Also among the crowd, it is believed, stands Alexander the Great: "good" in medieval legend because he closed up the Antichrist's hoards beyond the Caucasus, "bad" in that, obsessed with pride, he sought to conquer the world. The Antichrist seeks to create his empire by seducing earthly authority and validating it against the true, otherworldly monarchy of Christ.

Seduction occurs in still further ways. To the left and just out of view, a Jew, swarthy like the Antichrist himself, works the crowd, offering money to an impoverished woman. Here is the seduction of material wealth and of Jewish usury, combined with the still more physical seduction of the "carnal" Jews. Savonarola's anti-Judaism was real enough, though it appears to have been qualified to the extent that he had a serious interest in Jewish learning and the Kabbalah. Signorelli's anti-Judaism is far more medieval, far more virulent.

Perhaps most important of all is the seduction of the clergy. Behind the preaching Antichrist gather a group of clergy, one and perhaps two of them visibly Dominicans. They dispute the meaning of these events, and perhaps with the others become cooped co-conspirators in the empire of the Antichrist.

Signorelli created what may well be the most developed eschatological vision ever to occur within Western art. Yet its entire purpose is to undo the central achievement of Western apocalyptic: the validation of the material world. It is hard to imagine another moment in the history of the West when the apocalypse had ever been turned so monumentally against itself. (*Scala/Art Resource, NY*) acute need combined with extraordinary social imagination could visualize these huge interlocking authorities as dynamic communities participating in sacred time. It was one thing for dynasties to promote themselves at moments as bearing sacred mission or for their publicists to portray a crowned head as the Last World Emperor. It was quite another for the apocalypse to penetrate the tissues of political culture and to define society as a whole. A great many Europeans, both Jewish and Christian, anticipated events of prophetic moment to follow on the year 1492, and these duly took place in ways both uplifting and horrific. No one anticipated the European Reformation. It proved far more difficult for Antichrist to take center stage in the atemporal climate of the north. But when he did, the world changed forever.

CHAPTER 2

APOCALYPSE REVIVED: THE REFORMATION

IMAGINING CHANGE

Between 1517 and 1525 Martin Luther and the reformers associated with him achieved something truly extraordinary, a new spirituality articulated through an altogether new religious vocabulary. The "priesthood of all believers" undercut more than a thousand years of ecclesiastical development. During the course of those centuries the clergy had successfully abstracted itself from medieval Latin society in order to dominate that society—and thereby created what they believed to be the true Christian world. Now the reformers had radically reimagined both. At a stroke the clergy had become the creatures of the community, in a real sense public servants. Moreover, the claim that salvation could be achieved by faith alone subverted the sacramental system, the foundation of clerical power and the flashpoint for dispute about priestly authority. But faith in what? Where, without clergy, could anyone perceive religious truth? Supernatural truth could only come from beyond nature itself, directly from the deity—God's specific statements made in scripture. By reading or hearing the text, anyone—literally anyone—could grasp the fundamentals of Christianity, and notably the Nazarene's redemptive mission. By having faith in that mission, salvation would occur as an act of grace.

By faith alone, by scripture alone, by grace alone, this unbending insistence on direct personal contact with the divine overturned the logic of religion. Authority now oscillated from radical individualism—with subsequent reformers generating highly developed preoccupations with both internal and external "discipline"—to a no less radical preoccupation with society and civic responsibility. Religious services for the Protestant could only take place in public, and community coercion supplanted clerical coercion as the central instrument of social control.

Here indeed was revolution. Here was also an enormous epistemological problem: why in the world was there the medieval church at all? If the church at Rome embodied false Christianity, indeed anti-Christianity, then how did this come about? How could something so profoundly wrong possess such complete power and authority? Any radical reformer, any revolutionary—at any time—needs to address just this question. It has never been an easy question to answer.

And if that were not enough, the question came with a corollary. Why was *now* the time to set it right? and who appointed you, the would-be reformer, to do so? How could so many previous generations of intelligent people be so blind, so misled? The great conservative, Catholic charge—where was your church before Luther?—does not even need to be posed. The very circumstance of reform requires the reformer to answer this question to himself. The Catholic canard, however long-lived, polemically effective, and rhetorically important within the sixteenth-century upheaval, is ultimately irrelevant.

Today, modern people all but instinctively respond to such questions with secular historical analysis and the powerful insight of social science. But no such intellectual tools were available to the sixteenth century. Quite the contrary, the reformers would lay the foundations from which such categories of analysis eventually arose. For early modern people the problem was gigantic. Change required a vocabulary of development, history, and time. It demanded ways of imagining qualitative change.

Yet, as we have seen in chapter 1, the mainstream medieval world offered intellectual structures that were altogether unsatisfactory to this purpose. The dominant ways of thought spoke within two allied voices. On the one hand there existed an organic tradition, a form of naturalism variously labeled but famously known as the Great Chain of Being. Concerned with the manipulation of timeless categories, it undertook deductions from universal propositions. Universal propositions, however, could only generate still further universal propositions. They offered no insight into particular circumstances, no mechanism for conceiving of change or process. Only an angelic intellect might intuit particulars from universals. Only angels, the medieval successors to Plato's imaginary philosopher king, might perceive the individual within the general. The human mind simply could not do it. The syllogism neatly illustrates the point. Major premise: Socrates is a man. Minor premise: all men are mortal. The conclusion tells what Socrates shares or might share with other men, but it tells us nothing whatever about what distinguishes Socrates from other individuals. It can tell us nothing of Socrates' uniqueness, nothing about his particular character, or, most important, nothing about his moment—his moment in time. No matter how skillful the logician, no matter how determined the thinker, no matter how subtle the reasoning, universals could never get beyond universals. And all such categories were inherently timeless. The medieval ratio provided a deeply atemporal set of analytical techniques and offered no insight into history.

Again as we have seen in the previous chapter, even when medieval people needed to speak of the individual, the particular, the context, they still did so in ways that were also effectively timeless. They talked of tradition, custom, ancient usage—procedures, directives, and characteristics that had existed "time out of mind." When, between 1468 and 1471, England's lord chief justice Sir John Fortescue described the realm, he spoke of its customs and of their vast antiquity. England's outstanding feature was that, despite all the political changes that had taken place over the centuries, nothing had really changed. All sorts of people had ruled the kingdom of England at one time or another: Britons, Saxons, Romans, Danes, and now Normans. Yet throughout this vast stretch of time, "the realm has been continuously ruled by the same customs as it is now, customs which, if they had not been the best, some of those kings would have changed for the sake or justice or by the impulse of caprice, and totally abolished them." But English law worked so well that no ruler did, not even the Romans. That law was consequently the oldest and most continuous in Europe. "Hence there is no gainsaying nor legitimate doubt but that the customs of the English are not only good but the best."[1] England's law was the "best" in the sense that it best fit the particular context that comprised the English kingdom. Other legal systems did not serve their environments as competently or effectively as did England's because they lacked comparable antiquity. They were not as "immemorial." They could not therefore possess comparable "wisdom." The ancient medieval maxim described it succinctly: old law is good law, and the good old law is valid as new law is not.

Of course things did change, as Fortescue and everyone else knew full well, but what impressed medieval people was the underlying structure, ultimately rooted in nature, that withstood change. Both logic and tradition were timeless, and that precise quality made the world rational and amenable to human cognition. Change was just the opposite and found its symbol in Lady Fortune's wheel. Kings and kingdoms were lifted up and cast down, but the archetypes of kingship, social hierarchy, and authority remained unaltered. Change, transience, decay, and mutation all obtained in the world below the moon. But they did not feature within the regular workings of the pristine, changeless heavens (see Figure 2.1). Rather, they were the measure of irrationality, the consequence of the fall of man—at once both painful and yet meaningless. For medieval people the wheel of fortune became their emblem of the absurd.

The entire weight of the medieval world thus bore heavily against any idea of meaningful, qualitative change. To envision that this day might be one way, but that tomorrow would be or should be radically different—or that things had once been right, but were now just the opposite and utterly wrong—required an act of deeply religious imagination. It required the spirituality of the apocalypse. Prophecy alone allowed this possibility in the pre-modern age. The prophets, the patriarchs, and the apostles had spoken of corruption and crisis at the end of days. Daniel in particular had seen a succession of kingdoms before justice and righteousness triumphed. Paul had warned of a false Christianity before the return of the Nazarene. Peter's letters had spoken frequently of the Antichrist, indeed of the Antichrists, that lay in the future. John of Patmos had outlined figuratively what appeared to be the narrative of the entire Christian experience, which simply brimmed with images of transformation, retribution, and justice. Surely if this vast array of prophetic symbols and pregnant promises possessed any meaning at all, it described the spiritual crisis of the sixteenth century and the rise of reform in the latter days. The apocalypse, eschatology, and prophecy became ever more important ideas for Luther and the early reformers and then a central theme within the Reformation. The apocalypse made the world intelligible.

Figure 2.1 Robert Recorde's *The Castle of Knowledge* (London, 1556) is the first English explication of Copernicus's new astronomy. The frontispiece illustrates the empire of fortune and its limits. To the left Lady Reason with dividers in hand charts the heavenly sphere. There lies the realm of certainty and stability, where motion can be calculated and the future projected. Accordingly, Reason stands in her shoes, her feet firmly planted upon a pillar, clear-eyed and wise. To the right Lady Fortune turns her wheel of instability while precariously standing barefoot on a ball. Blindfolded, and with her clothing in disarray, she rules a world transience, aimless change, mutability, contingency, and ignorance—a world without meaning or intelligibility. The verses in the lower cartouche indicate that Lady Fortune's empire does not extend beyond the sublunar realm, even within a Copernican universe.

As early as the summer of 1520 Luther had come to see the medieval church and its clerical defenders as a cruel inversion of the Christian faith, the anti-Christianity of prophecy. "Well may we fear that
Antichrist has been at work, or is completing his preparations." The
reformers confronted nothing less than "the community of Antichrist
and the devil." The extravagant claims made for papal authority
"surely is the work of Antichrist himself." Like a great many people,
including even those who rejected his reform, Luther had no doubt
that he was living "in these latter days of evil."[2] His reform, along
with his prophetic understanding of its significance, proved explosive
throughout Europe. Within a decade his major works saw translation
into languages across the continent. The new spirituality reached in
all directions and to all levels of society. By 1525 the peasants of Swa-
bia took up arms in the name of reform both religious and social, and,
also from Luther, they adopted the language of Antichrist. If, like
nearly all European elites, Luther continued to believe in the Great
Chain of Being and social hierarchy, which he saw as still obtaining
within the realm of nature, he actually had more in common with the
radicals than he found comfortable. Both sides agreed that there had
been a great falling away since the days of the apostles and the early
church. Prophecy had unfolded as a false church supplanted the true
one. If Luther rejected the peasants' demands, it was in part because
the world neared its end, and the propagation of the gospel within the
time remaining could hardly proceed within a context of class conflict.
An admonition to peace rather than to social justice, however conceived, met the urgent need of this decisive moment.

Luther's combination of theological radicalism with social conservatism made his thought vastly significant, reaching well beyond any
social reform that might be derived from it, and well beyond its
impact on the peasants who appealed to him. Now for the first time
in more than a millennium, apocalyptic expectations reached into the
European mainstream intellectually, socially, culturally. Not since the
Intertestamental period had this line of thinking commanded such
widespread adherence. No longer the property of marginalized intellectuals like the spiritual Franciscans, or the ideology of the occasional
community like Savonarolan Florence, or even the prism for moments
of dynastic pretension, apocalyptic expectations now acquired an
altogether new status. They had become integral within Western

intellectual and political life. Nearly the whole of Europe was aflame with the claims of reform, and reform inherently entailed the apocalypse. The apocalypse now so defined the world that, although it might be refuted or reread, it could never be dismissed or ignored. It was a matter of intense dispute in the sixteenth century whether the Protestant reform would recover a lost church and, for some, a lost civilization as well. But on one point the reformers's claims were unassailable: like their apostolic predecessors, the reformers looked to an imminent end, the return of the master, the triumph of righteousness. In this respect, if none other, the Reformation linked with antiquity in ways quite unlike the Middle Ages.

Yet something else happened that was largely without precedent. Medieval men had hesitated to call even their bitterest enemies the Antichrist, but when they did they almost invariably named individuals: Saladin, Frederick II, Pope John XXII (an Avignon pope with the dubious distinction of being judged most often the historic Antichrist). Even Joachim of Fiore, the most original of the medieval apocalyptic thinkers, and probably the medieval thinker with deepest sense of time and change, still saw the Antichrist as an individual. Small wonder that the Middle Ages witnessed the development of a luxuriant undergrowth of legend about the life and deeds of Antichrist. Even when they identified groups of heretics or spoke of the Turkish menace, the target was imagined as an individual leader or a particular sultan. By contrast Luther and the sixteenth-century reformers saw the Antichrist as the *institution* that was the papacy and the medieval church—its doctrines, its ceremonies, its spirituality. The reformers thus undertook a project of greater complexity, with wider intellectual sophistication, and with a deeper preoccupation with time.

We can see this transition throughout Europe, even in far-off Scotland. When the Scots theologian John Ireland spoke of Antichrist in 1490 or when the Scots poet William Dunbar did so about a decade later, in typical medieval fashion they both meant an individual. The term bore no political implications; there was nothing even remotely imminent about it. By 1550 all that had changed. We encounter a new landscape when the earl of Glencairn in 1539 denounced the Catholic clergy as "monsters with the Beast's marke." In 1550 John Knox outlined the apocalyptic programmatic underlying human experience in what would be his most remembered sermon. The 1559–1560

revolution that overthrew papal authority ensured that the new historical vision reached deeply into Scottish culture. By 1570 the apocalypse
had established itself as a commonplace in popular political literature.
By 1580–1581 Scottish Catholics, looking to the prospect of a counter-
revolution against the Protestant government, felt the need to invert
the claims of the Protestant apocalyptic—even if they could not develop an alternative analysis of the past. The Antichrist had emerged at
Geneva (not at the Vatican). By the 1590s Calvinist merchants in
Edinburgh decorated their homes with murals that offered complex and
highly politicized readings of the apocalyptic struggle in which they saw
themselves.[3] The apocalypse had now become immediate, urgent, and
omnipresent, for it brought a changing world into focus.

But something else followed on the reformed understanding of Antichrist, which had no precedent whatever. By the early 1530s Philipp
Melanchthon, Joachim Camerarius, and other humanist scholars associated with Luther began to develop *a historical vision* of the rise of
Antichrist as an institution. Working with Johannes Carion's *Chronica*,
initially a highly regarded chronicle of European events in traditional
medieval form, the Lutheran humanists constructed an account of the
Middle Ages as a step-by-step historical process. The European past
had ceased to be simply one event after another, but instead acquired
a central organizing principle. The story of Europe now possessed
direction and meaning well beyond anything previously imagined.
Quite literally, it was going somewhere. Now people wanted know
when and how papal claims arose and were made successful. They
wanted to know when and how the false doctrines—transubstantiation,
the intercession of saints, purgatory, indulgences, and so on—had
actually emerged and become persuasive. What had caused this great
"falling away," as Paul had called it? When and why did the princes of
the earth ultimately succumb and give over to these gross pretensions
and fabrications? The rise of the Hildebrandine popes became a central
element in the prophetic story, no less than did the royal and heretical
resistance to them. The records of the past suddenly assumed crucial
importance. Episcopal registers, court records, political papers, charters,
grants, chronicles, documents of all sorts and archives of every description, all acquired a significance and urgency that they had never
previously possessed. Institutional records became important to the sixteenth century no longer simply to establish title, document a right, or

confirm procedure and precedence, but now also to identify historical development. Documents lay the foundation for understanding not merely current issues, but human purpose. The story of the West had become a linear process, a great sacred drama. Europe's first historicism was born.

History and prophecy were one. Luther found himself amazed and delighted at this discovery. "Though I was not at first historically well informed, I attacked the papacy on the basis of holy Scripture. Now I rejoice heartily to see that others have attacked it from another source, that is, from history." "What I have learned and taught from Paul and Daniel, namely, that the Pope is Antichrist, that history proclaims, pointing and indicating the very man himself." At precisely this juncture Luther, his associates, and virtually all reformers began to correlate prophetic symbols from scripture with the course of the medieval past—politically, spiritually, legally, and even culturally. The great reformer could only applaud "this art and new language."[4]

The new sacred history—that is, institutional history—spread rapidly and became one of the intellectual staples of the Reformation. Such writers as Matthias Flacius Illyricus and his associates with the Magdeburg *Centuries* in Germany, to Francis Lambert and Jean Crespin in France, to John Bale and John Foxe in England, developed a new, purposeful, and increasingly articulated vision of the past. It is no accident that separate chairs of history were established at a number of Lutheran universities during the 1540s and 1550s, something that Luther himself had encouraged. Nor did this development limit itself to the Lutheran world. It is a matter of major significance that Edward VI's revolutionary regime in England tried to attract Melanchthon, one of the fathers of the new history, to a chair at the University of Cambridge. Even without the appointment Melanchthon's influence reached far beyond the German lands. Luther's words about history validating prophecy had prefaced a history of the papacy written by the early English reformer Robert Barnes, a work that grew directly out of the new intellectual project at Wittenberg in the early 1530s. Barnes's history laid the foundation for the Anglophone tradition. Melanchthon, famous as the *Praeceptor Germaniae*, was no less the *Praeceptor Angliae*—and in many ways the teacher of all Europe.

At the most practical and visible level, this new concern with time manifests itself in Germany after 1550 with the appearance of elaborate clocks intended to illustrate the divine governance of the world. No less telling, an altogether new preoccupation with world chronology emerged, which sought to date events literally from the creation. The learned might enlist still other kinds of knowledge to this end. Could not astrology, periodization derived from the sacred numbers and times within scripture, and the narrative of human experience join with the apocalyptic program to form one grand synthesis? Were there not historical moments fatal to government and rulers that would correlate the shifting configuration of the stars and the schedule of prophecy? The rhythms of human behavior, the shifting patterns of nature, and the linear course of grace might become integrated within a single historical system. Despite Calvin's hostility and Luther's deep unease about the subject, the prospect of a reformed astrology based on the latest astronomy became the project of mainstream intellectuals throughout Europe.

Robert Pont, Knox's close associate and one of the most esteemed and venerable fathers of the Scottish Reformation, undertook just such a grand astral sociology. For Pont the numerical patterns that could be keyed within history, astrology, prophecy not only pulled together human experience—its moments of strength and virtue, its moments of decline and corruption, its overall direction—but elucidated their purpose and part within the redemptive plan. Astrology and thus the processes of nature itself validated prophecy and history, and operated as "a concurrente cause." For Pont and others writing at the end of the sixteenth century, the apocalypse found itself anchored in naturalistic explanations. Pont insisted that the apocalypse, now rightly understood through the force of nature, would show the Jews when messiah simply *had* to come and when his return could be expected. It would also identify unmistakably the latter days of the world and delineate the significance of contemporary events.[5] Obviously all these inquiries, however widespread or intensely undertaken, could only prove intellectually barren. Yet they are symptomatic of the new time-oriented sensibility. And if this kind of scholarship became prominent in the emerging world of history and development, no less did it also validate that world.

Now the Reformation made manifest sense. It emerged from the logic of prophecy, embodying the implications of time and history rather than that of the syllogism. The reformers enacted the prophesied events of the end of days, the culmination of human experience. Luther and the magisterial reformers were emphatic that they received no direct revelation, unlike Daniel and John. There would be no further illumination before the end. But they had seen the meaning of the sacred text, now altogether unmistakable, and they would proclaim it to the world. In that sense they were indeed prophets, for they were the interpreters and explicators of prophecy. The reform movement, if not any individual reformer, had been announced by God centuries before. A remarkable number of people, men and women, clerics and laymen, elite and low-born, now became self-conscious "prophets," offering interpretations of the apocalypse. The Scottish aristocrat John Napier of Merchiston and the Scottish minister John Knox claimed to be such "prophets" and were accepted as such. Europe was alive with intellectuals, often more theoreticians than theologians, who expounded the meaning of the past and its implications for the present moment. Inevitably, the non-elite also participated and could prove themselves remarkably articulate. Bishop John Jewel spoke a palpable truism when he claimed, "There is none, neither old nor young, neither learned nor unlearned, but he has heard of Antichrist."[6] All kinds of people, from major intellects like Thomas Cranmer to humble working folk like Anne Askew, saw themselves directly enacting the apocalypse through their martyrdom. The actions of both realized the prophetic promises and fulfilled human destiny.

VISIONS AND REVISIONS

What we might call the magisterial model or master narrative provided all but universally accepted assumptions about anti-Christian decline. Through debate about the model's structure and parameters, reformers of all kinds contested doctrine, politics, and the future. Broadly it ran as follows. From the founding of Christian society and the overthrow of Satan's public kingdom with the emperor Constantine (c. 300) to the final triumph of the medieval papacy in the thirteenth and fourteenth centuries, the faith had undergone a gradual, ever deepening declension. Step by step, at moments quickly, at moments in the face of stiff resistance, the Catholic Church had climbed to power and systematically subverted the faith of the Nazarene and the apostles, the faith established by the great emperor.

Thereafter, false Christianity, the Antichrist, had been restrained, ever more tenuously, for a thousand years. The period ran roughly from 300 to 1300, from Constantine to Pope Boniface VIII. With Boniface's unfettered claims for universal papal monarchy, with his "Unam Sanctam," his "Clericis Laicos," and other great proclamations of clerical power, even the face of Christianity had disappeared. Antichrist, Satan's lieutenant on earth, his historical and institutional manifestation, at this point emerged fully to seek out and destroy the now hidden remnants of Christ's flock.

Here was the millennium of which John had spoken. Here was the meaning of all those prophetic symbols in scripture. The great beast symbolized the body of the church within Christendom. Its ten horns identified the kings of the earth who protected and maintained it. Babylon was the city of Rome. The whore of Babylon specifically figured the papacy, a prostitution of Christianity. She was adored by earthly authority, while the true faith was depicted by the woman driven into the wilderness. The whore's "cup of iniquity" could only invite thoughts of the mass and the sacerdotal claims of the clergy. The false prophet and dragon manifested still further aspects of papal tyranny and duplicity.

Scripture indicated that there would be more than one beast, more than one great agency of evil in human history. Of course there were many antichrists—the mendicant orders, the curia, all the members and promoters of the medieval church. But there was clearly something more, and that more had long been readily apparent: the empire of the Ottoman Turks. This external institution of evil had also been anticipated and portrayed in both testaments. Except for Luther, most sixteenth-century reformers found the rise of Islam and the Turks in the figures of Gog and Magog, and in passages from the Revelation that obviously denoted the Middle East. Here again the focus fell on the evil empire rather than on any particular sultan. Europeans, however, knew relatively little about Middle Eastern societies and their history, precious little even about Islam itself; few indeed spoke the languages of the region. What impressed the reformers was chronology. The Ottomans burst onto the scene just as the papacy was reaching its horrific fruition. The emergence of Muhammad coincided with early papal claims, and, for some, both offered insight into that most mysterious of biblical numbers, 666. Since antiquity the seals, trumpets, and vials or bowls, along with the numbers that appeared the prophetic parts of scripture, had stimulated speculation about the periodization of history. In the hands of the reformers they unmistakably indicated that these were the latter days, the autumn of the world.

The culmination of human experience could not be far off. For the reformers the end could be all but immediate. As Luther wrote: "For my part, I am sure that the Day of Judgment is just around the corner. It doesn't matter that we don't know the precise day ... perhaps someone else can figure it out. But it is certain that time is now at an end."[7] Some thought they had solved it. The Lutheran minister Michael Stifel declared that end would arrive at 8:00 AM on 19 October 1533.[8] Although Stifel provoked a "scandal" and needed to be reassigned, his calculations grew directly out of widespread contemporary concerns. This kind of phenomenon recurred even into the late twentieth century, but we need to view Stifel in context. Quite unlike most of his late modern successors, there was nothing in the least anti-intellectual or obscurantist about him. He was a significant mathematician who drew on the most advanced theory. He was surely extravagant, but hardly mad. Calvin, Zwingli, and later reformers did not share so severe a sense of imminence. They configured their expectations differently, but were no less apocalyptic. Rather, they focused on the new institutions and the new society that might emerge to bear witness in the twilight of history. Their outlook was in some respects more energized and less resigned, carrying a more articulated political agenda, especially after mid-century.

What would happen in the immediate future, in the run-up to the end of time? No specific answer was available. The false church might be overthrown. The truth might triumph on earth. Alternatively, the faith might spread, but so too would the ferocity of persecution, and the suffering would only end with the return of the Nazarene at the rapidly approaching end of time. Visions of the end shifted as Protestant fortunes rose or fell. For the hugely influential English reformer John Bale, conflicting endings could appear within the covers of a single volume. He offered a major interpretation of the Revelation in his *The Image of Both Churches* (written between 1541 and 1548), and at a number of junctures in the book projected a glorious final period at the end of days. Based on the "silence for half an hour" (Rev. 8.1), Bale argued that, "Then shall wretched Babylon fall, then shall the bloody beast full of blasphemous names perish, then shall the great Antichrist with his whole generation come altogether to nought, then shall the fierce dragon be tied up for a thousand years." "In the time of this sweet silence shall Israel be revived, the Jews shall be converted, the heathen shall come in."[9]

Bale did not develop a highly detailed vision of these last days, nor did he firmly indicate how long this period of peace actually would be. Like his colleagues Bale anchored the millennium in the historical past, thereby securing the master narrative of the European experience and the place of the Reformation within it. Still, the great moment did not lie far off: "Thus shall the glory of God be within a few years seen the world over, to the comfort many." During that time the godless majority would coexist with the faithful, but there would be no persecution. Only at the end of this period would the wicked rise again against the faith, and that could be expected to precipitate the Last Judgment at the very end of time. At one juncture Bale even intimated that the earth itself might become physically renewed: "so shall the whole face of the earth appear more beautiful than now."[10] Bale's powerful expectations looked to Edward VI's brief rule, when a radical and reformed England seemed in the offing. That had not always been the case. The reactionary final years of Henry VIII's reign (occurring in a context of European-wide repression) produced a very different set of expectations about the end. "For nowhere is it lawful rightly without superstition to confess the name and verity of Christ, a few cities except, unless men be torn by these wolves [the Catholic clergy]. And thus is it like still to continue to the end of the world, both by this prophecy [the Revelation] and also by the prophecy of Daniel." One book, two endings. Bale seemed untroubled by this fact, and even went on to state firmly, "Yet is the text [the Book of Revelation] a light to the chronicles, and not the chronicles to the text."[11] In one sense nothing could have been further from the case. The entire configuration of *The Image* was driven by political history, shaped and reshaped by the course of contemporary events.

Nor should this be surprising. A former Carmelite friar who had written a history of his order before converting to Protestantism, and a man always more interested in history than theology, Bale was typical of many mid-century intellectuals. Agitator, radical administrator, polemicist, controversialist, and a playwright who pioneered the Anglophone history play, Bale was above all an antiquarian and historical editor. One of his greatest concerns was to preserve the vast archives of the dissolved English monasteries. These records would provide the materials by which to construct the English dimension of the new history of Europe. But in themselves such records could not speak directly to the purpose because their authors were normally corrupt, self-serving clergy and, more important, individuals who had no idea of the meaning of the events in which they participated. The real point of Bale's remark about tuning history to prophecy was to fit the facts into the new organizing framework.

In a way Bale went still further. There was, he insisted, "not one necessary point of belief in all the other scriptures, that is not here also in one place or other." "He that knoweth not this book, knoweth not the church whereof he is a member."[12] The Revelation embodied all the essentials truths of the faith. Initially for many of the major reformers, for Luther, Calvin, Bucer, and others, the Revelation had been a most problematic text—as it been for humanists like Desiderius Erasmus and, centuries before, for the Nicene Council and Augustine. Was it authentic or canonical? What could all those symbols possibly mean? Although it soon became a foundational text for all Protestants, at first this particular book, unlike all the other prophetic parts of scripture, prompted consternation about its interpretation and status. Bale felt no such hesitation and in fact proclaimed just the reverse. We would find it all in the Revelation, and the Revelation formed but another way of saying that we would find it all in history.

Plastic in its finale, but highly etched in its picture of the past, the reformed master narrative provided the framework through which the present was both understood and contested. To dispute the vision or aspects of it was to reformulate the issues, priorities, and program of the Reformation. For John Foxe—Bale's colleague and successor, and a writer of defining importance for the English-speaking cultures— Constantine was one of the most momentous figures in human history. "A second Moses sent up and put up by God," and almost an apostle, the great emperor had overthrown paganism, established the true church, and, through his Council of Nicea, published authentic doctrine. His were the halcyon days, and the binding of Satan. "Great tranquility followed," and if in subsequent centuries the long decline began, still peace "continued in the church without any open slaughter [of the faithful] for a thousand years." Here too was the model for the latter days: a second, end-time Constantine might arise to protect and promote the faith. Antichrist's power might be "in a great part of the world overthrown, or, at least, universally in the whole world detected."[13] The young, intelligent, and truly radical Edward VI—Britain's only genuinely revolutionary king—seemed a promising candidate. After his premature death and then the religious counterrevolution that followed under Mary Tudor, the much less promising Elizabeth might yet fulfill at least aspects of these hopes. Reform required royal authority, and Foxe visually linked Elizabeth with the emperor at a key juncture in *The Acts and Monuments*. Elizabeth's image, with her feet on an overthrown pope, appears circumscribed by the large "C" that began the name Constantine. Elizabeth's mission was literally contained within the name (and story) of the great emperor.

Not everyone agreed. More radical reformers pushed the ideal moment, the purest expression of the faith, and the model for the future, back in time to an earlier period. The closer one got to the apostolic era, the nearer one approached Christ, and, at the same time, the more radical appeared the implications for the present. During the first centuries the government of the church seemed more egalitarian, and the concern seemed to be more with faith rather than ceremony. For many radicals corruption crept in when some clergy claimed authority over their brethren, and bishops were introduced into the church. Here lay the root of the problem, "for bishops would be archbishops, and they metropolitans and they patriarchs, and so popes."[14] Constantine was certainly a crucial figure in world history, but not at all what more conservative reformers had believed. The great emperor promoted bishops, hierarchy, clerical authority, and thereby *launched* the prophesied Antichrist. Superstitious blindness led him to crystallize corruption. Far from being one of history's most noble moments, it was one of its most disastrous. The implications for the present were no less great. Reform found guidance from a clergy all of whom enjoyed "parity" with one another and by lay leaders who were integrated with them into a structure of councils. Thinking along these lines became highly formulated in northern Europe in the wake of the upheavals that took place in France, England, Scotland, and the Netherlands during that revolutionary decade 1558–1568. Merchiston's *A Plaine Discovery of the Whole Revelation* (1593) provided one of the fuller explications of this re-reading of the reformed historical vision. This work, Merchiston tells us, grew out of lectures he had heard on the apocalypse at the University of St. Andrews in 1564. Thomas Brightman's enormous *Revelation of the Revelation*, appearing posthumously in 1609, provided yet another hugely influential revision. A remarkable range of still further possibilities arose from such alternate interpretations of the prophetic past. Congregationalism as well as all kinds of sectarian possibilities derived from shifts in emphasis and even minor alterations in the narrative.

The master narrative, however configured, inherently entailed a double process. The rise of Antichrist was only part of the story. For who had resisted this ongoing corruption of the Christian church? When did people first detect this rise of a false church and come to see the full enormity of what was happening? Earlier heresy and dissent became matters of burning interest. Did England's great critic of the papacy, John Wycliffe (c. 1370), first see the significance of what was going on and announce the era of Antichrist? Many in England thought so and saw the subsequent story of his followers, the heretical Lollards, to be of defining importance. If English experience seemed to lie disproportionately at the heart of the redemptive drama, it might imply that England had a sacred mission at the end of days. Alternatively, what was the role of Jan Hus of Bohemia (executed by the papacy in 1415), who in some ways seemed Wycliffe's successor? Did the abbot Joachim back in the twelfth century have an inkling of what was happening, or did he speak more wisely than he knew? The history of the Antichrist became at the same time the history of rising consciousness.

Moreover, recent humanist discoveries about the antique world further enriched the new apocalyptic history. From the late fourteenth century onward, Europeans reconstructed classical notions of the citizen and public life. As we have seen with figures as different as Cola di Rienzo in Rome or Savonarola in Florence, such values could inform apocalyptic expectations within the Italian city-states. Although these political vocabularies had entered into northern Europe by the outset of the sixteenth century, they assumed an altogether new and compelling meaning after 1560. In those years the Reformation brought with it ongoing upheaval and drastic instability. The reflexive directives of law, tradition, order, hierarchy, and all the familiar commonplaces either weakened or dissolved altogether before the relentless imperative to direct action in the face of unprecedented problems and unexpected opportunities. In such volatile circumstances articulate decision-taking could only supplant ancient formulae and challenge instinctive habits of mind. Scotland, France, England, and the Netherlands became effectively "monarchical republics," and the language of citizenship acquired unprecedented immediacy, relevance, and cogency. What for many had previously been no more than abstracted ideals, moral exemplars, or merely rhetorical postures, now became practical mandates. Late sixteenth-century religious revolution was also political revolution, and its leaders often enough found it both necessary and exhilarating to adopt the analytical insights of the Italian Renaissance. The redeemed saint and the virtuous citizen turned out to have much in common. The selfrestrained Stoic and the "disciplined" believer found themselves in many ways at one. Calvin and Cato emerged as remarkably similar. For the humanist scholar and poet George Buchanan the great villains of antiquity were the enemies of the polis and civic life: Xerxes, Alexander of Macedonia, Julius Caesar. The legendary Athenian king Codrus who sacrificed his life to save the city provides the classical exemplar. Julius Caesar, the great subverter of the republic, is his antitype.

> On his country's behalf Codrus hurls himself on the foe's drawn
>   swords.
> Against his country's peace Caesar brought flames and the weap
>   ons of war.
> Codrus strengthened his country's laws by shedding his own
>   blood.
> Caesar made himself rich by spilling the blood of his countrymen.
> Today there's not a king who vaunts himself in the name of
>   Codrus.
> One and all want to be called Caesar.
> What's the reason? The common wisdom of those who hold the
>   scepter,
> Is to hate the acts of Codrus, and approve the acts of Caesar.[15]

Constantine could become expanded to embrace the Caesars generally, his disaster part of a still larger catastrophe. The destruction of the republic and the launching of the great Antichrist formed part of a single process of spiritual degeneration. Conversely, the recovery of a lost religion now involved the recovery of a lost civilization. Reformed religion became thereby also a civil religion. Within the master narrative, now enriched with these new dimensions, redemption embodied a political act. This line of thinking would emerge as foundational to what we today call the Atlantic republican tradition. Within Scotland, Buchanan's humanist successors, most notably Andrew Melville and David Hume of Godscroft, sought to imagine just such a vision of the past. But its influence reached wider still. Merchiston bitterly denounced the pagan Roman Empire and its immediate antichristian successor, which he saw as virtually identical. He said nothing about republican antiquity. The lessons of the past seemed severely and all but uniformly negative. But in his arrestingly frank policy directives to King James that prefaced *The Plaine Discovery* we surely hear the voice of the concerned citizen.

No issue more exercised Protestant apocalyptic thinking than did the idea of the millennium. On the one hand, it provided the spine that held together the European experience and made it intelligible. On the other, there was the vague and shifting promise of the future, and the language of the millennium was almost inevitably also thought of as speaking to the culmination of human experience. But nothing more encouraged hesitation about a millennial future than did the brief and bloody episode at the German city of Münster, 1534–1535. There radical Protestants, led by Jan Mathijs and John Beukels (also known as John of Leiden), declared the inauguration of the millennial age. Vastly more fantastic in its claims and subversive in its social organization than Savonarola's Florence or Cola's Rome—involving what appears to have a deliberate inversion of all contemporary social norms—the city would be crushed with blood-curdling ferocity by combined Protestant and Catholic armies. In the decades that followed, any talk of a future millennium carried with it the Münster taint.

Only at the very end of the century did this constricting fear begin to relax. Renewed reflection about the future occurred from the 1590s onwards throughout Europe. This renewed interest arose, somewhat surprisingly, in a context of increasing political conservatism and authoritarianism, and frequently provided a counterthrust to these developments. Moreover, such reflection comprised a genuinely Western phenomenon, occurring largely independently in England, Scotland, the Netherlands, France, Scandinavia, in communities across Poland-Lithuania, and especially throughout the German-speaking world. Overwhelmingly Protestant, such speculation nevertheless emerged also within the far less congenial climate of the Counter-Reformation, in Italy, Portugal, Spain, and most notably the New World. These lines of thought continued to appear, in increasingly articulated form, through the early decades of the seventeenth century. Often this apocalyptic speculation linked with proto-scientific utopias as well as with traditional forms of the occult. What characterized virtually all such reflection was its emphasis on human agency.

Many writers, like Merchiston, did not actually propose a future millennium, but instead developed much more highly articulated and positive expectations for the decades ahead. Others, like Brightman, proposed a double millennium, one that not only framed the historical past but also projected the political future. Here was a real shift, one that reached in many intellectual directions. Expectations about a future millennium became increasingly widespread and more highly developed in the years leading up to the Thirty Years' War. Nor did such expectations diminish once the war broke out and the Protestant cause experienced unrelenting catastrophe during the first dozen years. Whether with Johann Heinrich Alsted, Johann Heinrich Bisterfeld, and Jakob Boehme on the continent or with Henry Finch and Joseph Mede in Britain, the apocalyptic future emerged with ever greater detail and philosophical sophistication. Neither the hope of triumph nor the experience of defeat seemed to divert the powerful intellectual currents that had appeared by the 1590s.

Yet none of these variations, increasingly complex as they were, actually displaced the historical vision that had first appeared in the 1530s. One might celebrate Constantine and imperial Rome, and look to a revitalized and genuinely reformed final empire. One might instead insist that latter-day Constantines, would-be Caesars, and self-proclaimed Augustuses hardly offered a future that anyone would want. Still, the organization of the past remained broadly the same, contested at crucial junctures and yet thereby also confirmed. Even the shift from a past to a future millennium involved less change and marked less of a break than we might expect. Attention turned from the past to the future, but the outlines of the European (and hence human) experience remained as cogent as ever. They would continue to do so right into the eighteenth-century Enlightenment.

THE IRONY OF IMAGE

With the sixteenth century, universal literacy became a European ideal—indeed an imperative—for the first time ever. Even before the outbreak of the Reformation humanist scholars like Desiderius Erasmus had wanted scripture to become universally accessible. As Erasmus famously declared in his "Paraclesis" to the New Testament, "Christ wished his mysteries to be published as widely as possible. I wish that even the weakest woman should read the Gospel ... And I wish there were translated into all languages, so that they might be read and understood, not only by Scots and Irishmen, but also by Turks and Saracens." "I long that the husbandman should sing portions of them to himself as he follows the plow, that the weaver should hum them to himself to the tune of his shuttle, that the traveler should beguile with their stories the tedium of his journey."[16] The rise of a religion like Protestantism—so resolutely text-based, so emphatically a religion of the Word—now made literacy a universal norm. In part Protestant's dispute with the medieval church—the religion of the mass—comprised an issue about the relationship between verbal and non-verbal symbols. It can hardly be any wonder that Luther had urged the reallocation of clerical wealth for the creation of schools, Erasmus's pious aspiration translated into a social program. Nor should it surprise us that reformers like John Foxe saw the press ensuring Protestant triumph: "either the pope must abolish printing, or he must seek a new world to reign over: for else, as this world standeth, printing doubtless will abolish him." In language that anticipated John Milton, Foxe went on to claim that "how many printing presses there be in the world, so many block-houses there be against the high castle of St. Angelo [the great papal fortress]."[17] For reformers from Luther to Foxe the press was a providential invention, reserved for the latter days, and integral to the unfolding of the apocalypse. Accordingly, throughout the century we encounter images of reformers confronting Antichrist with printed books, and in one instance breaking down the walls of Babylon-Rome with bundles of them.[18] All this might seem only natural in the new world of text, records, institutions.

If general literacy had now become mandated within Western civilization for the first time, it remained of course vastly far from a social reality. The success of the early Reformation turned to a significant extent on its ability to create powerful images that reached into the tissues of popular culture. Such images ranged widely indeed, literally from the scatological to the eschatological. Images of peasants defecating into a huge, inverted papal tiara could complement images of the Antichrist.

Very quickly images of the latter became incorporated into reformed literature. The eschatological mood, so much a part of the outset of the
sixteenth century and so closely associated with the expected revival of
piety, had appeared early on in Albrecht Dürer's apocalyptic engravings.
But they became transformed in Lucas Cranach's woodcuts that accompanied Luther's 1522 translation of the New Testament. Now they
articulated specific spiritual claims about the papacy and the medieval
church generally. Their significance extended still further. Not only was
it the sole illustrated book of the New Testament in this edition, Luther
himself was as yet far from certain of the Revelation's authenticity and
meaning. At this moment the power of the apocalypse seems to have
run ahead of the great reformer himself.

Even today these images will seem striking. In one, reformers, in
the figure of the prophets Elias and Enoch, confront the beast wearing
the papal crown. They speak with the voice of prophecy; flame shoots
from their mouths. They have exposed the Antichrist (Rev. 11.1–8).
Behind them other reformers take the measurements of the Temple,
the Temple to be rebuilt at the end of days. In another, the whore of
Babylon (Rev. 17), wearing the papal tiara, rides on the back of the
great beast offering the cup of iniquity to the princes of the earth,
some of whom worship her on their knees. These images became for-
malized with the 1534 full German Bible. With them the reformers
confront the papal beast with the opened book of scripture. In the
background the temple being measured has now turned into the Castle
Church at Wittenberg. The apocalypse has become immanent within
the political dynamics of the Reformation and immediate in its implications. With the 1534 image of the whore, the cup has come to contain a very generous measure of iniquity—and the lady herself is
emphatically papal, in addition to being well-fed and sensuous. As
early as 1522 specific figures can be identified among the worshiping
princes (notably, the German emperor, Maximilian I).[19] In the 1534
version all royal authority is on its knees, and specific individuals
emerge prominently (Figures 2.2 and 2.3). Politics, spirituality, and
history have merged into a compelling prescriptive analysis.

All of these images reached their culmination in 1545, the last year
of Luther's life, with perhaps the most spectacular representation of
the papal Antichrist. Engraved by Melchior Lorch, the picture com-
bines the medieval theme of the wild man with the apocalyptic papal
Antichrist, joining as well scatology with eschatology (Figure 2.4). In

Figure 2.2 This illustration from Martin Luther's translation of the Bible (1534) shows the reformers as the prophesied latter-day Elias and Enoch who expose the dragon, the papal Antichrist (Rev. 11:2–8). The dragon is confronted with the open book of scripture. From the mouths of the reformers comes the fire of the holy spirit, the inspiration of the Word. In the background lies Wittenberg Castle church, the place from which the Antichrist is announced and confronted. The apocalypse has acquired a living immediacy, for it is being realized locally with the Reformation. An earlier version of this illustration in the 1522 New Testament had shown the reformers and the papal dragon before the rebuilding of the temple. The temple has become Wittenberg. (*Rare Books Division, The New York Public Library, Astor, Lenox and Tilden Foundations*)

the center of the flames of hell stands a gigantic wild man-pope. He wears the papal crown, holds a decayed papal cross in his right hand, a damaged key for binding and loosening in his left. From his mouth he roars forth flame, fumes, frogs, lizards, snakes, and filth (in apparent reference to Rev. 16:13). In the upper left-hand corner appear verses attributed to Martin Luther, declaring

> From Satan in his bursting red
> come the most harmful sins and death.
> The pope is rightly named the wild man

Figure 2.3 This illustration, again from Martin Luther's translation of the Bible (1534), portrays Revelation 17. The whore of Babylon riding on the back of the great beast offers a generous measure of iniquity to the princes of the earth who kneel and worship her. Sleek and well-fed, she wears the huge papal tiara. If we look at the immediate physical environment in the illustration, we notice that all these figures—the whore, the beast, the worshipful princes—inhabit a swamp. Only the vision on the horizon seems to project a different world. Does the reformed world therefore lie off in the distance? The contrast with the temple at Wittenberg is drastic: meandering drainage, decay, and presumably corruption versus straight-lined order and rationality. The two environments offer a stark choice, truth against falsehood. The illustration also should be compared with illustrations in chapter 10 (10.1 and 10.1a). Fritz Lang's film *Metropolis* (1927) now presents the princes of the earth as decadent capitalists. In Albrecht Dürer's print (1498) the princes appear uncertain, while only the clergyman kneels in prayer, unreservedly embracing falsehood. (*Rare Books Division, The New York Public Library, Astor, Lenox and Tilden Foundations*)

> Who through false fiendish banishment
> Brought on all human unhappiness
> Which God and man cannot endure.

"Bursting red" refers to the clothing of the curia and the blood of their victims, the faithful. In the lower right-hand corner sits a demon wearing a cardinal's hat who defecates a papal bull with many seals, on which is written the verse, "Hebibsch Got undt Menschen Ferren / Ich undt Teufel sindt die Hern (God and man get far away. / I and the Devil are the lords)." The picture illustrates the papal tyrant. As the wild man beyond nature and reason, he "rages" irrationally, inverts the Great Chain of Being, is subject to no law. As Satan's temporal agent on earth, he no less confronts the order of grace and seeks to replace God's immediate authority. In the fullest possible sense the papacy has perverted all right, all justice, all rationality, and all hope of salvation. It is the ultimate tyranny.

Within the parameters of traditional European thought, all tyrants by definition "rage" and defy reason. Yet Lorch's tyrant has good cause to be cross. His power has now been challenged, his tyranny exposed.

Lorch's image is so utterly arresting that it appears in nearly every modern book on the apocalypse, even those that have nothing whatever to do with this period.[20] Yet images derived from apocalyptic symbolism became increasingly rare during the course of the century. Even John Bale's faintly erotic whore, large-bosomed and offering iniquity by the pitcher to the princes of the earth, failed to stimulate a trend (1548?). Nor did Martin Schrott's whore, also from the 1540s, who actually feeds iniquity from her cup to the kneeling princes.[21] We face no small irony here: people spoke more and more about the Antichrist, but images of this figure become fewer and fewer. We more frequently encounter such illustrations in the Middle Ages when apocalyptic thought was vastly more marginalized. The imagery of evil changed because the understanding of evil had also changed. In the sixteenth century the Antichrist was seen as an institution rather than an individual, and an institution that had developed in a densely linear fashion over an immense stretch of time. Simple prophetic images—however dramatic, even an image as spectacular as Lorch's—could never fully articulate a process of this complexity. Allegory could never substitute for history nor symbols for time.

Right from the beginning, specific political referents anchored scriptural images and made them immediate and compelling. In the 1522 New Testament the destruction of Rome (Rev. 18) clearly portrayed the capitol and the papal fortress in the background. Contemporary political and religious figures, and, increasingly, significant German settings also cropped up in them.[22] The dramatic struggle taking place in Germany found direct expression within the contours of scriptural

Figure 2.4 Melchior Lorch's engraving of the papal Antichrist, 1545. The figure explicitly conflates the medieval wild man with the prophesied anti-Christian tyrant. Following long-standing medieval iconography of the wild man, Lorch's figure is bearded, covered with fur, and carries an uprooted tree as a club. But the club is also the papal cross. In addition, the figure carries the papal key of binding and loosening (Matt. 18:18). On his head is the papal tiara. Out of his mouth spew forth flame, sulphurous fumes, frogs, lizards, snakes, and filth (Rev. 16:13). The engraving claims that the papal monarchy embodies the ultimate tyranny—that it seeks to overthrow both the order of nature and the order of grace. As the wild man the pope lives outside reason and the laws of men. As the Antichrist the pope seeks to overthrow divine law and usurp God's authority. Inherently irrational, he "rages" against truth, righteousness, and all who would uphold them. It is the very essence of tyranny.

The verses in the upper left-hand corner, ostensibly a statement of Luther's (or rather a summary of Luther's views), read as follows: "Al ander Herrshaft ist von Got / Zur Hülf dem Menschen in der Not / Von Satan undt sein imagery. Even if illiterate peasants could not identify a specific referent, they could be in no doubt but that the apocalypse spoke to their world and informed their lives.

By mid-century direct historical experience began to replace symbolic representations altogether. The transition becomes dramatically clear with John Foxe's massive *Acts and Monuments*. Begun in the exile during the religious reaction of Mary Tudor's reign, it recorded in detail and with extensive documentation the experience of the Marian martyrs. First published in English in 1563 and thereafter seeing constant expansion and reprinting, the volume told not only the story of the Marian martyrs but went on to narrate the entire experience of Christian martyrdom. Thereby it simultaneously laid out the apocalyptic narrative of European history. Each martyr's tale, each confrontation, each act of courage, each bearing of witness, each of the varied forms of triumph, all fleshed out, articulated—and furthered—the historical drama of human redemption. In 1570 the Canterbury convocation ordered copies of the book to be placed in each cathedral church alongside the

---

berstlich Rot / Seindt hersustenen [härmsteten] Sündt undt Todt / Der Pabst heist recht der wilder Man / Der durch sein falsches schalkes Ban / Al Ungluck hat gerichten an / Das Got undt Menschen nicht leiden kan" (All other power is from God (i.e., there is no other power than from God) / To help man in his need / From Satan in his bursting red / Come the most harmful sins and death / The pope is rightly named the wild man / Who through false fiendish banishment [i.e., fiendishly banishes the truth rather than being banished from heaven] / Brought on all human unhappiness [i.e., misfortune] / Which man God and man cannot endure). In the lower right-hand corner a demon, wearing a cardinal's hat and holding his buttocks, defecates a papal bull. On it is written the counterpoint to Luther's message, again in verse. "Hebibsch Got undt Menschen Ferren / Ich undt Teufel sindt die Hern" (God and man get far away. / I and the Devil are the lords). The papacy claims tyrannous authority. Luther rejects it.

Sources for Lorch's image are not easily identified. But there is at least one fifteenth-century German illumination of a priestly wild man who leads Alexander the Great to consult with the trees of the sun and the moon. In the picture this figure wears a miter, but as a hirsute wild man, Timothy Husband notes, he is "the very antithesis of piety." *Alexanderbuch*, Augsburg (1455–1465); Husband, *The Wild Man: Medieval Myth and Symbolism* (New York, 1980), pp. 54–56.

English Bible. Its influence during the early modern period is difficult to overestimate, probably second only to the Bible itself. It suffused the textures of the Anglophone cultures, endowing them with an apocalyptic character that proved remarkably tenacious. That character was also surprisingly populist. The martyrs were overwhelmingly common people: merchants, craftsmen, husbandmen, wives, widows, maidens, servants. Foxe's documented accounts show them to be articulate about their beliefs as well as undaunted by either authority or by the fate that awaited them. They know full well the social and spiritual reality they seek to create. They are emphatically of this world. The change from the earlier sixteenth century is momentous. It was one thing to portray the pope as the butt of populist scatological humor, quite another to portray simple people as the agent of history.

Foxe believed in the Great Chain of Being as much as any. But he also knew that the humble comprised the engines that drove the apocalypse and realized human destiny. For this reason Foxe's work appealed to reformers of every sort, from Edmund Spenser to John Milton, from moderate Episcopalians to fire-breathing Levellers and communist Diggers, from the British revolutionaries in the mid-seventeenth century to the American revolutionaries in the late eighteenth. He would underwrite the Anglophone achievement. For just this reason he would draw down the wrath and scorn of conservatives such as Richard Hooker and William Shakespeare—and of Counter-Reformers, notably, the Jesuit Robert Parsons. Today our poetry comes from Shakespeare but our central values do not. We will find them arising, instead, with John Foxe.

The this-worldly character of Foxe's martyrs, their active engagement in historical and apocalyptic struggle, manifests itself in the illustrations that fill the book. The martyrs are characteristically defiant. Often in their moment of suffering they look directly at their persecutors, confronting them. Sometimes they look out at the reader. Foxe's illustration of martyrdom of the reformer William Tyndale, executed by Henry VIII in 1536, is revealing. In his final moment Tyndale does not ask God to receive his soul but to open the king's eyes. He seems less concerned to join God in heaven than for God to join men on earth. Accounts of martyrdom in Foxe and others strongly confirm the illustrations. These martyrs therefore differ decisively from their late antique predecessors who, in their moment of death, find themselves transfixed by God and the world to come. The latter attest to the irrelevance of this world and the consuming importance of the next. No less do they differ from the martyrs of the High Middle Ages where status was so sharply defining. The Foxean martyr affirmed history and human agency within it. And he (or she) was highly conscious of both.

THE TEMPORALIZATION OF WESTERN CULTURE

The sixteenth-century Protestant apocalypse created the first genuinely historical vision of Europe. Its devisers based it on institutional development, and, if it incorporated allegory and the manipulation of mystical numbers, it became increasingly independent of them.

We need to see the new apocalypse as part of a broader cultural shift, the temporalization of Western thought and outlook. The world increasingly assumed meaning not through its underlying structure, but through its development. Integral to this shift, and hugely strengthening to the Protestant vision, was the relatively new phenomenon of humanism. The so-called *studia humanitas* did not simply entail a passionate interest in classical literature and learning—matters that had always interested the medieval world. Rather, its prime concern was how to read that literature. The whole point of scholasticism, indeed virtually the entire thrust of medieval civilization, had been to dehistoricize every text and to turn scripture, the fathers, the councils, all literature, Christian or otherwise, into a single, coherent statement of religious truth. The very techniques of reading undergirded just this objective. As Guibert of Nogent had explained about 1084 when he outlined the procedure for writing a sermon,

> There are four ways of interpreting scripture.... The first is history, which speaks of the actual events as they occurred; the second is allegory, in which one thing stands for something else; the third is tropology, or moral instruction, which treats of the ordering and arranging of one's life; and the last is anagogy, or spiritual enlightenment, through which we are led to a higher way of life. For example, the word Jerusalem: historically it represents a specific city; in allegory it represents the holy Church; tropologically, or morally, it is the soul of every faithful man who longs for the vision of eternal peace; and anagogically it refers to the life of the

heavenly citizens, who already see the God of Gods, revealed in all His glory in Sion.[23]

Still further literary techniques reinforced this approach to the written word. The ancient Hebrews (quite unlike medieval Jews) knew about Christ through scriptural intimations, served the faith, and were therefore saved—even if they had not quite heard of him. Characters in the Old Testament embodied "types," "patterns," "figures," and "shadows," through which the Nazarene and his truth could be known. Even pagan literature could be similarly de-contextualized and endowed with Christocentric meaning. Herakles as well as King David offered insight into Christ's rule and character.

By the sixteenth century we have crossed over into an altogether new intellectual environment. Erasmus had made this clear in 1516 on the eve of the Reformation. If we want to understand scripture and know the meaning of Christian truth, the Rotterdam scholar declared, we must reconstruct its context. Once again in the "Paraclesis," he laid out the points at issue with high resolution. "[I]f we from study of history not only the position of those nations to whom these things happened, or to whom the apostles wrote, but also their origin, manners, institutions, religion, and character, it is wonderful how much light and, if I may say, *life* is thrown into the reading of what before seemed dry and lifeless." Erasmus repeatedly insisted that students should "learn to quote Scripture, not second-hand, but from the fountain-head, and to take care not to distort its meaning as some do, interpreting the 'church' as the clergy, the laity as the 'world' and the like." To get at the real meaning, he declared, "it is not enough to take four or five isolated words; you must look where they came from, what was said, by whom it was said, to whom it was said, at what time, on what occasion, in what words, what preceded, what followed."[24] Meaning came from its moment, from context, and thus from time. The greatest Protestant intellectuals—such as Philipp Melanchthon in Germany, George Buchanan in Britain, François Hotman in France—and virtually all Protestant intellectuals after 1550 were utterly immersed in humanist linguistic analysis. The apocalypse became interwoven into grammar and lexicography. Rarely has any twentieth-century student of the period spoken more succinctly about the significance of the last two than did G. N. Conklin.

> The older query, so to speak, of 'What does God mean here?' became the far more arresting question, 'What has God said here?' Allegory, mystic paraphrase, tropology and the whole formal literature of interpretation were uncompromisingly attacked as doctrinal irrelevancies by syntax and lexicography. Grammar, not speculation, became the greatest heresy of the Christian world, and unhappily no fires could be kindled to consume the *rudimenta linguae* of Hebrew and Greek.[25]

Grammar and thus context had become the ally of history and heresy.

We would severely miss the dynamism of this extraordinary century if we thought for a moment that such matters—involving questions of time and its meanings—were somehow a sideline and did not enter directly into the period's most contested issues. In truth, theology and temporality confronted one another at the very heart of the confessional conflict. Thomas Aquinas's explication of the Eucharist became and still remains the central doctrine of Catholic theology. Its message, not simply for clerical power but also for history, is resolute and unmistakable. Transubstantiation, as Aquinas defines it, means that the participant in the sacrament encounters the divine literally and physically (and, for Protestants, "carnally")—an encounter at once immediate, intimate, total.[26] Consequently the Catholic sacrament constantly replicated exactly the same act in exactly the same way as when the Nazarene had (reputedly) said, "This is my body." On this central, all-important point Aquinas is emphatic: "from their first utterance by Christ these words have possessed the same consecratory power, provided they were spoken by a priest, as if Christ himself were actually present among us pronouncing them."[27] At the heart of Catholicism lay an unchanging moment constantly repeated.

All reformers joined issue. Christ's sacrifice was sufficient. Salvation derived from having faith in that act. It could not be replicated; efforts to do so would not only fail, but amounted to supplanting Christ and in the deepest sense could only be anti-Christian. One might believe with the conservative Lutherans in consubstantiation, and regard Christ as mystically present in the Eucharist even if the elements had not been transformed. One might believe with Calvinists that Christ was spiritually present in the sacrament. One might believe with the radical Zwinglians that the sacrament constituted no more than a memorial. But the sufficiency of the historical Christ was not in dispute. The Protestant communion contrasted utterly with the Catholic Mass, for it remembered the past rather than replicating it. Time and history informed the Protestant service to the point of defining it. One of the central axes of contention between the two faiths therefore involved the textures, contours, and significance of time. Protestantism, albeit hugely preoccupied with grace and faith, was nevertheless equally engaged in the saeculum—profoundly spiritual and yet irreducibly "secular."

Still another axis of contention grew immediately out of this one. The Protestant sacrament could only be a public undertaking, the community together remembering its spiritual past. There could always be a private mass. There could never be a private communion. Conflicting claims about time led at once to conflicting demarcations of the public and private. Protestantism's heavy emphasis on the public—and the public as manifestation of both history and salvation—encouraged, if it did not enjoin, a profoundly civic consciousness.

Privacy for Protestantism was also reconfigured as a result, and the self became at once radically individualized and radically temporalized. Diaries in something like the modern sense had emerged with the Renaissance and were hardly a Protestant invention. But they became very much a Protestant phenomenon. Diaries recorded spiritual development, which meant highly personal development. The individual became historical, and by the end of the century there appeared all sorts of manuals for charting and assessing just that development. Once one *thought* one had felt the spirit, it became imperative to watch its growth and its gradual transformation of the personality. There were twelve steps of justification (or was it thirteen?). There were perhaps the same number on the road to sanctification.

If an increasingly temporalized world reshaped the personality, it informed much else as well. The individual was also defined by history and his own redemption in some sense resulted from it. The ancient heresy of mortalism which, in one of its forms, had claimed that the soul "slept" at death only to be resurrected at the end of time, now resurfaced in the sixteenth century. Although numerous reformers vigorously rejected the notion, it still appealed to many Protestants. And well it should. For it strongly reinforced the notion that we could only achieve our own salvation when the apocalypse worked itself out and found its fruition. History would indeed redeem us. Mortalism underscored the importance of the saeculum and in every way the importance of the physical world—the growing preoccupation, in Amos Funkenstein's words, with "God's body."[28] In the next century Protestants as different as John Milton and Thomas Hobbes would find this doctrine compelling and intellectually essential. The latter days may well have been expected to prove the worst of times, and Catholic victories on the battlefield along with the gathering Counter-Reformation gave every reason for such expectations. Yet, in at least one sense, optimism became all but inescapable. People in the sixteenth century simply had to know more than mankind could at any earlier moment. What the prophets, the patriarchs, and the apostles had seen only darkly through symbols, signs, and "types," the latter age fully understood through the clear light of history.

Three distinct agents had joined together to reformulate the standard of the intelligible. The Reformation's apocalyptic vision of the past had combined with humanist text in context, and both linked in turn with the Protestant theology of memory to infuse Western civilization with a new and largely unprecedented sense of time as the measure of meaning. To understand something, it now seemed, required less a knowledge of its essence than of its process, less its structure than its development, less what it was than what it might become. This temporalization of the Western world would continue, overcoming the severest resistance, until the last decade of the nineteenth century.

CHAPTER 3

THE LAST WORLD EMPIRE AND ITS COMPETITORS

THE ADVENT OF THE FIFTH MONARCHY

If the apocalypse did not penetrate the fabric of Roman Catholic piety and theology in the way that it did with Protestantism, apocalyptic expectations did shape and suffuse Catholic political vision in significant ways. The signal geopolitical event of the late fifteenth and early sixteenth centuries was the emergence of the great Spanish and Portuguese empires, the first on a global scale. Breathtakingly gigantic and utterly unprecedented, they operated within the realm of grace no less than within the realm of nature, and were preoccupied with salvation no less than dominion—indeed with the historical redemption, prophecy, and eschatology rather more than mere rulership. The people of Spain and more generally of the peninsula had received the gift of "election," an act of divine favor that endowed them with a special destiny in what were perceived as being the latter days of the world. The expanding Spanish kingdom promised to be nothing less than Daniel's fifth monarchy, the final world order that presaged the return of the savior. The blind Jews would be converted in the end to the true faith; the "fulness" of the Gentiles would be called. Jerusalem would be retaken, the holy sepulture recovered. The true faith would be propagated throughout the world, which would be governed by this messianic empire. These expectations found reinforcement and articulation from the wide-ranging prophecies putatively derived from the sibyls of late antiquity and from the varied medieval legends of the great Last emperor.

It is far from incidental that Ferdinand of Aragon and Castile styled himself the king of Jerusalem. Nor is it in the least surprising that

Christopher Columbus saw his voyages as being of a piece with the overthrow of Moorish Granada and the simultaneous destruction of the centuries-old Jewish community in Spain, all occurring in the same fateful year 1492. Nor should it be surprising that Columbus too fixed his gaze on Jerusalem and the holy sepulture. His expectations, as well those of his patrons, found their sources in this dense tissue of antique, medieval, and biblical prophecy. Like them he increasingly saw his role as a prophetic one, the Christ-bearer to the Gentiles: even to the point of finding in his own name that messianic message, "Christo-ferens" (Christ-bearer) and which he signed laid out in the form of a cross. Like his patrons he saw himself fulfilling the great events of the last age.

And so it seemed to happen. By the 1530s the Hapsburg dynasty, now headed by Charles V, had met with such spectacular success—the conquest of the New World, the crusade against Tunis, the domination of Italy, the consolidation of power in central Europe, the Netherlands, and Spain, the turning back of the Ottoman Turks at Vienna—that this new superstate, unlike anything in history, might very plausibly be the prophesied Last World Empire. As early as 1525, following the defeat and capture of Charles's French rival Francis I at Pavia, Alfonso de Valdés had looked to the fulfillment of the imperial eschatology. Valdés served as the emperor's secretary and court Latinist, but his sentiments extended well beyond the court to virtually all reaches within these vast dominions. Earlier still, Charles's iconography proclaimed his having burst through the traditional boundaries of antiquity, the pillars of Hercules. That great terminus for the classical world, associated with the ancient motto *non plus ultra*, was cast as a columnar device with a motto that made just the opposite statement: *plus ultra—noch weiter* for the German-speaking empire—"still further" (see Figure 3.1). For Horace, Claudian, and other classical writers, the oceans were natural boundaries; crossing them was unnatural, violating the order of things. Now Christian mission had overcome pagan limitations, as grace transformed nature in the run-up to the eschaton. Spanish imperial power became synonymous with the *civitae dei*. Although during the course of the sixteenth century the great Hispanic design experienced setbacks, disasters, even catastrophes, such events merely curbed presumption and tested Spanish resolve. For all these reasons, royal policy categorically refused to surrender territory, and the century witnessed a trajectory of erratic but unmistakable growth.

Small wonder that Philip's famous *impresa* or emblem of 1555 portrayed him as Christ-Apollo in the chariot of the sun with his divine mission of bringing the light of the faith to the entire earth. With the motto "*Iam Illustrabit Omnia*" (Now he will illuminate everything), the impresa dramatically showed Philip as enlightening a hitherto darkened New World—darkened by its paganism, darkened by being hidden until its providential discovery in these last times (Figure 3.2). Contemporaries were altogether clear on the matter: God had "inspired this emblem which is an oracle or a prophecy that the whole world will soon be illuminated with divine light through the universal conversion of the infidel to the true Catholic faith."[1] Psalm 18.43, to which Columbus himself had appealed, was once again called into service: "[T]hou did make me the head of the nations; / people whom I had not known served me." Following the 1560s the same imagery and the same claims became further articulated with the acquisition of the Philippines and bore similar implications for the Orient. After the annexation of the far-flung Portuguese empire in 1580—itself a profoundly spiritual act—the Dominican preacher Hernando del Castillo expostulated, "[I]f the Romans were able to rule the world simply by ruling the Mediterranean, what of the man who rules the Atlantic and Pacific oceans, since they surround the world?" By now the phrase, an empire on which the sun never set, had long become a cliché. But then who, after all, was the sun? At this moment Philip chose to adopt the astonishing, if layered motto *Non Sufficit Orbis* (The world is not enough) (Figure 3.3).[2]

Contemporaneous Portuguese attitudes were strikingly similar. Portugal, the "Ensign" or standard-bearer of Christ, had received providentially the sacred mission to establish Daniel's fifth monarchy. Promoted by a series of papal bulls and brieves during the middle 1400s, documents that deeply and enduringly informed the attitudes of the political elites, Portuguese expansion by century's end had conferred on Dom Manuel I (r. 1495–1521) an enormous string of (self-awarded) African and Asian titles. Eschatological expectations led to the forced conversion of Portuguese Jewry in 1497 and to an ever more prominent missionary dimension to the growing empire. Moreover, by the later 1520s, familiar apocalyptic projections—the

Figure 3.1 Columnar device for Charles V, in Girolamo Ruscelli, *La Impresse Illustri* (Venice, 1566), 111–14. One of the many devices proclaiming the daring "Plus Ultra" on behalf of the Hapsburg monarchy. Originally designed for Charles V at his assumption of sovereignty in 1516, the emblem associated the prophetic Last World Empire with the Hapsburg dynasty. "Plus Ultra" became, in Marie Tanner's words, "Europe's most enduring symbol in the bid for universal theocratic monarchy." The image would have a long future before it—and an increasingly conflicted one.

Earl Rosenthal has described the origin of the device and provided a careful discussion of this and similar devices in his seminal articles: "The Invention of the Columnar Device of the Emperor Charles V at the Court of Burgundy in Flanders in 1516," in the *Journal of the Warburg and Courtauld Institute* 36 (1973): 201ff., and "*Plus Ultra, Non Plus Ultra*, and the Columnar Device of Emperor Charles V," *Journal of the Warburg and Courtauld Institute* 34 (1971): 204–28, esp. 228. Tanner, *The Last Descendant of Aeneas: The Hapsburgs and the Mythic Image of the Emperor* (New Haven, 1993), p. 155. *(California State Library, Sacramento)* conquest of Jerusalem, the overthrow of the Ottoman Turks—became elaborated and augmented through local prophetic writings associated with a small-town shoemaker, Gonçalo Eanes Bandarra, whose verse "Trovas" became hugely popular. Together such diverse sources formed a long prophetic tradition that found its apogee, though hardly its conclusion, in Portugal's greatest Fifth Monarchy Man, the Jesuit Antonio Vieira (1608–1697). This national eschatology penetrated the textures of Portuguese society and culture to shape politics, literature, and spirituality for centuries to come.

We might expect these two messianic empires, underwritten by potentially conflicting claims, to become bitter rivals. In fact, from the late fifteenth century onward, their relations seem to have been characterized more by symbiosis than competition. Similar administrative practices, common social attitudes, shared religious values, the same views on race and blood, a long practice of slavery—all further smoothed by papal partitions of the globe into disparate spheres of influence—combined with significant economic interdependence to make for cooperation rather than antagonism. Like the Counter-Reformation they so powerfully promoted in the later century, the new empires were obsessed with hierarchy, authority, order—with protection rather than participation. If humanist rhetorical conceits and historical scholarship celebrated these massive structures, especially before 1550, the Iberian preoccupation was with imperial Rome, not its republican predecessor. The classical values of the polis and the citizen did not intrude: *civic* humanism could hardly have been more alien or more unwelcome. The Iberian eschatology carried with it an authoritarian agenda that became manifest from Naples to Ghent, from the Spanish *Comuneros* to Chile. For all the classical myths and motifs, Spaniards (and Portuguese) remained a "chosen people," latter-day Israelites rather than latter-day Romans. Precisely because of their spirituality, they looked less to replication than to the unprecedented. The profoundly religious categories so foundational to this mental world made events intelligible rather more through that language of Moses than that of Machiavelli. No other dynasty embraced the prophetic with such energy and conviction. Never before—and nowhere else—did imperial claims and clerical vision, royal power and papal agency, the Sibylline and the Joachite, merge more seamlessly or more compellingly. Where earlier there had been rival visions and conflicted expectations,

Figure 3.2 Global device for Philip II, in Girolamo Ruscelli, *La Impresse Illustri* (Venice, 1566), 111–14. This remarkable image of Philip II portrays him as a messianic Christ-Apollo driving his chariot the sun through the skies. Accordingly, a ribbon above him bears the motto "Iam Illustrabit Omnia" (Now he will illuminate everything). He is the light to the world. Most notably, he brings light across the seas to the hitherto darkened Western hemisphere—dark in that it was unknown to Europe, dark in that lacked the true faith. The globe at the bottom shows the New World literally darkened. The globe at the top shows a view of the southern sky. Philip is nude, unprecedented in such iconography according to Marie Tanner. His substantial penis, possibly erect, emphasizes his power—that is, his manhood both as virtue and virility. (*California State Library, Sacramento*)

Figure 3.3 The reverse of the medal celebrating the union of the two world empires of Spain and Portugal under the rule of Philip II in 1580 shows the globe firmly contained within its equator and longitudinal lines below the astonishing motto "non sufficit orbis" (the world is not enough). Atop the globe charges a horse suggestive of the horses powering Philip's chariot in the 1555 engraving that had portrayed him as the *lux mundi*. The medal is thought to have been struck in about 1583. (*INCM, Museu Numismático Portugêus, Inv. no. 2918*)

Ferdinand and Isabella, Charles and Philip, Manuel and his successor João III, joined with the Vatican to discover integrated purposes and a great cooperative venture.

By any standard the great empires proved an all but unqualified success, and at moments their vast spiritual and political objectives seemed almost within grasp. Yet in both the Iberian realms, well-founded confidence had an edge of anxiety. It was one thing for Jews and Moors to become Catholic, at least nominally, and quite another for them to become Spanish, Latin, and medieval. As early as the mid-fifteenth century the *conversos* no less than the Jews found themselves the target of pogroms and restrictive legislation. The "offspring of perverse Jewish ancestry" were deemed "infamous and ignominious" and consequently unworthy "to hold any public office or any benefice." Fear of Jewish, and later of Muslim deceit, of converts being false Catholics, combined with a deep concern for community identity and authenticity, from which arose an abiding obsession with genealogy, with having pure blood (*pureza de sangre*) or clean blood (*limpieza de sangre*). Iberian authoritarianism thus found itself reinforced by claims of race. These lines of thought played out in both New World governance and European conflict. Heretics such as the Dutch could only be inferior people, agreement with whom would defeat Spanish spiritual mission and compromise Spanish honor.

To confront such awesome powers—with the best armies, the best generals, and seemingly limitless wealth—required an act of considerable courage. But, in a sense, that was the least of it. For any challenger needed also to confront these empires' apocalyptic claims, their political assumptions, their racial preoccupations. Both the Jews and the Moors developed counter-eschatologies—a "messianic backlash"—to oppose the apocalyptic of their conquerors and persecutors. In the first years of the new century, Jewish prophetesses appeared in Toledo and Seville. The one in Toledo, a fifteen-year-old, had a vision of the victims of the Inquisition sitting in heaven and predicted the coming of the Messiah. Forty-five followers of the "beautiful" one in Seville were burned. At Valencia prayers of vengeance cried out against the "Catholic monarchs": "Revenge us, O Lord, on this damned Queen of Spain, who has destroyed your people, and pushed it into evil, and has burned and killed it.... Come from your pity and give us miracles, that the Queen of Spain may be burned in the fire." From abroad, the émigré Isaac Abravanel wrote books predicting the imminent return of the Messiah (perhaps as soon as 1503), the restoration of the Jews to Israel, and their enemies consigned to eternal damnation. Other self-proclaimed Jewish prophets such as Solomon Molkho and David Reubeni confronted the Hapsburgs, the papacy, and the Portuguese daringly and directly—and with disastrous results.[3] Despite profound antagonism toward the Spanish and all Christians of the peninsula, the Jews found themselves enmeshed within a common messianic culture.

In broad terms, that would be true elsewhere as well. The Iberian colossus had defined empire for Europe as an entity at once spiritual and geopolitical, mapping the terrain within highly developed apocalyptic terms. No competitor, no opponent, no dissident could do other than speak to this central element in the West's new imperialism.

COUNTER-EMPIRE

Ranged against the Hapsburg superstate was the House of Valois and the French monarchy. The rival dynasty was not an alternative claimant to the Spanish mission and mantel—or so maintained a number of its publicists. Rather, they cast France as the protector of

European liberty, the upholder of boundaries, the promoter of Stoic self-restraint and limitation. The humiliating defeat of Charles's siege at Metz in 1552—one of the great French victories during the reign of Henri II (r. 1547–1559)—brought forth an outpouring of patriotic fervor. The Hapsburg eagle was now portrayed as chained between the Herculean columns, with the motto *Non ultra Metas* (not beyond Metz or not beyond these limits—punning on *metas*, meaning boundary markers). Poets celebrated the event, among them Pierre de Ronsard, Melin de Saint-Gelais, the future chancellor Michel de l'Hôpital, and, most notably, the Scottish humanist George Buchanan.[4] Buchanan's Latin verses, highly popular and immediately translated by Joachim du Bellay, portrayed Henry as even greater than Perseus and, significantly, Hercules in defeating monsters, for France had beaten back the Hapsburg Hydra. That world domination of which Charles had madly dreamed, and for which he brought such huge forces, now discovered boundaries and limits. And France alone had stood firm against this universal aggression. "The strength of the Germans gave way." "Italian liberty, unaccustomed to a tyrant's yoke, muttered and grumbled." "Restless ambition ... was dreaming of world empire." "But you the good leader of war-like France have put a stop to the arrogance."[5] At this juncture Buchanan seems to have envisioned a Gallo-Britannic counter-empire that would underwrite political societies and make possible civic life—and that, at least conceivably, just might enable a world of religious toleration.

George Buchanan (1506–1582) was one of the most radical thinkers of the sixteenth century and also one of the century's most determined critics of empire. By 1550 he had become convinced that these great empires were incompatible with civic life, and that civic life, the highest form of association, was prerequisite to realizing humanity's potential and purpose. Only as a citizen—as one who participated in political decision-taking by making moral judgments that at once determined the public good and defined his personhood—could any individual hope to achieve virtue and, crucially, become civilized. The monstrous congeries emanating from Madrid and Lisbon, far from achieving mankind's destiny, had in fact foreclosed what it meant to be human. The high points in history were the republics of classical antiquity and of quattrocento and cinquecento Italy ("Italian liberty," indeed). For Buchanan the founders and defenders of republics were history's great men; their subverters and enemies, its greatest villains. The legendary Codrus (who sacrificed himself to establish the Athenian republic) found his antitype in Sulla and Caesar. To strike down Caesar was to be a true citizen: "Such great virtue ... was deep-seated in the heroic soul of Brutus, / When the pious daggers were given him on behalf of his country."[6] For Buchanan spirituality was civil, piety derived from classical *pietas,* and salvation was integral to public life. He held Xerxes, Philip of Macedonia, and Alexander the Great in utter contempt, and he poured out venom on the Roman emperors. Empire could only be a spiritual and political catastrophe.

Buchanan developed lines of thinking that comprised a near total rejection of every element within the Iberian ideology. As he daringly told the Lisbon Inquisition, he had come to discount all forms of prophecy. The bishop of Rome might well be a "sacrilegious Judas," as he said in the 1530s; the doctrines of Catholicism might well be hellish and incompatible with salvation, as he clearly believed in the 1560s. But the apocalypse did not organize his view of history or of the current moment; the papacy was profoundly evil, but at no point emerges as the prophesied Antichrist. The prophetic never informs his extensive oeuvre, and, unsurprisingly, Buchanan's blistering rejection of popular, non-biblical prophecy was uncompromisingly thorough-going. Merlin was "an egregious impostor and cunning pretender, rather than a prophet."[7]

For the Iberians, crusade, conquest, global empire, the true faith, the extirpation of perverse heresy and sodomy, and mission-infused, "pure" blood, all comprised elements integrated into a single apocalyptic package—the ideology of the last age. To impugn any of these elements struck at the imperial eschatology, and, accordingly, Buchanan is perhaps the first of many British writers to invert the Iberian blood claims. Charles is "half Moorish" (*semimaurus*). John Knox, Andrew Melville, Edmund Spenser, David Hume of Godscroft, among others, subsequently turned the preoccupation with "pure blood" against its advocates. Further, Buchanan insisted, Iberian settlements across the ocean were utterly corrupt, not fulfilling some messianic mission but leading innocent people into "a shameful servitude." By resisting the Hapsburgs, the French challenged eschatological pretension and served mankind in almost every conceivable way.

There existed a third option, much less impressive at the time but considerably more consequential after 1560 when the prospects and persuasiveness of Gallo-Britannia precipitously evaporated. The English kingdom—revitalized and redefined by Thomas Cromwell, Thomas Cranmer, and Henry Tudor in the 1530s, and then radicalized during the brief reign of Edward Tudor—presented itself as an empire for liberty. Although overseas settlement never surfaced, the new England joined Christian liberty with political liberty in a powerful apocalyptic vision that projected universal reform. Just as Constantine the Great (d. 337), allegedly born in Britain and with his allegedly British mother Helen, had overthrown Satan's public kingdom and instituted the true faith, so his heir, a latter-day British Constantine, might overthrow Satan's successor, the Antichristian papal monarchy, in the final age of the world.

At the end of the 1540s, in the midst of a war with Scotland to secure the dynastic union of the two realms, this vision became fractured. On the one hand, the English government claimed historic feudal suzerainty over Scotland, a view bolstered by medieval mythologies and, to some extent, by medieval history. On the other, there also emerged the prospect of a British union of equals, founded on mutual solidarity, common reforming purposes, and a fusion of peoples. The most influential writing promoting the latter was an "Epistle Exhortatorie" of 1548, ostensibly written by the English regent, the duke of Somerset. Appealing to "the indifferent old name of Brytaynes," the "Epistle" offered realistic insight into contemporary politics, as well as genuinely powerful flights of rhetoric: "we offer equalitie & amitie, we ouercome in war, and offer peace, wee wynne holdes, and offer no conquest, we gette in your lande and offre Englande." The more egalitarian vision and the literature promoting it were no doubt shaped by émigré Scottish Protestants who passionately sought the creation of a radical, reforming Britain, one that might provide the model for mankind in the final era of the world.[8]

Like its competitors, the new Britain would also be imperial because it embodied multiple monarchies—and, more than that, multiple monarchies integrated into a new identity. Certainly it was no less apocalyptic in its aspirations, no less global in its horizon. Somerset's "Epistle," the centerpiece of this unionist literature, addressed a European audience through Johannes Sleidanus's Latin translation. Even Charles V read it and, hardly a surprise, found it distinctly displeasing. It also appeared almost immediately in German. The "Epistle" subsequently informed virtually all Scottish writing on the subject of Anglo-Scottish union—from John Knox in 1558 to Thomas Craig, Robert Pont, and John Russell in the wake of the 1603 regnal union. It did not matter whether they revered Constantine or repudiated him.

A WORLD REDEEMED, A WORLD WITHOUT EMPIRE

Whatever the ambiguities and contradictions within French aspirations or whatever the discrepancies within England's British vision, neither Henry Tudor nor Henry of Valois and their sickly sons proved capable of a sustained alternative to the Hapsburgs. Hapsburg domination in England during the disastrous reign of "bloody" Mary Tudor (1553–1558) and even the less repressive experience of French domination in Scotland during that same decade indicated that empire meant annihilation, not liberation. John Knox declared that God "hath not created the earth to satisfy the ambition of two or three tyrants, but for the universal seed of Adam; and hath appointed and defined the bounds of their habitation to diverse nations, assigning diverse countries." The Spaniards might see themselves as the elected successors to the Jews, but the Hapsburg policy of growth through "happy marriage" ran directly counter to the Hebrew experience and to the principles of the Old Testament.[9]

Such circumstances might have urged a renewal of the egalitarian version of Edwardian Britain—they certainly did for Knox—but events worked in very different directions. That extraordinary decade 1558–1568 saw the Reformation unleash a revolutionary upheaval that challenged authority throughout the region: authority became destabilized in England, twice overthrown in Scotland, radically contested in France, and violently rejected in the low countries. Moreover, the fortuitous emergence of female rulers with problematic claims to the throne further heightened the volatility of the moment. During these years direct action became all but inescapable, and legitimacy needed to be imagined anew, indeed to become self-generated. In such a context, classical political thought and the civic vocabularies, so promoted by Buchanan, acquired an urgency that would have been unthinkable in earlier decades. Appeals to fellow countrymen, to the common good, and, literally, to the *respublica*—more than custom or tradition—became insistent and frequent. By 1562 Chancellor de l'Hôpital had ceased to speak of France guiding the *totum orbem,* and instead appealed to the *cives* and the *citoyen.* In the 1570s the French had begun to construct a new vocabulary, one that enjoined the duties of *"bon patriottes et concitoyens"*—terms and concepts that soon thereafter entered English.[10] For Buchanan, Scotland now appeared an autonomous commonwealth, led by selfless aristocrats pursuing the public good, and where, ideally, citizens imposed law on themselves. In such a commonwealth, as Buchanan declared in verses written for the new-born James in 1566, the king would be a far more modest figure than the great emperors both past and present. But, as a self-ruled model for citizens, he would also be a more worthy and significant one. The virtuous Scottish republic, unlike its grotesque Iberian antitypes, had no place for empire, however imagined, and could only become corrupted by it.

Anti-imperialism did not foreclose global activism. Exactly during these years, Buchanan continued to be directly and passionately involved in both the French and English reformations. So too were such close intellectual associates as Andrew Melville and Philip Sidney. These early modern "patriots" were consistently internationalists, reformers in a great common cause at once religious and political, that ran everywhere within the region—and extended from there to all Europe and throughout the globe. Rarely did "patriots" become apologists for their home government, and normally they were at odds with it. Their civic world pointed to confederation and the most intimate collaboration in the struggle against the Hapsburgs and their papal ally. That global struggle, truly a world war, might in fact require colonies both at home and abroad. But such "plantations" needed to be conceived and structured in ways compatible with civic humanist ideals. Humanist attitudes invited autonomous or semi-autonomous communities, and made their founders latter-day law-givers. Liberty was a term integral to its vocabulary, and the overseas enterprises of the English, the French, and especially the Dutch were seen continually as being allied with the Amerindians and as seeking to achieve their liberation from the Iberian conquests. Liberation did not arise merely from strategic considerations; nor was it cynical posturing, as required by today's "post-colonial" historiography. It arose from deeply held intellectual commitments, no less sincere than naive. In the most strenuous terms, Spain's enemies could not possibly be conquistadors, but just the reverse. With few exceptions, they did not adopt the Spanish model but sought to overturn it.

During the later decades of the sixteenth century, the English, the Scots, the French, and the Dutch overwhelmingly and emphatically rejected the Last World Empire. So, too, did those among them who undertook to plant colonies. And yet a palpable change had taken place. Quite unlike Buchanan, they overwhelmingly and emphatically did *not* reject prophecy and the apocalypse. Their entire undertaking, like their homeland, like their allies abroad, was cast within a vision of struggle against the Antichrist. They countered the soteriology of universal empire and its claims to election every bit as much as its political and cultural assumptions. Their eschatology offered neither an alternative Last World Empire, nor an anti-apocalypse, but an altogether new apocalyptic program.

The Netherlands' life-and-death struggle against the Hapsburgs was understood, naturally enough, within the framework of the Protestant apocalyptic vision. Writers such as Willem Usselincx saw overseas colonization within such terms, and the Dutch estates seriously considered the prophetic interpretations of Joan Aventroot before launching their bold western venture to Brazil in the late 1620s. Both Elizabeth I and her successor, James VI and I, were greatly influenced by Reformation apocalyptic, especially James who wrote extensively on the subject. Yet both of them were also highly defensive and traditional, and hoped to reach an accommodation with the great super-state. When Philip II's messianic agenda made that impossible, Elizabeth reluctantly entered upon a global war. Much of the politics, literature, religious reflection of the late sixteenth and seventeenth centuries—in Britain and throughout Europe—concerned just this struggle against Universal Monarchy.

As with the Dutch, British colonial projects do not comprise competition for world empire but efforts to forestall such empire, a kind of anti-empire. Such was the case whether plantations were established in Ireland (to consolidate the British kingdoms), placed about the Baltic (to promote reformation ideals), or confronted the Iberians directly through transoceanic settlements. During the Elizabethan period the poet, planter, and political commentator Edmund Spenser viewed the Munster plantations in Ireland less as the conquest of that island than as part of the global struggle against Spain. His writing is intensely apocalyptic and patriotic. Anticipating Francis Bacon, he saw the discoveries in the New World specifically through Daniel's prophecy about the increase of knowledge from human travel during the last age of the world. Book II of the *Faerie Queene*—the Legend of Sir Guyon, or of Temperance—draws on Peter Martyr's account of the New World to create in Sir Guyon an anti-conquistador, whose story promotes the values of humanity and moderation against conquest, universal empire, and *Non Sufficit Orbis*. Even in the darkening days of the 1590s, Spenser's *A View of the Present State of Ireland* provides not a blueprint for violence, but, we now know, a remarkable protosociology of modernization that displays unexpected sympathy for the Gaelic Irish and an inclusive perspective. Like Buchanan forty years earlier, like Knox and Melville, Spenser inverts the Spanish preoccupation with blood. But he does more and goes on to reject the Iberian idea of race itself.[11] Like much contemporaneous literature, the *Faerie Queene* sought to imagine a coherent British response to the threat from imperialism, not to promote imperialism. For here was a desperate struggle, unquestionably the most dangerous war to confront the British Isles between the Norman conquest and 1939. In the end Spenser emerges as an opponent of empire rather than its apologist.

Philip Sidney's projected trans-Atlantic settlements, as described in the early seventeenth century by his friend Fulke Greville, fit this pattern. Sidney, a "wakeful patriot," Greville tells us, reflected on the possible strategies for the global war against Spain—"this devouring Sultan"—and concluded that the most effective one would be an attack on the Spanish possessions in the New World that would disrupt the flow of its treasure. English forces should focus on America, vulnerable to an attack, rather than being concentrated in an offensive in the Netherlands. The landing in America would not simply involve search, seize, and destroy, but the plantation of a colony in some convenient haven—possibly Puerto Rico. Sidney manifestly did not intend to found an alternate Protestant empire in the New World. He consistently speaks of forming "a generall league among free princes." At one point he envisioned a joint expedition with the Netherlands. Further, "hee contrived this new intended Plantation ... as an Emporium for the confluence of all nations that love or profess any kinde of vertue or commerce." Predictably he looks to an alliance with the Amerindians. The American undertaking, and perhaps much of the point of the war with Spain, was to lead Europe and the world "into a well balanced treaty of universal peace, restore and keep the world within her old equilibrium or bounds." This is the language of Knox and Buchanan. He repeatedly warns that England not over-extend herself as happened in France during the late Middle Ages: "I say, even when in the pride of our conquests, we strove to gripe more than was possible for us to hold: as appears by our being forced to come away and leave our ancestors bloud and bones behind for monu-ments not of enjoying, but of over-griping & expulsion." He is quick to dismiss "these wind-blown conquests of ours" that have "happily been scattered." The English expulsion from France had proven "happy" in large part because the rise of French authoritarianism would have corrupted England, turning English "moderate wealth" among social ranks into "the nasty poverty of the French peasants," bringing home mandates instead of laws, impositions instead of parlia-mentary freedoms. The Protestant agenda in France extended from the reformed religion to restoring constitutional institutions in "that once wel-formed monarchy." The issue in Europe and throughout the world was implementing boundaries to authority, limitations to power, and, implicitly, public participation.[12]

Buchanan, Spenser, and Sidney shared an emphatically British ori-entation and participated more broadly in what we might call a North Sea-English Channel *oikumene*, defined by a civic, reforming outlook, one informed, for most, by the Protestant apocalyptic framework. Yet within this group highly articulated impetus for a reformed British state surfaced in the 1590s from the Scottish north—outstandingly, with Buchanan's successor as court poet, the Presbyterian minister Andrew Melville (1545–1622). Melville embraced Buchanan's theories of resistance, endorsed his civic ideals, stressed his values of Stoic self-restraint. He adopted Buchanan's ideas, but he also did more: he endowed them with apocalyptic and signally British significance.

At some point early in the 1590s Melville undertook a Scottish national epic. Drawing on Scotland's medieval origin myths, Melville imagined the world contested between two competing "fountains," two competing spirits, arising from two sons sprung from a Gaelic Abraham. The Western counterparts to Isaac and Ishmael, the first wins praise for his modesty, seeking to preserve his father's laws and the practice of shared governance. He does not conquer nations, but,

Melville intimates, provides a model for nations. In contrast the latter is ruthlessly aggressive and bloodthirsty, striving "to extend his fame and his father's kingdom by whatever force, by whatever power." "Thirsting for gold and hungrier than Orcus," he "seizes all things by waging unbridled war." He "slaughters great numbers of people and overturns kingdoms." The first spirit will find its fruition in the emerging British kingdom, the latter in the enormous Spanish empire.[13] Herein lay the stark choice facing mankind in what was the final act in the epic drama of human experience: satanic empire or a world without empire altogether.

Instead of empire, there would emerge a confederated world of "free" societies. Throughout the first half of the seventeenth century confederal anti-imperialism shaped politics across the Protestant world, literally from Transylvania to New England. Anti-imperial leagues saw the struggle in no less apocalyptic terms than did their Fifth Monarchy enemies. Melville addressed the matter in verses celebrating the birth of King James's heir, Prince Henry, in 1594. The prince would succeed with his father to the southern crown and unite the two realms "into a single body of Scoto-Britannic People." The new Britain that resulted would lead the world against the Antichrist and empire. For Melville, Napier of Merchiston, and virtually all Presbyterian intellectuals, the papacy and the Hapsburgs, the "proud crown of the twinned Hesperia," were the direct political and spiritual heirs of the pagan Roman Empire—a view strongly corroborated by contemporaneous papal iconography. What had grown for so long could be swept away "in one short hour." For now "rust blunts the edge of the sword Aeneas wielded." Prince Henry, Melville hoped, would one day rejoice at having "buried the insolent spirit of empire in its tomb."[14]

There is every indication that the young prince completely accepted the vision Melville mapped out at his birth, and after 1603 his short-lived court promoted an outlook and policies increasingly at odds with that of his conservative and timid father. Attracting Hugh Broughton, Andrew Willet, and other leading Anglophone interpreters of biblical prophecy, the court was suffused with apocalyptic expectation. It was said that the prince "cherished the true prophets," and there is no doubt that he genuinely enjoyed sermons and listened attentively. The implications were far-reaching. Broughton and Willet were leading philo-Semites, their thinking inaugurating a tradition that culminated in the 1655 Whitehall conference and the readmission of the Jews into England. In contrast, James during these years launched a mini-expulsion, commanding the earl of Suffolk to ferret out Jews living secretly in the realm—"which made the ablest of them to fly out of England."[15] In addition, Willet (among others) took an uncharacteristically positive view of Anglo-Scottish union, and described the two realms going up to Jerusalem together "as louing sisters and fellow tribes."[16]

There can be little doubt that Henry's court was developing the prospect of a union far more profound and egalitarian (and potentially radical) than anything his father could have comfortably contemplated. Looking back to the apocalyptic radicalism at the end of 1540s, a new Henrician union projected common purposes and a common destiny that reached deeply into the hopes of wide populations in both realms. Henry was by far the most popular Stuart prince of the seventeenth century. Unlike his father, the prince looked to a transformed future rather than a world merely stabilized within traditional and hierarchic terms. Central to Henry's vision was confrontation with the Hapsburgs, both on the continent and also globally: notably, a blockade of Spain combined with an attack on the West Indies.[17] The underlying spiritual dimension cannot be doubted, and, unsurprisingly, in 1618, six years after the prince's death, the apocalyptic exegete Willet would be jailed for anti-Spanish writing.

If apocalyptic expectations became increasingly marginalized in the thinking of King James, these lines of thought were far from absent at his court. It has been recognized only occasionally that Francis Bacon's program for science inherently mandated European expansion, indeed the conquest of the globe, and that both the new discoveries and the new science realized apocalyptic prophecy. At its heart science was soteriological and eschatological. Science meant salvation, for its advancement did nothing less than work the historical redemption. "It is a restitution and reinvesting (in great part) of men to the sovereignty and power ... which he had in his first state of creation." Bacon's words on the matter are frequent and clear. These were "the latter times" of which Daniel had spoken, when he prophesied that "many shall pass to and fro and science shall be increased" (Dan. 12:4). "The opening of the world by navigation and commerce and the further discovery of knowledge" came together in the same final age.[18] Bacon's famous frontispiece to *The Great Instauration* (1620) adopted and transvalued Charles V's columnar image whose motto now became Daniel's prophecy (Figure 3.4).

Bacon's expectations translated into his advocating aggressive prosecution of the war with Spain in the 1590s and his opposing the peace sought by Robert Cecil and James. In the 1620s, and now out of public office, Bacon again urged war with Spain. Yet defeating the Spanish Empire did not imply a *translatio imperii*. He never seems to have contemplated a new British order, and his well-known comment in "On Plantations" implied circumspection: "I like a Plantation in a Pure Soile; that is, where People are not Displanted, to the end, to plant in Others. For else, it is rather an Extirpation, then a Plantation."[19] Bacon is manifestly an imperialist, but not a British imperialist.

Accordingly, British colonial projects in the earlier seventeenth century from Lithuania to the New World were suffused with apocalyptic purpose. But their founders intended to obstruct world monarchy, not to realize it, while the settlements themselves were conceived as quasi-autonomous, humanist poleis, not mere extensions of the metropole. Few of James's courtiers can have reflected more on eschatology than did Sir William Alexander who authored a massive poem of some 11,000 lines describing in detail the events that would occur at the Last Judgment. Probably no one promoted colonies in America more indefatigably than did Alexander on behalf of Nova Scotia in what is today Canada. Ultimately, colonies for Alexander do not lead to a revived Constantinian empire at the end of days, but comprise an alternative to it—realizing, *inter alia,* prophecy but without bloodshed and dispossession. Robert Gordon adopted a distinctly Baconian tone when he promoted his venture by noting that all divines—that is, experts—agreed that "these are the latter dayes ... well knowne by the signes that were to come before, sett downe by God himself in his sacred Word, and for the most part alreadie manifested."[20] The popular travel writer William Lithgow went further, seeing both economic development and colonies as elements in the struggle against world empire—Turkish and, especially, Spanish. Philip II had been "the worlds usurper." His Hapsburg successors wished to "domineere / O're all the universe." Who or what might "this monsters monarchy confyne: / For if he could, he would himselfe invest, / From pole to pole, and so from East to West." Supported by the

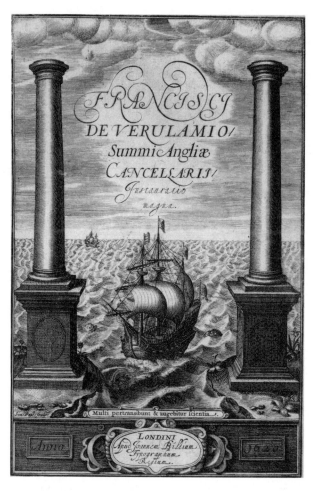

Within the image:

FRANCISCI
DE VERULAMIO,
Summi Angliæ
CANCELLARIS,
Instauratio
magna.

Multi pertransibunt & augebitur scientia.

LONDINI
Apud Joannem Billium,
Typographum
Regium.

Anno   1620

Figure 3.4 In the frontispiece to the *Great Instauration* (1620), Francis Bacon famously appropriates and transvalues Hapsburg iconography of the previous century. The conquest of the globe is a central and integral feature to the program for science and thus human redemption. All of these events embody the fulfillment of prophecy and culminate the apocalyptic narrative—as the motto from Daniel 12.4 indicates: "Multi pertransibunt & augebitur scientia" (Many will pass to and fro [in the latter days] and knowledge will increase). Yet no final empire, Hispanic or otherwise, assumes these momentous responsibilities. The "multi" Bacon has in mind may be not simply many people, but many peoples as well, and the scientific project will reconstitute the human mind empirically, without recourse to theological dispute. Even Jewish wisdom becomes important as humankind seeks a final truth that lies just over the horizon. Bacon's text coincides with the outset of the great religious war that would convulse Europe till mid-century.

Antichristian papacy with its unnatural clergy, Spain was the great threat to mankind. Plantations, both at home and abroad, comprised key parts of the alternative. Support for the colonial enterprise could be based widely across the British religious spectrum. Although Lithgow later strongly supported the Scottish Revolution of 1638 and the Covenanters, at this point he firmly identified with Laudian episcopacy and decried the "peevish, Puritanick show."[21]

Only with the mid-century revolutions and the coming of the English and then British republic did a centralized and coherent challenge to the Hapsburgs finally emerge. Parliament and then successive revolutionary governments between 1649 and 1660 understood themselves emphatically within the language of Foxe and Brightman. Domestically, that entailed an altogether heightened sense of public space, the citizen-saint, and radical social experimentation. Globally, it entailed confrontation with Catholic and counter-revolutionary Europe. Moreover, eschatological expectations assumed plausibility and telling potency because England and then Britain emerged as a world power, for the first time since the Middle Ages, and by many standards for the first time ever. The British republic is a spectacular success story, probably the most spectacular of the entire century. Not only did the republic defeat all of its enemies rapidly and decisively, but also its new capabilities and successively able leadership transformed it almost

←―――――――――――――――――――――――――――――――――――――

Edmund Spenser had anticipated Bacon's views (and Daniel 12:4) in his anti-imperial poem *The Faerie Queene*, Book II, "The Legend of Sir Guyon, or of Temperance" (1590):

> And daily how through hardy enterprise,
> Many great regions are discoverèd,
> Which to late age were never mentionèd.
> Who ever heard of th' Indian Peru?
> Or who in venturous vessel measurèd
> The Amazons' huge river, now found true?
> Or the fruitfullest Virginia, who did ever view?

> Yet all these were, when no man did them know,
> Yet have from wisest ages hidden been;
> And later times things more unknown shall show. (Proem, ii.3–iii.3)

(Courtesy of The Huntington Library, San Marino, California)

in a twinkling from a vulnerably isolated pariah state to a universally courted global power. Contemporary Englishmen might well be forgiven for believing that something quite special was taking place.

Did the revolutionary governments with their successive victories in England, Ireland, Scotland, against the Dutch, in the Mediterranean, and with their new navigation acts seek to establish a world empire, a British Fifth Monarchy? Was this the point in 1655 when the republic launched its huge (and, in the event, hugely disastrous) expedition to the New World? Did Oliver Cromwell, the key figure in this decision to attack the Spanish island of Hispaniola, actually imagine himself as a messianic Last World Emperor? The answer must be no. If Cromwell's contemporaneous enemies vilified him as a would-be "Emperor of the West Indies" or as "Imperator Augustus" of the British Isles, Laura Knoppers has shown the Protector to be extremely reluctant to embrace any such grandiloquent iconography—effectively weakening his authority as a result.[22] He manifestly did not intend to construct the Last World Empire and could only reject out of hand any prospect of becoming a Protestant Charles V. Cromwell's "union and right understanding" among nations that would realize humanity's political and spiritual destiny consisted of some form of confederal integration— much like the ideals of Sidney and Melville before him. The Lord Protector emerges a much more humble and idealistic person than is often imagined.

In 1658, during the last year of his life and at the height of his power, a remarkable emblem was produced that celebrated him within a completely different vocabulary (Figures 3.5 and 3.5a). In it Cromwell stands wearing an inconspicuous laurel and effectively bare-headed, presented as an emphatically modest figure, without ambition, without any dynastic claim. We encounter no imperial crown, no chariot drawn through the sky, no final empire. Yet if he is modest, he (and the new British republic) is also powerful, for he carries on his sword the crowns of the three British kingdoms. He has overcome the whore of Babylon and defeated division, thereby leading the country to both stability and freedom. Behind him stand the familiar two columns, but their message utterly inverts *plus ultra*. The left column is plastered with civic mottos and icons of civil rights, leading up to the sun and moon at the top, the true order of nature. The right column displays the three kingdoms offering him laurels. Atop the right column sit the Houses of Parliament that flourish along with the Lord Protector. Beyond the columns appear "Fame" and the New Model army. The defeat of Antichrist and the coming of the messianic age will issue in a world of the citizen, a world circumscribed rather than unbounded.

To be sure, English Fifth Monarchists were much in evidence on the authoritarian left. Christopher Feake imagined the English Revolution and subsequent successes in the most militant terms as an apocalyptic march on Rome. On 11 September 1653 in the midst of the war with the Netherlands, he held forth:

> Thou [God] gave a cup to the hand of England, and we drank of it. Then thou carried it to Scotland and Ireland, and they drank of it. Now thou has carried to it to Holland, and they are drinking of it. Lord carry it also to France, to Spain, to Rome, and let it never be out of some or other of their hands, till they drink and be drunk, and spew, and fall, never to rise any more.[23]

The authoritarian right also saw in the new world the prospect of empire and conquest. The Hobbesian Michael Hawke looked to Cromwell as a latter-day Caesar whose authority derived from providential triumphs. Cromwell conformed to neither imperial construction.

It is hard to imagine two more dissimilar figures than Oliver Cromwell and his Portuguese contemporary, the Jesuit Antonio Vieira. Although at opposite ends of the religious spectrum—with Cromwell vastly more tolerant of Catholics than Vieira was of "heretics"—they shared a number of overlapping objectives articulated through a common vocabulary. Both had met the Amsterdam Rabbi, Menasseh ben Israel, and drew on his messianic expectations (Vieira even appropriating the title of Menasseh's best known tract, *The Hope of Israel*). Both were variously philo-Semitic: Cromwell seeking the readmission of the Jews to England, Vieira seeking to mitigate the blood laws that discriminated against New Christians. Both sought curbs on the Inquisition in the New World, possibly as a prelude to its elimination. Both sought to liberate (or protect) the Amerindians and were genuinely appalled by their treatment at the hands of the Iberians. Both sought to legitimate and promote commerce within the region. Both knew that they lived at the end of days and understood their objectives in highly articulated prophetic terms. But Vieira saw all these objectives as leading to the Fifth Monarchy and projected Dom João IV of the

Figure 3.5 "The Embleme of England's Distractions, as also of her attained and further expected Freedom and Happiness" (1658). This engraving by William Faithorne, executed from Francis Barlow's pen-and-wash rendering (3.3a), portrays Oliver Cromwell as a figure who has brought both stability and freedom to the British Isles.

By far the most arresting feature of the emblem to contemporaries would have been the Lord Protector standing effectively bare-headed. Illustrations of the seventeenth-century House of Commons portray its members meeting with their hats on. Individual parliamentary officials also often appear wearing their hats. The point in the emblem is to show the Protector's modesty, his lack of ambition, and the truth of the Greek statement on the ribbon at the top that only God glorifies. At the same time the Protector's power is also manifest as he holds the crowns of England, Scotland, and Ireland by his restored House of Bragança as the prophesied Last World Emperor. Cromwell would have none of it. Despite their common apocalyptic vocabulary, Vieira emerges as one of the great imperialists, Cromwell one of the great anti-imperialists. The differences between them are in some ways subtle, and yet also decisive. Portuguese historiography has deemed Vieira an "elevated figure," and Anglophone treatments of him have often agreed.[24] Cromwell has been excoriated for more than three centuries.

Cromwell's savaged reputation owes much to the contemporaneous emergence of more populist, "left-wing" criticism of both his domestic and foreign policies. Outstanding among such critics was the republican political philosopher James Harrington. Harrington's *Oceana* (1656) envisioned a great agrarian republic and thereby criticized the

←————————————————————————————————————

sword—and yet wears none. Indeed the extraordinary power of the emergent British republic had become manifest at home and throughout Europe.

Within Britain the Protector has defeated the whore of Babylon (dumping her cup of iniquity) and overcome faction—and thereby brought the ship of state safely to its Mount Ararat. Nevertheless, the new Britain both contends with Catholic, counterrevolutionary subversion as well as the task of creating plenty for its citizens.

It also does more. Behind the Protector stand the familiar two columns. But they have ceased to be an imperial device, at least in the usual sense. The left column is plastered with civic mottos and civil rights, leading up to the sun and moon, the true order of nature. The one on the right shows the three British kingdoms offering laurels, leading up not only to the Protector but also to the British Parliament: atop the column sit the Houses of Parliament in place of any dynastic emblem. Beyond the columns appear "Fame" and the New Model Army. The thrust of the device is evident. The defeat of the Antichrist will bring liberation rather than empire, civic societies rather than hierarchy.

The emblem, far more than Bacon's frontispiece, confronts and inverts Hapsburg iconography: modest Cromwell versus Philip as Christ-Apollo; unbounded authority versus circumscribed authority. It is hard not to think that this was intentional. The earlier attack on the Spanish nerve-center at Hispaniola can only have seemed the logical outcome of these utterly conflicting visions of the human experience and human destiny. The activity beyond the columns would likely have been more elaborate had the expedition to the Caribbean succeeded in capturing Hispaniola—rather than merely Jamaica. (© *Copyright the Trustees of the British Museum*)

Figure 3.5a Francis Barlow's pen and wash prototype for Faithorne's "The Embleme of England's Distractions" offers a much more conservative image of the Protectorate. A younger Cromwell, now prominently laureled and promoted by a larger, more dominating figure of Fame, provides the focus. The revolutionary armies become accordingly diminished. A palace/cathedral stands atop the column unaccompanied by the Parliament of England, Scotland, and Ireland. Skulls impaled by long spikes at each end of the building further emphasize the Protector's awesome power. In Barlow's drawing only England wears an imperial crown, indicating London's superiority and, implicitly, its sovereign authority. If Cromwell's understated laurel makes him a citizen-legislator, the dramatic laurel makes him Caesar and looks to the principate. Barlow presents a heavily regal reading of the Protectorate, while Faithorne projects a more civic future. Both are immersed in competing visions of England's eschatological destiny. (*Courtesy of The Huntington Library, San Marino, California*)

seemingly monarchical drift within the Protectorate, as well as its reluctance to formalize land redistribution and to secure a more civic society with higher levels of public participation. Only with these arrangements in place could England (Oceana) hope to liberate the world and redeem mankind. Writing with the West Indies disaster very much in the public mind, Harrington even went so far as to provide the speech Cromwell should have given at the opening of Parliament in September 1656. Casting the Protector as at once a classical legislator and Mosaic prophet—and emphatically not as an emperor—Harrington's Cromwell would institute the republic and then lay down public office. Harrington's England would then assume the mission of liberating mankind through the creation of citizen societies, achieved by the overthrow of "gothic" feudal elites. Harrington may have had in mind the experience of the revolutionary armies in Scotland which saw themselves as defeating the nobility, gentry, and clergy, thereby creating independent landowners who might "live with a more comfortable subsistence then formerly, and like a free People, delivered (through Gods goodnesse) from their former slaveries, vassalage, and oppressions."[25] Both the radical military and Harrington saw liberation as agrarian, rather than commercial.

The emergent world of free republics comprised the kingdom of Christ, the historical redemption, for the democratic republic claimed soteriological purposes every bit as much as the Fifth Empire. But it reimagined the engines of salvation: the illumined saint and the articulate citizen became coterminous, as grace completed nature and the millennial world was achieved. Harrington's civil religion is even more thorough-going than Buchanan's; and, quite unlike Buchanan, its story for Harrington—from Jewish promise to Christian fulfillment—comprised sacred history. The triumph of civil religion lay at the heart of the apocalyptic trajectory.

In the messianic age the republican order for Harrington would be neither confederal nor imperial. Instead, there would exist unequal leagues. Liberated societies would tax themselves to pay for the armies that had secured and now maintained their freedom. The world would no longer be dominated by empire as traditionally understood, but patronized—in the sense of sponsored—by the great redeemer republic. Here was an imperial anti-imperialism. "Gothic" empire would not be "translated" from one realm to another, but would be supplanted and cease to exist altogether. Only a true republic, however, could realize such a world. Any effort to liberate mankind—like the West Indies expedition—emanating from a different kind of state could only fail or fail to liberate. It could achieve no more than the exact opposite of its stated purpose: a gothic empire that ran directly counter to spirituality and humanity. Moreover, even if all indications from history and the present moment assigned England the providential role of messianic liberator, there always existed the possibility that she might squander the opportunity.

In part for reasons of population, the most likely competitor would be France rather than Spain. A French republic would "assuredly govern the world," and consequently the Caribbean expedition was doubly misdirected. Later on, Harrington seems to suggest, teasingly, the terrifying possibility of French radicalism. A letter reaches the British Parliament about "his Phoebean majesty." The Sun King, it seems, has suddenly realized that "free states" were "incomparably better and more assuredly directed unto the good of mankind than any other." This prospect prompted "a violent passion of weeping and downright howling" at what was deemed "horrid news." Although the story turns out not to be serious, it nevertheless offered the people of Oceana / England "a great admonition."[26]

John Pocock has observed that Harrington wrote "at the last moment when it was possible to ignore the power of capital in the formation of states."[27] The land-based, self-supported citizen-soldier, who underlay Harrington's civic world, did not rely upon monied wealth. Quite the opposite. Like John Milton, Harrington was heir to the anti-commercial tradition associated prominently with George Buchanan. Accordingly, he contributed precious little to the emerging discourse of political economy. His vision of England allowed for trade but would not be defined by it. He offered no clear analysis of the contemporaneous Dutch republic—then the wealthiest society on the globe—and viewed its politics with unease. Steven Pincus has emphasized these dimensions of earlier republican political thought in order to describe and distinguish the rise of a new kind of radicalism and republicanism that came into its own after 1650.[28] Based on a commercial rather than an agrarian society, this radicalism looked to a more complex world, where trade and banking were the engines of power, where money, not self-armed farmer-citizens, created modern armies. Labor now generated value, and there existed consequently no natural limits to wealth. In this world people pursued their "interests" rather than moral autonomy, and promoted society through productivity rather than through civic virtue. Precisely because interests were varied, commercial society needed to be more deliberative in determining the common good, and thereby became potentially more democratic. Accordingly, its historical models also differed. The world of political economy looked to commercial Carthage rather than virtuous Rome, to open Athens rather than to moneyless Sparta, to the more populist United Provinces instead of severely aristocratic Venice.

Whether commercial republicanism was actually more radical than its rival remains an open question. What is not an open question are the apocalyptic preoccupations of the new trade-based radicalism. If imperialism and anti-imperialism were now cast within the vocabulary of commerce, the struggle against Antichrist and universal empire simply continued from this shifted frame of reference. This circumstance can hardly cause wonder, for commerce and apocalypse had a long association. The court of Dom Manuel had explicitly associated the two. Portuguese explorers were to proceed against aborigines if they refused missionaries (or their teachings) *and* if they rejected trade. For the Dutch this association was, of course, far closer. The interweaving of naive idealism, apocalyptic struggle, and global trade in Dutch thinking during the late sixteenth and early seventeenth centuries is truly extraordinary, and possibly never more so than with that tireless campaigner for a Dutch West Indies company, Willem Usselincx (1567–1647). Perhaps only the Dutch could promise to liberate the Amerindians, enact the sacred drama, and provide their new allies with the items they wanted at a better price than the minions of Antichrist could hope to offer.

In revolutionary England, too, the new economic writing, as Charles Webster observed long ago, possessed "an optimistic and utopian" character.[29] Indeed, eschatological values informed it. Even so ostensibly secular a figure as the Leveller Richard Overton (*fl.* 1631–1664), writing in the 1640s, shared a number of common assumptions of his more orthodox opponents. His plea for toleration, and notably of the Jews, arises from the philo-Semitic language of his erstwhile Presbyterian allies. He bitterly decried "Scotch Government" as the Inquisition's successor, but he had more in common with the Scottish Presbyterian leader Samuel Rutherford than either would have comfortably admitted.[30] He developed close connections with Dutch Mennonites. His printing career self-consciously looked back to Martin Marprelate and Elizabethan Puritanism. He proclaimed a "general Baptist" confession of faith, which, however unorthodox, arose from the Calvinist tradition. His mortalist doctrines were of a piece with contemporary radical piety. Such doctrines emphasized the apocalyptic program because salvation is only realized with the resolution of history, with the resurrection of the body at the end of time. The vocabulary of the apocalypse—"the mystery of iniquity"—can suffuse Overton's writings.[31]

Yet, if he spoke the language of prophecy, Overton also spoke the language of interest. From the earliest years of the Revolution, he sought free trade. The attack on clerical privilege and hierarchy connected directly with his attack on economic privilege and monopoly. He insisted "that every English Native, who hath goods, Wares, and Merchandize, may have freedom to transport the same to any place beyond the seas, and there to convert them to his owne profit." He was always much exercised about the "hinderance to Trade" which could only be "prejudiciall to the Nation."[32] Overton's model was the Netherlands, for its republicanism, its toleration, and, linked to them, its commerce and prosperity. The English now had the opportunity of becoming "the most absolute free people in the world." England might become the model for nations, stimulating revolution in Scotland and perhaps elsewhere. "We know wee have stoore of friends in our neighbor countries."[33] Already by the later 1640s, we encounter embryonic hints of global liberation arising within a world commerce. Religious liberty, political liberty, and economic liberty melded together as a common cause, and behind all of this proto-liberalism, this new world in birth, lay the apocalypse.

There is probably no better combination of the entrepreneurial and the apocalyptic than that exemplified by the Scot Sir James Hope of Hopetoun (1614–1661). With long-term trading connections in Holland and extensive mining interests in Lanarkshire, Hope was a highly successful entrepreneur, in many respects anticipating the "improvers" of the eighteenth century. In 1641 the Covenanting government made him Master of the Mint. During the revolutionary years, he would become a leading figure in the "left opposition" of Scotland's most radical parliament (1649) and then assumed much the same role in

England's most radical parliament, the Nominated Parliament of 1653. He was remembered during that parliament for his "speech for the Jews." Later he saw his mining interests as potentially off-setting the Hispaniola disaster. Hope was always known in England as a "good commonwealthsman."[34]

During the course of the extraordinarily fecund 1650s, there emerged two forms of radical politics, two forms of modernity, and with them two forms of resisting empire, each of which promoted expansion in order to do so. Both drew heavily on that resilient Western vocabulary, the Judeo-Christian apocalypse, a vocabulary that combated empire no less than creating it. Within the Anglophone world it did both, the second while seeking the first. The result would be an empire to end empire.

THE LATER CAREER OF THE FIFTH AND FINAL EMPIRE

The massive religious struggles of the seventeenth century comprise a face-off between conflicting apocalyptic visions—the imperial opposing the confederal, the hierarchical confronting the civic—and, underlying them, conflicting perceptions of mankind's political destiny. It is said that Philip III (r. 1598–1621) rejected his father's advice on just about every topic save one: the monarchy's overriding spiritual goal. He embraced messianic mission with no less zeal—and, it seemed, with the promise of still greater success. By 1629 the destruction of continental Protestantism seemed imminent, one of the great goals of the Hapsburgs finally at hand. Even if Spanish power declined in the decades that followed—and that power remained more formidable than is often recognized—Protestantism had declined far more precipitously in the face of a revitalized and highly aggressive Catholicism. In 1590 perhaps half of Europe was Protestant, by 1648 barely 20 percent. Moreover, neither the Portuguese secession nor the Catalan revolt seemed to dampen Iberian enthusiasm for messianic monarchy. Yet the mantle of the final empire would be assumed to powerful effect in later seventeenth-century France, and this enduring idea would only become dormant, if not completely defunct, with the 1713 Peace of Utrecht.

Against such powers emerged various continental analogues to Britain's Solemn League and Covenant or to the New England confederation. Again both like Britain and like their formidable opponents, they were immersed in eschatological expectations. They too looked to a world reborn. They too developed wide-ranging reform projects. Perhaps no one worked more tirelessly for the ultimate confederation that would precede the millennium than did the émigré Scot John Durie (1596–1680). In company with him also appeared an impressive range of continental thinkers who drew on the turn-of-the-century enthusiasm to develop ever more highly articulated projections of a future millennium. Inevitably these lines of thinking responded to the successive catastrophes of the 1620s. But their fundamental outlines derived from the earlier optimistic moment. What seems to be missing even at the most excited and hopeful junctures is confidence in a final monarchy. Neither Frederick V, Bohemia's brief "winter king," nor Sweden's remarkable Gustavus Adolphus enter the stage as Last World Emperors. Despite gigantic spikes in the pamphlet literature in 1620 and again in 1630, which assembled vast prophetic, astrological, and esoteric learning, the prospective new age seems rather collaborative than resolutely imperial. The constantly embattled House of Vasa did indeed seek to establish a final "*dominium maris Baltici*," and Johannes Bureus (1568–1652), the most determined promoter of Swedish expansion, developed a compelling eschatological-historical vision for the new Swedish order. But this was a considerable distance from universal monarchy. Even during the winter of 1630–1631 when, at the height of his success, Gustavus Adolphus held court in Germany and received emissaries from as far as the Ottoman Empire, the king's horizon was necessarily limited. He might have hoped to displace Hapsburg power in central Europe, but he was far too dependent financially and too defensive in outlook to contemplate global conquest. The Baltic might well become a Swedish lake, but only Philip II and his successors might work plausibly to turn the entire Pacific Ocean into a Spanish sea. When the driven Dominican prophet and polymath Tommaso Campanella (1568–1639) looked at the maritime power of Elizabethan England, he saw trouble for Spain's world empire. Nevertheless, "the English seem least of all to affect an Universal Monarchy."[35] He was right. But his words could have applied as well to the Palatine Elector and the king of Sweden. If the last monarchy proved largely a Catholic vision, it surely found no more devoted advocate than the friar Campanella. Throughout his surprisingly long life Campanella found it "evident that the prophesy concerning the end of the world, both according to nature and the art of policy, shortly to be fulfilled."[36] Both the course of history and the dynamics of nature, each elements within a common fabric, hurtled toward their eschatological resolution. Before that could happen or, rather, integral to these events, was the creation of a global papal theocracy. The agency through which this clerical order was to be achieved, or so Campanella believed until the late 1620s, was of course the Spanish Empire. Although he felt no special affection for Spain, only its global power could underwrite this eschatological project. It barely mattered that both Spain and the papacy treated him monstrously. Nor did it seem to concern him that his "natural" Catholicism fit poorly with the Aristotelian neo-scholastic climate of the Counter-Reformation. The sheer energy with which he approached nature, society, and salvation, no less than the manifest truth of his insight, would surely sweep all before it.

As early as the 1630s, visibly as the tide seemed to turn at last against the Hapsburgs and perhaps earlier still, a rival claimant to the role of the Last World Empire arose with the revitalized French kingdom. Anticipations of such claims had appeared in the earlier sixteenth century, and at the opening of the next century flashes of such French hopes can be detected as Henri IV consolidated power and prepared to move against the Hapsburgs during the years before his assassination in 1610. But a sustained and articulated vision only occurred under Cardinal Richelieu during the final phase of the Thirty Years' War. Perhaps surprisingly, Tommaso Campanella contributed significantly to its formulation, as he deftly developed a *translatio imperii*. For Campanella now came to believe that Spain had found its fruition outside of itself, in its external achievements rather than in events at home, and above all in preparing the way for its progeny, France. Spain, a plant without roots, had exhausted itself in the creation of global empire and in the confrontation with its ripening successor, thereby leaving itself drained, populated "avec seulement un clergé, des moines, des prêtres, des religioueses et des putains."[37]

Many contemporaries agreed with his conclusions, if not with the intricacies of his argument. So too have recent modern studies of the period. Current French scholarship draws on the work of Ernest Lavisse, and suggests that in both style and outlook Louis "fut un roi plus espagnol que français." Both his rule and that of his predecessor Cardinal Richelieu now appear much more religiously motivated than twentieth-century historians have often suggested. Moreover, both were specifically inspired by Hapsburg ideals. The Hispanic mantel was not adopted merely from personal taste of the ruling figures, but, it now seems, from a more general cultural penetration. It is within the hispanized eschatological framework—rather than the secular reading inherited from Voltaire and Alexis de Tocqueville—that we need to understand the war to extirpate the Dutch republic, the revocation of the Edict of Nantes, the campaign for Britain, the extraordinary iconography of Louis' reign. The Sun King trope dated from antiquity, held powerful Carolingian associations, and had become all but inseparable from messianic empire. Philip II had so completely identified himself with it and with its eschatological meanings that his contemporaries had to confront it, while his would-be successor could only adopt it. Similarly, Escurial and Versailles were not only defining structures, but strikingly analogous ones, and the parallels between Louis and Philip have today become matters of serious historical study.

By the second decade of the eighteenth century the Fifth Monarchy had become in many respects a spent force. If its vocabulary was resurrected and contested a century later with Napoleon, such thinking reemerged in a world that had well-developed secular constructs at its disposal. The Fifth Monarchy needed to compete with other modes of explanation, at once newer and vastly more sophisticated, and, equally, the apocalypse in any of its forms seemed increasingly archaic. Even those for whom such ideas remained vital and compelling knew that their thinking involved a choice. For most of the seventeenth century and for most of Europe such choice was simply unavailable: secular categories were only beginning to be constructed. Yet—in one of the great ironies of the Western experience—apocalyptic thinking proved decisive in creating the very modes of cognition that would subsequently supplant it.

CHAPTER 4

PROPHECY AND NATURE: SCIENCE, SEX, AND SALVATION

We will find nothing in the least scientific about the apocalypse. No specific discovery ever resulted from any of the many eschatological scenarios; no specific insight can be connected to apocalyptic claims or expectations. Prophetic numbers led to neither a constant nor a formula. Yet it is all but impossible to imagine modern science without its effect. For the apocalypse proved essential in creating what we can call the program for science; that is, the incremental process of testing, replication, and reformulation inherent in modern scientific discovery. In so doing, the apocalypse also proved essential in creating the scientist as a social type who participated in that program. Prior to the seventeenth century there were philosophers, magicians, shamans, witches, virtuosi, even university professors, but only at the end of that century can we identify figures whom we might legitimately call scientists. Only then did science emerge as a collective, time-bound process, like the sacred drama itself, and a process possessed of civic and public character like the Renaissance and Reformation values out which it arose.

Apocalyptic discovery also had a terminus, but, crucially, that terminus kept receding. Far from simply being a matter of problem-solving, the scientific enterprise involved human transformation. Science consequently acquired a legitimacy and centrality, as well as a structure and dynamism, that inherently extended beyond the solutions and answers it uncovered. All of these qualities distinguish it from earlier natural philosophy, whether in the West or elsewhere.

Between 1590 and 1650 there appeared an extraordinary outpouring of spiritualist-scientific utopias that envisioned the rapid expansion of human knowledge, and this enhanced understanding would restore Edenic man and work the historical redemption. In the event, more than a restoration was anticipated. Rather, there would be a "refounding," an "instauration" to use Francis Bacon's term, for man redeemed was something other, something more—something richer—than man innocent.

This train of thought cropped up just about everywhere in Europe, from Uppsala to Naples, Edinburgh to the Levant, Amsterdam to the wilds of Lithuania. It grew out of a context in which an increasingly articulated apocalyptic future and even the prospect of a future millennium became prominent in European culture. The Englishmen Thomas Brightman, Hugh Broughton, and, signally, Francis Bacon provide exemplars. So too do the Italian Tommaso Campanella, the Germans Tobias Hess, Johannes Piscator, Christoph Besold, Simon Studion, Johann Valentin Andreae, the Swede Johann Bureus, the Scots John Napier of Merchiston, Robert Pont, and James Maxwell. This growing preoccupation with the eschatological future culminated both in Britain and on the continent in the same year, 1627, with the first appearance of the great millenarian systems of Joseph Mede and Johan Heinrich Alsted.[1] Broadly analogous reflection occurred in Judaism with contemporaneous figures like Abraham Cohen de Herrera and Menasseh ben Israel. Frequently associated with such concerns was a newfound preoccupation with esoteric and magical traditions: astrology, Pythagorean number mysticism, alchemy, even Kabbalah. The decades straddling 1600 mark the high point of Lutheran astrology. The last years of the 1590s witnessed in Scotland the beginnings of Freemasonry. It is no accident that the first Faust book surfaced in 1587 and captured the European imagination during the decade that followed. European intellectuals have found themselves more attracted to magic at some periods than in others; Italians had felt its attraction a century earlier. But never before had magic been as widespread nor associated, as it now often was, with social reform and eschatology.

To be sure, the project was variously conceived. Some, like the Rosicrucian writers in Germany (1614, 1615), stressed esoteric learning and arcane symbolism; yet their expectations and vocabulary arose from the new millenarianism of the previous decade, especially at Württemberg, and was a far more mainstream and widespread phenomenon than scholars once believed. Others saw nature itself transforming as an integral element within the redemptive process. As humankind strove toward salvation, so nature labored toward its renewal and fulfillment. Campanella insisted memorably in 1598 and 1602 that the sun was "constantly coming nearer" to the earth and "is now ten thousand miles nearer"—a development that foretold of "grand mutations."[2] At the end of the 1590s masonic lodges appeared in Scotland which promoted Renaissance esoteric wisdom and also crossed class boundaries in unexpected ways. In these years Sweden's Johannes Bureus took up the first systematic study of the language of the ancient runes, around which he constructed a deeply apocalyptic understanding of the past and a millenarian vision for the future. Yet for all their differences in religion and program, the commonality of these undertakings remains decisive. All of them embraced mystical, indeed magical traditions, and all rejected scholasticism. All sought redemptive knowledge through an engagement with the physical world. All imagined discovery as a community undertaking involving individuals with different talents, abilities, and insight. All were deeply immersed in the apocalypse.

The validation of the physical world is particularly striking. Just as earlier Renaissance thought had been preoccupied with what God said rather than what he meant, so the late Renaissance sought to encounter God through his body rather than his essence. The traditional view that separated mind from body seemed less compelling as a result. The mechanical arts, skills that built things by human hands, acquired new status vis-à-vis the liberal arts, the mental categories through which phenomena were classified. Francis Bacon, by far the most influential of these thinkers (only Campanella approached his stature), famously observed that the mechanical arts "having in them some breath of life are continuously growing and becoming more perfect." Arts such as artillery, sailing, and printing improved over time, while just the reverse happened to the liberal arts that derived from the famous philosophers of antiquity. "Philosophy and the intellectual sciences on the other contrary, stand like statues, worshiped and celebrated, but not moved or advanced." The former provided the model. Bacon would (grudgingly) "let the great authors [Plato, Aristotle] have their due, [so long] as time, which is the author of authors, have his due, which is further and further to discover truth." The key was time—for "truth is the daughter of time"—and that time could only be sacred time. The purpose of it all was redemption: "the sovereignty and power ... which [man] had in his first state of creation."[3] Here indeed was the great instauration. Here was Campanella's City of the Sun, where the mechanical arts assumed central significance in the culminating world order. Here too was Bureus's eschatological preoccupation with artifacts and architecture.

If redemption was temporal, the time-bound discovery of a God immanent within his creation, it was necessarily a shared undertaking. The organization of the scientific project derived heavily from humanist traditions and specifically Niccolò Machiavelli's republicanism. The project was a cooperative, collaborative, almost a civic undertaking, requiring many talents working and interacting as part of an apocalyptic program. For the strategy of truth was so complex that no individual or any one generation could work out its secrets and structure. It could not be achieved "within the hourglass of one man's life." Science therefore went far "to level men's wit," because discovery resulted as much from location as from ability. "For however various are the forms of civil polities, there is but one form of polity in the sciences, and that always has been and always will be popular." Human knowledge and power—the refounding of humanity, which gradually recovered from the effects of the Fall—could only derive from "public designation," and "not through private endeavor."[4] For Denis Diderot in the next century, it had been Bacon's genius to see through genius (his underlying apocalyptic spirituality having dropped out of the picture altogether). If Bacon's scientific respublica was undoubtedly imagined as elitist, if meritocratic (as was Diderot's), it was also an open society quite unlike the authoritarian world of Philip II where science would be retarded more than a generation. In stark contrast to Philip, Britain's James, a latter-day Solomon, would launch this grand redemptive design as a classical legislator rather than the Last World Emperor. As he had joined England and Scotland to create the new society Britain, so he would join the new Britons in the great public project. Today we find it difficult to visualize James as such a grand figure. Yet Bacon was not alone in seeing the British union as a Machiavellian *occasione* through which radical innovation might be achieved. Nor was he alone in wanting James to be the radical legislator who would realize the potential of this extraordinary opportunity.

The apocalypse did more than provide the spine for the program of science and the vision of its purpose. It also transformed magic. All forms of magic viewed the universe as a web of hidden forces. These forces ranged widely, from chemical bonding, to electromagnetism, to personal magnetism, to emanations from the heavenly bodies, to much else as well. Magicians sought to manipulate objects (and, at times, people) by controlling or directing these forces. In so doing they not only achieved power but powerful spiritual insight and, potentially, might peer into the mind of God. The power element was important: manipulating nature, controlling nature, "vexing" nature as Bacon put it.[5] It would be hard to imagine a more compelling validation of the physical world or of physical operations within it.

But there was another dimension. The physical universe and the forces within it manifested themselves through one single substance, *spiritus*. In itself, spiritus was in no way esoteric. Either ultra-refined matter or ultra-coarse mind, spiritus within mainstream thought was an in-between material that connected these two great polarities. Through spiritus, mind was able to move matter. A long-standing commonplace within the Great Chain of Being, spiritus, as John Donne put it, would "knit the subtle knot, which makes us man." Spiritus was essential for the mind to work, "else a great Prince in prison lies."[6] For magicians, however, spiritus was not only an important ingredient but the central constituent—and for many the exclusive constituent—within the cosmos. The consequences were enormous, at least potentially. With the mind-body dualism pushed to the margins or eliminated altogether, the hierarchy of qualitatively different essences that derived from it was also marginalized. Instead of mind-body, the dualism became hot-cold, active versus quiescent matter, condensed versus rarified spiritus. It would be hard to find *teloi* in such a world, and the universe might be transformed simply by activating it. Further, if now all creation was composed everywhere of the same material, it could be then treated mathematically. For mathematics can only deal with things that are the same: we cannot add apples and oranges. The last was crucial: number became the measure of meaning, the language of God.

Manipulating nature, opening it to mathematics, finding the deepest forms of knowledge within it, all of this sounds very modern. And yet it is not, no more so than is the apocalypse. Magic offered a personal, spiritual journey, with its arcane power limited a handful of adepts. Acolytes and technicians did not make the trip. No graduate students need apply. These select cognoscenti communicated with each other only rarely and even then within a language deliberately obscured to keep its wisdom from falling into unworthy hands. Secrecy lay at its heart, obscurity permeated its discourse, irrationality informed its procedures. In each of these respects the apocalypse transformed the ancient magical traditions into something altogether unprecedented. For by making magic a public project that required "many wits and industries" over the course of time, replication became essential and magic necessarily became demystified. The apocalypse changed magic from an individual quest for private gnosis to a community quest for open discovery and the shared integration of multiple insights. Solitary salvation became overshadowed by the historical redemption, the occult and the secretive supplanted by the universal and the verifiable. As a result, a number of the key features in magic began to look strikingly different, as did the mentality behind it.

Bacon exemplifies this transition. He both arose from Renaissance magic and at the same time was deeply critical of it. Bacon looked to spiritus, believing that "everything tangible that we are acquainted with contains an invisible and intangible spirit, which wraps and clothes as with a garment." Nonetheless he vigorously discounted magic as "full of error and vanity which the great professors themselves have sought to veil over and conceal with enigmatical writings."[7] The mentality of the gnosis led to nothing—or worse. But magic, now transformed within the new apocalyptic program, stressed human capability and became powerful in turn. The language of power is everywhere evident in Bacon's writing. Scientific investigation was "not an opinion to be held, but a work to be done." It sought to "command nature in action." Knowledge became experiential, the result of interaction with the physical world, and from which arose the beginnings of experimental science. If Bacon's formal system of induction led to problems in logic—problems that would be taken up later by figures like J. S. Mill and Bertrand Russell—rather than shaping scientific practice, the implications of his program remain unassailable. There was also something more. Bacon's program pointed away from sterile theological disputes to forms of cognition upon which all could agree. "I am laboring to lay the foundation, not of any sect or doctrine, but of human utility and power."[8] Just as Bacon promoted empire, but not a specifically British empire (and was implacably hostile to Spanish pretensions), so too his program drew universally on the insight of many wits, and not necessarily Christian ones.

A number of these themes are developed emblematically in Bacon's famous though uncompleted utopia, *New Atlantis* (1612?). The tale begins with English sailors who have traveled both beyond the pillars of Hercules and beyond the New World as well—*plus ultra* in the fullest sense. There in the Pacific, in the outermost reaches of the globe, the sailors find themselves lost, becalmed, and in the most dire circumstances. At this point, and significantly at just this location, they encounter the island of Bensalem, inhabited by a community governed by the revelation of science. On the island they are freed by science from chance and fate, and healed by science physically and, it seems, mentally. They live in a world that controls nature rather than being controlled by it. Early on, as they experience Bensalem and learn about it, the sailors say, "It seemed to us that we had before us a picture of our salvation in heaven."[9] Their physician is a Christian priest: the Christian flock and the flock of science have become one. Accordingly, a visiting priest-scientist looks somewhat like an Anglican bishop.

Bensalem is the antitype to Jerusalem, the old and new dispensations. Located on opposite sides of the globe, they comprise the beginning of the sacred drama and its conclusion, literally and metaphorically demarcating the narrative of the human journey. As Jerusalem embodied the promise, so Bensalem comprises its fulfillment (with Bensalem's meaning of "offspring of peace," "safety," "completeness"). Judaism finds its completion in science-Christianity.

Or does it? Bensalem, it turns out, is not exclusively a Christian society, but has a Jewish community within it—quite unlike England which expelled the Jews in 1290, quite unlike Spain which expelled the Jews in 1492, and certainly unlike most utopias, especially early modern ones. Joabin, the Jew in the story and the only living Bensalemite described as "wise," plays a vital and complex role in Bacon's fable. Joabin and his co-religionists look to a further revelation, further discovery that remains as yet in the future. Like Bensalem itself, the final achievement of knowledge lies just over the horizon. The presence of the Jews inherently ratchets up the apocalyptic dimension of the story because the conversion of the Jews at the end of days had been a Pauline commonplace since late antiquity (Rom. 11:25–26). But Bacon had something else in mind. The "calling of the Jews" did not mean conversion, the vastly belated recognition of Christ. The final truth is not simply contemporary Christianity (in any of its forms), but something further, and the "called" Jews have a part in its discovery.

Joabin informs the sailors about Bensalemite customs, and in the process validates human bodies and, with them, human eroticism. He explains the "feast of the family" in which the father of thirty offspring "of his body" receives an award. What could be more "natural, pious, and reverend" than this celebration, exclaims Joabin's English companion, who had never heard of "a solemnity wherein nature did so much preside."[10] Be fruitful and multiply, indeed. Procreation is a virtue, an obligation, a civic act. Bensalem is a resoundingly un-Augustinian society, and, seen as a millennial projection, it directly inverts the greatest Latin father. Joabin also describes Adam and Eve pools where prospective spouses learn about each other's bodies—and what they might be getting into. Although an attenuated adaptation from Thomas More and Plato, the sexual in Bacon goes beyond that of all his contemporaries except for Campanella. That the erotic should be revalued by the Jewish Joabin is hugely significant. From late antiquity onward the Christian churches had decried Jews for being "carnal," for reading scripture literally and physically rather than recognizing the "higher" spiritual meaning of Jesus. Bacon's utopia utterly explodes the timeworn vocabulary. The "carnal" Jews recover and legitimate our carnality, quite literally the pound of flesh—and a great deal more. Hath not a Jew organs? Indeed. With Shakespeare's famous passage—utterly illiberal, utterly anti-Semitic in its intention—Shylock betrays the physical and thus contemptible nature of Judaism and its practitioners. Now, with Bacon, physical bodies, in every sense, acquire new meaning and significance. Most dramatically, validating the Jews has validated sexuality.

The prophetic character of Joabin becomes evident through the long-recognized source of his name in the biblical Joab. David's leading general, Joab, played a decisive role in the king's success, even his survival. Yet Joab was also an exceedingly ambiguous figure, for he would assist in David's adultery with Bathsheba by securing, on the king's orders, the death of her husband, Uriah the Hittite. The upshot was Nathan's prophetic curse on the Davidic dynasty and the flickering of the Hebrew promise.[11] For centuries Christian theology regarded David as a "type" foreshadowing Christ as king and judge, and made him, arguably, the most prominent typological figure in the

Old Testament. Now at the end of days with the Davidic presence looming once again, Joab/Joabin sets things to right and expunges the curse of Nathan. David's attraction to Bathsheba, we will recall, occurred when he happened to see her bathing, clearly a misdirected anticipation of Bensalem's Adam and Eve pools. But it is one corrected by Bacon's revision of More-Plato: a friend does the looking; desire becomes informed by another perspective. So imagined, a redeemed world extends to redeemed eroticism. The issue is not to repress desire with Augustinian restraint, but legitimate desire by lifting the burden of nature. It is not at all fortuitous that Bacon first introduces the Feast of the Family immediately after the sailors perceive themselves to be "free men."

Bacon is now recognized as one of the first early modern thinkers to assign positive value to passion and to propose a balance among the passions rather than their repression. Moreover, like Bensalem's priest-scientists, Bacon himself was hugely concerned to prolong life (and to prevent senility), at once a spiritual and physical undertaking. At the most practical level that challenging task involved condensing one's spiritus and at the same time preventing it from drying up. A variety of ways existed for achieving this result, among them, "Venus saepe excitata, raro peracta."[12] Erotic tension was a good thing, but Bacon could not recommend that people frequently expend their vital fluids. As the mind-body dualism faded within Bacon's intellectual world, so too to some extent did the allied and equally ancient duality of reason and passion.

Inevitably, life prolongation, achieved in part through widely varied processes of heating and cooling, comprised one of the most central tasks of Bensalem's science. For nothing else could more directly undo the consequences of the fall. All of the operations of Salomon's House, the institute of the Bensalem priest-scientists, are inherently spiritual and soteriological. Even though the Bensalemites have Solomon's natural history as Europeans do not, their institute is not a Solomonic foundation (despite its name), but the work of an indigenous prophet-legislator, Solamona.[13] The institute is not simply anchored in the Old Testament but possesses a broader, more universal base. It is significant that Joabin and his community are nice Jews, not meanies, which largely seems to entail that they are respectful about Jesus and embrace Bensalem and its laws—that is, the authority of science. Jewish apologetics do not intrude. Jewish messianism reinforces Bensalem's destiny, while the specifics of the "Jewish dreams" remain marginal. At the same time, Christianity reaches Bensalem swiftly and painlessly with a pillar of light, in a way somewhat resembling the revelation in Stanley Kubrick's film *2001*. The population receives the texts and little else—a minimalist Christianity and in that sense Protestant. In Bensalem we therefore encounter at the same time a stripped-down Judaism and a stripped-down Christianity, the barest essentials effectively devoid of theology, permitting the entire focus to be on nature. What remains from both faiths is the prophetic, the eschatological—that is, the program for science whose entire purpose is salvation. That salvation is now imminent, for the *New Atlantis* concludes with the scientific dispensation, hitherto hidden, on the verge of going out to the nations.

Bensalem's science offers the prospect of Jewish-Christian reconciliation by looking beyond formal doctrine to a spirituality to be found in the physical world. To be sure, Bacon believed or claimed to believe in an immortal soul. The universe did not resolve itself entirely into spiritus; the mortalist heresy is apparently not at hand. Still, the entire thrust of his thought so constricts soul and so emphasizes universally spiritualized bodies that the potential for radical heresy is always nearby. The physical dimension of salvation, the essential role of all bodies— prominently including the human body and its desires—assumes such defining importance that cognition has truly become intimate with the erotic.

It is hard to imagine two individuals more different than Francis Bacon and Tommaso Campanella. Bacon had a long and distinguished career in Parliament and on the Privy Council, eventually becoming the chancellor of England, a career only marred in his late years by impeachment from office. Campanella spent most of his adult life in Spanish and papal prisons, a confinement punctuated at junctures with unspeakable torture. Campanella long promoted the Spanish monarchy as the prophetic Last World Empire; Bacon promoted the struggle against it. Campanella's goal of a global papal theocracy embodied a crusade for Catholicism and sought the extirpation of all heresy, all dissent. Bacon's program allowed for difference, even required it in order to succeed. Campanella placed great store in astrology, astral influence, and horoscopes; Bacon accepted astral influence, but rejected horoscopes, and, like many contemporaries, sought to construct a reformed astrology, an *astrologia sana*.[14] Campanella inhabited a vitalist universe; Bacon's *spiritus mundi* proved much more restrained.

For all that, however vast their differences, their similarities turn out to be decisive and defining. Both see the historical redemption as achieved through an apocalyptic program conducted by a college of priest-scientists. Campanella's *City of the Sun* (1602)—a work on which Bacon's utopia visibly drew—similarly places in the Pacific a utopian community governed by science. The island's rulers clearly comprise a radicalized version of the Vatican: the curia is recast as the ideal scientific society. Its governor with whom "all decisions terminate," clearly a pope-like figure, is described as a prince-prelate (*principe sacerdote*). He is the ultimate scientist, the master of the greatest and widest knowledge of nature. To become pope one must be familiar with all the sciences, and, apparently first of all, have a firm grasp of world history, the history of technology, and all the mechanical arts. Happily, through Campanella's pictorial pedagogical techniques, each branch of the mechanical arts can be learned in merely a couple of days. Therefore papal capability arises from the basis of social science and engineering—that is, from the physical world. Campanella's rejection of Aristotelian scholasticism is emphatic: "knowledge which requires only servile memory and which deprives the mind of vitality because it meditates upon books instead of things" does not truly comprise knowledge at all.[15] The physical world provides the foundation for all truth, even the most lofty spiritual wisdom.

Accordingly, the mechanical arts become revalued and knowledge of them is required of everyone. Both science and education are experiential, demanding direct engagement and something beginning to sound like experimentation. To be sure, the prince-prelate must be a metaphysician and theologian "above all." Yet, crucially, metaphysics and theology involve grasping the structure of the cosmos and the physical linkages between heaven and earth as well as "the Power, Wisdom, and Love of God and of all things." Mind and body, grace and nature, become so interwoven with one another as to make dissociation difficult. Integral and essential to all of this is knowledge of astrology and prophecy—that is, knowledge of time, development, the future.[16]

The inhabitants of the City of the Sun, the Solarians, have inscribed all the sciences on the seven concentric walls of their city. One need only walk about the city to witness illustrations and demonstrations of the principles of nature. But living in the City of the Sun instills learning in subtler and perhaps still more pervasive ways. The very layout of the city replicates the structure of the cosmos, and even unconsciously the inhabitants absorb nature's fundamental patterns. Built on a hill, the city rises to a temple at its top where the scientist-cardinals work and where literally the heavens and the earth connect. The entire thrust of Solarian science draws together the cosmos into an integrated organic whole. Through their highly applied study of nature the priest-scientists "serve as mediators between God and man."[17] Toward the end of his dialogue Campanella notes that the Solarians have discovered "the art of flying, the only art the world lacks." Although the technique is not described, of course, this final art before the millennium presumably will connect human beings with the heavens and the bodies within it, literally with the divine.[18]

Despite his careful and detailed validation of mundane physical labor, Campanella is more tentative than Bacon in his elevation of the mechanical arts against the liberal arts. Notwithstanding this diffidence, his validation of the human body and human sexuality is vastly more thoroughgoing. It has remained shocking even into modern times and is all the more surprising from a monk and one for whom monasticism shaped his social vision. Even more than Bacon, Campanella sees procreation as a civic act because procreation occurs within a highly formulated eugenics program. The Solarian population is maintained through intercourse managed by a Council on Procreation. "Tall handsome girls are not matched with any but tall brave men." Fatties are joined with skinnies to balance things out. The appropriate astrological signs rigorously guide the timing. Prospective mothers gaze on statues of illustrious men to focus their thought and shape the conception process. Sex thereby becomes a means to "improve natural endowments, not to provide dowries or false titles of nobility." Though thoroughly distasteful to later twentieth-century sensibilities and scandalous to nineteenth-century Victorians, the Solarian solution would likely have seemed liberating within the stifling world of arranged marriages. Procreation occurs literally "for public, not for private ends," and the rules governing it are observed "religiously."[19] The Solarians have created a society where the civic has supplanted the familial, the *respublica* altogether replaced the *domus,* and within this society there exists neither private property nor commercial transactions.

Accordingly, Campanella takes an extremely severe view of cosmetics, high heels, and long gowns. He is apparently concerned that the Council on Procreation might be fooled into making bad decisions about which women really are tall and handsome. For beauty aids can serve as an alternative to getting in shape, and women who owe their beauty to makeup rather than exercise will bear sickly children.[20] Cosmetics therefore pose a serious danger not because they are "unnatural," but because they subvert efficacious procreation and undermine the state. By so doing they also frustrate the achievement of the millennial era. No wonder they are a capital offense. For the same reasons Campanella takes a surprisingly mild view of sodomy—quite unlike contemporary Spain where the Inquisition ferociously pursued "unnatural" sodomy and heresy as analogous crimes. Sodomy, after all, did not result in offspring. It might be "illicit" and a crime; it might divert energy. But it did not subvert the social order.

Campanella's eugenics program proved explosive from the outset. But in some ways his attitude to recreational (nonprocreative) sexuality is equally surprising. Good sex is essential for good health and to prevent sodomy. Young men even under twenty-one "are permitted to have intercourse with barren or pregnant women." Misbehavior, typically taking the form of ingratitude, malice, and bad attitude, is punished "by banishment from the common table or from intercourse with the opposite sex."[21] Even the elite priest-scientists at the temple, whose minds are normally focused on other matters, do on rare occasions have a good shag "for the health of their bodies."[22] The Solarians do celebrate males who abstain until they reach twenty-one, apparently not most. Females who cannot conceive and are able to have recreational sex do not enjoy the same status as other matrons, lest women deliberately make themselves barren "in order to become wanton."[23] But Campanella's purpose is entirely utilitarian rather than Augustinian. The point is to prevent distortion of the eugenics program and, in the fullest possible sense, to achieve the regeneration of humanity.

Thus Campanella's comments on sexuality are in no way frivolous or incidental, still less a species of mental exercise. Quite the contrary. His sexual program is a "matter of major concern" because it is integral to the redeemed millennial age with its new dispensation realized through the final fusion of nature and grace.[24] The renewal of nature occurs at every level of existence—cosmic, human, animal, vegetable—resolving historical tensions and burdens, and transcending inherent boundaries. Everything becomes revitalized and stronger: the Solarians have even found a "magical" way to make animals react to idealized paintings of themselves when they conceive. As we might expect, Solarian practices have prolonged the human lifespan, and they normally live between 170 and 200 years. Campanella emerges about as antinomian as the Catholic imagination could allow. He consistently found himself fascinated by the Anabaptist communities of the Radical Reformation and even held grudging respect for them.

However radical, Campanella like Bacon still insisted on an immortal soul. The millennial age is not the terminus. The world we know, even in its fulfilled and renewed form, will pass away. Human life, however strengthened, will not go on forever. But the millennial age remains real and compelling. Unlike Thomas More a century earlier, these writers have every intention of achieving human potential, of realizing prophecy. Their thinking is no *jeu d'esprit*. They offer not fantasies but blueprints. They seek human destiny, the resolution of history. Campanella's utopia would have emerged from political revolution, Bacon's from a great legislative act. Further, in 1516 More sought to discover boundaries beyond which unaided human reason could not go. How far might human society reach and how much might it achieve without the insight of the Christian revelation? What are the limits? A century later Bacon, Campanella, and so many others sought to do just the opposite: not finding boundaries but crossing them. How far might men through their own efforts overcome all boundaries, transcend all limits? What so decisively separates More from these later utopian thinkers is the apocalypse. That is what makes them modern—as More, for all his irony and charm, is not.

REACTION: THE APOCALYPSE ATTACKED—AUTHORITY, SKEPTICISM, AND THE DECLINE OF THE CIVIC IDEAL

At exactly this time, apocalyptic expectations, a future millennium, civic values, and the new science met with a ferocious reaction that profoundly challenged these cultural currents both politically and intellectually. By the 1590s Counter-Reformation attitudes with their emphasis on authority, hierarchy, and Aristotelian classification had begun to bite deeply into European assumptions. During just those years civic life waned as a compelling social ideal. Henri IV, the aging Elizabeth, and James VI adopted increasingly absolutist postures. The active citizen, so much a part of northern European political vocabularies between 1558 and 1588, became increasingly supplanted by the obedient subject. A world we create became displaced by a world we inherited, participation by protection, while political responsibility and pursuit of the common good fell before preoccupation with private right and local privilege. Livian virtue and Ciceronian autonomy faded as norms before Tacitean manipulation.

This privatized world, characterized by ironic detachment, cynicism, and the personal, would prove inimical to the scientific program every bit as much as to public culture. But, above all, it foreclosed the prophetic. Expanding hope therefore arose within a severely darkening environment, and these years per force witnessed an extraordinary push-pull. The new authoritarianism proved palpably more severe in the Catholic south, and its chilling effect—resulting most dramatically from Giordano Bruno's execution, Campanella's imprisonment, and Galileo's repression—would shift the scientific center of gravity during the course of the century from the Mediterranean to the North Atlantic.

Still other developments contributed to this powerful, almost tectonic cultural vector. Among them was what came to be called "mercantilism." Not a coherent theory of political economy, mercantilism simply enjoined royal economic activism. New technologies required big armies for military success, and big armies required big populations and big treasuries. These in turn required material wealth, not the illusory glitter of New World bullion. Commerce became crucial, as did large-scale economic strategies. Theorists like France's Antoine de Montchrétien (d. 1621) adopted Carthage, not Rome, as his model, and economic policies enacted for "reason of state," policies involving the big picture that only the crown could hope to comprehend. "Reason of state" inherently precluded politics and the public determination of public policy. Dynastic and jurisdictional consolidation complemented and further urged the new authoritarianism. The quest for religious authority would be joined by a comparable quest for royal authority that might "rise above" unresolvable, fratricidal, and manifestly catastrophic religious difference.

Underlying these changes was a "new humanism," an intellectual shift of the first importance. Far-reaching in both its origins and consequences, the new humanism involved such influential theorists as Francesco Guicciardini (1483–1540) in Italy, Michel de Montaigne (1533–1592) in France, and Justus Lipsius (1547–1606) in the Netherlands. Some of its central constructs and claims arose in response to the Reformation crisis. Protestantism forced questions about the foundations of religious knowledge hitherto unprecedented in Christian Europe. By what standard do we determine spiritual truth? Protestants had made the novel and stunning claim that the Bible alone provided access to Christianity. If a person—any person—read it with a sincere heart, its meaning and requirements would become clear. All theological intricacies were contained in it, but its basics were universally accessible. Catholics countered by asking how in the world could one know that he had read it rightly? Scripture was no easy text; it fairly bristled with obscurity, complexity, contradictions. There existed no inspired users' guide to the inspired text, no sacred *Cliff Notes*. The reformers replied, indeed had claimed from the outset, that one would know that he had truly encountered the Bible because that person would be warmed by its spirit. He would have an inner feeling. Catholics of course remained unsatisfied: all manner of strange people claimed to be inspired. Could any individual risk salvation on what might be no more than indigestion—or, far worse, the work of the devil? One needed authority; personal conscience would create chaos, as many faiths as there were people. Protestantism was simply self-justifying. All very well. But then, it emerged, so too was Catholicism. How did one know the true authority? Was that man on the balcony actually the pope? How could one know that the pope actually was the vicar of Christ?

Skeptical arguments cut two ways and threatened to be equally damaging to both faiths. Against our expectations, however, devastating doubt actually became the great ally of Catholicism. If one does not know, one cannot judge, and if one cannot judge, one can hardly seek change or promote reform. Skepticism enjoined a lowering of voices, protected the status quo, dissipated eschatological visions. Its power was recognized early on and had kept individuals like Erasmus within the traditional church. But in 1569, during the French wars of religion, skepticism became systematized as an intellectual structure, a "weapon of war" in the crusade against Calvinism. That year the Counter-Reformer Gentian Hervet turned to an extreme strand of skeptical thought from classical antiquity: specifically ideas that were associated with Pyrrho of Elis (c.365–270 BCE) and that had been preserved through the writings of Sextus Empiricus (c. 200 CE). Pyrrhonist skepticism was distinguished by its insistence upon suspending judgment. In that way it differed from its classical rival, the Academic skepticism formulated by the Platonic Academy during the third century BCE. The Academy had met the challenge of Stoicism by using Socratic questioning to claim that nothing could be known. To the radical Pyrrhonists even this claim was still too great. It was a kind of "negative dogmatism," for at least one knew that one did not know. Serious men could only suspend judgment in the face of conflicting dogmatic claims.

Pyrrhonism encouraged conservatism and passivity, and thereby suited the Counter-Reformation well. The young Spanish Jesuit Juan Maldonat (1534–1583), who had arrived in Paris in 1565 to accept a post at the newly founded Collège de Clermont, quickly adopted these techniques to dispute with the University of Paris's great Protestant professor Pierre de la Ramée. Pyrrhonism informed the thinking of still other Counter-Reformers, including no less a figure than the future saint François de Sales. It probably reached its apex with the dialectical strategies developed by François Veron, who became effectively the official debater for the crown.

No Pyrrhonist would prove more influential or of greater service to the Catholic cause than Michel de Montaigne. Although a friend of Hervet and Maldonat, Montaigne also differed from them. His immersion in the great classical texts was much more thoroughgoing. Hervet, Maldonat, and Veron attacked the use of reason and "inner feeling" to produce a coherent religious message *sola scriptura*. But they were careful not to repudiate the larger significance of reason and sense perceptions. As mainstream neo-medieval Counter-Reformers, all of them firmly accepted Aristotelian scholasticism as a mode of cognition and the Great Chain of Being as the structure through which to perceive the world. But Montaigne did not simply use the ancient arguments. He entered their mental world and challenged human reasoning universally. His thought emerged vastly more humanist—and vastly more devastating—as a result.

For this reason Montaigne's actual religious beliefs are hard to pin down and even today remain a matter of dispute. There may be evidence to suggest that under all those layers of ironic doubting Montaigne held deeply to an a priori faith in Catholicism. But he unquestionably regarded Calvinism as incendiary and subversive—and genuinely terrifying. He would have no part with religious revolution, political revolution, or even intellectual revolution. How could anyone seek reform, much look to a new heaven and new earth, when the watchword was *que sais-je*? His famous essay "Of Cannibals" argued that the people of Brazil in many ways lived more virtuous and honorable lives than the people of Christian France. Yet, he took care to point out, a society like theirs had completely surpassed the imagination of Plato and the laws of Lycurgus. The best minds in Europe could not have anticipated it. How much, then, did we really know about society and politics?

Further, it was crucial for Montaigne's argument that these people were cannibals, always the hallmark of the barbaric. For even Brazilian cannibalism evinced a kind of virtue: captives were treated kindly in the hope of making them regret their impending death (and then being eaten); in turn, the captives showed themselves stout-hearted and mocked attempts to corrupt their courage. Of course Brazil was not a model for France. The point was not to recommend cannibalism, but to undermine self-confidence—lest in decrying cannibalism's horror and the faults of Brazilian society, "we should be so blind to our own." During the current religious wars within Christian France, people were burned at the stake, broken on the rack, torn apart by dogs. Which was more barbarous—roasting people alive or doing so only after they were dead?[25]

Categories so fundamental as civilized/barbarous no longer seemed secure, and our ability to judge (and thus act) became similarly qualified. The Brazilian utopia/anti-utopia served to make any utopia impossible. Quietist introspection and personal withdrawal could be the only conclusion. Montaigne's unflinching deconstruction of contemporary values and shared perceptions led not to openness or toleration but to just the reverse: authority and repression. If the monstrous horrors of the religious wars were perpetrated, overwhelmingly, by the Ligueurs and militant Catholicism, the cause could only lie with the reformers, with activist and destabilizing Calvinism. It was no accident that Montaigne's Brazilians make a point of dispatching "false prophets."

Accordingly, there existed no room for the citizen. If on occasion Montaigne spoke of the *concitoyen* (fellow citizen), as he did in "Of Cannibals," he used the term in its older medieval sense of regional inhabitant. That is, an extended neighbor. He did not mean French-man, an individual who, seeing beyond the patchwork of the realm's tangled jurisdictions and privileges, recognized and helped define the overarching public good. "The good patriot" entered French, English, and Dutch vocabularies during the 1570s and 1580s, but it would not enter Montaigne's. Quite the contrary. Montaigne urged the wise man to "withdraw his soul within, out of the crowd." Social responsibility, public office, civic values were irrelevant to the life of the mind and to the seemingly mundane things that made living worthwhile. "La société publique" can do without our thoughts.[26] Thereby the Stoicism of his sometime teacher George Buchanan had become transvalued. Where Buchanan had encouraged citizens to repress private passion in the interest of higher civic purposes, Montaigne wanted people to repress any such misdirected inclination to engage in public life. If there existed any question about the matter, Montaigne's own experi-ence in Bordeaux and, as he tells us, that of his father should lay it to rest. The focus could only be quietist and on the intimate, the private, the personal: family values, not public values.

Montaigne's contemporary, Justus Lipsius, came to adopt similar attitudes. Lipsius looked at the Dutch struggle against Spanish domina-tion and, astonishingly, came to regard it as a civil war—and a war in which he wanted no part. "While the cruel fighting troubles us and the trumpets summon us to civil war, may I (forgive me, my country) dwell free from care in Hauten's garden, and may my gardening make me forget my sorrows."[27] A generation earlier Francesco Guiccardini had anticipated elements within this line of thought. As he watched the Italian city-states implode and collapse before the European super-powers and, signally, the Hapsburg empire, he increasingly lost confi-dence in human agency. "The future is so deceptive and subject to so many accidents, that very often even the wisest of men is fooled when he tries to predict it."[28] History did not offer rules for effective behav-ior or how one might realize one's personality as a citizen, but instead created a philosophic attitude that would help one survive its vicissitudes. Time was not something in which we participated, but something we withstood.

Montaigne's assumptions and agenda were altogether incompatible with the emergent program for science. The physical world continually eluded our knowledge. For nature was "feverish" and forever changing. Those who described its workings normally tried to create a whole physics from a "little scrap of knowledge." "From this vice spring many abuses." We have "more curiosity than capacity." "We embrace everything, but we clasp only wind." Worse still, "l'étude des sciences" compromised the spirit, making men effete and ineffectual.[29] If the study of nature was futile (and worse), the methods for doing so were downright dangerous. Montaigne precluded from the outset Bacon's emphatically public project because all judgments, all reflection, all opinions other than those prescribed by authority should only occur in private. In his *The Advancement of Learning* (1605), Bacon enjoined "the good patriot," and claimed that "the conservation of duty to the public ought to be much more precious than the conservation of life and being."[30] The contrast could hardly be greater, far greater than gulf separating Bacon from Campanella.

Yet the full magnitude of the differences between them only emerges when we consider their reaction to the New World. For Montaigne the discovery was humbling, chilling, even shattering. It displayed as few things could just how insubstantial human knowledge was and how severely qualified acceptance of it must be. If we were so profoundly certain and so profoundly wrong in the past, how could we have any assurance that we were not equally wrong right now?

> Ptolemy, who was a great man, had established the limits of our world; all the ancient philosophers thought they had its measure, except for a few remote islands that might escape their knowledge. It would have been Pyrrhonizing, a thousand years ago, to cast in doubt the science of cosmography, and the opinions that were accepted about it by one and all; it was heresy to admit the existence of the Antipodes. Behold in our century an infinite extent of terra firma, not an island or one particular country, but a portion nearly equal in size to the one we know, which has just been discovered. The geographers of the present time do not fail to assure us that now all is discovered and all is seen.... The question is,

if Ptolemy was once mistaken on the grounds of his reason, whether it would not be stupid for me now to trust to what these people say about it; and whether it is not more likely that this great body that we call the world is something different from what we judge.[31]

In this respect as in so many others, Bacon was the polar opposite of Montaigne. For Bacon the discovery of the New World was exhilarating, the fulfillment of prophecy, the redemptive coming together of human knowledge. Modern readers sometimes regard Montaigne as liberal or progressive, but he is nothing of the sort. Like his distant descendant, Michel Foucault, who is also mistaken for a *gauchiste*, Montaigne powerfully fueled an intensive reaction. Apocalyptic faith, not radical doubt, founded science and opened the way to modernity.

PROPHET, MAGUS, WITCH

Historians have generally agreed that the European fascination with witchcraft largely centered on the two centuries between approximately 1480 and 1680. Within that lengthy period, by far the most intensive reflection about demonology and the greatest preoccupation with witches occurred during the late sixteenth and early seventeenth centuries. The phenomenon in these years needs to be seen as part of the great reaction against the prophetic described in the previous section. Witch beliefs and witch-hunting did not involve a confrontation with the Roman church, or with any institutionalized agency of evil. For Protestants to focus more on witches rather than, say, the papacy or the Society of Jesus, entailed a major shift in priorities. Demonology inherently marginalized the historical, the political, the prophetic. It inherently deflected the apocalypse.

To be sure, the Revelation ensured that there would be "necromantic" popes, and Protestant apocalyptic historians readily identified a substantial number of them. But wicked popes from past centuries were interwoven into historical analysis and grand narratives rather than providing present prescriptions. No pope ever slipped into little old ladies' bedrooms at night to spirit them away to kinky parties in the neighboring woods (possibly to their disappointment). No Jesuit invested his time in elderly, impoverished nobodies. Witchcraft meant the Devil and his demons, not Antichrist, and the Devil was the universal tempter, a far less timebound figure, a figure far less immersed within the course of history. Encounters with the Devil and his demons were always intimate, personal, private, and their implications conservative, authoritarian, and normally approached through Aristotelian scholasticism. More than that. For Catholics the demonic validated the efficacy of miracles, thereby validating a transcendent God, while it exposed the poverty of prophecy, thereby discounting an immanent one. For Protestants witch prosecutions affirmed "discipline" and promoted a regulated society, while in the process it reconfigured reform and distracted from the apocalyptic conflict against the papal monarchy. In a very real way witchcraft proved a wedge issue for Protestantism, to use modern parlance, for to go after witches was to play a Catholic game.

France during the religious wars produced only one Protestant demonologist, Lambert Daneau. It produced one demonologist with a distinctive faith all his own, Jean Bodin. All the rest—and they were many—were militant Counter-Reformers. Outstanding among them was the selectively skeptical Father Maldonat and his students, the most prominent of whom were Louis Richeome, Pierre de Lancre, and Martin Del Rio. Del Rio (1551–1608) became the most influential demonologist of the seventeenth century, whose writing, among much else, informed Philip II's 1592 order on witchcraft. Far from a dispassionate theological study, French demonology served to attack Protestantism every bit as much as did Pyrrhonist skepticism—with which was closely allied. As Jonathan Pearl has shown, validation of such witchcraft beliefs as the transportation of witches to sabbaths, the use of ointments created from murdered infants, the ability of witches to make themselves invisible through the help of the Devil, also validated the mysteries of the church. Seeing was not believing, for the senses deceived. Transubstantiation remained true despite appearances. Did not Jesus himself at moments make himself invisible? For Maldonat, Protestantism with its historical spirituality seemed to undermine the immortality of the soul. Faith in authority was the necessary precondition in theology and the precondition for salvation.[32] Witches and Protestants were traitors to that faith and its God.

To be sure, the Devil and his demons worked through natural means to alter the appearance of things. Only God could actually suspend the laws of nature. But that in no way impugned the reality of demonic "false miracles," as Maldonat called them. Such naturalism was important, for the witch phenomenon became amenable thereby to scholastic reasoning. Hierarchy could be shown a common principle obtaining in all planes of being. Daneau's demonology contrasted sharply with that of Maldonat and his followers. As a Protestant Daneau had argued his case from scripture and from human experience, avoiding the philosophic structures of the Counter-Reformers. More important, if Catholic demonology carried heavy religious and political implications, its effects nevertheless were drastically depoliticizing. By stressing authority, stability, tradition, even accepting folklore, against those who would overturn them all, demonology reinforced a consolidating monarchy, for it helped turn active citizens (or subversive ideologues) back into obedient subjects. Although all the demonologists were determined Ligueurs (even the politique Bodin at one point enlisted), it is no wonder that their writings, almost without exception, saw print during the years of Henri IV's rule. It hardly mattered that the Ligue had been defeated and discredited. Demonology promoted absolutism, and in the process curiously paralleled Pyrrhonism. If Montaigne seemed ambivalent and ironic about witchcraft, it is striking how gentle the demonologists' criticisms of him turned out to be.

Only exorcism, that most dramatic and successful form of ultramontane rite-theater, faded along with the Ligue. With demonic possession, as with all matters demonic, what we see and what we have were two different things. Always uneasy about possession, miracle-bereft Protestantism could only offer prayer as a solution. Catholicism claimed something far more powerful, and that power depended on the reality of demons. If demons disappeared, so too, it seemed, might Catholicism. The stakes could hardly be higher: at issue was the *verba operanda* confronting the bare historical word in context. Protestants constantly denounced the "conjuring mass" as anti-Christian and even Devil-inspired, but the rite itself remained inert and fraudulent. Demonic possession, in contrast, reached out to other worlds. The thunderously successful 1566 exorcism of Beelzebub from a young woman at Laon was a major Catholic triumph that confounded Protestant scoffers. The "miracle of Laon" made demonology a major weapon in the Catholic arsenal and thereafter an exclusively Catholic property. But possession was potentially explosive: could we always count on Beelzebub to be there, saying the right things about "my Huguenots" (whom the great demon regarded as more damaging to Christ "than the Jews")? Del Rio and others worked to promote and at the same time contain the phenomenon within naturalistic terms that the clergy might control. But, in the end, this form of demonology, unlike the others, largely fell before its inherent political dangers.[33]

Much the same pattern emerged in Counter-Reformation Germany. The Catholic heartlands in Bavaria and Franconia remained the only areas where significant intellectual interest in demonology continued after 1600, for demonology was integral to the struggle against the Reformation. In an important article William Bradford Smith has described how the infamous witch-hunter Friedrich Förner (1568–1630) helped to lead the successful struggle against Protestantism in Bamberg, and how much of his attack focused on the prophecies—or "divinations," as Förner called them—of the reformers.[34] Against Protestant apocalyptic Förner offered miracles: the former was the work of false prophets, the latter the visible hand of God. The attack on the prophetic was integrally linked with Förner's use of that now truly shopworn charge: where was your church before Luther? To discredit prophecy was to discredit a crucial element in Protestant apologetic and in the Protestant vision of the world. Again like the French, Förner stressed the incendiary character of Protestantism and its prophetic claims. His objective was to secure peace, order, security, authority.

Following the destruction of Bamberg Protestantism, Förner became obsessed with large-scale witch-hunting. For heresy and witchcraft formed part of a common package, both being assaults from the Devil on the true faith. No wonder the most vigorous opponents of witch-hunting were Protestants. It is difficult not to think that the false prophets, *magi,* and *veneficii* Förner had in mind were the Protestant millenarians, Rosicrucians, astrologers, natural magicians, and apocalyptic exegetes—Alsted, Studion, Besold, Andreae, and so many others—who shaped German Protestantism in the opening years of the seventeenth century. The severest moments in the witch-hunt, Smith observes, coincided with dramatic moments of Catholic activism: the Catholic victory at White Mountain at the outset of the Thirty Years' War and later the imperial edict restoring secularized church lands.

The contrast with the other side of this titanic struggle is illuminating. Apocalyptic excitement never reached more deeply into the cultural tissues of Swedish society than during the contemporaneous reign of Gustavus Adolphus (r. 1611–1632). Yet this period, "so choked with eschatological expectation," saw little witch activity.[35] The world of Bureus, like that of Bacon and Campanella, had another agenda, and the great Swedish hunts lay over the horizon.

Accordingly, we encounter a broadly similar dynamic in lands like prophecy-soaked Scotland, where the Tridentine decrees constricting prophecy and the apocalypse did not obtain and where "miracles" were no longer compelling. Many people certainly did talk about witches in sixteenth-century Scotland. The witchcraft charge (or smear) formed part of Queen Mary's opening salvo in her famous first meeting with John Knox, while Knox himself clearly preferred to talk about Antichrist. The great reformer faced that charge from Catholic priests throughout his life, and long afterwards. Virtually every Scottish reformer did. Although Knox seems never to have accused anyone in this way, it had long been a political commonplace.

However, demonology and witch-hunting were another matter altogether, and those involved with them consistently turn out to be religious and social conservatives. Scotland's greatest demonologist was Mary's son, King James VI. The king, we now know, was the driving force behind the great witch panics of 1590 and 1597. Nor was he alone in this interest. Earlier in 1568 John Erskine of Dun had initiated a major witch-hunt throughout the shires of Angus and Mearns. Erskine, the superintendent of that region, was solidly Protestant, but no less solidly conservative. Committed to clerical hierarchy, he stoutly resisted "parity" among ministers and the new Presbyterian church polity from France. Hume of Godscroft believed that he was the key figure in the effort to reintroduce bishops into Scotland (just as Knox was inveighing against them). Always a friend of the crown, Erskine tried to prolong negotiations with the regent during the 1559–1560 revolution, and in Knox's view was too "addicted" to pleasing her. When Knox reduced Mary to tears, it was Erskine who dried them.[36] Powerful Roman Catholics also pursued witches. The great Catholic earls Errol and Huntly, the would-be leaders of the Counter-Reformation in Scotland, joined with the king to play a major role in the events of 1597, one of the bloodiest hunts in Scottish history.

Knox was, famously, one of the first to adumbrate the Protestant apocalyptic in Scotland, a subject about which Erskine seems to have been silent. Unlike Erskine, Knox had no real fear of any witch menace, and he could never be described as a witch-hunter. Certainly he expected the eradication of the black arts; certainly he would support the prosecution of the odd witch whom local authorities turned up from time to time. But witchcraft was only one part of the wide range of abuses that the reformer hoped to correct through the institution of "discipline," and even "discipline" was but one side of the cataclysmic upheaval in which Knox saw himself participating. His reaction to the passage of the Scottish witchcraft statute in 1563 shows just how marginal his interest in the subject really was. Knox had broken with the key Protestant leader, the earl of Moray, because of the earl's compromises with the ungodly Queen Mary: the enactment apparently was an attempt by Moray's party to smooth relations with the kirk. Knox was utterly unimpressed by this "new shift." Such a sop constituted no substitute for the reformer's sweeping objectives. Knox seems to have accepted conventional demonology, and at one point had given thought to "why mannes nature is afrayed for spirits, and so vehementlie abhoreth their presence and company."[37] Tellingly, he never wrote about the subject, and witchcraft rarely surfaces within the six volumes of his collected works.

Witchcraft seems still more marginal with Knox's radical Presbyterian successors, all of whom had developed far more highly articulated apocalyptic expectations. Andrew Melville is not recorded as having commented on the subject at all. The major contemporary Presbyterian historians James Melville and David Calderwood barely notice it. Although the king could stampede the kirk and enlist significant Presbyterian leaders to join him in the cause, on the whole witch-hunting seems to have been more an episcopal preoccupation. When the Presbyterian intellectual Hume of Godscroft dismissed Bodin's absolutist *Les six livres de la république* (1576), he twitted the Frenchman's *De la démononmanie* (1580) in the process. To be turned into a wolf might be truly unfortunate (it would certainly complicate one's life), but to have a wolfish disposition, especially in a king, was vastly more serious. Hume was well aware of how authoritarian kings cynically manipulated witch beliefs against their enemies, most notoriously James V's efforts against the House of Douglas through the trial of Janet Douglas, Lady Glamis in 1537.[38] As Hume tells it, the incident sounds like a test run for the 1590 crisis. It is impossible to say what Hume's attitude toward the witch phenomenon actually was. What is not in doubt, however, is that witch prosecution and tyranny came together.

In 1597 King James would turn up in St. Andrews both to purge the university's Presbyterians and to hunt witches.

The contrast with the Scottish king is arresting. During the Armada crisis in the late 1580s, James entertained a serious, if fairly traditional interest in the Protestant apocalypse. A decade later that interest had waned considerably, a lessening that continued for the rest of his life. In the later 1590s he had entered upon a confrontation with the Scottish Presbyterians to establish his untrammeled authority over the church, to anchor his legitimacy in sources derived from blood and right rather than from revolution and civic action, and to have done with what he regarded, with some justification, as the chronic instability of the previous thirty years. To this end, he produced a remarkable series of tracts: the *Daemonologie* (1597), the *True Lawe of Free Monarchy* (1598), and the *Basilikon Doron* (1599). All three asserted in the most emphatic terms that there existed an underlying natural order that withstood all the flux of time and contingency, that maintained hierarchy and authority against all claims for parity, whether civil or clerical, and against all claims of custom and privilege, however "ancient." All three works are deeply atemporal, seeking to found authority beyond the reach of time. All three are also deeply anti-prophetic.

The *Daemonologie* is the most interesting in this regard because in it we can see the transition in James's thinking. On the margins the tract still offers the hint of the historic and even a trace of the apocalypse. In pagan times, James tells us, devils were more apt to confront people directly, but with the coming of the gospel people better understood the nature of good and evil. Apparently as a result, most people were better equipped to resist the assaults of devils, while those unreservedly perverse would actively them seek out. Now the same process was again taking place with the Reformation, the truth of which "we finde by experience in this Isle":

> For as we know, mae Ghostes and spirits were seen nor tongue can tell in the time of blinde Papastrie in these countries, where now by the contrarie, a man shall scarcely all his time here once of such things. And yet were these unlawful artes farre rarer at that time: and never were so much harde of nor so rife as they are now.[39]

In the future, however, James expected a still sharper increase in witchcraft. There were two reasons for this. On the one hand the great disorder and lack of discipline among the people would cause many to turn to the Devil—a circumstance that clearly pointed to the need for authority. At the same time the Devil himself would redouble his efforts with the latter days at hand and time running out: "the consumation of the worlde, and our deliverance drawing neare, makes Sathan to rage the more in his instruments, knowing his kingdome to be so neare an ende."[40]

For all this talk about "the latter daie," the entire thrust of James' tract is to foreclose prophecy and all possible discussion about the future. Again and again he emphasizes, all prophecies, oracles, and visions have ended. Those who pretend otherwise are "evil." Scholars who seek "to creepe to credite with princes by fore-telling them manie greate thinges" are agents of the devil—and, he might have added, the Scottish universities abounded with such scholars. Astronomy is acceptable and honorable, but astrology must be curtailed, a claim that is misleadingly modern-sounding. His reading of the apocalypse is severely Augustinian. Antichrist is nowhere to be found. "All the sciences of the Ægyptians," if they involved the occult, are proscribed. Moses either never learned them or left them with his sins in Egypt.[41] The *Daemonologie* speaks to a land immersed in the apocalypse and seeks to lead the inhabitants away from it. Other than the shifting frequency with which cases occurred, witchcraft is a timeless phenomenon, each story much like the one before it, building in no direction at all, largely disconnected from the Christian time sequence. Preoccupation with witchcraft is not a manifestation of apocalyptic interest, but of its decline.

When James thought of the Devil, he thought of "God's ape," an inverted parody of God himself, about whom much could be learned by examining his "contrarie."[42] Only the king's Calvinist principles—along with the jibes of the contemporary English critic of witch beliefs, Reginald Scot—prevented him from positing an inverse hierarchy comparable to the heavenly one. Even the demonic and the damned had to participate in the underlying logic of creation. These features, which stress nature rather than history, provide the substance of the witch theory for James and hallmark his discussion of it. Just these dimensions lie at the heart of the *Daemonologie* and link it with the *True Lawe* and the *Basilikon Doron*, making all three a coherent and integrated political statement.

The reply to the *Daemonologie* came, effectively, from the venerable Robert Pont (1524–1606) who proposed in 1599 an involved synthesis of reformed astrology, apocalyptic analysis, and chronology. The reply to the *Basilikon Doron* and the *True Lawe* came, effectively, from Hume of Godscroft who proposed a radical, alternative Britain, at once deeply civic and resolutely apocalyptic. Probably the most telling British reply to Del Rio came from the Scot James Maxwell (*fl.* 1600–1635), in some ways Scotland's counterpart to Campanella, who promoted not only biblical prophecy but also Merlin and just about every historical seer.[43] Witch-hunting was challenged by the apocalypse, for that was the heart of the matter.

In England James gradually found his most congenial allies among the conservatives within the church hierarchy. He and his son, Charles I, would promote them, ultimately with disastrous consequences. Unknowingly, the king also had allies among some of the English Puritans. In the 1590s William Perkins emerged as one of the great Calvinist theorists, developing what came to be known as covenant theology. Its influence was huge, literally from Transylvania to New England; his major works would be translated into perhaps half a dozen languages. Nevertheless, Perkins seems to have had no connection with the English Presbyterian movement of the 1570s and 1580s, had precious little to say about the apocalypse, and, according to Patrick Collinson, manifests an inward-looking, "diverted" spirituality that arose in the wake of Presbyterian defeat. In a way the neo-scholastic Perkins too formed part of the general cultural reaction, and it therefore only makes sense that he should have become a demonologist. If his theology would find itself grafted onto revolutionary programs in Scotland, central Europe, and across the ocean, such was manifestly not his intention. His contemporary, George Gifford, a more thoroughgoing Calvinist, opposed witch beliefs on the ground that proclaiming oneself a victim of witchcraft absolved one of moral responsibility. Misfortune came from God directly, not ill-disposed neighbors, and one should behave accordingly. Still more separates Perkins from other puritan contemporaries like Thomas Brightman and Henry Finch who pioneered new millenarian readings of the apocalypse. In the end, Perkins like James comprises part of the movement away from eschatology. The new conservatism, like the Counter-Reformation, looked to the demonic and rejected the prophetic, promoted neo-scholasticism while discounting natural magic and proto-science. Not even Francis Bacon could turn it around.

Despite the massive, far-reaching reaction, Protestant apocalyptic remained a cultural force of vast power both on the continent and in the British Isles. So the Hapsburgs discovered in 1630. So too did the House of Stuart in 1638 with the outbreak of the British Revolution. In the British Isles apocalyptic expectations reached their apex with this mid-century upheaval that convulsed the entire archipelago and subsequently shook all Europe. In the process were laid the groundwork of modern politics.

CHAPTER 5

THE BRITISH REVOLUTIONS: THE RISE OF MODERN POLITICS

When people today think of the American Revolution or the French Revolution, clear and powerful images spring immediately to mind: the Declaration of Independence, the Minutemen, the Continental Congress, and the Liberty Bell; of the Rights of Man and Citizen, the Sans Culottes, the Tennis Court Oath, and the red liberty cap. But mention the English Revolution or the British revolutions, and we draw a blank. At most, these revolutions are events against which people define themselves, not things in themselves. Since the late nineteenth century, Irish nationalism has fed on a mythic "curse of Cromwell" and a rhetoric of victimization to promote clerical traditionalism and political reaction. Scots only occasionally and with considerable ambivalence recall the Covenanters. For the English these events are locked away in a far-off "puritan" past, so excised from the present that it is as if they never happened. The British revolutions simply do not form part of modern public consciousness.

Yet between 1638 and 1662 the British Isles experienced an upheaval that shook them to their foundations. No political event of comparable magnitude has since occurred there. The upheaval led to the basic patterns of modern politics, patterns that triumphed with the Enlightenment and the democratic revolutions of the following century. Modern notions of civil liberty—freedom of the press, religious toleration, freedom of assembly—largely arose in the modern world through these events. Democracy, not as a theoretical option but as a moral imperative for humanity, does not predate the British revolutions. The republic, founded on a territorial basis rather than as a city-state, is almost entirely a mid-seventeenth-century English invention. The sovereign state—indeed the state as distinguished from the Great Chain of Being's body politic—does not arise from earlier claims for royal absolutism, however authoritarian, or earlier celebrations of monarchy, however fulsome. Only with revolutionary England were the epistemological foundations of the state hammered out. Only within revolutionary England would the metaphors of the state be developed. To an extraordinary extent, modern politics began with this upheaval. The apocalypse reached its high mark within the English-speaking world during just these decades and proved integral to each of these developments. And more. It made all of them possible.

THE SCOTTISH REVOLUTION

The British revolutions began in Scotland in 1637. The revolt had been sparked by the imposition of an Anglo-Catholic prayer book onto the realm by conservative elements within the English episcopal hierarchy. The latter had sought to restore clerical authority in ways that had not existed anywhere in Britain since the Reformation. To this end they sought to sacramentalize worship and discount humanist-Protestant apocalyptic history. They buttressed their new religious conservatism with a determined anti-Calvinist theology that underwrote the necessity and importance of the sacraments—and, in so doing, broke with what had been an all-but-universal consensus within Anglophone Protestantism. To this end they also sought to control administration of the British kingdoms through domination of the prerogative courts that were not subject to English common-law procedures. In Scotland, legally linked with England since 1603 through the Stuart dynasty, they worked to secure their objectives through like-minded administrators and episcopal surrogates. The explosive service book was but one manifestation. Their purpose was an emphatically hierarchical and authoritarian social order that secured political, intellectual, and religious conformity through systematic repression. The movement comprises part of the great European reaction described in the previous chapter.

The 1637 revolt against it met with stunning success, and during 1638 royal authority in Scotland effectively evaporated. The country was governed by the Scottish parliament and, between sessions, by its executive committee in conjunction with standing committees in all the shires of the realm. Episcopacy would be swept away and in its place emerged the radical French church polity that had initially reached Scotland in the later sixteenth century: ministerial equality, administration through a system of committees or courts that paralleled the new lay governance. The National Covenant—a great legislative act between people and king (at least nominally) as well as between nation and God—mobilized the country, harnessing its vitality in ways that were completely unprecedented (and never have been subsequently duplicated). Like the Jews of the Old Testament, Scots had acquired a sacred constitution, a divine mandate. They also acquired something more, for as Christians, albeit highly Judaized Christians, they not only reenacted the Old Testament but worked to realize its promise in the new dispensation. Where Israel had pointed, Scotland would go. What Israel had seen in the distance, Scotland would travel. The Covenanting movement was imbued with apocalyptic expectations, and within this Old Testament vocabulary it is hard to imagine how their outlook might be otherwise.

The Scots certainly rose up against the anglicizing consequences of Charles I's religious policy, the provincializing consequences of his political policies. The National Covenant revitalized and reconfigured Scottish politics and spirituality; there is far more than a hint of religious revivalism. Yet it would be a grave mistake to see the Scottish Revolution as a nationalist uprising, or the National Covenant as a quest for "identity." Scotland's revolution was a pan-British phenomenon both in practice and perception—involving from the outset radical reformers in both Ireland and England. From the earliest stages Scots also looked to long-standing allies in the Netherlands, Sweden, and throughout the Baltic as part of a great common cause. Their purposes were emphatically universal. Scotland was not unique among nations but a model for nations. Scots were consumed by mission, not self-actualization. For the next decade the revolutionaries would work tirelessly to achieve a great confederation to defeat universal monarchy, both imperial and papal. Their objective went well beyond any network of treaties and alliances. They sought nothing less than an alternate world order. Extra-national structures were essential, and we get an indication of what they had in mind with the joint committees

that were created by the 1643 Solemn League and Covenant with revolutionary England—the first genuinely British institutions. They were
self-consciously the heirs of Sidney, Melville, Spenser, Hume, and still
others throughout Europe. Their goal was seen to be world liberation,
understood as a world of reformed polities, and that in turn could only
mean the eschaton.

In 1639 and 1640 the revolutionaries thoroughly defeated Charles's
campaigns to reconquer Scotland, and by 1641 the king was forced to
recognize (tentatively, in his view) the new order in his northern
realm. Scottish success energized English radicalism with which it had
been so closely associated. It led to the calling of what later would be
known as the Long Parliament. That parliament swept away the conservative officials, along with the prerogative courts and eventually
the Episcopal church structure itself, root and branch.

But Scottish success precipitated something else as well: counter-
revolution in Ireland. Ireland was a land inhabited by four distinct cultural communities, two Protestant, two Catholic. In 1641 the two
Catholic communities formed a confederation that rose against the
crown and the emerging Protestant radicalism. The Confederates borrowed heavily from Scottish political rhetoric and administrative practices. Like the Scots they too were in no sense nationalist and found
it difficult to think beyond a reconfigured British world. Yet they also
differed decisively from the Scots. The Irish were fractured at their
social base and did not share Scotland's intellectual and political coherence. Nor did they share the scriptural and apocalyptic vocabulary
so defining to the Scots. The Irish Confederation, however solemnly
and dramatically sworn, could never be comparable to the Scottish
Covenant. The Counter-Reformation's preoccupation with Aristotelian classification and neo-scholastic hierarchy also precluded an independent Ireland and, most emphatically, a republican one. The Irish
rising comprised a British Vendée, not a proto-Eire. It sought traditionalism and historic "graces" rather than radicalism. As the struggle
deepened, a number of the more militant Confederates looked to integration within the Hapsburg or Bourbon empires, not to independence. The Irish conducted a crusade, but their mission was hardly
eschatological. Only if Ireland had been absorbed into the Spanish
Fifth Monarchy might that have been imaginable, and for the most
part Irish Catholics looked to London rather than Madrid. The great

continental monarchies might provide aid. They did not provide purpose.

Reforms in England undertaken in conjunction with a king who patently despised them (and whose duplicity seemed boundless) raised larger questions of governance and the roles of crown and parliament. The Irish crisis and, with it, the crucial issue of controlling the military forced these issues to a head, precipitating civil war and then revolution.

PROGRAMS OF LIBERATION: FREEDOM OF THE PRESS, RELIGIOUS TOLERATION

The collapse of authoritarian monarchy in large parts of England, and notably in London, brought with it the collapse of state censorship and the 1640s witnessed an extraordinary range of political publication, a phenomenon that was, again, altogether unprecedented. Almost inevitably, more conservative parliamentary leaders found this development seriously troubling. Unbridled calls for reform, for "liberty and reformation," for a new order appeared to threaten the fabric of society itself, and by 1643 the reimposition of censorship seemed all but inescapable. In this context systematic arguments for freedom of the press—not on behalf of a beleaguered minority but as a universal principle—first surfaced.

The most notable by far was John Milton's *Areopagitica* (1644). In that work Milton inverted some of the most deeply held assumptions in European culture. After all, if there existed one truth, on what possible basis could conflicting opinions and manifest falsehood be tolerated? Milton's answer was fundamentally Baconian because it insisted that the strategy of truth was so complicated that no individual, no authority, no single generation could possibly master the full range of its intricacies and complexity. Its discovery required the public interaction of many minds, many abilities, many conflicting insights. Truth was indeed the daughter of time. "Where there is much desire to learn, there of necessity will much arguing, much writing, many opinions; for opinion in good men is but knowledge in the making." It required "a perpetual progression."[1] Whether civil or religious, knowledge could have but one purpose. Again like Bacon, that purpose was the reconstruction of the human mind, the historical redemption.

Milton surveyed the history of the West and wondered when had there been censorship. He found it largely absent from classical antiquity, the biblical world, the early church—and especially absent from civic societies, the great republics. Censorship, it turned out, was a relatively recent invention. Censoring became prominent in the time of John Wycliffe and Jan Hus, the discoverers of the false church. It became systematized and ferocious with the Council of Trent. Censorship had arisen with the Antichrist. And well it might, for censorship did nothing less than forestall Christianity and salvation. The familiar landmarks suddenly shifted. All the pluses now turned into minuses, for censorship, far from being the guardian of truth, was its greatest enemy—much like the false church itself. The struggle against censorship became an integral element in the apocalyptic drama and in the effort to realize human destiny.

Milton looked at the history of the past century and a half and found a steady improvement in human knowledge, an ever closer approach to truth. Wycliffe and Hus had identified the false church. But Luther had improved on their understanding. Subsequently Calvin had improved on Luther. Still better insight had come in the days of Elizabeth. "The light which we have gained was given us, not to be ever staring on, but by it to discover onward things more remote from out knowledge." The worst possible thing anyone could do would be to call the process to a halt and claim that the final answers were in hand. There would be no final truth before the coming of Christ. So too, there could be no limit or terminus to human learning before his return. "He who thinks we are to pitch our tent here, and have attained the utmost prospect of reformation that the mortal glass wherein we contemplate can show us till we come to the beatific vision, that man by this very opinion declares that he is yet far short of truth." Now it seemed that through the English Revolution, "God is decreeing to begin some new and great period in his church, even to the reforming of the reformation itself." The prospect of the millennium might lie just ahead.[2]

Milton's much more highly articulated millenarian expectations marked a significant departure from Bacon. Still more did Milton's emphasis on England's historical role in the sacred drama and his projection of England as, potentially, the theater through which the final stages of human redemption might find their achievement. As his often-cited words had it, "What does he [God] do then but reveal

himself to his servants, and as his manner is, first to his Englishmen."
For England, Milton famously insisted, was "a knowing nation, a
nation of prophets."

> Behold now this vast city, a city of refuge, the mansion-house of
> liberty, encompassed and surrounded with his [God's] protection,
> the shop of war hath not there more anvils and hammers waking,
> to fashion out the plates and instruments of armed justice in the
> defense of beleaguered truth, than there be pens and heads there
> sitting by their studious lamps, musing, searching, revolving new
> notions and ideas herewith to present, as with their homage and
> their fealty, the approaching reformation: others as fast reading all
> things, assenting to the force of reason and convincement.[3]

At this excited and hopeful juncture, Milton was prepared to imagine
most of the nation involved in the great project. Not everyone could
generate the powerful insights or foresee the larger meaning. Yet every
person—or almost every person—might assess, judge, evaluate, verify.
The matter concerned "not only our seventy elders, but all the Lord's
people are become prophets."[4]

For all his patriotism Milton remained no nationalist, and these well-
known remarks are far from nineteenth-century celebrations of John
Bull. England had seized the time and undertaken the mission, as it had
before at crucial times in the past, but the mission, not England, was
the point. Failure in the past had led the spirit to move elsewhere, and
it might do so again. Milton's confidence in England's determination
and even its capacity for civilization was never unshakable. But his confidence in the millennium and in republican government would not flag
even in the darkest moments. Still more important, Milton's hopes in
1644 did not simply derive from the present excitement, but were anchored in his understanding of the apocalyptic past—that is, in the Calvinist historical traditions of Brightman, Foxe, Bale, reaching back to
Melanchthon and Wittenberg. In this respect, crucially, Milton is at
one with his censorious opponents. The argument for a free press not
only derives from an apocalyptic vision (and could not exist without it),
but the whole dispute is conducted within a shared eschatological tradition. That common vocabulary and that sense of common cause made
Milton's arguments far more telling than they could otherwise have
been, even to those who angrily rejected them. Humanity rather than

"diversity," public purpose rather than detached self-discovery, had made dissent valuable and even essential. They still do.

Bacon surely shared this historical apocalyptic that had become so deeply rooted within the Anglophone cultures, but it does not appear prominently in his writings. Instead, his scientific program may be read legitimately as a variant on it. Milton, like nearly all the great English revolutionaries, was a mortalist, and in this he differed from Bacon and the would-be parliamentary censors. In a world permeated with spiritus, bounded by soul-slumber, and looking to the millennium, politics became enormously important, indeed redemptive. Religion became increasingly a civic dimension of human experience. Public debate and public dissent would be inescapable, and the story of civil liberties—their loss, recovery, and ultimate triumph—might well lie at the core of the sacred drama.

It would require but a short step to transform this eschatological narrative for a free press into an analogous defense for liberty of conscience and religious toleration. The minister John Saltmarsh (c.1612–1647) directly connected the two: "Let there be free debates and open conferences and communication, for all and of all sorts that will, concerning difference in spirituals; still allowing the state to secure all tumults and disturbances. Where the doors are not shut, there will be no breaking them open."

Even if there were to be a national church, as in 1646 appeared only natural, there still needed to be a multiplicity of voices. "Let there be liberty of the press for printing, to those that are not allowed pulpits for preaching. Let that light come in at the window which cannot come in at the door, that all may speak and write one way, that cannot another." As we had yet to arrive at the final doctrinal truth, it was necessary to wait "till the Lord enlighten us." Even within churches people should eschew "soul-compulsion" and attend on what will be revealed and on "the revolution of Providence."[5] Virtually all arguments for religious toleration during the 1640s turn at least in part on this notion of further revelation, the full answers lying as yet over the horizon.

For all their intellectual and spiritual differences, the great advocates of toleration are consistently immersed in the apocalypse. Roger Williams (1603–1683) has long become iconic as a promoter of liberty of conscience. Yet his outlook differed considerably from that of

Saltmarsh. With a severely Augustinian piety Williams rejected any connection whatever between the Old Testament and political life. The "antitype" or Christian-era counterpart to biblical Israel was the church of the genuinely faithful, and that church exercised no authority over men's bodies. There would be no Fifth Monarchy, no latter-day Jerusalem, no holy commonwealth—and no persecution. Moreover, the whole of scripture itself offered precious little political guidance. It spoke about the spirit and provided a vision of history, but said nothing about social organization. By the 1640s Williams had become convinced that since the days of the apostles, no church, no sacrament, no ordinance, no clergyman was authentic or carried any legitimate authority. Only in the imminent millennial era would new apostles arise to recreate true churches. In the meantime there could only be toleration for everyone. Now was no time, however, for quietist passivity or earnest waiting, for there existed an apostolic imperative. Now was to the time to seek out the latter-day apostles, for such apostles to discover themselves—and, inevitably, Williams hoped he might be one of them. Such "ministers or messengers of the Lord Jesus ought to let them [the unfaithful] alone to live in the world," assailing them neither by prayer nor prophecy. Nothing should be done before "the great harvest," for only the Lord might judge things of the spirit.[6] Toleration, whether understood in positive terms with Saltmarsh or negative ones with Williams, derived from millennial expectations and could make no sense without them.

One consequence of this line of thinking was the redefinition of social connections and a broadening of the notion of public life. As Saltmarsh put it, "We may be friends though not brethren, and let us attain to union though not to unity."[7] What drew people together, what made them English, then arose less from shared religious doctrine than from shared civic purpose. But shared civic purpose still demanded a shared eschatology, a civil religion rather than modern secularism. Thomas Edwards, one of the fiercest conservative critics of such views, got it right when he called their proponents "civil heretics."[8] Outstanding among these figures is Richard Overton whose remarkable *Mans Mortalitie* (1643/1644) had laid the intellectual foundations for a transformed politics that included toleration. With Rabelaisian laughter and with language that curiously anticipates Voltaire's *Philosophical Letters* (1733), Overton developed a comprehensive mortalism, predicated on a cosmos solely composed of spiritus and animated through natural magic. There existed no immortal soul. The mind-body dualism that underwrote the Great Chain of Being was a fancy and a fraud. The mind died with the body; there would be no afterlife. Drawing heavily on the Old Testament (and a historically accurate reading of such texts as the Psalms and Job), Overton looked instead to the resurrection of mankind at the end of time. The apocalypse, Jewish history rather than Greek logic, was therefore central to Overton's universe. It is hard to imagine how the physical world could possibly be more thoroughly validated, and within this world an activist political life became paramount.

As Jesus partook of the creation, so he too must be within its "compasse," "for there is no *beyond*": outside the physical universe, "*place and being* is impossible." Overton was convinced of the location of the risen Christ: "he must be in the most excellent, glorious, and heavenly part [of the universe], which is the Sun." Copernicus had made not only a physical discovery but also a spiritual one, and Overton's language and religious excitement parallel that of the great astronomer.[9] Overton's notion that light is the reflection or shadow of God locates him squarely within traditions of Renaissance magic reaching back to Marsilio Ficino in the fifteenth century, traditions of which he is self-consciously a part. Within this mental world it made sense for Overton to accept astrology. But, like Bacon, Overton has taken esoteric tradition and transformed it through the apocalypse—not into the program for science, but into radical politics.

Overton's cosmology precluded the Great Chain of Being and natural hierarchy. His emphasis on human reason and agency resisted the authority of "ancient" custom. For Overton, as with Saltmarsh, people join together through civic decision-taking, the creation of shared policies, perhaps even through what we might call common sense. Public space remained sacralized, necessarily so as we have seen, but specific religious doctrines became private matters and thereby even peripheral. It was hugely difficult to imagine toleration for Roman Catholics in revolutionary England, and understandably. Catholicism lay at the heart of the historic tyranny, both spiritual and political, against which the revolution was being fought. Consequently, "Catholic" carried the meaning that "counter-revolutionary" would have in the twentieth century. On this basis Milton had rejected extending civil liberties to them, and specifically freedom of the press. But once faith lost its political agenda and became merely private belief, toleration became possible and perhaps even mandated. Once that happened, all people might come together and pursue a political program that was at once liberating and redeeming, utterly apocalyptic and yet also increasingly tolerant.

Like Milton, Overton spoke of the incremental growth of spiritual knowledge, "for no man knoweth but in part, and what wee know, we receive it by degrees, now little and then a little." He accordingly defended the "liberty of printing, writing, teaching." Like Williams, he spoke of judgment being reserved for the Lord "untill the Day of Harvest or desolution of all things."[10] He was resolutely anticlerical, lambasting clerical taxes, clerical privilege, clerical pretension, the power of clerical assemblies. He writes as young "Martin Mar-Priest, the son of old Martin the Metropolitane" (i.e., the Elizabethan anti-episcopal pamphleteer, "Martin Marprelate"). He contrasts the huge prosperity achieved by the tolerant Netherlands (despite a desperate struggle against the Hapsburg colossus) with the horrific desolation in persecuting Germany. Yet his central preoccupation lies elsewhere: with "the common good," and "such as stand for the good of others as well as their owne, and have hazarded their lives for the publicke good."[11] The creation of a civic society lay at the heart of the sacred drama. Here was the real story portrayed in Daniel and Revelation. This struggle comprised the true meaning of the Mystery of Iniquity, the woman driven into the wilderness, Daniel's fourth beast with the "iron fangs" being none other than Presbyterian persecution.[12] "Scotch Government" was the direct spiritual successor to the Spanish Inquisition. Both and all like them traced their roots back to the medieval papacy.

A sectarian at least from 1643, Overton saw the "Separates," those abused as Anabaptists and Brownists, as the vanguard in the struggle for the public good, the historic witnesses to the truth, who, like salamanders in the fire, were consumed by liberty and consumed for it. John Foxe, a radical John Foxe but completely recognizable nevertheless, stalks Overton's pages. In the end the spirit of persecution and the agencies that upheld it would perish along with the Beast and False Prophet in the Revelation's prophesied lake of fire and brimstone.[13] The "late Solemn League and Covenant" had been hijacked by the Presbyterian interest. In its place, at home, there should be a National Covenant "to engage all in this publicke freedom." Abroad there should be a "Civill League and peace" that promoted these values, with Scotland and with all nations.[14] Rather like the peace proposals of the Enlightenment, Overton's tract purported to originate from "Europe."

Nothing more thoroughly illustrates the eschatological framework through which Overton saw political events than his almost obsessive quest for Jewish toleration. One might almost say emancipation. The Jews, Overton believed, had an enduring covenant with the Lord, quite independent of the Christians, and they continued to be "the apple of his eye." If they had "stumbled," exile and gentile domination would only persist "for a time." Overton seemed to believe that there was something authentic about the Jews that the Gentiles did not share. He even felt a kind of gratitude toward them. Deicide became less the monstrous crime of all time than simply the great opportunity of non-Jews. "Shall we that have received vantage by their rejection, thus recompense them with tyranny?" When Isaiah spoke of kings and queens being their nursing fathers and mothers (49:22, 23), the prophet meant nothing less than that the rulers of the world would assist the Jews "in their return to the land of their forefathers." Persecution of the Jews was especially heinous. At one point he seemed to intimate that the horrors of the English civil war comprised punishment for the 1290 expulsion of the Jews and the persecutions that had occurred in medieval England. "How then can we complain of the vengeance that is at this time upon us and our children, that have been so cruel, so hateful, so bloody minded to them and their children?"[15] Steeped in the Old Testament—and utterly hostile to the scholastic methods through which it had usually been approached— Overton gave the Jewish text Jewish readings, and in the end dreamed Jewish dreams.

To be sure, Overton looked to the conversion of the Jews. It would be virtually impossible to think otherwise in a religious age, and especially when the event was so deeply inscribed into the Christian apocalypse. But persecution was the problem, not the solution. 'What hopes then is there the Jewes should be converted, where this tyrant [persecution] is in force?" Even so, conversion was not an immediate expectation. It required longer than "a minute." Ultimately, far more was at issue than simply conversion, for Overton expected the Jews to play a major role in the events of the latter days, not least the restoration of the Hebrew commonwealth. The redemption of humanity did not comprise merely a Christian event. The Jews were the key or at least one of the keys to the future, and Overton's fascination with them seems to have persisted throughout his career.[16]

The most arresting feature of Overton's apocalyptic philo-Semitism was its pervasiveness within revolutionary Britain. Roger Williams "longed for some trading with the Jews themselves (for whose hard measure I fear the nations and England hath yet a score to pay)."[17] More surprisingly, such attitudes extended right across the political spectrum to Oliver Cromwell and on to the Scottish Presbyterians. Ostensibly there could hardly be people more different than Richard Overton, the General Baptist who thought everyone had a chance to be saved, and the Scottish leaders Samuel Rutherford, George Gillespie, James Durham, and Archibald Johnston of Warriston, all double predestination, supralapsarian Calvinists. Nevertheless, Scots held very similar attitudes about the Jews. At least as early as the 1630s Rutherford visibly ached for a rapprochement with "our elder brethren, the Jews." Durham, the Scots' most prominent commentator on the apocalypse, looked to a restored Jewish state in the Middle East that might overthrow the Turkish Empire.[18] Overton and the Scots comprise variants on a common British apocalyptic tradition that was anchored in Calvinism. They shared a common philo-Semitism, common eschatological assumptions, common revolutionary principles, a common vision of Europe's historical development, even common hopes for political developments in the Middle East. Here were erstwhile allies whose common cause had made the revolution possible in the first place. Their drastically conflicting agendas had grown out of a single apocalyptic vocabulary, which, despite ever-deepening anger, they could on occasion still recognize. In the end Oliver Cromwell's Protectorate convened the 1655 Whitehall Conference to consider the readmission of the Jews to England, which marks the founding of modern British Jewry. Yet Overton regarded the Protectorate as a betrayal of the revolution and worked to overthrow it.

Throughout Britain the more an individual's outlook was informed by apocalyptic expectations, the more likely he would hold positive attitudes toward the Jews, possibly to the point of seeking their participation in the emerging commonwealth. By contrast, the more circumspect an individual was about the apocalypse, the greater the circumspection about the Jews. The pattern cut across national boundaries: the more qualified expectations of the Englishmen Thomas Edwards and William Prynne and of the Scot Robert Baillie made them far more fearful that Jewish beliefs would encourage heresy, both spiritual and civil, as well as promote rampant "carnality." All three prominently supported the revolution, but, equally, all three proved inveterate heresy-hunters—and were no friends of the Jews. If we go further and look at the enemies of the revolution, we will encounter an anti-Calvinism, an anti-apocalypticism, and an anti-Semitism that has persisted within British culture into modern times.

CIVIL RELIGION, DEMOCRATIC PROJECTS

During the 1640s revolutionary England witnessed the emergence of the first democratic party, and by almost any standard the first genuine political party in history. The Levellers, as they came to be called, developed a highly articulated political program, organized demonstrations, collected huge petitions, continuously published manifestoes, established their own newspaper (*The Moderate*), charged membership dues, had political colors (wintergreen), wore political ribbons, and, crucially, identified with no particular church or religious dogma. At several junctures they attracted thousands to their cause. Almost without exception, however, the Levellers saw their objectives in terms of the apocalypse, for political life and the citizen bore a spiritual and soteriological character that made their achievement a prophetic and eschatological event. The illumined saint realized himself as the articulate citizen. Human reason, to which the Levellers constantly appealed, was fiercely distinguished from the medieval *ratio* and the university "learning" that both founded the Great Chain of Being and divided the lower orders from their lettered, Latin-trained betters. But reason was also closely associated with the mind of God. Inspiration had to inform and thus, at least broadly, conform to shared forms of cognition—to common sense—because salvation itself had become a public endeavor. The central aim of the revolution, like that of its successors in the eighteenth century, was the creation of civic life: the unprecedented trial and execution of the king, like the unprecedented

Whitehall Conference to readmit the Jews, both manifested a developing public culture and worked to create one. These events were at the same time apocalyptic and millenarian. The Levellers took all these objectives to what seemed, for them, to be their rational (and spiritual) conclusions.

From the beginning, therefore, Leveller writing would often be characterized by highly practical claims interspersed with abstract argument and dotted with still larger eschatological reference. Arguments for free trade could coexist, comfortably it seems, with the Mystery of Iniquity. One of the earliest tracts of the future Leveller leader John Lilburne (c. 1614–1657) described his punishment in 1638 at the hands of Archbishop William Laud. The tract offers a straightforward story of his being whipped through the streets on London, placed in the stocks, and his own holding forth there with remarkable success against the injustice of the Laudian regime. We have a dramatic, accurate, and completely secular account of these events—except for the title, *A Work of the Beast*, which frames the account in ways going well beyond its ostensibly simple narrative. The scripture verses from Hebrews quoted on the title page talk about suffering and injustice, but are unexceptional. However, the title page also indicates that it was "printed in the year the Beast was wounded 1638," which identifies Lilburne's trials with both the Revelation and the revolution in Scotland. Further, we can see this writing as self-consciously locating itself within the grand narratives of John Foxe and Thomas Brightman. Lilburne's tract is at once historical, eschatological, patriotic—and also British. In it we encounter the bedrock of the Leveller movement. The later writings—variously urging toleration, civil liberties, annual parliaments, universal manhood suffrage (or suffrage anticipating the franchise of the 1881 voting act), and a great many social reforms—frequently never mention God, much less prophecy, and will strike moderns as entirely secular. The political world they sought to construct, however, was not a secular one. Civic life demanded civil religion, and that religion could only be time-based, and hence sacred, the work of providence, the manifestation of divine purpose. Anticlericalism, even antiscripturalism, arose most often from spiritual motivations, and could even be profoundly Christian.

Perhaps no individual can illustrate this civic spirituality more dramatically than Gerrard Winstanley (1609–1676?), the most radical political figure in the English Revolution. Winstanley was a more thoroughgoing mortalist than either the sixteenth-century Reformers or his Leveller contemporaries, for death brought neither soul-slumber nor the prospect of resurrection. Death meant the end of the personality, the rejoining of the universal spirit that underlay all creation. Drawing on the great Lutheran mystic Jakob Boehme (1575–1624), Winstanley did not claim that all humanity *might* be saved. Far more. All creation *would* be saved—eventually. The rising up or "unfolding" of the spirit manifested itself in people and struggled to become actualized through the course of events throughout time. That process was the sacred drama which people experienced as history. Realizing that spirit was the huge obligation of mankind, which would liberate humanity as it overcame the heavy burden of the sin lying on the whole of nature itself.

Obviously, there existed no such place as heaven or hell. These were simply the invention of the clergy, used to intimate people into accepting an unjust and inegalitarian society. Such doctrines were "a cheat," and so too were the clergy who proposed them, the real meaning of a witch. "For while men are gazing up to Heaven ... or fearing Hell after they are dead, their eyes are put out, that they see not what is their birth rights, and what is to be done to them here on Earth while they are living."[19] The clergy, all clergy, were nothing else but the key element within the historic Antichrist of prophecy. Through these false claims, that "they preach to keep both King and people in aw of them ... they are become the god that rules." "This subtle divining is the Whore that sits upon many waters." Not only did the rulers of the earth worship the great Whore—that is, organized religion—so too, tragically, did all mankind.[20]

The whole of Christian theology was a fraud: Winstanley only occasionally mentions Christ, whose story comprised an allegory about the spirit rising within individuals, rather than a historical event. So too the story of Eden, though not directly discounted as myth, nevertheless became less a historical occurrence than a metaphor for the advent of private property and human inequality. The perpetrators of theology were then the subverters of human liberty and the spirit. In the end he backed off, just slightly, about the existence of heaven and hell. Winstanley, long recognized as a kind of "practical Baconian," insisted that all knowledge could only derive from direct experience.

He did not doubt that heaven and hell were destructive myths, but to know what actually happened at death required an experience that no human could claim. For this reason, such answers were "beyond the line or capacity of man to attain to while he lives in his compounded body." "For every one who speaks of any Herb, Plant, Art, or Nature of Mankind, is required to speak nothing by imagination, but what he hath found out only by his own industry and observation in tryal."[21] As with Bacon, Winstanley viewed the growth of knowledge as public and soteriological, but the eschatological dimension became intensified because the Creator lies so near the Creation and is so immediately manifested in it. Further, the public has become universalized to include all mankind. The artisan now became hugely relevant to human potential, a notion no more than implicit in Bacon—though subsequently becoming prominent in Diderot and an eighteenth-century commonplace.

If the rulers of the world were in awe of clerical mythology, they also profited from it and therefore propagated it. Kingship thus was not only anti-Christian, but the true engine of Antichrist. It was the malign force that upheld social inequality against reason and nature, and employed highly developed falsehood to do so. Kings also upheld the law (and its practitioners), which defined and maintained social inequality. This was the catastrophe of 1066 when Duke William conquered England, gave the land to his colonels, and legitimated this theft through the creation of the church and legal system. Kingship was incompatible with salvation and what it meant to be human.

Winstanley went still further. His anti-medievalism did not lead to a commercial society, but to the common ownership of land and what it produced. Agrarian communism was integral to redemption, and the creation of a public society now extended even to its most significant product. There would be universal manhood suffrage as a result. Classical theory required that a citizen be independent, for only then could anyone make moral judgments that were genuinely his own. Only then could he determine the public good and help formulate policy. This independence could only be achieved, it was widely believed, by owning a sufficient amount of property, though how much and in what forms much exercised the revolutionary imagination. Winstanley's collective ownership cut through the Gordian knot. Public property created public man. In this world the minister became a kind of postmaster, announcing the news, teaching politics, creating effective citizens. In this world there could no longer be any need for trade secrets, and knowledge of nature, art, and God would advance apace. In this world "men of publick spirits, as Moses was," would be elected to parliament. Public life would unite "both Jew and Gentile into brotherhood" and reject none. It did not matter whether or not an individual was "in church fellowship," for all were one in the (allegorical) Christ. There could only be universal toleration of private belief. In a society that so validated this life, funerals would become simple matters without any exhortation or reading—and no intimation of an afterlife. The age of the spirit would be the age of politics.

As we might expect, the overthrow of the monarchy convinced Winstanley that the millennial era was at hand. Initially that meant direct action: Winstanley and a number of his fellow "Diggers," as they came to be known, began working wasteland in Surrey within three months of Charles's execution. The Digger commune was intended as a "sign" of the rising spirit and model for the future. Violence and expropriation formed no part of their program. But that was not the case for the local landed elite who felt greatly threatened. When the revolutionary government saw no danger or any reason to intervene, the gentry destroyed the Digger project through lawsuits and organized physical assault. Thereafter Winstanley appealed to Oliver Cromwell to achieve what the spirit had not. Cromwell, Winstanley hoped, would prove a prophet-legislator, a latter-day Moses, and implement the communal republic. In so doing, Cromwell would "rather exceed Moses." Where Israel of the Judges had been a communist democracy and comprised the promise, revolutionary England would provide its fulfillment in the latter-days.[22] Israel had been powerful as a republic, but failed when the monarchy was introduced—as described in 1 Sam. 8:10–19, for the seventeenth century probably the most fraught passage in the Old Testament. But the new England would succeed in bringing the light "to all the nations of the world."[23]

The Diggers saw themselves as the fulfillment of the revolution, the "true Levellers," as one of their pamphlets had it, and in some ways they were surely right to do so. They grew out of the same Calvinist tradition as all the other revolutionaries. It is no accident that Foxe is the only author Winstanley cites other than the Bible. Their impassioned quest for "the publique spirit" lies at the heart of the upheaval.

The contrast with Montaigne and the Counter-Reformation is arresting. Winstanley began with the most intense apocalyptic faith and ended by completely rejecting all clergy, all theology, and the God beyond the moon. Montaigne began with the most thoroughgoing skepticism and then completely validated traditional religion and uncompromising authority. Winstanley's resolute spiritualism led to universal toleration. Montaigne's drastic doubt bolstered militant intolerance. Winstanley validated the study of nature; Montaigne precluded it. Winstanley's great design sought to create a civic culture in which everyone participated. Montaigne's great design was to close down any such possibility. Winstanley's mysticism mandated an appeal to reason. Montaigne's reason informed against itself and led to fideist piety. Winstanley does not seem to have possessed a sense of humor; Montaigne's charm continues to beguile. Yet Winstanley's eschatological civil religion led to modernity, while Montaigne's ironic, skeptical faith has shaped the repressive, postmodern reaction against it.

One partial exception (and apparently the only one) occurs in the person of the Leveller leader William Walwyn (1600–1681). Unlike his closest colleagues and virtually the entire revolutionary spectrum, Walwyn held to a relatively attenuated apocalyptic. He undoubtedly accepted the Protestant historical vision. Like all the English radicals, his resolute anticlericalism was founded upon the priestly (and anti-Christian) usurpation of civic capacity. Historically and archetypally this disruption had occurred with the papacy, but the same anti-Christian spirit informed all clerical organization and all claims to religious authority derived from special revelation. So far we encounter the standard stuff of English radicalism and of what became the European revolutionary tradition. Still, his references to "these latter times," Antichrist, and the Revelation do not lead to a highly articulated scheme for the sacred drama. Nor does he evince a developed interest in any sacralized reading of the English experience. English liberties, whether in the early British church or in Anglo-Saxon society, whether manifested in Magna Carta or in John Wycliffe, do not seem to have impressed him. He does not focus on historic struggle, human destiny, sacred schema. The apocalypse does not seem to suffuse his objectives and expectations in the way it did with so many others.

Again unlike most his contemporaries, whether Winstanley, Lilburne, Cromwell, the Scottish Presbyterians, or even Thomas Hobbes,

Walwyn rarely refers to the Old Testament. "I am not a preacher of the law, but of the gospel." "The law was given by Moses, whose minister I am not."[24] Accordingly, Walwyn shared none of the Revolution's philo-Semitism and preoccupation with the Jews. Walwyn rarely mentions them, and when he does his comments are uniformly negative. He is unlikely to have endorsed the mission of Menasseh ben Israel, the Amsterdam rabbi who sought Jewish readmission into republican England. Nor is it likely he approved of the 1655 Whitehall Conference, set up to consider the proposal. Extremely religious, Walwyn was committed to a thoroughgoing antinomianism. Christ's "love" had totally abrogated the law and, with it, the law's terrors: all would be saved. Judaism challenged his radically Christocentric vision of universal salvation, and anti-Judaism became inescapable as a result. Walwyn is celebrated today for the wide range of religious toleration he urged, running from radical sectarian "Brownists" to Roman Catholics. Ostensibly, even pagans and Muslims might qualify. Any opinions, Walwyn insisted, were acceptable so long as they were "not destructive to humane society" and, crucially, did not "blaspheme the worke of our Redemption."[25] The last could only mean the Jews.

The tenor of his thought inherently qualified his apocalyptic. If all men were saved, then there could hardly be a Last Judgment at the end of time. Walwyn's thinking became still more detemporalized through his rejection of mortalism. History did not redeem you. Salvation arrived immediately at death. Like all the Leveller leaders, Walwyn was an anticlerical layman, a radical democrat, a fervent, undaunted campaigner; yet even at the time contemporaries saw him as a man apart. His attitudes might almost look back in some ways to the underground Family of Love that accepted any political or religious government (practicing religion in detached, private conventicles), or forward in other ways to some interiorized aspects of Quaker spirituality. Walwyn dissented from his closest colleagues not only in theology, but, from that, in his attitude toward authority. He subscribed the Solemn League and Covenant, refused to vilify Cromwell and other republican leaders, and remained a member of his parish rather than withdrawing into a gathered church.

In view of his bifurcated outlook, limited eschatology, and severely relativist attitude toward formal religious doctrine, it makes sense that he looked to Montaigne and particularly liked "Of Cannibals."

Walwyn blasted the pretension and, to him, dishonesty of the Congregationalist clergy, his erstwhile allies, in part by appealing to "this honest Papist" and to "these innocent Cannibals" who knew not the meaning of "lying, falsehood, treason, dissimulation, coventousnesse, envy, detraction, and pardon." Walwyn went still further and took strength from the Counter-Reformer Pierre Charron (1541–1603), Montaigne's adoptive son, whose *De la sagesse* (1601) subverted all religious dogma in the interest of an a priori traditional faith.[26]

Such thoroughgoing relativism might well undo clerical claims, indeed all claims, and certainly compromise any progressivist historical time sequence. It would also unhinge any hope of reform, just as the Counter-Reformers had intended. But if Walwyn had "been long accustomed to read Montaigns *Essaies*," he nevertheless did not "approve of him in all things." To say the least. Walwyn completely inverts French skepticism, making Montaigne liberal and Charron tolerant. The entire thrust of Walwyn's writing was to promote assurance, not to subvert it. Whereas Montaigne sought to undermine confidence, forcing recourse to authority, Walwyn sought to create confidence, enabling recourse to human agency. Seen through Walwyn's post-Calvinist eyes, we encounter a Montaigne made tolerant, active, and altogether civic-minded. This Montaigne, drastically different from the historical figure, is well on his way into the liberal canon—and onto the papal Index of Forbidden Books (1675).[27] Walwyn's residual apocalypticism—the man is in no sense secular—manifests itself less in grand historical narratives than in the course of open debate to discover the truth: "onely freedome will in time cause the truth to shine upon them."[28] In the end Walwyn endorsed the Baconian project and enlisted Montaigne in its service.

AGRARIAN REPUBLIC AND SOVEREIGN STATE

The apocalyptic framework which so guided the thinking of Milton, Winstanley, Lilburne, Overton, and all the Leveller leaders, including Walwyn, extended to two giants of the English Revolution, James Harrington and Thomas Hobbes.

Probably no previous European theorist had more closely identified the redeemed saint with the articulate citizen than did James Harrington (1611–1677). As one realized one's humanity through political decision-taking that identified and achieved the public good, so an individual transformed himself in a process that was ultimately saving. The construction of a world of such political societies at the end of days comprised the historical redemption, literally "the kingdom of Christ." Harrington agreed with Winstanley and other radicals that it appeared to be the mission of revolutionary England, the redeemer republic, to bring about just this prophesied millennium of "free" states. The promise of Israel and of the Old Testament was the democratic republic that Harrington saw as constituting the Hebrew Commonwealth: that is, the Commonwealth of the Judges, before the days of Samuel and its destruction with the creation of the Jewish royal dynasty. Here was the "sign" of the human future: "For as the kingdom of God the Father was a commonwealth, so shall be the kingdom of God the Son." The coming of hierarchy—both royal and clerical—overthrew the sacred order. It had been a staged process: Mosaic democratic congregations were supplanted by a proto-Presbyterian Sanhedrin. That in turn led to a proto-papal monarchy with the high priest Hillel. Thus the long transition from synagogue to temple culminated in "the first papacy." Christ emerged as a figure rather like Martin Luther who pierced clerical pretension and restored liberty, at once Christian and political. The mission of the apostles, and most prominently Paul, was to set about creating the classical *ekklēsia*. Historically, such assemblies of all adult male citizens had the ultimate decision-making power in the Greek state, and now, for Christians, became at once religious "congregations" and political societies.[29]

It was crucial for Harrington that Paul possessed both Roman citizenship and identity as a Jew, thereby combining in his person Jewish prophetic mission with classical political values. In a real sense the overthrow of the Hebrew commonwealth directly paralleled the overthrow of the Roman republic (and, presumably, the Macedonian destruction of the Greek poleis). The coming of Saul, Caesar, and Philip were events of the greatest eschatological moment—and of *equal* eschatological moment. As the catastrophic Hebrew monarchy led to the Jewish papacy, so the catastrophic Roman monarchy found poisonous fruition in the Roman papacy. George Buchanan had asserted that monarchy and empire inherently foreclosed human capability and, accordingly, attacked antique and modern kingship in uncompromising terms. His fellow Scot, Napier of Merchiston, saw the medieval papal monarchy as the Roman monarchy's immediate continuation both politically and spiritually. The classical struggle against hierarchy became, effortlessly, the Christian struggle to the same purpose. Harrington drew these perceptions into a historical analysis of unprecedented sophistication.

Harrington did still more. He went on to inject, famously, an altogether original proto-sociology into this historical vision. The ability to make moral judgments and thereby political decisions required personal independence. Obviously, being dependent on someone's will—either as a client or servant, or through the corruption of bribes—prevented such judgment and thereby political capability. Landed property, Harrington argued, made possible just that independence, and the distribution of land provided the foundation for any society and defined the character of its politics, literally, its "superstructure." In the antique world, and notably the Roman republic, widely distributed land led to large-scale political participation and the creation of public culture, the "ancient prudence" as Harrington called it. At Rome a great agrarian republic had emerged, populated with independent small farmers. Their personal autonomy enabled them to participate in politics and determine the public good. But they could not stop there. They not only identified public policy, but, Harrington added, as self-armed citizen-soldiers they possessed the power to turn judgment into social reality. Politics therefore involved both speech and action, simultaneously realizing the personal and the communal.

The coming of monarchy and, with it, clientage and dependence, events subsequently compounded by barbarian tribalism, overthrew the public morality of antiquity. In its place arose medieval hierarchy, feudal competition, the false spirituality of the Antichrist, in a word the "modern prudence." That gothic "order" began to come apart in England when Henry VII and, still more, Henry VIII redistributed land on a large scale, the latter doing it quite spectacularly with the dissolution of the monasteries. These kings had done so to secure their vulnerable dynasty, but the long-term consequences proved far otherwise. In time they made possible, even inescapable, the English Revolution and now the great, latter-day territorial republic that Harrington saw as emerging. That republic would be both meritocratic and democratic: Harrington envisioned a franchise nearly as broad as that proposed by the Levellers. Above all it would be soteriological and redemptive.

Revolutionary England would restore the "ancient prudence." In so doing, it fulfilled the promise and achieved human purpose. Revolutionary England, at least potentially, would lead the world into the final era of righteousness, morality, and public life.

On the face of it, we would be challenged to imagine a figure more inimical to all these lines of revolutionary apocalyptic than Thomas Hobbes (1588–1679). A royalist exile between 1640 and 1651, with strong connections to the court of Charles's Catholic wife Henrietta-Maria, Hobbes utterly blasted "Prognostications from Dreams, false Prophecies, and many other things depending thereon." These concerns were of a piece with belief in fairies, ghosts, and goblins, and the "superstitious fear of Spirits."[30] Divine revelation, whether inspiring an institution as in Catholicism or an individual as in radical Protestantism, could never be authoritative because there existed no independent way to validate it: "God Almighty can speak to a man, by Dreams, Visions, and Inspiration; yet he obliges no man to beleeve he hath done so that pretends it; who (being a man) may erre, and (which is more) may lie."[31] Prophecy lay well beyond human capability, "for the foresight of things to come ... belongs only to him by whose will they are to come"—that is, the supernatural. Among people the best prophet was simply "the best guesser; and the best guesser [is] he that is most versed and studied in the matters he guesses at: for he hath the most *Signes* to guesse by." Those with the most experience in any field could best predict a particular outcome, "though," Hobbes adds with laconic irony, "perhaps many young men think the contrary." So much for a nation of prophets.[32]

Further, Hobbes utterly rejected classical politics and the civic tradition, indeed public life itself. "These Greek and Latin Authors" had encouraged men from childhood in school to "a falseshew of liberty" and thereby constantly destabilized society.[33] He might almost have had Buchanan in mind. The alternative to the Great Chain of Being, Hobbes insisted, was not the world of the citizen but sovereign authority. Against John of Salisbury's body social, Hobbes proposed the modern state. The universe did not comprise a hierarchy of qualitatively different essences, each with its unique and interfacing function. Instead, there existed only matter and motion. It was all the same stuff and thus could be treated by the quantitative methods of mathematics.

So too, social differentiation derived from an act of will rather than a priori structure. Society needed to be imagined not through a biological image of interdependent organs, but through a mechanical image of the automata comprised of wheels, springs, and pulleys. As an engine or a watch, society became much more the consequence of human agency and the product of power.

In some ways the contrast between Hobbes and Winstanley, at the opposite ends of the political spectrum, could hardly be greater. Winstanley saw the republic as integral to human salvation, kingly power being anti-human and anti-spiritual. Hobbes announced, initially with royalist intentions, a single sovereignty that most contemporaries would find hard to imagine outside the rule of a single person. Where Hobbes sought authority (Job's irresistible Leviathan), Winstanley sought democracy. Winstanley wanted the participating citizen, activist and socially engaged; Hobbes wanted the protected subject, private and passive. Where Hobbes looked to private property secured by the sovereign, Winstanley looked to common property secured by the public spirit. For Hobbes, liberty in the largest sense needed to be overcome; for Winstanley liberty in the largest sense needed to be achieved. The world of the good guesser confronted the world of the illumined saint.

Conflicting politics joined with no less conflicting visions of nature. For Hobbes nature was entirely material, its image mechanical. For Winstanley nature was fundamentally spiritual, its image vitalist. Hobbes saw spirit as simply a refined form of matter; Winstanley saw matter as simply an attribute of dynamic spirit. Debate about society inherently enjoined debate about the natural order.

For all that, both Hobbes and Winstanley inhabited the world of revolutionary Britain, necessarily drew on common intellectual structures, and shared more than we might have at first expected. However sharp the contrast between them, both were immersed in the apocalypse and looked to a final millennial world on earth. Both were philo-Semitic at least in the sense that the Jews would initiate the last age—and, more generally, looked to Judaic rather than Greek categories. Both were determined mortalists. Both rejected heaven and hell as actual places; there existed no parallel universe. Both were resolutely anticlerical and saw human purpose realized through the unraveling of priestly power. Both understood Christianity to be a civil religion. Perhaps surprisingly, Hobbes, as well as Winstanley, has been described as a utopian thinker.

To be sure, Hobbes's last age differed significantly from Winstanley's. Quite unlike Winstanley's expectation of eventual universal salvation, the Hobbesian millennium would be inhabited by both the saved and the damned, the former living forever, the latter (and their offspring) facing the prospect of final death. That world would ultimately be ruled, presumably as a sovereign state, from Jerusalem by the risen Christ. Even so, Hobbes's eschaton may be, potentially, less harsh than it first appears. The signal purpose of the sovereign is to provide security and thereby reduce fear to the greatest extent possible. The mandated beliefs in Hobbes's civil church are in fact quite minimal, and these requirements, at once political and soteriological, provide security in several senses. The true sovereign will reduce the need for fear both in this life and also the next; and Leviathan, however awesome, turns out not to be a fully secular structure. Consequently, the redeemed may number quite a multitude, and a multitude who populate a physical world much like the one we inhabit today. Hobbes, another post-Calvinist Protestant, will have us discover yet one more thing we need not fear. Even Hobbes's pope has ceased to be the fearsome historical Antichrist: rather, he heads the "Kingdom of Darkness"—indeed, he is the "king of the fairies"—because his authority rests upon the "ghostly" non-knowledge of scholasticism, the Great Chain of Being, and the Greek tradition with its grotesque claims for an immortal soul. The papacy is the direct political and intellectual heir of the classical world, and, as Hobbes put it, now sits forlorn on the grave of the Roman Empire. The prophetic millennial age sweeps aside all of this rubbish, as it had in various ways for virtually all Protestants, and lies at the heart of Hobbes's vision.

In the end, the advent of the sovereign state no less than the advent of political democracy seemed to require the apocalypse, but in both instances the divine has become problematic. For Winstanley, the Creator seemed to dissolve into his creation. For Hobbes, the *present* location of God, prior to his promised return, defied all explanation. In a universe where only the physical world existed, as Hobbes firmly maintained, the deity had well and truly absconded. Religion, however powerfully felt, had begun to qualify its very foundations. But the eschatological remained completely intact, centrally important, altogether vibrant.

OLIVER CROMWELL: CLASSICAL LEGISLATOR, OLD TESTAMENT PROPHET, MESSIANIC PRINCE

By almost any standard Oliver Cromwell has been the most effective ruler of post-medieval England (and Britain)—and also the most excoriated. Within his own time, radical critics portrayed him as the betrayer of the republic and, with it, some form of social revolution. They provided a vocabulary that has persisted remarkably unchanged into modern times. During the past thirty years, Cromwell has also been taxed by a "post-colonial" critique, at once shrill and seriously distorting. Since the 1660 Restoration conservatives have seen Cromwell as emblematic of the British revolutions, whose effects they have bitterly sought to counteract, in part by minimizing these events as an unfortunate interlude. After 1850, with the defeat of the Chartist movement, the revolutions did indeed become excised from British public culture and ceased to be a vital element within politics. In fact, Cromwell presided over the foundations of the modern British state and over the dynamics by which it emerged a world power. He embraced and embodied many of the central values of the revolution, and outstandingly its eschatology.

The trial and execution of Charles Stuart, "that man of blood," resulted from his bottomless, truly Nixonian duplicity that had betrayed the nation to a foreign power and precipitated a second civil war. These decisions were suffused with the experience of the Old Testament, and notably the Book of Numbers (35:33). Contrary to revisionist historiography, the final offer to the king after his trial in January 1649 did not manifest hesitation, weakness, or doubt. It comprised no desperate effort to come to terms and thereby avoid an act no one wanted to take. Everyone, including Cromwell, knew that Charles would never accept any such compromise. Rather, it allowed Charles to rush to his own destruction as biblical precedent prescribed. At the same time, the event was no less suffused with eschatological meaning, for the end of kingship opened the way to prophetic fulfillment and, potentially, the millennial age. Revolutionary England did not simply replicate Israel, but realized its promise, a promise to all mankind at the end of days. The key to Cromwell and his contemporaries lies in the evident thrust of history, the divine program. The spectacular successes of the revolutionary armies and of the republic not only linked with the Protestant historical vision, but opened up providence and the prophetic future.

The regicide involved still more. Eschatology, we have seen, is by its nature communal and, normally, open rather than secret or hidden. Charles's trial was a public act, his execution a public event and, as such, completely unprecedented. The end of the monarchy was therefore a profoundly *civic* undertaking. The public culture that the apocalypse had done so much to create made possible (in fact, necessary) that Charles be tried and judged by the people of England. At the same time, these events in turn promoted public culture. The classical and the eschatological inextricably adhered to one another. Citizens were saints, or at least potential saints. Here Cromwell was unbending. It was essential for parliament "to be as just towards an Unbeliever as towards a Believer." "I had rather miscarry to a Believer than to an Unbeliever," for the purpose had to be, visibly, "the whole people!"— the common good. Moreover, saints came in many forms, and possibly even conflicting forms. "When I say the People of God, I mean the *large* comprehension of them, the several Forms of Godliness in this Nation." So too, the moment required activeness rather than passivity, civic engagement not quietist reflection or passive waiting. Cromwell's language was exclusively scriptural, but its message was irreducibly classical.[34]

At just this juncture before the Nominated Parliament in July 1653, Cromwell's eschatological expectations, as well as those of the nation, seemed most energized and urgent. "Indeed I do think ... we are at the threshold."[35] The final era of righteousness and justice appeared in the offing. Human potential would be realized, mankind's destiny fulfilled, God's purposes achieved, through public debate and the political responsibility of the citizen-saint. Nor was that all. The great expectations extended of course to the Jews, and the years 1649–1653 witnessed the cresting of the apocalyptic philo-Semitism that had originated with Brightman and Broughton in the 1590s. Now the monstrous injustice of the 1290 expulsion would be reversed, and Jews would be readmitted to England. In addition, prophecy clearly pointed to a restored Jewish state in the Middle East, and that too, somehow, might now come to pass. Cromwell made himself explicit on the matter.

Integral to the great designs at the latter days was the grand union of "free" (i.e., reformed) states—as Melville had envisioned back in

1594. Whether that would take the form of observer-participants on each other's councils of state, or a European parliament (for which the British Nominated Parliament might provide a model), or some other sort of federal or confederal arrangement remained to be seen through the working out of providence. A range of possibilities would come to be proposed. The centrality of a new radical European order to so much revolutionary eschatology lies beyond dispute.

The coming of the more conservative Protectorate in January 1654 is all too often regarded as the first step on the road back to the restoration of the monarchy. This view is seriously misleading. No less than the Nominated Parliament and the Long Parliament before it, the Protectorate was driven by idealism and apocalyptic expectation. As Cromwell told the first Protectorate parliament in September, "And truly, I believe I may say it without hyperbole, you have upon your shoulders the interests of all the Christian people of the world."[36] The concern of his government would be "settling"—that is, stabilizing—the republic and the revolution. For only then could the prophetic promises ever hope to be achieved. As Andrew Marvell presented it in his well-known poem celebrating the first anniversary of the Protectorate, Cromwell differed from other heads of state—from kings—because he, unlike them, operated in sacred time and saw reality clearly through the lenses of the apocalypse. Kings are subject to inert nature, to heavy tradition, to pointless routine. Cromwell, an inspired and inspiring classical legislator, could harmonize all the conflicting interests, the competing objectives, and countervailing forces within England to create what begins to sound like a great Graeco-Roman polis. Ordinary rulers cannot imagine what they now confront: despite two bloody civil wars, the English were able to "rig a navy while we dress us late, / And ere we dine, raze and rebuild their state" (ll. 350–51). Commonplace rulers had every reason to be perplexed, for "When for his foot he thus a place had found, / He hurls e'er since the world about him round" (l. 100). The world awakened one morning to discover a new politics. The future was British, not in the sense of Fifth Monarchy world conquest—though Marvell was understandably impressed with Britain's emerging might—but through leadership to world redemption. Revolutionary Britain had grasped the logic of providence, and universal renewal lay at hand—if European rulers could only recognize it. Legislator, prophet, and a Gideon-like ruler-citizen, Cromwell defied all definitions, while he opened all vistas. Precisely for this reason, Marvell maintains, ordinary rulers puzzle over the fact that "Abroad a king he seems, and something more, / At home a subject on the equal floor" (ll. 389–90). Something more, indeed. Cromwell's eschatological calling separated him from the realm of nature, the world of the Great Chain of Being, along with the boundaries and limitations that went with it. To be a king was to be subject to sin and death, not redemption, as ordinary rulers themselves recognize: "O could I once him with our title see, / So should I hope that he might die as we" (ll. 391–92). Cromwell and the British state seemed to operate in a different dimension, a different time.

The underlying apocalyptic character of the Protectorate is evident with the 1655 Whitehall Conference to consider the readmission of the Jews to England. If, in the face of ferocious anti-Semitic lobbying from conservatives, the conference proved inconclusive, it nevertheless met with limited success and marks the beginning of modern British Jewry. The Conference involved still more, for it too comprised a fusion of the civic with the apocalyptic, so characteristic of the civil religion that underwrote the British republic. As David Katz has observed, "the willingness of the English government to take the political risk of holding a public debate on the Jewish question transforms the English case to one of striking originality and makes it almost unique."[37] Other powers, in contrast, had occasionally admitted Jews, but through private negotiations and for commercial purposes. The key word in Katz's remark is "public"; the eschatological future remained central, and, more than that, it was embedded in genuinely social discourse, genuinely political decision-taking.

Cromwell rejected the crown in 1657 for reasons that follow exactly the same lines of thought. He would not retreat to some fanciful "Halcyon Days of Peace" as imagined under Elizabeth or James. He would not abjure the evident logic of history: "I will not seek to set up that which Providence hath destroyed, and laid in the dust; I would not build Jericho again!"[38] Cromwell's reference is in part to the sin of Achan, the sin of personal covetousness and self-absorption that will stain the commonwealth and defy divine mandate (Josh. 7:10–26). Achan took sacred spoils for himself. Conversely, the danger is to neglect the public good and ignore the sacred drama, to reject the apocalyptic for the commonplace, to disavow grace for nature. Here would be a grave sin indeed.

THE ENGLISH FIFTH MONARCHY

English Fifth Monarchy Men shared nothing in common with the Last World Empires projected by Philip II and then Louis XIV, beyond the Book of Daniel. "All earthy governments and worldly governments," they insisted, would be "broken and removed by the first administration of the Kingdom of Christ." "The Lord Jesus Christ" was "the only absolute single person," the only legitimate king. The Fifth Monarchists did not comprise a church, and they embraced a range of theologies from General Baptist universalism to, most often by far, a firm commitment to Calvinist predestination.[39] They were a shifting, unstable movement, lacking a common program and possessing none of the coherence of the Levellers. Still, their grand visions combined effortlessly with highly practical social reform proposals. Their voice would be heard nationally and especially in the Nominated Parliament. Like the Levellers, most would be implacably hostile to the Protectorate.

The Fifth Monarchists believed firmly in the imminent prospect of the millennium. However, wide differences of opinion existed about what its nature: Christ might come at its outset; alternatively he might not come at all, his spirit alone permeating the world. Most imagined the millennium as having two periods, a "morning" and an "afternoon": the first would be realized through direct action and for a while it seemed as though Cromwell might be its key agent. Once prophecy had been fulfilled and perfection reached, Christ would arrive to govern. England and eventually all countries would be ruled on the model of ancient Israel and through a Great Council or Sanhedrin that would represent both Jesus and "the whole body of the Saints." The members of this "Representative"—composed of "princes under Christ, from whom, with his people, their power is derived"—would be drawn from and be elected by "the Lord's freemen [i.e., those that have a right with Christ in and according to the new Covenant]." Citizenship was restricted then to the spiritual elite, and although great efforts were made to ensure the rotation of office, the Fifth Monarchy movement possessed a pronounced authoritarianism. But authoritarianism and elitism apparently did not prevent the movement from being reformist: law reform, more equitable taxes, and, most incongruously, the protection of personal property and private liberties. Still more striking, Christ's new government would not undertake "to prescribe forms of worship for their brethren, nor to take the power upon them given to the church."[40] However, Christ's regime would eliminate church taxes (tithes), and consequently no church could be other than voluntary and "gathered." In the end, the most thoroughgoing theism, the most intense preoccupation with casting the Beast, False Prophet, and their armies "alive into a lake of fire," the most determined rule of the saints led to civil religion rather than organized religion.

Again and again, in so many directions and in its most creative moments, the common denominator of the British Revolutions would prove the apocalypse. We can hear its echoes quite clearly today because its signal achievement was modern politics.

CHAPTER 6

PROPHECY AND SCIENCE II: PHYSICS, GEOLOGY, AND THE ESCHATON

In 1973 John Pocock observed that "scholarship has suffered until recently from a fixed unwillingness to give the Hebrew and eschatological elements in seventeenth-century thought the enormous significance which they possessed for contemporaries."[1] Since that time there has been an impressive start in uncovering this defining dimension within early modern culture, and perhaps never more so than in the history of science. But it remains surprising how reluctant scholars have been to consider the apocalypse as having a history integrated into broader cultural patterns. We have already encountered an indication of the Judaic and apocalyptic dimensions to the rise of science with our examination of Francis Bacon in chapter 4. Their role in shaping scientific practice and outlook persisted throughout the century and figured prominently in the work of a great many individuals, including such familiar figures as Isaac Newton, Robert Boyle, and Thomas Burnet. These three, like so many of their lesser-known colleagues and competitors, were born in the years running up to the British revolutions, but their work spoke to the intense political and cultural conservatism that followed the restoration of the monarchy in 1660. Modern science acquired many of its central attitudes not only contemplating the physical world but also the implications of that world for the fraught environment of the great reaction.

THE GREAT REACTION: JOHN DRYDEN

Within two years of Oliver Cromwell's death in 1658, the British republic disintegrated. Its downfall was far from inevitable, as recent studies have made increasingly clear, and resulted from conflicting visions of the republic and the meaning of its revolution. The result was political implosion which in turn precipitated an economic implosion, a response to the burden of world-power status. By 1662 the British Isles had become a much more authoritarian place. Hierarchy and clientage had become the norm, passive obedience its watchword. The social attitudes of the Great Chain of Being were now constantly proclaimed and made frantically reflexive. Institutionalized mechanisms of repression were securely in place within two years of the proclamation of the restored monarchy. The English church, now restored along with the monarchy, permanently lost its Calvinist moorings; the conservatism that found its faintest origins no earlier than the 1590s would hereafter define the official Protestant future. Still further buttressing authority was the new cult of Charles I, the "martyr king," envisioned in the "figure" of Christ. Anti-revolutionary and anti-Calvinist iconography, literature, festivals suffused society in all parts of Britain. From public burnings of "Jack Presbyter" and a reconfigured calendar to the creation of high art, the message was one of authority and counter-revolution—while radicalism and dissent most often manifested themselves through rhetorics of disguise.

Events in Britain formed part of a general European reaction. In 1660 Louis XIV assumed the reins of government and initiated a revived program for the Last World Empire. The destruction of surviving French Protestantism became a mandate, not simply a goal. Protestant "heresy" throughout Europe could expect the same fate. Dutch republicanism did not long survive, and, it briefly seemed, neither would the United Provinces themselves. Where the Hapsburgs had failed, the Bourbons came very close to succeeding. The British kingdoms became, albeit covertly, a French satrap. More generally, Hapsburg-Bourbon culture, Catholic and absolutist, became universally defining norms, even if universal monarchy did not.

In England, however, unlike the continent, reaction meant not only the elimination of religious dissent, but also the destruction of civic values and public life, which both underwrote the revolution and lay at its heart. It meant an all-out attack on the "patriot." For John Dryden (1631–1700)—the leading poet of the reaction and the counterpoint to Marvell—the term was the "All-attoning Name." It served simply to disguise self-serving private interests, greed, and usurpation.

> So easie still it proves in Factious Times,
> With publick Zeal to cancel private Crimes:
> How safe is Treason, and how sacred ill,
> When none can sin against the peoples Will:
>
> Gull'd with a Patriots name, whose Modern sense
> Is one that would by Law supplant his Prince:
> The Peoples Brave, the Politicians Tool;
> Never was Patriot yet, but was a fool.[2]

The point was to marginalize the political and the civic as being almost always bogus, and to supplant them with the familial and the paternal. Cold impersonal equality would be replaced with the warmth of personal dependence, patriotic posture by heartfelt gratitude, public values by family values, the fraudulent by the authentic. Against the revolutionaries' ungrateful, unnatural, indeed satanic rejection of authority, a David-like Charles II might need to turn from mercy to judgment and show the other side of his divine paternity. "Why am I forc'd, like Heaven, against my mind, / To make examples of another kind? / Must I at length the Sword of Justice draw? / Oh curst Effects of necessary Law!"[3] Authority was both double-edged and unassailable. Can one elect one's father? Is God a political choice?

The new authoritarian regime sought to terminate what had formerly been the daily life of civic society. Petitioning had formed the most immediate and commonplace form of political expression during the revolutionary period, and with the Restoration petitioning became proscribed. Dryden was firm on the matter. He has the king link petitions to treason and irreligious behavior.

> From plots and treasons Heaven preserve my years,
> But save me most from my Petitioners.
> Unsatiate as the barren Womb or Grave;
> God cannot Grant so much as they can Crave.[4]

Petitions framed the issues and constructed political debate. They had been probably the preeminent Leveller activity. Direct action, going to the seat of government, public responsibility, the fundamentals of citizenship, were precisely what the new order sought to foreclose. The American Bill of Rights, if not the Constitution itself, can be read as a resolutely anti-Stuart document.

In a profound way the revolution could not be completely undone, for the Restoration simply could not abolish civic society by fiat. Ironically, then, Dryden and people like him had no choice but to enter the public realm in order to discredit it, or at least to counteract it. Doing so could only enjoin a public vocabulary. Although the "patriot" was associated with republicanism and radical religion, the term could never be completely suppressed and abandoned. Efforts were made, especially in times of political crisis, to co-opt it and give it a royalist reading. Even Charles himself had used the term in the first, fragile moments of the Restoration. Despite these efforts, the world of the patriot could not sit comfortably with the reaction. When Dryden began speaking positively of patriots after the 1689–1691 revolution had swept away his patrons (along with his title as poet laureate), he gave the term an antipolitical twist: "There are Times and Seasons when the best Patriots are willing to withdraw their Hands from the Commonwealth."[5] Dryden's statement is, of course, an oxymoron. It anticipated a conservative strategy that marked much of the eighteenth century, that period's ultimate oxymoron being, "the patriot king."

The efforts to attack and deflect the "patriot" inevitably extended to the apocalyptic thought with which the civic had become intimately associated. But political eschatology had reached so deeply into English and British self-consciousness that it needed to be redirected and reconfigured rather than rejected. Only the truly prophetic could identify false prophecy and expose its dangers. Only the apocalypse itself could upend the apocalypse. Again, Dryden took up the challenge. Right from the beginning in 1660 Dryden portrayed the restoration of Charles II as the return of King David: divine in his authority from both the commonplace scriptural "type" and the pattern of nature. But, like David, he was more: a prophetic and eschatological figure, the true leader of latter-day Israel and the legitimate king of the redeemer nation. False prophets and notorious rebels, analogues to Korah, Balaam, Shimei, and Zimri, had led the English

Israelites to perverted faith, the most monstrous abominations (the regicide), and the Egyptian bondage that was the republic. "Priest-craft" came after the days of the monarchy's true Davidic piety and had led to the radicals' "old belov'd Theocracy"—a total inversion of Overton, Harrington, and the Revolution, yet a canard so power-ful that modern scholars still somehow accept it.[6] English Israel, still the elect nation, required the restored prophetic order; and "Th' Al-mighty, nodding, gave Consent; / And Peals of Thunder shook the Firmament. / Henceforth a Series of new time began, / The Might Years in long Procession ran."[7] David-Charles will lead England into a new era, a new order of the ages. Dryden has embraced the apoca-lypse in order to neutralize it and subvert its alarming implications. Calvin may have become eclipsed, but eschatology had not. Modern people will likely prefer Marvell's moral edge to Dryden's ironic cleverness. But both poets shared a common denominator that had suffused their age.

Empirical falsification has rarely, if ever, buried the apocalypse. Instead, the apocalypse (in this respect like witch belief) had become supplanted through alternate ways of thinking, rather than being marginalized or rejected through refutation. Restoration royalism in itself did not provide such an alternative—even if King Charles rather than King Jesus had in fact returned.

ISAAC NEWTON AND THE POLITICS OF GRAVITY

The British Revolution had proven drastically disturbing politically, religiously, and, integral to this upheaval, even in the understanding of nature. So too had the ferocious reaction, and the patently fractured society that had resulted from it. Few reflected on these matters more tellingly than did a group of moderate Anglicans—known then and since as Latitudinarians—among whom Isaac Newton (1642–1727) emerged by far as the most prominent.

On the one hand, the Revolution had led to a radical spiritualism that achieved one of its fuller expressions with Gerrard Winstanley. Religiously, Winstanley's Creator seemed to disappear into his creation and become irrelevant. Politically, this line of thought pointed to de-mocracy and to the subversion of organized religion. On the other, a no less threatening materialism had appeared with the thought of Thomas

Hobbes. There the deity seemed to disappear altogether. Furthermore, the sovereign state might provide security, but it did so in a way that utterly threatened the churches. Beyond both of these lay the growing Counter-Reformation, the Great Chain of Being, and neo-scholasticism, which received highly skilled and hugely effective poetic promotion to English Protestants from John Dryden.

It would be signally Newton's mission to foreclose the world of radical spirit: "This Being [God] governs all things, not as the soul of the world, but as Lord over all." He did not rule over "his own body ... but over servants."[8] At the same time, Newton was no less concerned to reject a purely mechanical world of matter and motion which, he believed, could only lead to infidelity and atheism. A universe imagined as a great machine, held together through physical causes and totally separated from spirit—as René Descartes had proposed (and Hobbes had pushed to its logical conclusions)—made the deity a "dwarf God."[9] Newton's God was a powerful and providential figure, not a being abstracted away into some parallel universe. This "Lord God of Dominion," as Newton called him, governed and sustained the universe. He was very much the God of Israel, possessing an emphatically Jewish and, we might add, neo-Calvinist character. He was a God of history and prophecy, manifested through his will, not through Greek logic and human contrivance.

Newtonian mechanics assumed the task of redeeming just this God. To be sure, Newton did not invent gravity simply to justify his notion of the deity. His concept of nature and his religious (and political) commitments are enmeshed within a single intellectual complex. But God and gravity went together. Newton's science synthesized Winstanley and Hobbes, while avoiding the terrible dangers inherent in each. Put another way, Newton had a foot in both the magical and mechanical traditions, and from them succeeded in creating something altogether new.

Newton's connections with British radicalism have only recently received serious examination. His notion of hidden active spirits, literally the occult, has sat poorly with post-Enlightenment science, and rightly so. Consequently, his voluminous alchemical writings after having long met with neglect, if not embarrassment, have become the subject of significant study within the past fifteen to twenty years. Moreover, Newton's all-consuming Lord God of Dominion precluded the notion of the trinity: Jesus might be God's prophesied agent, but to make him divine compromised God's sovereignty and comprised the grossest idolatry. It was in fact anti-Christian. Accordingly, the Athanasian creed marks the rise of Antichrist—making the Church of England (in which Newton remained a life-long member) a false church. From this belief, the difference between Judaism and Christianity became surprisingly marginal. Jesus emerges a Moses redivivus, a unique prophet and lawgiver but disconnected from the godhead. Again like the revolutionaries, Newton is philo-Semitic in that his thinking draws heavily and self-consciously on Judaism. Newton's intellectual radicalism manifested itself in still other ways: mortalism. Soul-slumber at death made salvation occur only at the resurrection and the completion of history. One modern scholar has suggested that Newton's source for this doctrine may actually be the Leveller Richard Overton.

Whatever his spiritualist heresies, Newton was nevertheless emphatic about the autonomy and uniformity of matter, as well as the crucial role of mathematics in describing nature. Gravity held the universe together, Newton insisted, by operating through a vacuum without any evident physical connection. Universal attraction was a hidden force; one domino did not strike another domino, in turn striking yet another, and so on to cause motion. Rather, motion comprised an effect that resulted from some unknown agency. Such attraction might be a universal property of matter, but that property, that behavior, *could not be deduced from matter itself.* We could describe gravity quite well through a series of highly effective formulae: most notably, the inverse square law, which held that attraction between two bodies was directly proportionate to their mass and inversely proportional to the square of the distance between their centers ($f = \Sigma m_1 \times m_2 / r^2$). But these formulae offered no explanation whatsoever why matter needed to behave that way. Nothing within the structure of matter required this relationship. Not a thing within Newton's mechanics assured us that the sun would in fact rise tomorrow. What was gravity? What caused gravity? Newton famously failed to answer: "hypotheses non fingo" (I don't fashion [= invent, fabricate] hypotheses). The structure of the universe was thus completely arbitrary, an act of will. And there was little doubt as to whose will that might be. The universe was therefore at once utterly certain (we could predict its behavior confidently) and utterly contingent (there existed no reason for any of this). Newton had created a world of effects without cause—beyond of course the all-powerful, unknowable Jewish God.

God and gravity therefore came as a package. More formally, empiricism and theism became not only allies, but inextricably entangled. Precisely for this reason, John Locke (1632–1704) has been associated then and now with Newtonian science. Locke did not share Newton's religious convictions at all. But he did argue at considerable length that our knowledge came entirely though our senses. We could only work with what we encountered, for effectively there was nothing else, and that fit very well with a world, like Newton's, offering no final answers, no ultimate truths, no complete coherence. In the next century the debate about human reason and its ambivalent connection to nature, about empirical science as against rational science, would generate a number of the assumptions underlying modernity and secular culture. People such as Gottfried Leibniz objected strenuously to Newtonianism because it seemed to validate the occult and, still more, because it appeared to make the universe "a perpetual miracle." Others such as Jonathan Edwards found Newton attractive precisely for that reason, the utter contingency that made us all "sinners in the hands of an angry God."

Newton's God, however, maintained the creation in still other ways. Even if nature's laws sustained the universe, brute matter still had a way of running down, and at moments that required restorative intervention from the divine which, Newton theorized, manifested itself in the form of comets. But the laws of physics themselves, being arbitrary, were contingent and could be changed. That could and indeed would happen, resulting in a new heaven, a new earth.

Newton insisted that the Bible was to be taken literally and could not be allegorized away, except where allegory was obviously and manifestly intended. The events described in it about the end of days could only be literal. They therefore had to be anchored in nature and in a restructuring of the physical order. That restructuring would result from the effects comets once again had on all the heavenly bodies, fully realizing the ancient prophecies. In this epoch, the risen Christ would literally rule from Jerusalem for a thousand years over a believing world, and, in addition, over what Newton significantly called "the mortal Jews." The millennial era, he believed, comprised the fulfillment of God's covenant with Abraham.

Christ would not rule alone. Interspersed among "the mortal Jews," would appear "the children of the Resurrection": the saints, martyrs, and heroes of the faith would awaken from their slumbers and assume a physical form. That form, like Christ's, would be both material and spiritual: as Christ immediately after his crucifixion had hovered for a time invisibly about the earth assuming physical shape at will, so too would Christ and his saints during the millennial age. Not only would Christ and his saints have this dual nature, but the latter would travel with Christ about the heavens—"that no region in the Univers may want its inhabitants."[10] At the end of the thousand years there would occur a revolt of the nations, now deceived by the unleashed "dragon"; "the beloved city" would find itself surrounded by these forces, but ultimately overthrow them (of course). Thereafter the general resurrection would take place, along with the final transformation of the earth.

Newton's contingent universe mandated the Lord God of Dominion while at the same time it opened the prospect of alternative universes governed by alternate physics. Prophecy became plausible by being resoundingly natural. The present universe, however, was governed neither purely by radical, vitalist spirit nor solely by materialist necessity. At the same time, it was a quantitative universe amenable to mathematics. Thereby it totally undid the Great Chain of Being, with its hierarchy of qualitatively different essences, its interlocking teloi, its organic integration, its grand cosmic purpose—and its idolatrous mass. It is surely suggestive that Newton's great *Principia* appeared in 1687, arguably the darkest moment for seventeenth-century British Protestantism. Newton had constructed a cosmos that at once dispatched Winstanley's radicalism, Hobbes's infidelity, and Dryden's conservatism. Yet, despite all their disagreement about politics, human nature, the physical universe, despite all their profoundly conflicting objectives, each one of them remained centrally engaged with the Anglophone apocalyptic. It had long become the cultural bedrock that might be reinterpreted, but could never be simply dismissed. Moreover, the Judaic proved defining both intellectually and politically for each of them: for the revolutionaries, for Hobbes, for Newton, even for Dryden, as it had for Bacon before them. It shaped not only notions of divinity and history, but no less the structure of the eschaton.

If Newton's universe was constructed from common material with that of his opponents, it nevertheless also differed drastically. His, unlike theirs, offered no final answers. Truth could only be worked out experimentally and arrived at through replication and consensus. There simply existed no other standard. Unlike Bacon and Winstanley, whom he most resembles, there could be no full resolution or complete restoration through human agency. The contrast is sharper with Hobbes, who, for all his radical brilliance, proved no friend of science at all. The practice of science could be seen as requiring "moderation" where the elites came together civilly if not civically, where discussion and dissent were essential. At the same time, many Newtonians looked to the new science to generate technology and social wealth. Thereby the populace (who did not participate in the scientific enterprise) would be led as "by an Orphean charm" to contented obedience. Newtonianism further reinforced the "moderate" Whig establishment that triumphed with the 1688–1691 revolution, by concluding that the millennium, however certain, was not in the least imminent. Newton's hugely complex calculations, integrating scripture, history, and nature, indicated that the millennial age would not commence for centuries. Even so, although the "calling" of the Jews, the ruin of the wicked nations, and other such human events would comprise the run-up, Christ himself will initiate the millennium. It will not result from human agency. It should not form the basis for contemporary political strategies.

Newton remains one of the West's greatest heretics, whose thought held multiple seeds of subversion. Voltaire, David Hume, and others seized on his science, revalued its assumptions, and laid the foundations of secular culture. His eschatology would be embraced by various evangelical traditions to endorse civil religion and social revolution—and, later on, also to repudiate them. The most powerful advocates of modernity and its most powerful critics find, legitimately, their sources in Isaac Newton.

THOMAS BURNET: APOCALYPTIC GEOLOGY AND THE CHALLENGE TO CONTINGENCY

Newton's contemporary, the Anglican clergyman Thomas Burnet (c. 1635–1715), pressed the integration of the apocalypse with nature still further, and much further in fact than the great physicist approved. Burnet was a thoroughly establishment figure: master of Clare Hall, fellow and proctor of Christ's College Cambridge, chaplain to William III, master of the Charterhouse, a leading intellectual light within the Church of England, and, for a while, a serious candidate to become the archbishop of Canterbury. Being part of the establishment in no way qualified his commitment to the Protestant apocalypse. Quite the contrary. Burnet insisted that the apocalypse comprised the central principle in the history of the planet: the processes it described were not only inherent within the story of mankind, but also immanent within what we today call earth science. As he explained at length in his hugely popular *The Sacred History of the Earth* (1681–1690), the Bible quite literally described what had happened to the earth and what lay in its future. Burnet had no patience with conservative divines, such as Henry Hammond, who, however learned, would allegorize the apocalypse or mystify its meaning. The apocalypse "never pleas'd the Church of Rome," Burnet pointedly (and rightly) noted, "and so far as the influence and authority of that [church] would go, you may be sure it would be deprest and discountenanc'd." Roman Catholics characteristically minimized the Judeo-Christian eschatology, vigorously disputed the notion of a future millennium, and had long sought to "suppress the *Northern Heresie*, as they call it."[11] The apocalypse lay at the heart of the (reformed) Christian faith, at the heart of human experience, at the heart of our physical world.

Burnet's frontispiece neatly outlined the course of the history of the globe (Figure 6.1). Atop of the picture stands Christ, the alpha and omega, the beginning and the end. Beneath his feet the successive stages of the earth's history are portrayed. At the upper right is the world as chaos before creation, darkened without the light, undifferentiated without the articulation of the Word. The next sphere is the Edenic world. Looking something like a billiard ball, it lacks all irregularities, all mountains, all oceans, all seasons. Its axis is perfectly aligned with the ecliptic to the sun, the climate of its temperate zones is altogether salubrious, the land is hugely fertile, and the inhabitants lead lives of Methuselan longevity.

But of course this happy state did not continue. The perpetual summer gradually dried the thin crust of the earth, marking it vulnerable to the "abyss" of water that lay beneath, a layer of vast multiple oceans that in turn surrounded the inner core of the globe. Eventually cracks formed and the water gushed forth, inundating and shattering

Figure 6.1 The frontispiece to Thomas Burnet's *Sacred Theory of the Earth* (London, 1681, 1684) depicts the stages of the physical history of the planet, a history that coincides with its moral condition. The book offers a resolutely naturalistic explanation of the earth's experience and thereby of the Christian eschatology—despite the throngs of angels appearing in the corners. Burnet's book also insists that the apocalypse involves planetary rather than cosmic history. It consequently makes the sacred drama a local phenomenon. (*Courtesy of The Huntington Library, San Marino, California*)

the world. The geological explanation was essential. Burnet calculated that it required some eight oceans to create the scriptural deluge; forty days and nights of even the heaviest earthly rain by itself could never have achieved such massive flooding. The third sphere portrays this flooded and ruined earth, its survivors borne afloat in the great ark. It was of the utmost importance for Burnet that the physical decline of the earth coincided with the moral decline of its inhabitants. Such was the genius of God that the world's convulsions required no super-natural act and at the same time were fully integrated into mankind's spiritual condition. "This seems to me to be the great Art of Divine Providence, so to adjust the two Worlds, Humane and Natural, Mate-rial and Intellectual, as seeing through the possibilities and futurities of each ... should all along correspond and fit one another, and espe-cially in their great Crises and Periods." Burnet's naturalism is as reso-lute as his apocalypticism. Although he acknowledges the role of divine intervention, remarkably little takes place. The hosts of angels, posted in the corners of the picture, never emerge as more than a kind of coworker who reinforces things that are already happening. "We must not fly to miracles, where Man and Nature are sufficient."[12]

Burnet comes the closest to providing angelic agency when dealing with the deluge: here, after all, traveled a "Ship whose *Cargo* was no less than the whole world; that carried the fortune and hopes of all posterity, and if this had perisht, the Earth, for anything we know, had been noth-ing but a Desert, a great ruine, a dead heap of Rubbish."[13] Guardian angels came down to look after the ark at this dangerous juncture rather than simply observing "as idle spectators," but we never learn what they actually did beyond hovering. Here as in the end of days they appear more as cheerleaders than as decisive actors.

The fourth sphere in the frontispiece portrays the world as it cur-rently exists. Here was an earth "torn and mangled." The waters became the modern oceans, surrounding the upturned, uneven land-masses we know today. The planet, now with its axis shifted in rela-tion to the solar ecliptic, has become a much harsher place, marked by seasons, infertility, drastically reduced lifespans, hard labor, cruelty, barbarism, ignorance. Of course, hope of better things comes with the Old Testament and the Gospel, bringing the promise of redemption and, with that, the truth. Among the greatest truths was the story of what had happened and would subsequently come about, hitherto

known only dimly to mankind through traces in the world's philoso-
phies. With scripture came the literal truth, not the invention of
poets, albeit a truth that spoke to eras lacking modern science. Poets
had written of "a Romantick state, that never was, nor ever will be."[14]
Prophets outlined the natural history *of this world*, leaving out only the
astronomy and geology.

Ahead lay a massive conflagration (illustrated by the fifth sphere),
one of such intensity as to liquefy the globe's surface (rather than
merely scorching or charring it). In this way the paradisiacal earth could
be reconstituted. The great fire would extend from the top of the atmosphere to the caverns beneath the oceans and result, Burnet theorized,
from large-scale volcanic activity, in turn igniting the world's underground fossil fuels, reinforced by "fiery meteors" generated in the atmosphere.[15] Burnet thought a great drought in the preceding years might
intensify the inferno, making tinder of what had previously been the
goods of the earth. The event is emphatically terrestrial rather than cosmic: contrary to Campanella's expectations, the sun remains in place;
no comet appears; other heavenly bodies do not participate. Even the
earth's core remains unchanged. As in the deluge, the angels once again
seem almost redundant. They do not sit idly; yet their activities hardly
emerge as decisive, or perhaps even necessary. "This ministry of Angels
may be either in ordering and conducting such Natural Causes as we
have already given account of, or in adding new ones if occasion be; I
mean, encreasing the quantity of Fire, or of fiery materials, in and about
the earth."[16] Burnet strains to find a job for them. But they seem super-
fluous, once again. The apocalypse is altogether essential, organizing life
on earth, no less the inhabitants than their habitat, but the miraculous
has become severely marginal.

Burnet expected the great conflagration to begin, appropriately
enough, at Rome, the seat of Antichrist. This expectation made sense
because Italy was a volcanic region, famously so through Vesuvius and
Aetna. Divine judgment found itself "supported by Natural Cause."
The burning at Rome would be more intense than elsewhere—the
lake of fire and brimstone—presumably again occurring for geological
as well as moral reasons. Burnet could not anticipate where the fire
would next spread, but it would eventually engulf the entire planet.[17]

Only in the millennial age of the restored earth, the sixth stage,
does divine intervention become prominent. The purifying fire of

course destroys all life, and the world becomes populated through "the Sons of the First Resurrection," the truly righteous of history. The world, once again righted on its axis, becomes a paradise without irregularity, no longer needing "Military affairs, Sea-affairs, most trades and Manufactures, Law, Physick, and the laborious part of Agriculture." The righteous will spend their time in devotion and contemplation of the ever-awesome divine mysteries. They will also be quite sociable: "Imagine what a Congregation will be there of Patriarchs, Prophets, Apostles, Christian Martyrs, and Saints of the first rank, throughout all Ages. And these all known to one another by their Names and History. This very meeting together of such Persons, must needs create a joy unspeakable." So too, "the Corporeal Universe" will be studied and at last understood: mechanics, light, geology, politics, history, scripture, other worlds and their populations, will all be discussed, thought through, understood. Burnet did not think "it necessary that Christ should personally be present and resident upon Earth in the Millennium. I am apt to believe that there will be then a celestial presence of Christ, if I may so call it; as the Sun is present to the Earth, yet never leaves its place in the Firmament." That presence enlightens and enlivens the world, but does not immediately guide it. Angelic spirits, however, might well turn up directly. "Why did I except Angels? Why may not they be thought to be present at these assemblies?"[18] Angels join the conversation, apparently turn up at seminars, drop in at academic cocktail parties, but, once again, fail to dominate the scene or provide the answer-book.

This, "the last Act" in the great human drama, will "satisfie the Spectators and end in a general applause." But end it must. At this point Burnet becomes self-consciously speculative. The millennial era will conclude after a thousand years, just as scripture indicates. A crisis will occur. There will be, it seems, "a double race of Mankind in that *Future Earth*," and "this Earth-born race, encreasing and multiplying after the manner of men, by carnal propagation," will seek to overthrow the community of the righteous. Burnet imagines them like the barbarians who invaded Christendom in late antiquity or like the stories of the giants who made war on the gods.[19] But he does not comment on their origins or say much at all about them. As all life had perished in the great conflagration, they cannot be Scythians or Turks, and we are left to wonder who they might be. Their invasion, along with its accompanying defeat, closes the last period of human history, initiating the general (second) resurrection and the Last Judgment. With these events terrestrial time ends. The earth is transformed into "a liquid flame," moves to another part of the universe, and becomes a fixed star, like the sun, shining in the firmament—pictured as the final sphere in the frontispiece.[20]

Burnet contrives to be intellectually radical and also socially conservative. At the same time he is completely committed to the apocalypse as history's defining framework while being no less determined to see nature as an autonomous structure. Familiar materials have created an altogether new landscape. The radical dimensions to his thought are striking. Scripture speaks only about the Earth—not the cosmos which, from all appearances, will go on forever. Life on other planets might well see the conflagration on Earth as warning or lesson, but these events did not affect them. The physical appearance of these similarly "Teraqueous" orbs suggested that, with the exception of Jupiter, they too had experienced a deluge.[21] But the Bible spoke neither to their condition nor their prospects. Less than a century earlier, Giordano Bruno proposed comparable lines of thought, which claimed the existence of other worlds and thereby made revelation and the incarnation distinctly parochial phenomena, and in 1600 had met a horrific death at the hands of the Roman Inquisition. Further, Burnet's theory mandated a corpuscular universe like that of Newton and Boyle, and, like theirs, his too was informed by the spiritual energy of hidden forces. Burnet speaks of the sun in terms long familiar, reaching back to the neo-Platonism of Ficino. "A mass of light and Flame, and Ethereal matter, ten thousand times bigger than this Earth: Enlightening and enlivening an orb that exceeds the bulk of our Globe, as much as that does the least sand upon the Sea shore, may reasonably be presum'd to have some great Being at the Centre of it." We seem to encounter, once again, the voice of the Leveller Richard Overton.[22]

Although Burnet declines to identify that being, clearly it is Christ who resides in the sun. Christ's "celestial" presence during the millennial age literally emanates like the rays from the sun. Burnet becomes excited and perhaps just a bit pagan when he contemplates the final stellar status of the earth. "What is there in Nature, or in the Universe, that bears any resemblance with such a Phaenomenon as this [the description of the final order in the Revelation], unless it be a Sun or a fixt Star?" "The Earth and all its dependencies [= the creatures who inhabit it]: are absorpt into a mass of Fire; and converted, by a glorious Victory over the power of darkness, into a Luminous Body and a region of Light." "The Heavens and Earth shall flie away at the Day of Judgment" [Rev. 20:11], which "must be understood as our Heavens and our Earth. And their *flying away* must be their removing to some other part of the Universe." Like Newton, Burnet has planted a foot firmly within the magical tradition, and done so in the interest of the Judeo-Christian eschatology. A recent historian has listed Burnet as a precursor of the Enlightenment, a modernizing *érudit*.[23] Perhaps so, but all of his erudition was in the service of the apocalypse.

For all their intellectual and confessional similarities, Newton and his associates found themselves outraged by Thomas Burnet. He may have upheld the literal reading of the Protestant apocalyptic, but to do so he had to qualify severely the biblical account of the earth's history. What the prophets described and what actually took place were just not the same thing. Simplified and perhaps even falsified accounts of the great events had been required for primitive people in a prescientific age. In a world without mechanics and calculus, what else could one do? With Burnet scripture informed against scripture, literalism against literalism, and that was just not acceptable to English church leaders—or to Isaac Newton. If there existed any doubt about Burnet's implications, the eager use of his work by the early English deists Charles Blount and Anthony Collins quickly laid it to rest. Worse, Burnet's efforts to rationalize scripture succeeded in creating a public spectacle. Ribald popular verses had Burnet claiming, "that all the books of Moses were nothing but supposes."[24] That, perhaps more than anything else, cost him his chaplaincy and ended, precipitously, his prospects of becoming the head of the Church of England. Respectability rather than heresy (or even promiscuity) has always proven decisive for the Anglican communion.

Still more troubling for the Newtonian sensibility was Burnet's firm system of secondary causes, hovering angels notwithstanding. Part of Burnet's purpose, like Newton's, had been to overthrow René Descartes' atemporal rationalism, his severe partition between matter and spirit, his dictum: give me matter, give me motion, and I will deduce the universe. Jewish history, Christian revelation, the dynamism of time offered a more reasonable view of the cosmos than mere mathematical deduction. Burnet's arc of plausible hypotheses, however, seemed to foreclose the Lord God of Dominion every bit as effectively as Cartesian mechanics.

The Sacred Theory of the Earth, quite like the *Principia*, addressed urgent political problems of the Restoration as well as undertaking to resolve fundamental questions about nature. Burnet's book grew directly out of the Exclusion Crisis (1680–1681) and the subsequent triumph of reaction that soon led to the accession of the Roman Catholic, French-sponsored king, James II. Burnet joined a range of writers throughout Britain and on the continent who promoted the Protestant eschatology in the face of manifest, growing, and imminent danger to all reformed religion. Burnet's own position was directly threatened, and he would endorse the 1689–1691 revolution, becoming one of the earliest Anglican churchmen to preach before William. Nevertheless, Burnet, a committed social conservative, shared with many contemporaries a morbid fear of the revolutionary republic and mid-century radicalism. His validation of the apocalypse may have threatened heresy, but it did not encourage political activism, in part because of its thoroughgoing naturalism: the forces of nature dwarfed human agency. Burnet is emphatic on this matter. The revolutionaries had been misled by what they took to be direct revelation from God, by inspiration that increasingly came to be called "enthusiasm." Such misconceived "revelation" had convinced them that the millennium would happen in this world. Nothing of the sort. The millennium would only arrive with the new heaven, new earth—that is, in the wake of the great conflagration. "Princes need not fear to be dethron'd, to make way to the Saints: nor Governments unhing'd, that They may rule the World with a rod of Iron. These are the effects of a wild Enthusiasm; seeing the very state which they aim at, is not to be upon this Earth." It could occur only in the *next* earth. This circumstance, Burnet insisted, did not preclude a "melioration" of the world, the promotion of reformation, piety, purity, peace.[25]

But none of this could be identified with the millennial era. Even so, the millennium apparently did not mean democracy, even among the righteous: "not that we suppose an universal equality of conditions in the Millennial state."[26] Burnet did not delineate the organization of the millennial order, no doubt because those beneficent times did not require toil and highly articulated social structures to direct it. In the end, the apocalypse emerged as central and still politically safe, literally true and yet socially sanitized. For all his careful conservatism, however, Burnet remained an exceedingly radical intellect, and behind this too lay the apocalypse.

Late twentieth-century readers of Burnet will almost reflexively find parallels between his ideas and those of modern Creationists. Both he and the Creationists find Christian eschatology in the Earth's geology. In fact they are completely opposite. Burnet sought to minimize the supernatural within the processes of nature; Creationists seek to inject the supernatural into the processes of nature. Burnet's thought led to the Enlightenment; the Creationists specifically reject the Enlightenment, their thought leading only to obscurantism. Burnet adopted the largely shared property and common sense that was the apocalypse in order to open new intellectual vistas and succeeded in raising potentially troubling questions about the autonomy of nature; the Creationists enjoin the apocalypse to close down common sense and foreclose troubling questions. The Creationists' apocalypse seeks to subvert what Burnet's apocalypse achieved.

The most powerful anticipations of science and its real foundations arose from a sense of limitation and even awe, a preoccupation less with validating ancient prophecies and hoary mythologies than to see where they might take us. That sense of limitation and also that sense of the future proved central elements within secular modes of explanation and modern science when both emerged in the eighteenth century. The sense of the future went well beyond any particular information about nature or any analysis of natural processes. Without it there would not have been either science or modernity.

CHAPTER 7

APOCALYPTIC CONSCIENCE IN CRISIS: QUAKERS, JEWS, AND OTHER SUBVERSIVES

THE REVOLUTION FROM WITHIN: THE RISE OF THE QUAKERS

When English-speakers today think of the Quakers, one image springs immediately to mind: oatmeal. The wholesome, kind-hearted man on the Quaker Oats package—at once elderly, yet vigorous—attests to stability, reliability, even security. In reality the Quakers could hardly have been more different. The product of the English Revolution, they arose in the late 1640s and proliferated throughout the 1650s. Their (well-founded) image was that of an ecstatic counterculture, a living denial not only of the Great Chain of Being, but, in the view of many, also a denial of all order, even civic life in almost any form, however radical. Like many of their revolutionary contemporaries, they firmly rejected all clergy, for God spoke directly to each individual through what they called "the inner light." The Quakers went still further. All church buildings were in no sense sanctified, but fraudulent "steeple-houses"; each individual comprised a church within himself. All church services and sacraments, however conceived, were equally fraudulent and idolatrous; instead, Quakers gathered in "meeting-houses" to await the direction of the spirit.

The Quakers called themselves the Society of Friends, one of the very few early modern designations that did not immediately imply hierarchy. They pointedly refused the everyday symbolism that articulated the Great Chain of Being, rejecting all the social glue and commonplace textures of traditional Europe. Every individual was addressed by the singular, informal "thee" and "thou"; all titles went unrecognized and unused; they neither tipped their hats before putative superiors nor accepted such gestures from others; the secular law (and the social structure it defined) was altogether discounted. The inner light made all oath-taking vain and irreligious, and at a stroke removed the customary guarantor of truth and social cohesion. The inner light even served to create a species of gender equality, thereby striking at the "sanctity" of the family and traditional authority.

In many ways the Quakers anticipated attitudes and daily practices during the French Revolution. However, civic ideals and the classical citizen would not be found among the Quakers, quite unlike the French revolutionaries. The Quaker leader George Fox declined to enlist in the revolutionary armies. Nor did he identify with the revolutionary cause. He condemned the "earthly" Leveller program. Fox only developed something roughly approaching a coherent political program in that climactic year 1659. Even so, his social objectives always remained highly ambiguous, even contradictory, because his preoccupations pointed in other directions. During the 1650s Fox claimed at several points that the children of the inner light would "be made kings upon the earth" in the imminent millennial age, expectations not unlike those of the Fifth Monarchists, but he never worked to seize political power.[1] During that decade Quakerism did appeal to revolutionary soldiers, but it never encouraged them to join up (Quaker pacifism would only develop later). Public culture afforded an opportunity to decry the "priests," but held no intrinsic value of its own. The republic enabled Quakers to defy ecclesiastical sanctions but in itself was hardly a cause worth adopting. The new faith offered extraordinary radicalism, but it did not offer a political vision. Its coherence lay elsewhere.

If Quaker politics is in some sense an oxymoron, the Quakers were in no sense quiescent. They were hugely confrontational and acted out the spiritual reality they understood themselves as experiencing. They directly challenged clerical authority in the more mainstream churches, apparently upstaging sermons at times through dramatic displays of female public nudity (Figure 7.1): chicks up front! The singularly spectacular occasion of acting out occurred at Bristol on 24 October 1656, when the most prominent Quaker, James Naylor, led his largely female followers—indeed, groupies—into the city in a manner that replicated Jesus' entry into Jerusalem. Naylor saw the event as externalizing Christ's spirit within, and serving as a sign of the promise. At least one of his followers, however, actually did think him to be the risen Christ. The ferocious, altogether barbarous reaction of the local authorities and Parliament indicates the perceived subversion resulting from the Quakers and the opportunity for repression that Naylor's action provided.

Eventually, the Quakers did establish a successful society in British North America, one that Voltaire's *Philosophical Letters* later celebrated in the most fulsome terms. "William Penn could boast of having brought forth on this earth the Golden Age that everyone talks so much about, and that probably never was, except in Pennsylvania."[2] That was a contained and commercial Quakerism, modified and transformed in ways that did not lead to democracy; and in time Pennsylvania acquired the brutal English common law—more sanguinary than the legal system in any other colonial society. In the explosive context of the mid-seventeenth-century revolution, Quakerism provoked reaction and contributed materially to the Restoration.

From the outset Quakerism was, centrally, a millenarian movement. The Revelation, with its time and eschatology, acquired such importance as to make other parts of scripture potentially obsolete, becoming anachronistic by being the products simply of their historical moment. Fox's thinking was explicit from an early date.

> I had also great openings [spiritual insight] concerning the things written in the Revelations; and when I spoke of them the priests and the professors would say that was a sealed book, and would have kept me out of it. But I told them Christ would open the seals, and that they were the nearest things to us; for the epistles were written to the saints that lived in former ages, but the Revelations were written of things to come.[3]

Much of scripture addressed the past and might have only limited significance for the present. But the apocalypse spoke to the future and the future was now. And besides, who would want to read other people's mail, anyway? Did John and Paul actually give out copies of their

THOMAS VENNER,
ORATOR CONVENTICULORUM REGNI
MILLENARII ET LIBERTINORUM, SEDUCTOR
et CAPITANEUS SEDITIOSOR. ANABAPTISTARUM
ET QVACKERORUM IN CIVITAT. LONDINENS.
Decollato in quatuor partes dissectus D. 19. Jan. Anno 1661.

Figure 7.1 *Historia Fanaticorum, oder Eine vollkommene Relation und Wissenshafft von denen Schwärmern, als alten Anabaptisten und neuen Quäkern...* (Frankfurt, 1701). This anti-apocalyptic image portrays the Fifth Monarchy Man Thomas Venner (d. 1661) who led several millenarian uprisings, the last and most remembered against the restored Charles II in 1661. Venner holds the Bible in his hand and the devil in his heart, simulating piety and poverty (i.e., his "mad" social program). Armed for battle with Bible, helmet, and pike, he raves insanely—as his uneven eyes and open mouth visibly indicate. The image is of English origin.

Superimposed on his pike is another English image, showing Quaker direct action: a woman upstages a preacher by publicly disrobing. The pretended piety (and poverty) of Baptists and Quakers—now made synonymous—only seeks to disguise the total inversion of rational society and the order of nature. Social radicalism, direct inspiration, and insanity come as a single "enthusiast" package.

The *Historia Fanaticorum* is a German translation of Richard Blome's *The Fanatick History: or An Exact Relation and Account of the Old Anabaptists and* private correspondence to provide "rules to all saints to the worlds end," expostulated the Quaker scholar Samuel Fisher.[4] This severe temporalizing and contextualizing of scripture was hardly new to Christian and Jewish eschatology: it lay implicit in the thought of such varied visionaries as Joachim and John Bale. The Quaker reading differed because, increasingly, it closely fused institutional time with personal experience, the eschatological with the soteriological, redemption at the end of days with the redeemed saint in the present. The apocalypse became bifurcated in that it offered a historical vision and at the same time a "realized eschatology" with the inner light of every individual. The latter dimension grew in importance and resulted in Quakerism becoming at once both drastically destabilizing and drastically depoliticizing. For this reason, thwarted revolutionaries like John Lilburne became Quakers, and eventually, it seems, even Gerrard Winstanley became a sympathizer. Quakerism was not the only option available in the face of reaction, far from it; but it did allow some individuals to be less radical than radically self-absorbed.

Something broadly parallel has happened in recent times. The defeat of the Equal Rights Amendment led to reactionary feminism and Gloria Steinem's *Revolution from Within*, but needed not have done so. Nevertheless, with Quakerism, if not modern feminism, the radical never fully disappeared, and the two forms of millennium continued to exist in dynamic tension—as the name "Philadelphia" attests. That tension underwrote Quaker creativity from the late seventeenth

←───────────────────────────────────────

New Quakers (London, 1660), supplemented with additional materials. The *Historia* provides an indication of the pan-European character of "enthusiasm" and its critics.

Blome (c. 1635–1705), primarily known as a geographer, herald, and plagiarist, drew several responses that year, including comment from Samuel Fisher. Notably, Blome's *History* did not dispute the Protestant apocalyptic. Luther and the Reformation had dealt the "Romish beast" the prophesied "deadly blow" (p. 3). The sole illustration in the *Fanatick History* is an imperial-looking engraving of Charles II. The point is to cast the exiled king as a figure strong enough to stop the spread of Quakerism—"which none but a regal authority can stifle" (sig. A2ᵛ). As literally the defender of the faith, Charles may emerge implicitly as a latter-day David or Constantine, his restoration endowed thereby with eschatological significance. (*Rare Books Division, The New York Public Library, Astor, Lenox and Tilden Foundations*) century onward, notably with the beginnings of abolitionism. Still, Quaker disquiet with messianic politics persisted through the eighteenth century, now reinforced with pacifist commitments. Only a minority of "free Quakers" became activists on behalf of the 1776 revolution. As in the 1650s, the Friends shared that fateful decade's apocalyptic excitement, but not its resolute *civisme*. If the Quakers abjured politics in the seventeenth century, they nevertheless found themselves heavily involved with contemporary Judaism and, quite unexpectedly, associated with radical Jewish eschatology.

THE HOPE OF ISRAEL: JUDAISM IN THE MESSIANIC AGE

Nearly all seventeenth-century British radicals—from Scottish Presbyterians to English Diggers, from the Quakers to their most angry critics—were immersed in the Old Testament, wanted to imagine themselves as latter-day Jews, and often in a great variety of ways sought to connect with contemporary Jewry. With few exceptions the more apocalyptic an individual's outlook and the more articulate and heartfelt his eschatological expectations, the more interested in the Jews and, in that sense, philo-Semitic he would likely be. People who experienced reservations about the apocalypse would also experience reservations about the Jews. Those who backed off from earlier apocalyptic expectations or discovered second thoughts about their meaning would likewise develop second thoughts about the Jews. We need to see this pattern as a general phenomenon that characterized European Protestantism.

Jews during this period proved far from passive bystanders. Nor was Judaism at all disconnected from these early modern intellectual currents and religious upheavals that ultimately gave rise to secular civilization. To be sure, there existed foundational differences between Jewish and Christian eschatology. Even though apocalyptic expectations totally penetrated the tissues of Judaism, there would be no Jewish millennium, for the doctrine only occurs in the New Testament Revelation. It might prove more difficult, then, to imagine a period of triumph prior to the coming of the messiah. Further, the messiah could not be founded on a specific historical personality—no Jesus, no Hidden Imam—and this figure's potential attributes were necessarily less formulated. Finally and most important, no Jewish state had existed since late antiquity, and, as a result, Jewish apocalyptic reflection inherently focused more on the intellectual rather than the institutional, concerning itself more with ideas than with politics. Despite these differences, the underlying similarities between the two faiths, especially in matters of prophetic expectation, are manifest and compelling. Salo Baron was surely right when he long ago observed that the two faiths need to be seen as variant interpretations of a common tradition.

Medieval Judaism replicates (or, more accurately, anticipates) the pattern of its Christian rival with remarkable closeness. Atemporal Aristotelian scholasticism faced off against apocalyptic projections and esoteric traditions. Thomas Aquinas and Joachim of Fiore find their counterparts in the scholastic Moses ben Maimon ("Maimonides," 1135–1204) and such apocalyptic mystics as Abraham Abulafia (1240–c. 1291) and Eleazer ben Jehudah of Worms (1165?–1230?). Maimonides, the premier Jewish scholastic, worked strenuously to minimize and even disguise the eschatological dimensions within Judaism. We would only recognize the messiah once he had overthrown the enemies of the faith, rebuilt the Temple, and gathered all the exiles— events that seemed utterly remote in the twelfth century. Israel could do nothing to prepare for, much less precipitate, the messianic era. Activism, the great rabbi insisted, was manifestly not the answer.

> Concerning these things and others like them, no one knows how they will come about until they actually happen, since the words of the prophets on these matters are not clear.... [a man] should not regard [these matters] as of prime importance, since devoting himself to them leads neither to the fear nor the love of God.

Even so, Maimonides continued, "do not think that in the days of the messiah there will be any departure from the normal course of things or any change in the cosmic order."[5] We will recall that Aquinas, in many respects his Christian successor, insisted that hierarchy so permeated nature and the cosmic order that it would continue (albeit without coercion) even among the redeemed in heaven. Like all scholastics, Aquinas and Maimonides inhabited (or sought to inhabit) a cosmos of changeless structure that was amenable to the medieval ratio. Certainly there would be a terminus, just as there had been a beginning, but true spirituality looked to an ordered world governed by a changeless God.

Rabbi Eleazer thought otherwise. The messianic age was at hand: it would start in 1226 and culminate in 1240. The new order might entail the abrogation or even an inversion of the law of Israel. The anti-scholastic Moses ben Nahman ("Nahmanides," 1194–c. 1270) had set the date much further ahead, but no less precisely, to the year 1358. The thinking of Abraham Abulafia in the next generation was equally specific: the final redemption would occur in 1290, and then "The heaven will become earth, / And the earth will become celestial."[6]

In medieval Christendom, with the Jews everywhere a beleaguered minority and acutely powerless, the Roman pontiff often appeared as a latter-day pharaoh. This image fit readily within the medieval messianic imagination. As Moses had confronted the pharaoh to initiate Jewish liberation, so the Messiah would confront his counterpart at the culmination of history to realize Jewish redemption. Accordingly, Nahmanides proclaimed the pope as integral to the eschaton. "When the end of time will have come, the Messiah will at God's command come to the Pope and ask him for the liberation of his people, and only then will the Messiah be considered really to have come, but not before then."[7]

Jewish apocalyptic speculation might well find this prospect to be the only plausible one. To this end, Abulafia, fired with eschatological expectation, actually set out to visit Pope Nicholas III in 1280. Precisely what Abulafia expected to achieve is today a matter of dispute. Did he intend to convert the pope to Judaism? Did he simply wish to tell the papal pharaoh to free the Jews?—Let my people go. Abulafia undoubtedly believed that he personally was the Messiah, and recent scholarship has proposed that he wanted the pope to recognize his status as king/Messiah of the Jews. Through Kabbalistic meditations Abulafia had achieved union with the divine intellect, and that spiritual achievement needed to be actualized in the physical world. Messianic "potential" in the supernal order required translation into the corporeal realm below. As it happened, Nicholas had withdrawn to a small castle not far from Rome. The pope was aware of the strange Jew's plan to meet with him and quickly dispatched the matter: if Abulafia dared to show up, he should be arrested immediately, taken outside the walls, and burned. Abulafia duly arrived, on the eve of the Jewish new year, only to learn that the pope had died suddenly the night before. The Franciscans had him arrested, but, inexplicably, released him some twenty-eight days later. During the early modern period, at least two more Jewish messiahs (and a Judaized Christian one) subsequently turned up in Rome to confront the papacy. The road to

Jerusalem, it seemed, began at Rome—as Jews and, later, Protestants (as well as a range of Catholics) came to agree. Perhaps it is no accident that all three individuals—Eleazer, Nahmanides, Abulafia—lived contemporaneously with Joachim or his immediate successors.

Abulafia and others like him were major intellects within medieval Judaism. Their confrontation with scholasticism entailed conflicting concepts of God, nature, and human cognition. Abulafia's career illustrates some of the tensions between apocalyptic and scholastic thought. As a young man, he found himself exhilarated by stories of the Mongol invasions of Europe and the Near East. Who were these unknown people coming from the ends of the earth, who so smote the Christian and Muslim oppressors? Abulafia thought they might be the Ten Lost Tribes of Israel whom many expected to reappear at the end of days. In this belief, apparently, he left his native Iberia in 1260 at age twenty and traveled the length of the Mediterranean to Palestine. There he set in search for the legendary Sambatyon River, reputedly the impenetrable frontier that separated the Lost Tribes from the rest of the world. Recent scholarship has suggested that he might have sought to witness the great crossing of the Tribes into the known lands. His stay in the Near East, however, was brief and must have been severely disappointing. No Lost Tribes, no Sambatyon. He subsequently returned west where the study of "philosophy" supplanted his interest in eschatology.

It did not last. Sometime before 1280 he became immersed in ecstatic Kabbalah and had found in it messianic meanings that involved his own spiritual ascent. Abulafia ceased to be an observer and became an actor; his reformulated apocalyptic would lead to the pope and to eschatological preoccupations that dominated the remainder of his life. "Philosophy" now became the handmaiden of history and prophecy. As one late thirteenth-century Kabbalist text put it, in the messianic age "the natural, philosophic sciences will be canceled and concealed, because their supernal power is canceled, but the science of names and letters, which are now unknown to us, will be revealed." The mystical and eschatological would supplant the Jewish formulation of the Great Chain of Being. Accordingly, the text went on to cite Joel (3.1): "Your sons and daughters will prophesy."[8]

Despite all of this reflection, the apocalypse only appeared on the margins of medieval Judaism. Writings on the subject during the period comprised no more than a modest element within the Jewish corpus. At moments they strike us as spectacular, not unlike those of Joachim and his successors, but they never were defining. Overwhelmingly, attention focused upon "philosophy," law, tradition.

From the end of the fifteenth century that situation changed rapidly. In mirrored symmetry with the Christian experience, apocalyptic speculation now became mainstream. What had been confined to limited circles of initiated adepts now became common property. In previous centuries, messianism and the kabbalistic spiritualism frequently associated with it, needed to be deliberately obscured, for the vulgar could only misunderstand and degrade its wisdom. By the sixteenth century the apocalypse, messianism, and Kabbalah had become matters of general interest. The private assumed a public character; the intimate became the communal.

That transformation brought still further change, for it ensured that religious and even social activism acquired central importance—while scholasticism increasingly appeared to be intellectually irrelevant. Prophets such as Schlomo Molkho (c. 1500–1532), who called upon the pope, and David Reubeni (c. 1490–c. 1535), who visited the king of Portugal, both with eschatological purposes, now attracted mass followings. Moses Cordoveto (1522–1570), Isaac Luria (1534–1572), and their disciples developed theologies and spiritual exercises that worked to achieve the restoration of the cosmos and the redemption of humankind. The Jewish people must not passively wait for a messiah who would find recognition after the fact. Jews, potentially all Jews, had become agents in the reintegration of the universe and, in the language of the Kabbalists, "repairing the faces of God." Kabbalist cosmogony had imagined fundamental flaws occurring at the creation, when the divine emanation shattered the physical vessels meant to contain it. This broken universe required spiritual action, and that action had now become everyone's responsibility. Piety—everyday piety—carried messianic meaning, the most powerful eschatological implications.

In part the apocalyptic upsurge comprised a response to the expulsion of the Jews from Iberia (1492–1498) and the abrupt end to their vibrant and ancient communities—what Jonathan Israel has called "the single greatest disaster to descend on the Jews between the destruction of the Second Temple and Hitler's holocaust."[9] But only in part. Apocalyptic thought provides a mechanism for conceiving qualitative change, and therefore arises in moments of expectation and hope rather than despair, and virtually never simply from deprivation. At issue is not calamity but intelligibility. The fall of Constantinople in 1453 and the collapse of Christian power attracted significant Jewish eschatological interest, far more than did the bloodiest medieval pogroms. The extensive messianic writings of Isaac Abravanel (1437–1508) doubtless did respond to the Iberian catastrophe. Hayyim Vital, Isaac Luria's most significant student, however, spoke more generally, explaining the wide dissemination of messianic Kabbalah as the consequence of troubled times: "The disclosure of this lore nowadays, in these bad generations, is to safeguard us by its means ... because in those [earlier] generations, the majority was [constituted by] men of deeds and piety, and even scanty [parts of Kabbalah] were able to save them from all opponents."[10] Still others only occasionally reference the Iberian crisis, if at all, and those events do not provide the focus of their apocalyptic.

Early modern Jewish eschatology needs to be seen within a broader framework. The most arresting feature of the period is the level of cultural interpenetration with regard to the apocalypse (and much else), in part the consequence of the breakdown of Iberian Judaism. More widely, a growing "osmotic" interaction was occurring in many places as a result of the Renaissance, Reformation, and the new preoccupations with text and time—quite beyond the extraordinary intellectual and social fluidity that constrained conversion created on the peninsula. These newly emerging forms of spirituality brought with them a spectrum of eschatological vision, which in turn embodied a range of activist programs. The great apocalyptic upsurge of the sixteenth century comprised a cultural shift within the European experience of tectonic proportions—and one that involved Jews every bit as much as Christians.

Whether Christian messianism, shaped by adoptive Jewish elements, served to reinforce Iberian notions of the Last World Empire or whether Jewish messianism angrily rejected Iberian monarchical pretensions altogether, core commonalities remained inescapable in ways untrue of the medieval period. Even the interpreters of the apocalypse most hostile to Christianity and the Hapsburgs adopted a broadly common vocabulary but might best be understood as seeking to claim the rhetoric. Jewish counter-eschatologies were true, the Hapsburg Last World Empire false. Jewish genealogy was founded on genuinely "clean" blood; the Iberian *limpieza* arose from a lie. Yosef Kaplan has described Jewish thought in this last respect as a *mimesis de l'antagonisme*, replicating and inverting the dominant ideology. Spaniards such as Abravanel or the young *converso* prophetesses of 1500 and 1501, for whom vengeance provided the apocalyptic focus and continuing leitmotif, could attract interest beyond their intended audience. Abravanel's works, despite their militant Jewish purpose, spoke to both Jews and Christians for some two centuries. Another Jewish writer saw the fall of Naples to France's Charles VIII in 1495 as initiating Judaism's messianic age, no more than a modest variant on widespread Christian perceptions promoted by such commentators as Ficino and Savonarola. The similarity between elements in Abravanel's eschatology and that of his contemporary Savonarola (as well as that of late medieval Christian heretics) has long been recognized. Abravanel's resolute insistence that the papacy formed the direct continuation of the pagan Roman Empire anticipates, astonishingly, the thought of Scottish Calvinists in the 1590s such as Napier of Merchiston and Andrew Melville.

Like their contemporary Christian counterparts, Renaissance Jews could produce republican or quasi-republican eschatologies. Despite the Jews' almost reflexive recourse to the protection of monarchy, their struggle against the Hapsburgs might promote not only counter-empire, but, alternately, a future with no empire at all. Abravanel's comments reveal an almost visceral desire to span the two sides of the Renaissance world.

> ... the government of Venice is a mistress *that is great among nations, and princess among the provinces* [Lam. 1:1]; and the government of Florence *is the beauty of all lands* [Ezek. 20:6]; ... Lucca, Siena, and Bologna and other lands that are without a king, but are governed by leaders who are chosen for a limited time, are ... just governments *in which there is nothing perverse or crooked*" [Prov. 8:8].[11]

In the pulsating, supercharged atmosphere of early modern apocalyptic expectation, there were not two self-contained streams of thought and interpretation that occasionally interfaced, but, instead, Jewish and Christian expectations experienced continuous interaction and a mutual reshaping of one another. Both Jews and Christians looked to the end of the evil empire—which, despite all the prophecy, somehow failed to occur.

There exists a broad messianic arc at the center of early modern Judaism. It began most visibly with individuals such as Abravanel, Molkho, and Reubeni and continued through Isaac Luria and his disciples later in the sixteenth century. Subsequently Jewish messianism reached its apogee with the extraordinary upheaval in the next century precipitated by Sabbatai Şevi (1626–1676) and Nathan of Gaza (1643–1680). It would culminate thereafter in the rise of Hasidism and, less directly, in Judaism's Enlightenment, the Haskalah. Although the impact of Luria's vastly intricate mystical system is a matter of modern scholarly dispute, the apocalyptic trajectory is not at issue. That spiritual experience continuously reinforced and refracted contemporaneous Christian expectations. One such instance involved the Amsterdam rabbi Menasseh ben Israel (1604–1657) and his mission to revolutionary Britain.

Menasseh ben Israel and Oliver Cromwell

From the 1590s onward a growing philo-Semitism became palpable throughout the British Isles. It correlated directly with apocalyptic expectations, with Calvinist commitment, and generally with "Puritanism." The English exegetes and reformers Thomas Brightman, Andrew Willet, Hugh Broughton, Henry Finch, and William Gouge joined with Scottish counterparts, among them John Napier, William Alexander, Patrick Forbes of Corse, and Samuel Rutherford, in becoming greatly interested in contemporary Jews. They were persuaded that the Jewish people would play an important and perhaps decisive role in the great events at the end of days—who thus were critical in the achievement of human destiny. A general reconciliation of two faiths would occur. As early as 1648 Oliver Cromwell found himself aching for such a coming together of peoples and creeds: "I profess to thee I desire from my heart, I have prayed for it, I have waited for the day to see union and right understanding between the godly people (Scots, English, Jews, Gentiles, Presbyterians, Independents, Anabaptists, and all)."[12] Such union of purpose could only occur within the framework of the apocalypse. Many British commentators became convinced that Old Testament prophecies simply had to refer to a restored Jewish state in the Middle East. Here was one point on which they and their Jewish contemporaries agreed. An excited sense of the imminence of these events was another.

To be sure, the eschaton would also involve the "calling"—that is, the conversion—of the Jews to Christianity. But even in its simplest and least sophisticated form, the puritan reading of this event differed decisively from the traditional one. Since late antiquity Paul's oft-cited lines in Romans had been understood as the Jews at last recognizing the truth and their own perverse blindness—a final triumph for the Christian faith, a final humiliation for Judaism. For the Protestant and especially the Puritan, Christianity was a dynamic, changing phenomenon: only the reformed Christianity of the final era could be worthy the Jews' conversion. If the Jews had been blind in the Age of the Apostles, that blindness experienced confirmation and validation in the Age of Antichrist. Perhaps then Jewish "stubbornness" turned out to be well-founded, a firm rejection of idolatry—and, from the more militant Scottish perspective, a rejection of jumped-up paganism. Even so, radical Protestants were prepared to admit that Christianity had yet to arrive at its final and truest form, and that this apocalyptic achievement might well require Jewish wisdom: language, commentaries, Kabbalah and other esoteric systems, magical traditions, ancient prophecies. Reconciliation in the largest possible sense.

This line of thinking led English commentators such as Roger Williams to conclude that Edward I's expulsion of medieval Jewry from England in 1290 had been a profound mistake. The Jews should be readmitted, for, at the crudest level, only then could they witness an unfalsified Christianity and therefore be expected to convert. Some, including Williams, went further. If Old Testament prophecy genuinely spoke to the Jewish future—and could not be allegorized away through medieval techniques to mean the Christian church— then that expulsion from England had served to frustrate the divine program and God's evident purposes. The 1290 edict did not simply constitute bad judgment but was morally wrong, even a crime of almost apocalyptic magnitude. The grave misstep needed to be rectified, and Jewish readmission became a moral and even eschatological imperative. If the Jews truly did enjoy a privileged relationship with God that would find fruition in a new Israel, then any gentile Israel— any English Israel—became inherently linked to it.

Philo-Semitism and the call for readmission translated into action with the revolution. In early January 1649, as Charles faced trial and the republic was in birth, the widow Johanna Cartwright and her son formally petitioned Parliament to have the 1290 edict rescinded and the Jews readmitted. From that point onward to the Whitehall Conference, summoned in late 1655 to discuss the matter, the issue continually resurfaced and became one of the registers in which the revolution and its objectives were debated. That debate echoed everywhere throughout the English-speaking world, from Scotland to North America to Anglophone communities on the continent. It had active supporters in every one of the successive revolutionary governments— the most notable supporter being Oliver Cromwell himself.

The debate was enriched and promoted (if also complicated) by various Jewish overtures and then signally by the arrival of Rabbi Menasseh in 1655. Menasseh met with leading intellectual and political figures in England, becoming effectively Judaism's de facto ambassador to the republic and to English-speakers generally. As with many Jews at this moment, his outlook was intensely messianic. Rumors and stories ostensibly from beyond the Sambatyon circulated once again in 1641. The appalling massacres in Eastern Europe that resulted from Bogdan Chmielnicki's Cossack revolt in 1648 were seen by many as the "birth-pangs" to a new era. Did not the Zohar, according to some readings, identify 1648 as the date of deliverance by the Messiah? The evacuation of the Dutch New Netherlands in Brazil in 1654 brought with it the end of the Jewish community at Recife. The displaced population urgently required resettlement and in perhaps every sense new beginnings.

England was only one such possibility for settlement among a number, but a combination of circumstances gave the English prospect an eschatological cast. In the previous decade word had reached the Amsterdam congregation that a Jewish community had been discovered deep in South America, living just beyond a great river (as we might expect). Could these people be one of the Lost Tribes? The possibility stoked Jewish messianic excitement, naturally enough. Menasseh carefully collected the testimonial evidence. He and a number of associates became persuaded that Jews now living in the New World—both as settlers from Europe and apparently Lost Tribes (having crossed, it seemed, from Asia)—fulfilled the lines from Deuteronomy (32:26) that Jews would be scattered to the furthest ends of the earth before the messianic age. Only one corner of the world still remained unfilled, England. The new state now seemed vital to Jewish redemption. As Menasseh assured the English public in his "Declaration to the Commonwealth of England" (1655), the Jews had been dispersed everywhere "except only in this considerable and mighty island." "And therefore this remains in my judgement, before the MESSIA come and restore our Nation, that first we must have our seat her[e] likewise." Harold Fisch rightly insists that Menasseh's claims are neither flattery nor a promotional ploy, but comprise the rabbi's core beliefs.

Almost immediately after the founding of the republic, Menasseh drafted his famous appeal for Jewish readmission to England, *The Hope of Israel* (1650). It appeared in Spanish, Latin, Hebrew, English, and a few years later in Dutch, and thereby addressed at once all Christians and all Jews. The English translation (1650, 1651, 1652) was undertaken by the fervent millenarian and associate of Milton, Moses Wall. Menasseh's tract breathes messianic expectation. "It is about to be the end of this age." "We judge [the redemption] to be near. For ... we see many prophecies fulfilled, and others also which are subservient to a preparation for the same redemption." "The time of redemption is at hand."[13] The rabbi's bubbling enthusiasm did not foreclose caution. Unlike Abulafia, Eleazer, Nahmanides, Molkho, Abravanel, and so many others, Menasseh refused to set a date for the arrival of the new era. Yet its imminence remained beyond doubt, for this reticence did not qualify expectations. Just the opposite. It bolstered them because it underscored the need for activism. The eschaton demanded human agency, and, in the best Lurianic tradition, Menasseh's mission was an instance of it.

Precisely this outlook made revolutionary Britain all the more important to the Jewish imagination. Menasseh regarded the Spanish Inquisition as the fourth beast described in Daniel (7:7, 19), effectively what guided "the Spanish tyrannical empire," the order just preceding the messianic age. It is a matter of the utmost significance that in Menasseh's report from the Americas the Lost Tribes intend an alliance with the Indians to overthrow the Spanish colossus. Here was the same strategic vision that had exercised Dutch, English, and even French anti-imperialism from the late sixteenth century. In so doing, the Lost Tribes will fulfill prophecy, and these events then will lead to Jewish freedom and redemption—and, with it, freedom and redemption for the righteous among all mankind. The report from the west therefore hugely promoted policy in Europe. Moreover, the English republic had just burst upon the world stage with extraordinary power and with the prophetic mission of world liberation. Its apocalyptic energies were not merely comparable to those of the Jews. The two in fact converged in a grand program to realize human potential, human destiny. The "Western Design"—the expedition to Hispaniola and then Jamaica—emerged for both the Jews and the British as a project providential rather than narrowly profitable. Small wonder that Menasseh looked at the English republic and exclaimed, "And truly it is from hence, that of late you have done so great things valiantly, and by an unusual attempt, and things much to be observed among the Nations. The whole world stands amazed at these things, and the eyes of all are turned upon you."[14] Modern conservative and revisionist historiography belittles the English-British Revolution to the point of denial. But contemporaries to these events certainly did not. In a letter to Sephardic Jewry Menasseh was emphatic that the English had changed. "Today this English nation is no longer our ancient enemy."[15] Quite the reverse. The crimes perpetrated by medieval England in 1290 would be expunged—and a surprising number of Englishmen completely agreed. Revolution had transformed everything.

Jewish hopes and Christian hopes—Israel messianic and Israel millenarian—thus seemed to coincide in aspirations of universal liberation. Or did they? Were not both sides being somehow disingenuous? The Jews sought a world that validated Judaism, the British a world that validated Christianity. The point was to avoid conversion; the point was to achieve conversion. Who was fooling whom? In fact, Jewish and Christian expectations could turn out to be remarkably close, at least potentially. Moses Wall maintained that he was not trying to convert the Jews by translating *The Hope of Israel*. Conversion would occur at some indefinite point in the future by a supernatural act, much like Paul's conversion en route to Damascus. Consequently, there was not much for Englishmen to do, and apparently no need at all for them to hassle their new neighbors. Conversion was God's responsibility, not the state's. There simply existed no way in pre-modern, pre-secular Europe for people to imagine anything other than a final coherent structure of philosophical and religious truth, an ultimate resolution that was unassailable and compelling to any but the most willfully perverse. An increasingly temporalized culture made that final answer a collaborative project and, crucially, one that might continually recede.

"Ultimate" truth became more a process than an arrival, something rather sought than achieved. The time-soaked environment of both revolutionary Britain and the messianic Jewish "nation" at Amsterdam inherently stressed common purpose and minimized underlying difference. It made possible a proto-liberal world, though not a modern one.

Richard Popkin rightly noted that Menasseh's "messianism turned out to be one step away from the Christian millenarian position." Both sides were genuinely ecumenical and sought to formulate versions of their faiths that could reinforce rather than confront or offend one another. Far from some sort of tactical accommodation, their objective was passionately eschatological, the creation of a Judeo-Christianity that might realize the prophetic future.[16] Both sides, philo-Christian and philo-Judaic, saw themselves as participants in a great joint endeavor that went well beyond formal doctrine.

In the Netherlands Menasseh inhabited an ecumenical environment, and he had long been emphatic that the righteous of all nations would achieve salvation. The triumph of Israel was the triumph of humanity. There he knew many of the leading Christian philo-Semites, and was close to Adam Boreel (1603–1665), who claimed that no organized church adhered to the truth. Instead, pieces of the truth were scattered through all faiths, including Judaism. The prospect of reassembling them invited millenarian projections, in ways sounding somewhat like Bacon and Milton.

Just before departing for England Menasseh published his messianic treatise *Piedra Gloriosa, O Estatua Nabuchadnosor* (The Glorious Stone, of the Statue of Nebuchadnezzar). The work connected the little stone "cut out by no human hand" in Nebuchadnezzar's dream (Dan. 2:34) to crucial moments in Israel's struggle and triumph. Rembrandt van Rijn (1606–1669) famously illustrated the volume with four etchings (Figure 7.2), the first collaboration on a book involving a Protestant artist and a Jewish intellectual. Rembrandt's connection with Menasseh is thought to have gone back more than twenty years. The artist's specific religious beliefs are uncertain. He was raised in a Remonstrant (non-Calvinist) Protestant family. But, unlike his brother Adriaen, he never joined a Remonstrant congregation. He executed works for anti-Trinitarian Mennonites, Remonstrants, Calvinists, Roman Catholics, and Jews. He had a close working relationship with the Mennonite art dealer Hendrick van Uylenburgh, and it was later said that he adopted their views in the 1640s. By the time he did the illustrations for Menasseh's *Piedra Gloriosa* in 1655, he had embraced an unmistakable Protestant philo-Semitism. He clearly shared what Simon Schama has called Menasseh's "feverish ecumenism."[17] Other work by the artist may also suggest ecumenism and reconciliation. Undoubtedly, Menasseh brought with him to England the experience of collaboration and the expectation of a joint undertaking. Accordingly, he opened *The Hope of Israel* with the language of common purpose, an appeal to the "public good."[18] It was founded on overlapping visions of the future.

To be sure, postponement of the grand scenario inevitably brought tension and disappointment. If the British republic had met with spectacular achievement, vastly more spectacular events had been awaited—and had not occurred. The totally fictional tale of some three hundred rabbis meeting in Hungary to consider Christianity in 1650—who might well have converted but for the want of Protestant divines at the conference—is a sign of felt need. By the time the fantasy saw print in 1655, it already had rocketed about the Anglophone communities. Indications of rethinking appear in many places. James Hope of Hopetoun, one of the key radicals in the 1653 Nominated Parliament, had resigned himself by 1657 to "present dispensations" rather than looking to far-reaching transformations. Moses Wall expostulated in a letter to Samuel Hartlib, "Well, Sir, 1655 year is passant, & yet what hath God wrough[t]?"[19] Both retired into private life, Hope into international commerce and Wall into experimental agriculture. They both resurfaced briefly in 1659. Both regarded the Protectorate as a betrayal of the revolution and the spirit of God. It was too traditional, no more than the old monarchy re-emergent, "corrupt" in the sense of being insufficiently apocalyptic.

More than anything else the fraught questions of the apocalypse and its implications undermined the 1655 Whitehall Conference, a gathering of both clergy and lay leaders summoned to consider the question of Jewish readmission. In the end the conference closed inconclusively. There would be no great charter opening the way to Jewish settlement, no eschatological Anglo-Jewish mission, no new era of reconciliation, liberation, and redemption. The background drumbeat of royalist anti-Semitism and ugly aspersions was not decisive. Instead, the most powerful challenge to the conference came from former supporters of Parliament, individuals once deeply immersed in the apocalypse, but

who now feared that prophetic expectations had unleashed social and religious radicalism. Outstanding among these was the lawyer William Prynne (1600–1669). His *A Short Demurrer to the Jews* appeared in its full form only in 1656, but Prynne did manage to distribute the first part to the delegates before the final meeting. Its effect was devastating. For it not only presented what appeared to be a researched and scholarly account of Anglo-Jewish relations, one that rehearsed all the medieval tales of the blood libel and well poisonings. Much more tellingly, it stressed again and again that Jewish readmission would mean large-scale conversions not from Judaism but *to* Judaism. The lower orders in particular would "turn Jew." That prospect, remote to the point of absurdity from today's vantage, seemed at least broadly plausible then in a context of burgeoning and socially threatening heterodoxy. Jewish arguments against the trinity and the foundations of Christianity might well appeal to the populace "in this giddy, unsettled, apostatizing age." "It was now a very ill time to bring in the Jews, when the people were

←——————————————————————————————

Figure 7.2 Rembrandt's four etchings for Menasseh ben Israel's messianic *Piedra Gloriosa, O Estatua Nabuchadnosor* (The Glorious Stone, or the Statue of Nebuchadnezzar; Amsterdam, 1655). Menasseh drew together four moments when the little stone "cut out by no human hand" (Dan. 2:34) saved Israel and indicated its destiny: the overthrow of the four-part statue in Nebuchadnezzar's dream, the four great beasts or empires that would successively appear before the end of days (Dan. 7:3, 17), the stone on which Jacob rested his head when he had his vision of the ladder (Gen. 28:11, 12), and the stone by which David defeated Goliath (1 Sam. 17:49). The identification of the stone that overthrows the huge statute in Nebuchadnezzar's dream with the stone that David used against Goliath was particularly important. The stone symbolized the messiah.

There is reason to believe that Rembrandt very much endorsed Menasseh's book. The rabbi, notoriously impecunious, could hardly have offered a substantial commission, and Rembrandt did not come cheaply. Moreover, alterations in the etchings seem to suggest that Menasseh and Rembrandt collaborated closely on them.

Rembrandt's working relationship with Menasseh is not in doubt. The artist is thought to have consulted with Menasseh in laying out his painting "Belshazzar's Feast" (1635), as well as with the divine warning in Aramaic that the Babylonian king receives at the occasion. Rembrandt is also believed to have done an engraving of Menasseh. (*The Pierpont Morgan Library/Art Resource, NY*) so dangerously and generally bent to apostasy, and all sorts of novelties and errors in religion" constantly appeared. "The desperate and atheistical actions of sundry eminent professors have caused many English Christians to turn Antiscripturalists, Seekers, Atheists, and like the Jews, to repute Christ and Christianity meer fables."[20]

The scientist Robert Boyle, a man also immersed in the apocalypse, felt much the same way: "those numerous unprincipled (and consequently) unstable souls" who typically comprised the common people might find themselves seduced—"specially in a Time & Country, where that Profane Thing call'd Learning is so discountenanced."[21] The fears of individuals like Prynne and Boyle drew some credence from the fact that Diggers, Quakers, and other radicals often called themselves "Jews" and could even adopt the title "rabbi"; for Samuel Fisher, one of the most learned and perhaps the most intellectually significant of the early Quakers, "rabbies" simply referred to teachers and professors in general. Assuming a kind of Jewish persona (if not actually adopting Judaism) inherently drew together a variety of troubling images and invoked multiple specters of subversion.

Possibly the most bizarre of Prynne's claims was the assertion that England would find itself flooded with Spanish and Portuguese Jesuits posing as Jews. In its way Prynne's alarm possessed a kind of logic. Independent of the Jewish question, Prynne had come to believe that Quakers were often disguised Franciscans. The Counter-Reformers had worked tirelessly to overthrow English society, its church, its state, its values, its historic role. Guy Fawkes's conspiracy in 1605 to blow up king and Parliament embodied both instance and emblem. Did not the Quakers similarly seek to explode English society and everything for which it stood? Judaized Englishmen offered much the same prospect. There actually was the case of Alexander Ramsey, the "false Jew of Newcastle," a Jesuit *agent provocateur* who sought to create tensions among the Protestant churches.

Prynne had embraced Brightman at the outset of the revolution in 1641. Whether or not he accepted Brightman's philo-Semitism, he was necessarily aware of it, and he believed passionately in Brightman's formulation of England's apocalyptic mission. During the civil war Prynne had promoted the doctrine of parliamentary sovereignty. But in 1648 a purged Parliament that tossed out respectable MPs like "galley-slaves" (Prynne among them), the abolition of the House of Lords, and then the prospect of ending the monarchy caused him to reject the revolution—and increasingly to retreat from the apocalypse as well. Prynne would play a visible role in bringing back the king and subsequently came to terms with the Restoration reaction. His violent hostility to Quakers and Jews continued for the remainder of his life. He could be described as arriving at a more "secular" outlook only in the limited sense that his apocalypticism became more muted in the face of increasingly radical readings of it. For Prynne, Boyle, and so many others in the British context, qualifying the apocalypse would also qualify expectations about the Jews.

These concerns proved a basic fissure within the revolution itself. Sir Edward Spencer, who became the MP for Middlesex in 1648 and later, it seems, a rather conservative Cromwellian, challenged Moses Wall's optimistic assessment of Jewish and English prospects. Where Wall had seen the readmission as a divine mandate, Jewish learning as essential to understanding the future, and the restoration of a Jewish state as a central element in the sacred drama, Spencer utterly rejected the prophetic basis of all these expectations. Although he agreed that England was "the lykelyest nation under heaven" to accomplish Jewish conversions, "this very glorious action" did not mean that the Jews would ever convert as a nation or ever achieve a state of their own. Wall had far too high a regard for "learned Jewes writing" and for Jews generally. "I would not see them too much yeelded unto." Where Wall looked to a kind of reciprocity, Spencer imagined only Christian triumph and vindication. At bottom the issue was eschatological. Wall unflinchingly promoted a millennial future; Spencer altogether re-jected it and urged the anti-apocalypticism of the counter-revolutionary Henry Hammond, whose writing expounded the "reasonableness of Christian religion."[22] Like Prynne, Spencer too raised the specter of conversion to Judaism and cited the notorious example from the 1620s of the Judaizing sectarian John Traske. In fact, Spencer wrote in favor the proposed readmission, or at least nominally, for he hedged it with such severe restrictions as to make his writing actually subversive to the project. His book, *A Breife Epistle to the Learned Manasseh Ben Israel* (1650), was said to have been a bestseller, and must have contributed to the later defeat at Whitehall. Spencer's point was to puncture both Messianism and Millenarianism, both Jewish and Christian hope—and the radicalism that they entailed. The purposes of the revolution would be far more modest, far more conservative than had at first appeared.

We should not underestimate the extent to which philo-Semitism had reached into the aspirations of British Protestantism. One of the more damaging events for the cause of Jewish readmission resulted from the activities of a relatively obscure individual called Paul Isaiah. During these years Isaiah became a kind of professional convert and went about bilking churches and a number of significant government figures on the basis of their expectation for the Jewish future. It is easy to see how news of his fraud undercut the credibility of the Jewish cause and compromised its moral imperative. At the same time, it also indicates how much this kind of expectation informed everyday life. The Isaiah escapades could only work because apocalyptic expectations about the Jews were so much a part of the public culture. Small wonder Prynne needed to insist that England had no mission to convert the Jews and that the Jews as a nation would not be called in any case. Isaiah also went further and produced several angrily anti-Jewish works between 1652 and 1655 that provided polemical counterpoint to Prynne's scholarship.

Despite all these embarrassments, the Whitehall Conference succeeded in legitimating the presence of the hitherto-underground Jewish community in London, and it marks the beginning of modern British Jewry. To contemporaries like Menasseh and his associates, however, the mission was an utter failure and crushing disappointment. A despondent Menasseh departed for Middelburg in Zeeland, the most Calvinist of the Dutch provinces, where he died in late 1657. The magnitude of this reversal must have made it devastating: no great charter, no Anglo-Jewish "Western Design," no apocalyptic fulfillment. Most of the Jews in London also returned to the Netherlands. In Middelburg another New World colonial project was afoot, Nova Zeelandia, although Menasseh seems to have had no connection with it. The new project certainly responded to urgent Jewish needs and social upheaval: the Recife community displaced by the collapse of Dutch Brazil, the seepage of Marranos from Iberia, refugees from the east. Even so, Nova Zeelandia cannot have had an eschatological investment comparable to that of the British Israel.

The Sabbatean Apogee: 1666

In some respects Christian millenarianism crested with the British Revolution and the founding of the republic. The apocalypse continued to permeate British (and European) culture. But, if it still shaped the creation of modernity in decisive ways—perhaps most dramatically in Anglophone America during the 1770s and again during the 1860s—it never again penetrated politics so profoundly or so drastically shifted the foundations of Western civilization. Jewish apocalypticism similarly climaxed in the decade immediately following, years which witnessed the greatest messianic movement in the history of Judaism, excepting only that of Jesus. From May 1665 through September 1666 Sabbatai Şevi and his prophet Nathan of Gaza ignited fervent messianic expectations throughout world Jewry, from Amsterdam to the Yemen, Persia to Morocco, London to Lithuania and the Ukraine. Neither class distinctions, nor differences of language, nor level of education, nor any ethnic divide created discernable barriers to the rush of enthusiasm. The movement would have an enduring impact on both Judaism and Christianity, as well as, less directly, on the Enlightenment.

The son of a merchant in the Ottoman city of Smyrna, Sabbatai became a rabbi and immersed himself in ecstatic Kabbalah. Given to moments of intense spiritual fervor, he traveled restlessly about Turkey and the Middle East, becoming increasingly convinced that he was the prophesied messiah. His thinking grew out of the widespread expectations that had become so much a part of early modern Judaism. It will not surprise us that a Spanish edition of Menasseh's *Hope of Israel* was published in Smyrna in 1659. Christianity too may have reinforced these ideas. There were Protestant millenarians among the European merchants in Smyrna, and one (admittedly hostile) account claimed that Sabbatai's father had worked for Quaker traders. Unquestionably, Quaker missionaries had turned up in Smyrna, Constantinople, and Jerusalem during 1657–1658, and, they claimed, created considerable stir. Millenarians everywhere inevitably focused on the Christian year 1666, embodying that distinctly Christian number from the Revelation. Can it simply be fortuitous that the Sabbatean movement erupted at that moment? Although the specific impetus for Sabbatai's religious experience remains obscure, Jewish eschatology in this period is best seen once again as part of a broader cultural dynamic.

Things took a decisive turn in early 1665 when Sabbatai encountered Nathan of Gaza while traveling in Palestine. Another ecstatic Kabbalist with pronounced eschatological preoccupations, Nathan became Sabbatai's John, convincing him to recognize and announce his messiahship. At the same time Nathan was his Paul, pulling Sabbatai's spiritual experiences into a coherent and powerful theological vision. As the articulate Paul had turned the Jesus movement into Christianity, so the articulate Nathan turned Sabbatai's ecstasies into Sabbateanism. Both Paul and Nathan drew out the antinomian implications of the messiahs in which they so completely believed. Nathan constructed a compelling connection between inner personal renewal and the historical redemption—and one that concentrated this process onto the person of Sabbatai. In the language of the Kabbalist, the messiah joined with his "saints" to collect the divine "sparks" buried within the "husks" of the physical world. The restructuring of the self linked directly with the restructuring of nature; repairing the personality repaired that terrible shattering of the cosmos which had occurred at the creation. Soteriology joined with cosmogony in a great eschatological work directed toward the emergent messiah. The activism of the previous century and a half coalesced into accessible formulas, engaging piety, and a manifest point of messianic departure. At once familiar and yet also radically new, Sabbateanism tapped into the energy and vitality of Jewish people everywhere.

The movement necessarily turned on the plausibility of Sabbatai's messiahship. That made faith in the redeemer an essential ingredient, integral to Sabbatean spirituality. The emphasis on such faith, rather than on good works or other merits, gave the movement an unmistakably Christian tone, and at moments almost a Calvinist character. Sabbatai, after all, was a humble figure, a "suffering servant," rather than the conquering hero imagined by so much eschatological tradition. Accordingly, Isaiah 53 assumed an increasingly important place within Sabbateanism, initially with Nathan and notably with one of the movement's greatest thinkers, Abraham Miguel Cardoso (1626–1706). This famous chapter from Isaiah had long served as a Christian proof-text, and one of the flashpoints between Sabbateanism and its enemies would be their quasi-Christian reading of it. At a practical level the movement's adherents exhibited intense penitence and intense exhilaration, mortification combined with joyful exuberance. They now rejected theater and yet became theater.

Sabbatai formally announced the dawn of the messianic era in May 1665. The announcement soon met with spectacular success throughout the Levant. The emergent messiah left Palestine shortly thereafter and returned to Smyrna where he became the head of the city's Jewish community. By October word of the good news had swept through western Europe. Nathan emerges as a truly Pauline figure, throughout the remainder of his life visiting congregations, giving sermons, writing letters. The effectiveness of his correspondence is astonishing, for there would be no legion of missionaries, no bands of eager young converts seeking to propagate the word. Sabbatai's message addressed audiences long primed to receive it. From the beginning, to be sure, there appeared scoffers, skeptics, and those who found the upheaval to be genuinely threatening—notably the Hamburg rabbi Jacob Sasportas (c. 1610–1698) and the exiled Marrano physician Isaac Cardoso at Venice (1604–1681). But such individuals made little impact on the general euphoria and excitement.

Even though Sabbatai emerged as a suffering servant, the messianic age would be a monarchy, a Jewish version of the Last World Empire. In exile most Jews had all but instinctively looked to temporal monarchy for survival; and so monarchy seemed natural as well as biblical in the age that supplanted it. We are very far from the mental world of Harrington, or even Abravanel. Accordingly, at Smyrna messiah-king Sabbatai received embassies from world Jewry and began to appoint sub-kings who would subsequently rule the nations. His name replaced that of the sultan in the public prayers at synagogues every Sabbath. He was now the king of Israel, the "sultan Sabbatai Şevi." Ceremonies for Sabbatai in the streets replicated customary reverence for the Ottoman rulers. And the current sultan in Constantinople? Sabbatai would assume his crowns, taking "dominion from the Turkish king without war, for by [the power of] the hymns and praises which he shall utter, all nations shall submit to his rule." The great Turk would become *his* Grand Vizier. Thereafter the messiah would proceed to the Sambatyon leaving the former sultan in charge during his absence. Then and only then would the messiah become the warrior-conqueror of promise.[23] Confidence in the mystical harmonies and the tonal sympathies of the universe would seem to know no bounds.

When word of the Sabbatean upheaval reached him, the Scottish Protestant millenarian John Durie read the news as suggesting that Sabbatai might become the king of a Jewish state *under* the sultan within the Ottoman Empire. Apparently, anything more than that seemed preposterous to an experienced negotiator like Durie. Still, he observed that the French church at Basel received reports that the king of the Jews was conspiring against the sultan. Jewish confidence that the messianic era had arrived proved amazingly robust, manifesting itself in efforts to introduce a new time-reckoning, a new measure of experience, a new order of the ages. Books now appeared under the date: "the first year of the renewal of prophecy and of the Kingdom." Again and again, Sabbatai inverted the liturgical calendar, turning fast days into feasts, days of atonement into days of jubilation. The messianic calendar needed to differ from that of the exile; its experience of time would possess a new quality, a new rhythm.[24] It sought to articulate a transformed reality, for the redeemed world was one of celebration rather than of suffering. Although Sabbateanism could not develop a formal politics, utopian elements unmistakably appear. Sabbatean soteriological claims are strikingly universalist and large-spirited. Virtually all humankind will find redemption. Jesus himself would be restored to his "root," and, by implication, so too would even those rabbis who had rejected Sabbatai. There is very little sense of retribution for the wrongs perpetrated against the Jews during the exile; only in Poland, with the memory of the Chmielnicki horrors and their aftermath much in mind, would the unrighteous be avenged. In Sabbatean Smyrna popular prophecy reigned, and the words of Joel assumed a reality that had been matched perhaps only in British Israel.

Most striking to moderns and probably to contemporaries as well is the appearance of notions of gender equality. There had always been a physical dimension to Jewish ideas of salvation and reintegration, and the Christian charge of "carnality" neither comprised an aspersion nor troubled the Jews—as Francis Bacon seemed to appreciate in the *New Atlantis*. In addition, Jewish mysticism had long imagined a "feminine principle" that required eschatological liberation, and found Christian analogues in some forms of radical Joachism and in Campanella's *City of the Sun*. Sabbatai's eschatology emphasized these implicit antinomian implications, announcing the restoration of Eve's freedom in quite direct terms. "Woe unto you, miserable women, who for Eve's sin must bring forth your children in sorrow [the pain of labor], and are subject to your husbands, and all you do depends upon their consent. Blessed are you, for I have come to make you free and happy like your husbands; for I have come to take away Adam's sin."[25] The messianic age would redeem Adam and, with him, Eve, thereby liberating both men and women. Sabbatai's spiritual antinomianism proclaimed parity between men and women or something that seemed to approach it; yet the result remained far from Enlightenment values. The product of ecstatic religion, Sabbatean claims about gender addressed only the domestic and appear to have possessed no public or civic dimension. The abrogation of the old law might only be made real through its inversion, and inverted sexual norms could entail profoundly disturbing consequences. Nevertheless, the overwhelming sense of an unprecedented era that lifted ancient burdens could only be exciting—and even by modern standards seem liberating.

Inevitably, the Sabbatean movement stimulated great interest and excitement among Christians, especially among apocalyptic-minded Protestants. Few went as far as the Dutch millenarian Peter Serrarius and the French ex-Jesuit Jean de Labadie who saw Sabbatai as not the messiah but certainly his precursor and who became a kind of Christian Sabbatean as a result. Fewer still persisted in these beliefs. The restoration of a Jewish kingdom in the Middle East at the end of days, however, had become a commonplace within reformist eschatology across Europe since the 1590s. It now seemed to be happening right before everyone's eyes. A keen desire for the latest news from the Ottoman Empire ensued, no easy matter in the seventeenth century. Robert Boyle, the Royal Society's secretary Henry Oldenburg, John Durie, Jan Commenius, obscure Fifth Monarchists to officers within the English government, all followed these developments closely. Similar interest radiated across Europe. Rumors abounded, often fantastic and utopian in character: the Ten Lost Tribes were on the march in North Africa; their vanguard had just seized Mecca; the Tribes or some of them had now docked in Aberdeen, apparently en route to the Levant. During 1666 the Dutch version of Menasseh's *Hope of Israel* reappeared in two new editions at Amsterdam.

Debate about events in the east in many ways replicated the debate about the readmission of the Jews to England during the previous decade. To discredit the Jews was to discredit reform, the possibility of change, and, implicitly, the revolution; above all, it undermined confidence about the future. To validate the Jews was to validate the possibility of alternate vistas. Conservatives such as John Evelyn and Paul Rycaut dismissed these "Carnal Expectations" and decried radical fantasies about the downfall of the papal Antichrist and, with them, allied fantasies about "the greatness of the Jews." Anti-Semitic riots and demonstrations erupted across central and eastern Europe in the face of Jewish jubilation. Jesuits felt threatened; Calvinist leaders saw the movement as a prelude to conversion.[26]

The slowness of the Turkish government to react to this massive social breakdown, at once utterly unarmed and yet altogether revolutionary, is surprising. Government leniency is downright amazing, all the more so given the habitual brutality in suppressing uprisings. Finally at the end of 1665, the Smyrna authorities expelled Sabbatai from the city, whereupon he traveled with a small party to Constantinople, possibly intending to meet the sultan. There he was immediately arrested, met with the Grand Vizier, and, against all expectation, was not executed but returned to prison where he soon lived in comfortable conditions. In April he was transferred to a prison in Gallipoli where in lavish circumstances he held court as though he were the impending messiah-king. In September the government at last decided to act and had him taken back to Constantinople. In some respects this is the high point of the Sabbatean movement because many believed that the sultan would now relinquish authority to the messiah. Events proved otherwise. Sabbatai was given the choice of either execution or conversion to Islam. The deeply religious Mehemed IV and several Muslim clerics apparently hoped that Sabbatai would lead the Jews en masse to Islam. Faced with this stark choice, Sabbatai and his wife did indeed convert. Even so, they did little to encourage others to follow their example and wore their new faith lightly.

It is unlikely that Sabbatai's decision was either cynical or craven. He seems to have believed that his apostasy comprised a spiritual act, a final confrontation with sin, a drawing out of the last bits of divine light from among the shards of evil, and that thereby he had begun the final stage before the messianic age. He had taken on the greatest burden, assumed the greatest guilt to achieve the fullest possible redemption. Two of his most loyal and prominent followers, Nathan and Abraham Cardoso, subsequently developed highly articulated theologies about these themes. Nathan also did more. He visited congregations, shored up faith, and eventually traveled to Rome where he performed some sort of magical rite that exorcized the other great center of spiritual wickedness. Here was the counterpoint to Sabbatai's sacrifice. Here too was an odd analogue to long-standing Protestant eschatological objectives, a spiritual confrontation with the two great Antichrists which would lead to their final overthrow.

From the modern perspective, Sabbatai's decision must have been surely the right choice. His martyrdom could only have resulted in extensive bloodshed. For most Jewish contemporaries, however, the reaction was disbelief, shock, and then shame. The affair resulted in ridicule and the greatest humiliation. How could the Jews have rejected Jesus and then be taken in by such an obvious impostor? In Amsterdam the Jewish congregation confiscated Sabbatean prayer books and imposed a ban even on pronouncing his name. That became the view almost entirely throughout Europe: the utter execration of the great "false" messiah. Jewish messianism had a long life ahead of it and still informs the modern world, but Sabbateanism continued in an organized way only among the extraordinary sectarian groups known as the Dönmeh ("converted") Jews. The Dönmeh followed Sabbatai into apostasy and assumed a comparable messianic responsibility. Outwardly they were in every respect orthodox Muslims, but privately they practiced Sabbatean Judaism. This world, like the messiah's, was drastically inverted, an outward lie lived on behalf of an inward truth. For the present, the messianic age was realized within the community, but under cover. This redeemed world had restored the body along with the spirit, and at times expressed that restoration through radical and transgressive sexuality. Profoundly pious and surprisingly cohesive, these groups persisted largely undetected into the middle twentieth century.

The later actions of Sabbatai and Nathan against Constantinople and Rome may have paralleled Protestant aspirations. The effect of the Sabbatean debacle, however, was disastrous for radical Protestantism and millenarian expectations. Conservative voices sounded loudly, often triumphantly, in the decades that followed, discrediting messianism and millenarianism as fundamentally linked (which in significant ways they were). As one anonymous author put it: "I the more willingly give Readers the History of this Impostor, because it borders very much on the Ground with the Pretensions of our *Prophets*."[27] The derisive German illustration of Naylor and Sabbatai (Figure 7.3) made the point emphatically. As early as that climactic year 1666, Sabbatai had already earned the epithet "a Quaker Jew." Radical reformers of all sorts found Sabbatai an acute embarrassment and, not unlike most Jews, sought to distance themselves from the painful episode. Serrarius almost alone among Protestant intellectuals kept faith with Sabbatai even in his apostasy.

Figure 7.3 *Anabaptisticum et Enthusiasticum; pantheon und geistliches Rüst-Haus wider die alten Quacker, und neuen Frey-Geiste* (n.p., 1702), attributed to Johann Friedrich Corvinus (d. 1724). This illustration seeks to discredit millenarian eschatology. "The new monarchy" (i.e., the fifth from Daniel) is associated with the self-proclaimed messianic kings James Naylor ("King of the Quakers, in the year 1657"—actually 1656) and Sabbatai Şevi ("King of the Jews, in the year 1666"). Folded into Naylor's cloak is "Bossheit" (malice), "Quacker" (a play on "Quackelei" meaning silly talk, nonsense, or babble, and "Quacksalber" meaning quack or charlatan), "Frey-Geister" (free spirit), and "Ehrgeiz" (ambition). Lying across Sabbatai's cloak are the Talmud and the Koran. On the table lies an orb, over which are a crossed scepter and sword; these in turn support an imperial crown. Despite Sabbatai being Jewish-Muslim, the crown is Christian. It would be hard for Europeans to imagine the symbolism of the Last World Emperor in any other way.

Linking Quakers with Jews had become a fairly standard way of attacking radical religion. Even before the debacles initiated by Naylor and Sabbatai,

The parallels between Sabbatai's movement and that of the Quakers may have proven still greater than either they or their critics ever realized. Both in their way had discovered a "realized apocalypse," an eschatology that manifested itself as personal salvation, what Gershom Scholem has called the "retroversion of the Messianic doctrine."[28] Arising from Sabbatean centers in eastern European, this interiorized faith, subsequently known as Hasidism, found the messianic in daily life, in a charismatic spirituality, and even in the natural order rather than through the Fifth Monarchy. Sabbateanism had such spectacular success because it tapped into the powerful apocalyptic expectations suffusing the Jewish world. These spiritual energies did not simply dissipate after 1666, but became redirected. Like Quakerism, Hasidism looked to

←—————————————————————————————

that association had already played a part in undermining the Whitehall Conference of 1655, that had been convened to consider readmitting the Jews into England. Sabbatai himself seems to have acquired the epithet "Jewish Quaker" as early as 1666.

"Enthusiasm" (Enthusiasticum) became a buzz-word by the late seventeenth century for direct inspiration, fanaticism, madness, and social upheaval. We have already encountered the term in the 1680s with Thomas Burnet in chapter 6 and will consider its eighteenth-century meanings in chapter 8. The illustration comprises a warning against the dangers of "enthusiasm."

Nevertheless, these figures comprise no small irony. Not long after Naylor's entry into Bristol and Sabbatai's into Constantinople, both movements developed an interiorized faith, an internalized apocalypse. These theologies—later Quakerism and Hasidism—became increasingly quietist rather than disruptive.

Further, if the commonplace association of Quakers, Baptists, and other "enthusiasts" with Jews had become a way of discrediting radical religion, there actually were connections between these religious groups (of which the author was probably unaware). The apocalyptic expectations of early Quakers such as Margaret Fell and Samuel Fisher made them much exercised by the Jews. Sabbateanism, it now seems, drew on Christian ideas—as the year 1666 (greatly resonant for Christians, not in the least for Jews) might suggest.

This crude, mocking, *fin-de-siècle* caricature contrasts with the engravings that Rembrandt van Rijn created at mid-century for Menasseh's messianic *Piedra Gloriosa, O Estatua Nabuchadnosor* (The Glorious Stone, or the Statue of Nebuchadnezzar). None of these pictures is actually secular, but the earlier apocalyptic idealism has come under attack, and the caricature forms part of the effort to marginalize it. As with the choice between Marvell and Dryden, moderns will probably feel closer to mid-century radicalism than late-century reaction. (*Rare Books Division, The New York Public Library, Astor, Lenox and Tilden Foundations*) prophets rather than professors, disdained clerical pretensions for direct illumination (and illumined leaders), and on that basis discounted textual authority. In the case of the Hasidic movement, the Torah faced subversion; in the case of the Quakers, it would be scripture itself.

From the outset, Fox had claimed that the most significant parts of scripture lay in its prophecies and eschatological visions, and that in exactly the same way present illumination rather than ancient texts were decisive. No Quaker pressed this line of thinking more systematically or more devastatingly than did the university-trained Samuel Fisher (1605–1665). In his extraordinary and dense *Rusticus ad academicos ... The Rusticks ALARM to the Rabbies* (1660; reprinted 1679), Fisher attacked a leading Congregationalist critic, John Owen (1616–1683)—along with such other mainline clergy as Thomas Danson, John Tombes, and Richard Baxter—for their narrow focus on the language of scripture. Owen had missed its spirit for linguistic technicalities, and that had left him "poor, and wretched, and miserable, and blind, and naked."[29] At issue was not getting the passage right, but whether *any* reading of scripture could be right. Fisher argued with formidable erudition that a serious examination of the versions of the Bible now extant and a serious consideration of the book's history and transmission could only lead to one conclusion: the original text of the Bible had become hopelessly corrupted. The constricted humanist debate, for all its learning, fell before still larger humanist considerations. The only true religion consequently came from within, and that "inner light" could be found everywhere.

Accordingly, in 1656 Fisher had set off to convert both the pope and the sultan to Quakerism—much in the pattern of Molkho and Abulafia before him, and of Sabbatai and Nathan subsequently. It should not surprise us that Fisher was strongly philo-Semitic and bitterly criticized those lukewarm philo-Semites who had hesitated and hung back during the Whitehall Conference. Nor should it surprise us that, en route to Italy and the Near East, Fisher visited the Quaker mission to the Jews in Amsterdam and, reportedly, met amicably with Jewish leaders. Inward faith need not foreclose direct action.

These interiorized forms of apocalyptic piety in Judaism and Christianity did not arise from "the experience of defeat," but had always been present. The events of the 1660s merely intensified and developed this dimension. Further, there are some indications that European spirituality generally became more inward-looking during these years. Even so, apocalyptic activism continued to manifest itself in a great many ways. There had existed all along alternatives both to the British Republic and to Sabbatai Şevi.

Alternate Polities and Alternate Messiahs

While in England Menasseh encountered the royalist millenarian Arise Evans. Evans told the rabbi that if he sought the messiah, he needed look no further than to the exiled Charles II. Menasseh remained unconvinced, but the proposal was not a priori preposterous. From biblical times Jewish tradition had allowed for an alternate kind of messiah, one who was neither a religious leader nor even a Jew. There might appear a political figure, a latter-day Cyrus, who would protect the Jews and perhaps, still more, restore the Jewish state thereby ending the exile. Messiahship was available in a variety of forms, and just about all of them cropped up in the charged religious culture of early modern Europe.

Menasseh may not have found himself impressed by Charles Stuart, but others did. One such was the Sephardic Rabbi Judah Leon (1603–1675). A noted biblical scholar, Leon had become famous and acquired the surname "Templo" for constructing what was thought to be an exact model of Solomon's Temple. Here was a matter of huge importance because the building was supposed to have been designed by God himself and thus its structure allowed observers to enter directly into the divine intellect. Leon took his model to England and presented it to the restored Charles because of the role the king was expected to play in achieving the messianic age. Presumably that would entail rebuilding the Temple. The king, yet another latter-day Constantine, now conveniently had at hand the model for the project. Similarly, John Durie and, briefly, Petrus Serrarius placed their hopes in Charles to perform acts crucial to the millennium, and as always that involved the Jews. Serrarius told Durie of his hope that the king's restoration prefigured the Jewish restoration and bore "some Shadow and Type of that Great Restitution of the Kingdom in Israel."[30] The great reaction restored "order" and combated "enthusiasm," but apocalyptic expectations and eschatological hopes remained very much alive, and such as Dryden could manipulate to telling effect.

Other potential messiahs manqués of this sort were available. Among them was Christina, Gustavus Adolphus's daughter and abdicated queen of Sweden, whose developed eschatology and Jewish connections gave some plausibility to such claims. By far the most compelling candidate in the later seventeenth century was Louis XIV. Louis was, quite self-consciously, the direct heir of the Hapsburgs and their eschatological mission. Unlike them, however, he was not burdened by the problem of New Christians and the preoccupation with "clean" blood. There were heretics aplenty, but none doubted the efficacy of conversion; there were no cultural fifth columnists. The French environment allowed for philo-Semitism; for many, the Last World Empire enjoined it.

In mid-century France Isaac La Peyrère (1596–1676) pressed apocalyptic philo-Semitism to conclusions in some ways more subversive than anything produced by the contemporaneous British Revolution. Originally a French Calvinist, La Peyrère is part of the Protestant eschatological preoccupation that began in the 1590s. The new eschatology, especially prominent in Calvinism, became strongly future-oriented, often specifically millenarian. It would also become increasingly bipolar. On the one hand the struggle against the papal Antichrist in the West became ever more articulated and detailed; on the other, the activities of the Jews, culminating with the restoration of Israel in the East, developed as a prophetic narrative altogether unprecedented within Christianity. This bipolarity is very visible in Brightman. Protestant writers, such as Henry Finch in 1621, could write about the latter quite independently of the anti-Roman struggle. La Peyrère—whose eschatological thought, he tells us, had begun the 1620s—went still further and focused exclusively on the story of Jewish conversion, Christian-Jewish reconciliation, and the creation of a Jewish kingdom that would initiate the millenarian-messianic age. Antichrist, for La Peyrère, dropped out of the picture altogether. Accordingly, the creation of an acceptable Judeo-Christianity became the decisive event in the culmination of the human experience. La Peyrère devoted his life to devising such a recast faith, and, inherently with it, harmonizing the Jewish and Christian understanding of the sacred drama—their historical pasts, their apocalyptic visions of the future. Only this profound integration of the two traditions could realize La Peyrère's all-consuming millenarian hopes.

The result proved extraordinary, and extraordinarily explosive. Probably La Peyrère's least controversial proposal was a drastically stripped-down Christianity that would prove minimally offensive to the Jews and to which they could convert. This church for the Jews offered the fewest possible ceremonies, with sacraments reduced to baptism and the Eucharist (the latter serving as a means of social control). Doctrines, creeds, dogmas, theology would be of the barest sort, and derived from Old Testament sources. Pagan accretions would be eliminated. The Jewish church would therefore resemble the early Christian church which, after all, had comprised a highly Jewish form of Christianity; at moments La Peyrère's proposed new faith almost sounds like puritan simplicity, a Judeo-Calvinism. Still more like the early church, and again like Protestantism, the focus of La Peyrère's Jewish Christianity was on history, eschatology, and the immediate future. That, of course, was its entire purpose. La Peyrère went further than any Christian contemporary in projecting an integrated faith. Although his formulation still remained Christianity's triumph, it could only have given pause to even the most determined philo-Semites.

Integrating biblical history and competing eschatologies into a common vision proved much more subversive. The story of mankind, La Peyrère maintained, involved four stages: the period under nature, the period under the law, the period under grace, and the period under glory. Humanity had at the outset lived literally in "the State of Nature," a condition that was utterly brutish, bestial, and much as La Peyrère's contemporary Thomas Hobbes had proposed it. Life in it was inherently sinful, but not unlawful because there existed no law. At some subsequent point God in his mysterious wisdom created the Jews, and the first Jew was Adam. Adam was the "first parent" of the Jews and the "mystical prince" to the remainder of mankind. With Adam came the Law, the standards of right and wrong that applied to everyone. Thus there had been men before Adam, and these had existed for an indefinite period. Further, human beings had arisen from more than one act of creation. La Peyrère made clear that God had created the Jews from the same stuff as everyone else and consequently there could be no physical or racial superiority. But, crucially, the Jews were an elect people, literally and uniquely the children of God. Finally, it followed that the story presented in the Old Testament simply narrated the history of the Jews. Everything it described was no more than a regional phenomenon. Mosaic law pertained only to the Jews. The sun stood still only for the locals. The Great Flood comprised a

Palestinian inundation. Jewish history in the Bible now ceased to be the master narrative for the human experience. At the same time, the Jews stood squarely and alone at the center of the sacred drama and human redemption—history insofar as it had cosmic meaning.

Adam's transgression of the law became "imputed" to everyone else, including, La Peyrère emphasized in a Calvinist voice, all children. Moreover, Adam's violation also "imputed backward" to the wild primitives who had inhabited the earlier State of Nature. All of this was necessary, even benign, for, as La Peyrère put it, "They had perished, had they not perished."[31] Only legal transgression could be exculpated and redeemed by the savior, the second Adam, who fulfilled the Law of Adam (not Moses), and launched the era of grace. Because the Jews rejected Jesus (and indeed killed him), they were themselves rejected. They had been grievously punished by God through the exile and also through the darkening of their skins. But their status basically remained unchanged. It was a grave sin for Christians to persecute them. If the Jews had sinned by persecuting and killing the son of God, so the Christians now came close to the same thing by persecuting and killing the sons of God. The rejection of the Jews had the positive consequence of opening the door for the Gentiles, allowing them to participate in the historical redemption.

The coming of Judaism's Messiah, Jesus, and the return of Christianity's redeemer, also Jesus, lay in the immediate future. This event required the conversion of the Jews, something unlikely to happen in a context of persecution and cruelty, actions which therefore obstructed human redemption and destiny. The creation of the pure Judeo-Christianity was also an obvious imperative. Still more was needed for the transition from the time of grace to the time of glory. La Peyrère turned at this point to a highly traditional idea, the French version of Last World Empire. By the mid-sixteenth century the French vision carried potentially conflicted meanings, while subsequently during the crisis of the religious wars it became eclipsed by civic values and anti-imperial vocabularies. Signs of change occurred after 1600, however, when Henri IV consolidated power and imperial aspirations recovered their voice. Very much a part of the world of Richelieu, the imperial eschatology had a long future ahead of it. European Jewry had historically looked to authoritarian monarchy for protection, and, in its desperate struggle for survival, seventeenth-century French Protestantism might well do the same. It is from this context that La Peyrère visualized the future and the transition to the Messianic-Millenarian era. The Jews would be recalled when they joined with Christians, especially in France. The French kingdom made sense because it was the land of freedom, for the country had no slaves—the contrast apparently being made with Hapsburg Iberia and the Ottoman Empire.

Once they converted, the king of France would lead them back to Palestine which then would inaugurate the time of glory, the period of universal redemption that apparently continues forever. Christ would return to rule the world with the French king from Jerusalem, and they would do so through the Jews. Although salvation is universal, the Jews would comprise the spiritual elite who guide the world as Christ's agents or courtiers, just as historically they had comprised the elect and in some sense never lost that status. A number of special Jews, seven thousand of them, would not even need to convert. Their spirituality is such that they can intuit the Christian message through Judaism, and in the final age they would play a uniquely elevated role even among the Jews.

La Peyrère's understanding of scripture derived, he insisted, from scripture itself. Further, viewed within La Peyrère's framework many of the long-standing problems in the text now could be solved. If the Bible's message still seemed at times unclear or contradictory, that resulted from the corruptions that had occurred through "the carelessnesse of the Transcribers." "Who will make it good ... that these are the originals we now have?"[32] La Peyrère devised many of the critical arguments about the history and condition of the extant text that Samuel Fisher was concurrently developing. Both agreed that Moses did not write the Pentateuch. Both agreed that much of scripture was unreliable and corrupted. Yet they differed fundamentally in their conclusions. The Quaker Fisher confronted his Calvinist critics with the proposition that the meaning of the Bible has been irretrievably lost: whether we "have the 20th or 100th part" of what the prophets and apostles wrote "is more than you or I or any man knows."[33] The Calvinist La Peyrère firmly believed that its meaning, message, and significance could in fact be confidently restored. Once we saw what the Bible was, its meaning could be made clear. The results might be shocking, overturning commonplace verities, but people should not find themselves troubled as a result. Like the Copernican hypothesis, the new reading of scripture did not change or in any way unhinge daily life or the order of society. La

Peyrère also saw his biblical analysis as similar to Columbus's search for new worlds. Unlike Columbus who had suffered dearly, La Peyrère believed himself born "in a better age" and prayed that his argument, an essay in every sense, might "fairly be received."[34]

Despite his disclaimers, La Peyrère's analysis of scripture, *Prae-Adamitae* (1655), translated as *Men before Adam* (1656), brought forth a ferocious reaction. It also brought personal disaster. In February 1656, while residing in the Spanish Netherlands, he was arrested at the behest of the archbishop of Malines. With the prospect of an indefinite imprisonment and possibly with the experience of Campanella in mind, La Peyrère agreed to convert to Catholicism, abjure his claims about the Bible, and apologize to the pope. In his abjuration he maintained that he had been misled by Calvinism: "Donc si j'estois Calvniste, je serois Preadamite."[35] He had relied on reason and conscience in reading scripture rather seeking the judgment of the proper authority on such matters, the papacy. We should surely take La Peyrère at his word at least in one sense: Calvinism indeed had initiated his eschatological preoccupations. His conversion did not eliminate them, however, and he continued to research and reformulate his views in an effort to make them acceptable. His abjuration, after all, indicated that his reading scripture was wrong because it conflicted with authority, not because it had been directly refuted. In these new circumstances, La Peyrère, rather like Campanella, gave the pope the organizational role formerly assigned to the French crown. In the end the Last World Empire would prove papal rather than royal, governed by an angelic pope instead of a messianic prince.

Despite La Peyrère's flattering vision, Pope Alexander VII declined to become a latter-day (Christian) Alexander the Great. Louis XIV did indeed take up the mantel of the Last World Empire, but not the Jewish cause. La Peyrère probably would have found the most sympathetic ear in Oliver Cromwell, but the Lord Protector steadfastly refused to be an emperor or even a king.

BARUCH DE SPINOZA: APOCALYPSE CONFRONTED

The three earliest works of recognizably modern biblical criticism, all of them foundational, were written by men deeply immersed in the apocalypse: Thomas Hobbes's *Leviathan* (1651); Isaac La Peyrère's

Prae-Adamitae (1655), and Samuel Fisher's *Rusticus ad Academicos* (1660). More than simply the apocalypse, all three authors were millenarians. All three were philo-Semitic in the sense that they expected the Jews to play a major role in the events that initiated the millennium. In other ways they could hardly have been more different. Fisher was an illumined Quaker spiritualist. Hobbes was archetypally the anti-illumined mechanist. La Peyrère was a Catholic convert whose thought arose in a Calvinist environment. Nevertheless, all three made eschatology defining rather than incidental to their thought. All three developed their critiques of scripture as a direct consequence of their millenarian commitments. The apocalypse, far more than humanism, made the Bible a historical text—and consequently a vulnerable text.

Ostensibly nothing could differ more completely than did the millenarians from Baruch de Spinoza (1632–1677), whose *Tractatus-Theologico-Politicus* (1670) systematically eliminated all revelation and any cognition beyond human reason. Hobbes, La Peyrère, and Fisher accepted that there existed an inspired text. The issue was its meaning or what might be gleaned from its extant remains. Spinoza flatly rejected the Bible's special status as a divine oracle. Yet the transition from radical religion to the radical critique of religion—or radical irreligion, to those outraged by it—may be less than first appears.

Spinoza, we know, encountered the millenarians intellectually and even personally during the 1650s and early 1660s when his own thought was gestating, and, while questions of "influence" with so original a mind are unlikely to be sorted out, similarities between their arguments can prove arresting. Like La Peyrère, Spinoza saw the Old Testament as a purely Jewish history, in itself largely irrelevant to the rest of humanity. Both agreed that Mosaic Law spoke to the Jews alone. Moreover, Spinoza's analysis of the current state of the text makes many of the same points that Samuel Fisher had developed at length. Both Fisher and Spinoza further agreed that the Word of God would remain recognizable even if all scripture disappeared. Both found in the central message of the Bible to be an ethical statement, effectively the Golden Rule. The overlap can hardly have been simply fortuitous.

The corpus of new criticism that emerged after 1650 shifted forever the ways in which people viewed and debated the Bible and its meaning. A sacred text became for all sides, inescapably, a historical document. The new criticism differed utterly from late sixteenth-century skepticism. The issues concerned history rather than logic. They comprised puzzles about events and society rather than about human reason and its limitations.

Spinoza's personal connections with the millenarians also appear telling. It is thought that after about late 1654, nearly two years before his excommunication from the Amsterdam Jewish community, Spinoza was in contact with Adam Boreel and may have participated in meetings of the "college" that Boreel had helped to found a decade earlier. The Collegiants were members of an ecumenical, nondenominational discussion-prayer group that rejected all ceremony, all theology, all dogma, and all clerical pretension. They sought to attract people of many persuasions, including Jews. Established in a number of Dutch cities, the Collegiants clearly supported toleration but lacked the political aspirations of contemporaneous English revolutionaries. Rather like Quaker meetings, their gatherings were egalitarian conventicles where anyone could speak and "free prophesy" reigned. The membership was radical in yet another way. They were overwhelming millenarian— chiliast Christians, unconfined by any church at all. By the time of his excommunication, Spinoza was not only speaking with Collegiant millenarians, he was living with them.

The Collegiants found Spinoza appealing because of his knowledge of Hebrew and the Torah, and doubtless also because he carried a special status by being a learned Jew who seemed sympathetic to Christianity. From Spinoza's perspective, their focus on ethics, toleration, and a world without a clergy or organized religion spoke to what would become prominent features of his thought. Spinoza's connections with the Quakers expanded during 1656 when he became familiar with the Amsterdam Quaker leader William Ames (d. 1662) and possibly also with Fisher; it has long been thought that at this time Spinoza translated into Hebrew two tracts addressed to the Jews by the "nursing mother" of Quakerism, Margaret Fell (1614–1702).

Despite their criticism of orthodoxy, their shared values, their overlapping intellectual projects, their common sense of what was wrong with contemporary society, Spinoza of course differed decisively from his Anglo-Dutch millenarian acquaintances and friends. If he always maintained strong connections with millenarians and individuals immersed in the apocalypse—Oldenburg and Boyle come to mind— his thinking nevertheless altogether rejected the religious foundation of their assumptions. All of these people except Spinoza understood the reality they perceived about them, its prospects and meaning, through sacralized and eschatological terms. For Spinoza, God inhered within a single substance accessible solely through reason. Consequently, there existed no elect people, for "in respect of understanding and true virtue there is no distinction between one nation and another."[36] Nor did any institution, text, or history enjoy special status. The gulf could only be profound. However, an extraordinary range of English revolutionaries could derive highly rational, secular-sounding outlooks from mystical and eschatological foundations. Winstanley's Behemist spiritualism consistently led to an appeal to the reason all men shared. In the Dutch context Spinoza's intimate friend, Pieter Balling (d. 1664), can illustrate how close the transition from universal "inner light" to universal "inner reason" could be. Balling was a Mennonite merchant of some substance, a Collegiant and also a Cartesian. In 1662 he published *Het Licht op den Kandelear* (The Light on the Candlestick) which spoke at length about the "inner light," and its "Quaker-like" character persuaded many that its author was William Ames. Yet Balling's "inner light" elided into the "clear and distinct ideas" of Descartes. The *Licht* subsequently appeared in an English translation produced by the Quaker Benjamin Furly (1636–1714) and thereafter entered the Quaker canon. Spiritualism and rationalism were not for Balling the polarities we would instinctively think them today. Nor were they for a number of Quaker intellectuals. The inner light, Fisher insisted, did not simply comprise a private revelation, the mystical illumination of the individual, but was rather "the Common Light and Publick Spirit of God, which is one and the same in all."[37]

The trajectory of Spinoza's thought is surely not that suggested by Balling's tract—even if the philosopher may have helped shape the piece. Spinoza is the first genuinely secular individual to be encountered in these pages. He did not decry the apocalypse, nor did he spiritualize the apocalypse, nor did he doubt the apocalypse. Spinozist metaphysics precluded the apocalypse. No earlier thinking so anticipates this conclusion. Nevertheless, Spinoza's outlook, objectives, politics, and sensibility have much in common with the radical millenarians.

Spinoza's Bible criticism, like that of La Peyrère and Fisher before him, emphasized context: the Bible was what it was and required no rationalization, no scholastic integration with Greek thought, no Great

Chain of Being. It spoke to the people of its time and enjoined laws in order to promote morality where such would not otherwise exist. But its status did not differ from Livy's histories or from any comparable litera-ture. It was time-bound, limited, language-based, as the truths of Euclid were not. If Spinoza did offer an analysis of the Bible's development, its constituencies, and its contextual meaning, the philosopher's "geo-metric" method did not offer or encourage an alternative to sacred his-tory. For all of its power, Spinoza's system remained fundamentally atemporal. A world without the apocalypse remained a world without a master narrative. The creation of a secular account of qualitative change—truly secular history—still lay ahead.

For many Quakers and Jews, radicals both east and west, an inter-iorized faith gradually pushed back the eschaton. It sacralized or ener-gized the everyday, sought a utopia of the commonplace. It made everyman his own messiah, redeeming a world that was all his own. Unlike late twentieth-century analogues, however, these developments proved neither quietist, nor nihilist, nor narcissistic, nor reactionary. Rather, they both contributed to an intellectual revolution of the first importance, challenging scriptural authority and subverting clerical power. In so doing they shaped the foundations of the Enlightenment.

The Quakers also did more. Neither as a confrontational counter-culture nor as a sectarian one did Quakerism ultimately undermine civic life and public values. No more than did Dryden. Nor did the Quakers subsequently neutralize the apocalypse or simply personalize sacred time. Just the reverse, they would become a part of politics—bringing with them all their extraordinary radicalism.

CHAPTER 8

PROPHECY, ENLIGHTENMENT, AND THE DEMOCRATIC REVOLUTIONS

Ever since the late eighteenth century militant reactionaries have sought to debunk progressivist ideologies and revolutionary programs by portraying them as consisting of recast eschatologies, warmed-over religious fantasies. The theocrat Louis viscomte de Bonald greeted (and dismissed) Condorcet's *Sketch for a Historical Picture of the Progress of the Human Mind* in 1795 as "l'*Apocalypse* de ce nouvel *Evangile*." Here was the sacred drama for the new gospel of the rights of man and democratic republicanism. In much the same way a century and a half later, the Cold Warrior Norman Cohn found in Marxism a "subterranean revolutionary eschatology." Both Bonald and Cohn intended to discredit the revolutionary past and thereby foreclose the prospect of a radical future. Neither Condorcet's "social mathematics" nor Marx's political economy mattered very much, for they merely overlay the fanaticism of a debased spirituality.[1] Condorcet and Marx, however, were profoundly secularizing thinkers, integral figures in that singular European achievement, a genuinely secular culture—and quite the opposite of such primitive and self-serving caricatures. The intimate connection between the apocalypse and modernity lies elsewhere and requires a much different approach.

Many of the central constructs and most powerful insights created by radical eschatology during the seventeenth century became key elements within the Enlightenment in the century that followed. But its programmatic heart, however immanent, would disappear. The argument from design, however subtle, would gradually dissipate. The cause of events overtook the course of events, human agency supplanted the divine plan. Deism made any such design unknowable, and successive deisms made it remote to the vanishing point within a universe inhabited by thinking matter.

FRANCIS BACON TO DENIS DIDEROT

Perhaps no one provides a better illustration of the transition from apocalypse to secular culture than does that pillar of the radical Enlightenment and leading *philosophe*, Denis Diderot (1713–1784). Co-editor of the Enlightenment's foundational *Encyclopedia* (1751–1765), Diderot found his model for the great work in Francis Bacon. Specifically citing *The Advancement of Learning*, he insisted that knowledge comprised a collective undertaking and could never fit within the hourglass of one man's life or that of a single generation. Truth was indeed the daughter of time. It required public effort, not private endeavor, the uncompromisingly civic space that the apocalypse had so powerfully injected into European culture. It consequently required as well the interaction of a great many men endowed with widely varied "special talents," all joined together "by their zeal for the best interests of the human race and a feeling of mutual good will." These needed to be men "of different sorts and conditions."[2]

Again like Bacon, Diderot strongly validated the mechanical arts: Let us pull "the mechanical arts up from the debasement where prejudice has held them for so long.... Artisans have believed themselves worthy of scorn because we have scorned them; let us teach them to think better of themselves: it is the only way to obtain more perfect productions."[3] With Bacon's revolutionary successors, Diderot imagined artisans actively engaged in the great project. Artisans were proto-scientists, and their empirical experience was needed to verify any mathematical hypothesis. Contributors to the *Encyclopedia* would enter the workshops armed with questionnaires to ferret out information and insight that undergirded even the most rarified natural science. Accordingly, once more like both Bacon and the English revolutionaries, Diderot too projected a leveling of wits. He evinced an abiding distrust of "genius."

> I have often thought how fortunate a nation would be if it never produced a man of exceptional ability under whose aegis an art still in its infancy makes its first too-rapid and too-ambitious steps forward, thereby interrupting its natural, imperceptible rhythm of development.... When the arts and sciences advance by imperceptible degrees, one man will not differ enough from another man to inspire the latter with awe, to lay the foundations of a new style or form the national taste.[4]

If the West's encounter with Aristotle had taught anything, it surely taught that. It might well take a Newton or a Leibniz to invent calculus, but any schoolboy could learn calculus, verify it, and, quite possibly, correct its applications. The genius of Bacon was to see through genius. Relative equality became crucial to the advancement of learning and to human progress.

Public life as proposed in the *Encyclopedia* mandated openness. There could be no place either for trade secrets or for state secrets. Like the Enlightenment of which he was so centrally a part, Diderot's undertaking could only be unflinchingly universalist. Those who worried about national interests surely knew "as well as anyone that the average duration of empires is less than two thousand years, and that in a briefer period of time, perhaps, the name *Frenchman*—a name that will endure forever in history—will be sought in vain on the surface of the earth.... it seems the word *humanity* is for them a word without meaning."[5] Diderot doubtless saw himself as a patriot, a term that had entered French (along with the modern meanings of citizenship and the public good) during the 1570s. Romantic nationalism and the preoccupation with "identity," however, lay as yet well over the horizon. Still again, he is at one with Bacon and the revolutionaries.

Nevertheless, despite his claims, despite his adoption of so many concepts originating with Bacon, despite his manifest admiration for the English chancellor, Diderot was no Baconian. The apocalypse had dropped out of Diderot's vision, and consequently so too had Bacon. For the same reason, despite their shared hostility to clergy, monarchy, and aristocracy, Diderot was also distanced from the radicals of the British Revolution. Diderot stood on the other side of the Newtonian divide where society and nature had become fundamentally detached and where no apocalyptic program would ever draw them together. The human mind and the reality we inhabit are not coterminous; our understanding of that reality is inherently and forever limited by our capabilities. As Diderot put it,

> if one banishes from the face of the earth the thinking and contemplating entity, man, then the sublime and moving spectacle of nature will be but a sad and silent scene; the universe will be hushed; darkness and silence will regain their sway. All will be changed into a vast solitude where unobserved phenomena take their course unseen and unheard. It is only the presence of men that makes the existence of other beings significant. What better plan, then, in writing the history of these beings, than to subordinate oneself to this consideration? Why should we not introduce man into our *Encyclopedia*, giving him the same place that he occupies in the universe? Why should we not make him the center of all that is?[6]

Knowledge thus becomes a social construction and can never be other (or more) than man-based. Here was a proposition that neither Bacon, nor the most determined revolutionary, nor the most radical intellect from the previous century could have imagined, much less accepted. Diderot would organize the *Encyclopedia* around the main human faculties, but he readily agreed that another arrangement might work every bit as well—that is, so long as it was founded on human bases and not on "a cold, insensitive, silent being in the place of man." Here too was less a celebration of human grandeur than a recognition of human limits, and, as Keith Baker noted long ago, a tone suggestive of Blaise Pascal's "disproportion" between mind and reality.[7] Unlike Pascal, however, Diderot looked not to solitary Jansenist faith but to "public effort" that would produce better answers even if not final answers.

NEWTON TO VOLTAIRE: ENDING THE *ESPRIT DE SYSTÈME*

Few people can have been more different than Isaac Newton and his French promoter and interpreter François-Marie Arouet, Voltaire (1694–1778). Newton's providential, universe-sustaining Lord God of

Dominion conflicts utterly with the absent God of Voltaire's deism. Naturally enough, Voltaire had no time for Newton's apocalyptic speculations; the great Englishman's interest in "chronology" was merely a hobby, something "he played with for relaxation."[8] Newtonian eschatology—to the extent that Voltaire knew of it through his published work—need not be taken seriously; such silliness reassured us that this remarkable mind was, after all, only human. Newton's physics, in stark contrast, was of the utmost importance, for it not only described the mechanics of the universe, but also provided the standard for what constituted an adequate explanation of natural phenomena. Still more and crucially, it made scientific inquiry a public and temporalized undertaking—mandating nothing less than the idea of progress.

Voltaire laid out the Newtonian system with compelling clarity (and little mathematics) in a range of works, but none better known than his *Philosophical Letters* (1732–1733). In this influential work Voltaire declared that since no one could ever agree on what a "soul" was—much less whether it was immortal or if it could be distinguished from matter—all questions about it were not worth asking. This kind of debate was altogether *mal posée*, the reddest of herrings. Worse, it impeded the pursuit of knowledge concerning matters where we could agree, and, by implication, we should leave the Great Chain of Being to Dr. Pangloss. These remarks might carry devastating implications for organized religion, but Voltaire remained undeterred. "Theologians," he continued, "have a bad habit of complaining that God is outraged when someone has simply failed to be of their opinion."[9] Theologians in the French Catholic Church did indeed take these observations rather badly, and in 1734 the work was condemned, banned, and publicly burnt. Voltaire himself fled to relative safety in semi-autonomous Lorraine.

Obscurantist clerics, however powerful, were the least of Voltaire's problems, at least intellectually. Voltaire's comments on the "soul" really served to underwrite the Newtonian universe against sophisticated, anticlerical critics, most notably Bernard de Fontenelle (1657–1757) and Bernard-Joseph Saurin (1706–1781). Unlike the British, French intellectuals saw the cosmos operating on fundamentally Cartesian principles. The planets circle the sun propelled in gigantic vortices or whirlpools of "subtle matter." No such fluid existed for the Newtonians across the channel; as Voltaire trenchantly put it, the skies over London were empty, while those over Paris were full. Everyone knew that Cartesian mechanics entailed serious problems: comets that moved in the wrong direction, problems with Kepler's ratios, the prospect of different fluids in different parts of the cosmos, and much else. But Newton's concept of gravity confronted what appeared to be one insurmountable obstacle. His formulae might well describe celestial behavior, but they could not *account* for it. What actually *caused* gravity? It was one thing to posit universal attraction as inherent within matter, quite another to explain it. On Newtonian terms the sun would rise tomorrow simply because ... well, it had always done so. To the Cartesians in France Newton's hidden force was in every sense an "occult quality," and in significant ways they had called their man. Despite all its difficulties the Cartesian view offered rationality, a physical operation of cause leading to effect, dominoes hitting other dominoes. Newton offered only an unexplained and perhaps unexplainable general effect. At issue between rational science and empirical science was the question of what constituted an adequate explanation. What did a "law" of nature actually tell us? Was not Newton the great reactionary threatening to overthrow the new science by making the universe a perpetual miracle—as Gottfried Leibniz and others had objected from the outset?

Voltaire faced a hard sell, as he full well knew. At one point he tried to weasel that the debate between Cartesian "impulse" and Newtonian "attraction" was no more than a quarrel about words. Newton had warned "that there would be resistance to the mere name of it." But of course the difference was fundamental. Subsequently, Voltaire has Newton say, "I use the word *attraction* only to express an effect that I have discovered in nature: the certain and indisputable effect of an unknown principle, a quality inherent in matter, of which cleverer men than I will find the cause, if they can." That prospect seemed altogether remote in 1733. The reality of gravity resulted from "its effects" being "demonstrated and proportions calculated." "The cause of that cause is in the bosom of God," and Voltaire then paraphrased Job 38:11, "Hitherto shalt thou come, but no further."[10] Here in an important way was truly Isaac Newton, the great limitation that was the Lord God of Dominion; yet it was Newton without the eschatology. What had been provisional, awaiting the eschaton, had now become the enduring standard of truth. Without the apocalypse,

Voltaire had no choice but a completely uncompromising commitment to modest Lockean empiricism. Only the familiar proposition, "what you see is what you get," could make Newton plausible. The requirements of Newton's Judeo-Calvinist God had become Voltaire's secular mandate.

Descartes' massive blunder had been to seek final answers, first principles, an overarching rationality, to indulge in metaphysical speculation. This was the tragic mistake of "the systematizing spirit," which could only lead to romance and folly, dogmatism and error. Descartes was a dreamer, Newton a sage. The human mind was not coterminus with the order of nature, and our understanding of it could never be unqualified. Voltaire put it succinctly in his dialogue between a philosopher and Nature. The philosopher asks, "My dear mother, tell me something of why you exist, of why there is anything." Nature replies, "I will answer you as, for so many centuries, I have answered all those who have asked me about first principles. I know nothing about them."[11] Nature's answers simply did not fit our questions. The worst possible option, then, would be to invent answers that we do not have or demand a design that we cannot see. But what could we actually see? With neither revelation nor final principles available to us, the standard of truth could only be our ability to agree upon it—through replication, publication, public discussion, civic society. Accompanying this standard came the assumption that people were largely the same—certainly more the same than they were different—and thus "humanity" carried enormous cognitive and epistemological weight, going well beyond allied notions of humaneness, dignity, and right.

A single remarkable generation worked this transition from rationalism and revelation to empirical contingency and the social construction of cognition. The sensationalist psychologist Etienne de Condillac (1715–1780) insisted that we were forever imprisoned in our perceptions. We could not penetrate first causes that remained forever hidden. The great naturalist Georges-Louis Buffon (1717–1788) saw general effects rather than causes as the true laws of nature. Diderot's co-editor Jean Le Rond D'Alembert (1717–1783) acknowledged that nature was not obliged to conform to our ideas. We deal with the nature of things as we know them, not as they are in themselves. Diderot's haunting observations about man providing meaning needs to be seen as part of this larger cultural transition. Scotland's David

Hume (1711–1776) spoke to the matter with characteristic directness. "While Newton seemed to draw off the veil from some of the mysteries of nature, he showed at the same time the imperfections of the mechanical philosophy, and thereby restored her ultimate secrets to that obscurity in which they ever did and ever will remain."[12]

Colin MacLauren (1698–1746), Newton's man at the University of Edinburgh, was no less emphatic. "We can never be sure we assume the principles that really obtain in nature; and that our system, after we have composed it with great labour, is not mere dream and illusion."[13]

Accordingly, Voltaire indicated in the "Micromegas" that, in the end, the book of nature was utterly blank.[14] People now occupied a contingent world, knowable through "laws" that described general effects rather than causes, and thereby told us both what we knew and what we did not. Modernity retained a distinctly Calvinist edge even after its apocalyptic catalyst had fallen away.

FROM APOCALYPSE TO PROGRESS: CONDORCET AND HISTORICAL PROBABILITY

Ever since the viscomte de Bonald sneered at the final section of Condorcet's "Sketch" for sounding "la trompette prophétique," the great philosophe has been characterized as the "prophet of progress."[15] The idea of progress was indeed one of the signal achievements of the eighteenth century, seemingly unique in world history. Increasingly a commonplace during the course of the century, the idea inevitably found expression with different emphases and different levels of confidence. Professor MacLauren thought that progress was God's compensation for denying humankind access to ultimate truth; knowledge would continually improve, even if it might never become more than provisional or perfected other than within the distinctly circumscribed terms of human capability. A rich range of variants appeared from thinkers as dissimilar as the philosophe-politician Anne-Robert-Jacques Turgot (1727–1781) and the Scots social theorist-academician Adam Ferguson (1723–1816). Among all of these figures no individual has been more closely associated with progress or become more an emblem of the historical inevitability of human triumph than Condorcet. Bonald had targeted the doctrine's foremost exponent.

Condorcet devised a psycho-linguistic theory of historical processes. Humans "attach signs" to the objects they perceive and construct linguistic interconnections among them and among subsets of them, what Condorcet called "languages" and "grammars" of knowledge. Such languages are continually reconstructed as perceptions and their symbols become more refined and are combined in ever more sophisticated and complex ways. This kind of cognitive development was natural to human beings.[16] The emergence of language in the simplest sense transformed the brute to the primitive. The invention of the alphabet transformed the human horizon by simplifying and hastening this process at an exponential level. With Greek antiquity had emerged the first secular vocabularies. Since Descartes, secular thought had become highly articulated and now at last gone on to triumph against its religious competitors.

This achievement had been spectacularly evident in natural philosophy and all but universally applauded. Similar achievements in moral philosophy, in politics, had acquired far less prominence and had been far less accepted and, in part for this reason, Condorcet was centrally concerned to construct a science of man using the powerful techniques that had been created in the study of nature. The new science had become compelling through the power of quantification: the Great Chain of Being, a hierarchy of qualitatively different essences, became transformed into mere matter and motion, understandable through mathematics because it was, simply, all the same stuff. Something similar could be done in the study of society, Condorcet believed, by adapting the new probability theory of Pierre-Simon de Laplace (1749–1827) to create a "social mathematics." Trained as a mathematician, Condorcet succeeded in devising precocious theories of decision-taking and even in laying the intellectual foundations for elements within the modern welfare state. Human knowledge, Condorcet insisted, comprised a single coherent fabric, one that resulted from a collective, public undertaking founded ultimately on the model of scientific advancement and suffused with values that had arisen from the religious dynamics of the seventeenth century.

Was there then a "subterranean" apocalyptic underlying Condorcet's historical vision? Condorcet's comments in the "Sketch," written frantically while in hiding from Robespierre's police during the final months of his life, do suggest, at moments, a built-in program. "This progress will doubtless vary in speed, but it will never be reversed as long as the earth occupies its present place in the system of the universe, and as long as the general laws of this system produced neither a general cataclysm nor such changes as will deprive the human race of its present faculties and its present resources." The invention of the alphabet "assured the progress of the human race forever." Condorcet's "general cataclysm"—at one point imagined as "a new invasion of Asia by the Tartars" that would halt the spread of enlightenment— seemed remote, even "impossible." "This progress of which we entertain a hope ... is almost a certainty."[17]

Remarks like these have shaped the reading of Condorcet from the outset with Bonald to the present; yet, as Baker has shown, any such interpretation is seriously misleading. If it was natural for people to construct ever more sophisticated language systems to describe reality, it was no less natural for them to concoct still more intricate systems of speculative invention. The "systematizing spirit" was inherent in the human condition because there would forever exist a "disproportion" between what humanity "knows, what it wishes to know, and what it believes it needs to know." Although there could be nothing inherently wrong here, a potentially devastating problem arose because these speculations served the interests of their inventors, as well as the political powers that sponsored them. Error consequently possessed a life of its own from which liberation was by no means guaranteed. "Certain prejudices have necessarily come into being at each stage of our progress, but they have extended their seductions or their empire beyond their due season, because men retain [their] prejudices ... long after they discovered all the truths necessary to destroy them."[18]

Insight was at once generated and retarded, if not defeated, by intellectuals past and present. The obstacles to progress literally comprised a *trahison des clercs*, for the primal intelligentsia of course were none other than the clergy. The ancient priestly castes had been overthrown in antiquity. Their Christian successors had experienced a similar revolution in modern times. At each juncture, however, the defeat of the sacerdotal language systems, whether devised by ancient and current religions, had occurred only through bitter struggle, revolution, and counter-revolution. History therefore provided no more than a probabilistic basis for belief in progress. It had happened in the past— admittedly a limited sample—and it might therefore be expected to occur again in the future. Progress possessed a statistical advantage, but seemingly none other. The future turned heavily on human volition rather than any pregnant past. History had no other "law" or offered any other lesson than freedom. It attested to human capability but possessed no other trajectory. Like the young Karl Marx, Condorcet sought less to analyze the world than to change it.[19] His "social mathematics" enabled men to do just that.

Along with Diderot and Voltaire, Condorcet drew directly on the thinking of the seventeenth century while completely abandoning the prophetic expectations that underwrote and informed it. Accordingly, he might celebrate Algernon Sydney, John Locke, and Francis Bacon—even writing observations on the *New Atlantis*—but the British Revolution remains a black hole. We never encounter the republicans, the Levellers, Milton, Harrington, Marvell, Cromwell—all the founders of the Atlantic Republican Tradition of which Condorcet himself was so prominently a part. This circumstance, at once anomalous and yet quite understandable, becomes highlighted by Condorcet's comments on Bacon. The chancellor not only lived "in a century still covered in the darkness of a superstitious ignorance," but also "at a time when events had not yet determined whether the inevitable fall to which kings were condemned by reason" would proceed from gradual enlightenment or violent upheaval.[20] The British Revolution occupies the room like the great elephant that none dares to mention.

As with Diderot, Condorcet could be no Baconian. Bacon's apocalypse had a terminus, Condorcet's progress was "indefinite." Bacon's apocalypse centrally envisioned the rise of Antichrist, while Condorcet's progress involved incremental improvement, comprising a straightforward linear process. The historic defeat of successive *trahisons*, the probabilistic future, and the possibility of backsliding differed qualitatively from any prophetic program. If Bacon's apocalypse validated human agency, history, the physical world, Condorcet's progress required no such validation and could only reject it.

Precisely this circumstance created for Condorcet another intellectual black hole, this time located inside the contemporaneous American Revolution. The American republic had been a beacon to the world, and, prior to the French Revolution, the freest society in the world. Its principles could only lead to the end of slavery. Even if ideas about Benthamite "convergent interests" conflicted with more civic notions and natural right, America's importance was of the greatest magnitude. But Condorcet could not recognize that its values were not always Jeffersonian, or that the engines that fired its revolution and ideals could involve far more than the new secular radicalism. The city of the eighteenth-century philosophers, of Condorcet, Voltaire, and Diderot, proved a good deal less heavenly than fashionably imagined at the height of the Cold War. But a significant number of early modern English-speakers did indeed conjoin democratic revolution and universal reform with the historical redemption. Eschatology continued to flourish powerfully and creatively in the "city on a hill."

APOCALYPTIC RADICALISM REVITALIZED

Apocalyptic expectations and eschatological frameworks not only survived the great reaction after 1660, they had proven integral to it. Even so, the Glorious Revolution of 1689–1691 that overthrew James II and brought William of Orange to the British crowns could only go further and revitalize strains within such thought that had been unfashionable and submerged. And no wonder. William and now all Britain were engaged in a global struggle against the Bourbon Last World Empire. Perhaps nothing better illustrates the changed order than the reissuing of the 1658 "Embleme of England's Distractions" (see Figure 3.5), now with Cromwell's face supplanted by William's, bewigged but still uncrowned.

Williamite Britain comprised a more conservative world than that of the 1640s and, still more, the 1650s. It had also become a changed one. If the Revolutionary Settlement was significantly less tolerant than the republican era, if the aspirations for civic polity and global liberation were visibly more attenuated, there now appeared a commercial and financial dimension to society that had only hesitantly been anticipated at mid-century. William's great wars would be funded through the creation of the Bank of England (1694), a sinking fund, and public debt. William's pre-emptive strike in 1689 sought to resist universal empire through a network of commercial plantations, far different from the great territorial state imagined by Louis XIV and his Stuart satrap. The emergent monied world of credit and fiscal promise entailed a cultural transition of the first importance. The prophetic future now became transmuted into a commercial one, and significant elements within the British elites abandoned the redemptive scheme for an economic narrative, moving from contingent grace to contingent credit. For them the apocalypse was not refuted, "disproven," somehow falsified by events, but supplanted and refocused.

There existed no inherent reason why political economy needed to be de-sacralized. If the classical citizen and the illumined saint had converged since the Italian Renaissance, then why not the prophet and the entrepreneurial actor? The creation of an economic *oikoumene* might well be imagined as the millennium where now-liberated human potential achieved sanctification while realizing virtue and the public good. Nevertheless this line of thinking constituted a severe departure from earlier assumptions, especially those of the classical world. It hugely expanded the realm of the public: the private *oikos/domus* and public *polis/respublica* division had now decisively shifted in favor of the latter with the advent of "oeconomics." John Locke (1632–1704) was, if not unique, uniquely prominent in developing the intellectual and psychological foundations for this transition, and thus the basis for what is often called the financial revolution. No less important for the shape of public culture, this development arose during the turmoil in the later 1670s as a struggle about clerical power. At that time Locke drafted at least initial versions of his two treatises on government and his *Essay Concerning Human Understanding*. Both subsequently triumphed with the Williamite revolution in 1690, the last underwriting not only Newtonian mechanics but also, it now seems, the commercial world. Because religious authority featured so centrally in the English confrontation during these years, the sacred became absorbed into the social—a circumstance largely unduplicated in Scotland and British North America, regions that, as a result, proved more amenable to civil religion and public life as mechanisms of salvation.

From the Cambridge Platonists to "Plain Mr. Locke"

These developments began somewhat improbably with three Restoration academics known today as the Cambridge Platonists, John Smith (1618–1652), Ralph Cudworth (1617–1688), and most notably Henry More (1618–1687). In his *The Immortality of the Soule* (1659), More undertook several objectives. First he sought to solve important epistemological problems within Cartesian thought, not withstanding "the excellency of Des-Cartes his philosophy." At the same time he was much exercised to discredit mortalism which he saw as "atheistical" and, more to the point, a threat to the clergy and organized religion. Hobbes was the obvious target, and More went on at length seeking to refute him. But, implicitly and at least as important, More wanted to explode Richard Overton's *Mans Mortalitie* (1643 and numerous subsequent editions) that shared lines of thought dangerously similar to More's own neo-Platonic preoccupations with the sun and astral mysticism. No less troubling, we may believe, was Overton's universalist antinomianism that directly confronted the conclusions of More's clericalist Arminianism. Mortalism, that central doctrine of the revolutionary, anticlerical republic, found its answer in the counter-revolutionary monarchy and the re-established church that succeeded it. For More, restoring the offices of Moses and Aaron, monarchy and episcopacy, after 1660 was itself an apocalyptic event. "Can there be a more fit fulfilling of the prophecy of the resurrection of the witnesses than this?"[21]

More met all these challenges by positing that bodies and souls, spirit and matter, never became disjoined. At death the spirit assumed shape within an "airy" body or "vehicle" that inhabited the atmosphere in a world very much like our own. Even if the physics was different, these "aerial inhabitants" were not "less active then the terrestrial, nor less busie, either in the performance of some solemn exercises, or in carrying on designs party against party, and that either more Private or more Publick." As these comments imply, government and politics would continue—if for no other reason than that bad genii as well as good ones populated the airy realm. There would be, at least for genii "of the better sort," music, dancing, and, oh yes, seminars and lectures. But the truly physical character of these "daemons" manifested itself through the "recreation" of "amorous propension" and eating. Bits from the "vehicles" would wear away or come off and need to be restored.[22] The physical reality of this higher realm also manifested itself occasionally on Earth through "apparitions and witchcrafts"—different from Counter-Reformation witch belief because these events did not involve satanic temptation but only reflected the higher realm and offered traces of it. Was a coven simply a seminar gone bad? None of these phenomena comprised a spiritual crisis. Quite the reverse. They supplied validation of the natural order rather than posing a threat. The genii did not effectively intervene at the terrestrial level. Instead, they aspired to transcend the aerial regions and arrive at the "aethereal" reaches still further beyond in Descartes' vortices. There alone lay the prospect of eternal felicity, safely away from any apocalyptic catastrophe that might await the nether planes of existence. The whole point was the rationality of creation and the reasonableness of God.

More's extraordinary conjunction of spirit and body served to naturalize grace and socialize the sacred. This unity made for a rational universe—all the more remarkable for having arisen on the basis of neo-Platonist and even Kabbalist mysticism. With matter and mind so inseparably linked, More could dismiss George Fox's inner light as well as also the source for so much radical religion in Britain, the German spiritualist Jakob Boehme, because on earth "vehicles" could not occupy the same spot simultaneously. Further, More's rationalism joined easily with a thoroughgoing Arminian theology: all men, as rational beings, might potentially be saved. The operative term, however, was *potential*. If salvation was universally available, people still needed to made aware of that opportunity and called upon to desire it. Here was a task only a learned clergy might perform. More's theology, the Cambridge theology, foreclosed private revelation, sectarian claims, social radicalism, enthusiast fanaticism by transforming the status of the prophet. The prophet became an institutional figure, the expounder of universal reason. The contrast with the universalism of the revolutionaries—of Winstanley, the Levellers, Harrington, Milton, even Cromwell—could hardly be more stark. Antinomian universalist liberation from the clergy (realized through toleration and politics) confronted Arminian universalism that mandated clerical authority. Post-Calvinism faced off against anti-Calvinism.

In 1668 More declared that "the first reformers talked much of the *word* and of the *spirit*: but this present Age are great Challengers into the field of Reason."[23] His commitment to universal reason in no way prevented him from embracing the Protestant eschatology or from being a committed millenarian. As was perhaps only appropriate for a former student of Joseph Mede, the rise of Antichrist, the Reformation in the latter days, and the universal triumph of sincere religion in the future millennial era would be delineated at length. Further, the evident fulfillment of prophecy through the course of history, More claimed, would validate the reformed cause to any rational mind that gave the matter serious attention. History, universally accessible, validated the faith even more compellingly than the miracles of the apostolic age that, for most, could only rely on report. More continually describes his analysis of prophecy as "very natural" or the result of "reason and prudent sagacity." There was nothing in the least inspired about it. The truths of the apocalypse were available to any learned man—certainly any learned Cambridge man—and could be made evident to all. If cracking the text required techniques only available to the educated elite, the message scripture provided also pointed to the central importance of the clergy. The Revelation and biblical prophecy in general did not describe political revolution, violent upheavals, and bloodshed. Despite its graphic images, "the *Apocalypse* is not so bloudy and boisterous a Book as I have heard some represent it to be."[24] The millennial victory turned on effective preaching and competent exposition. It demanded clerical action, "Holy Men," not fire and brimstone, not military confrontation, not political reform. Romanism would be defeated, but that would not mean the destruction of the Roman church, only its false doctrine. "This Light of Nature, I say, is abundantly well appointed ... to be subservient to that *Truth* and *Life* that is really *Divine*."[25] The future lay with monarchy, at once sacerdotal and royal, with hierarchy, with a rational clergy.

The clerical students of the Cambridge Platonists took this line of argument still further. Where More had hesitated, insisting that reason did not encompass the whole of the spirit—though "I understand by the *spirit*, not a blind unaccountable Impression or Impulse, a Lift or an Huff of an heated Brain"—his followers felt no such compunction.[26] Simon Patrick (1626–1707), bishop of Ely, George Rust (d. 1670), bishop of Dromore, William Sherlock (1641–1707), dean of St. Paul's, and others made reason not the dominant faculty, but the sole route to the spirit. In their furious efforts to marginalize dissent during the struggle leading up to the 1680 Exclusion Crisis—with prospect of revolution on one hand and a legitimate but Catholic king on the other—these Anglican clergy rejected all inspiration that could not be made visible, comprehensible, and so validated by contemporaries. "Visible demonstrations" of miracles in the apostolic age had been replaced altogether by no less visible reasoning in the present era. There simply was no inward operation of the spirit independent of ministerial influence. The standard of religious truth became social acceptance, and the guardians of any such acceptance could only be an "administrative priesthood," the institutionalized prophets of the established church. Professional clergy and inspired prophets became one. Patrick, a self-proclaimed "son of the prophet," who was prepared to believe that Christ might well return sometime between 1700 and 1734, enjoined an ordered world regulated "rationally" by men like himself.[27] Arminian universal reason assumed form as Anglican universal intolerance.

It would be in part against this clerical reading of the self and history that John Locke undertook his most celebrated writings. Soul became inseparable from body, reason from passion, and Christianity did indeed become "reasonable." But the prophetic dimension evaporated along with clerical pretension. Church office did not possess intimations of the holy spirit, and the great apocalyptic arc simply was no more. Reason truly became universal, truth a social construction. An amalgam of rationality and desire gave humanity confidence about the future, a future that was genuinely secular. Commerce became the alternative to religion in the sense that its civilizing "douceur" redirected passion into social cooperation rather than social conflict. At the Exchange in London, as Voltaire famously expressed it, "you will see representatives of all nations ... assembled for the profit of mankind." "There the Jew, the Mahometan, and the Christian deal with one another as if they were of the same religion, and reserve the name infidel for those who go bankrupt."[28] Universal empire and eventually empire in any sense—whether prophetic or proprietary—seemed unacceptable. An age of free men, Condorcet insisted, required free trade and independence in every sense; neither political nor commercial monopoly could be acceptable. What had begun in the later sixteenth century as an apocalyptic struggle against the Last World Empire concluded in the later eighteenth century with the end of empire altogether. Or, at least, so it seemed.

Civil Millenarianism

Did this eighteenth-century transformation also involve the decline of eschatology? Certainly we encounter all manner of marginalized millenarians during the eighteenth century. There were the Camisard prophets in London, refugees understandably hysterical at the destruction of their community, the last significant Protestant area in France, by Louis XIV in 1703. Jansenist millenarians crop up in France during the 1730s. Bizarre Britons, like Richard Brothers and Joanna Southcott at century's end, briefly attracted attention as well. But quixotic, "divinely appointed" figures such as these should not distract us from the abiding vitality of apocalyptic thinking within Europe, especially among Protestants and never more so than within the Anglophone communities. The apocalypse not only created modernity, it also survived it. Neither the 1713 Peace of Utrecht that ended, seemingly forever, the threat of eschatological universal empire, nor the obsessive quest for social stability, nor the intellectual achievements described above, dislodged apocalyptic thinking from the cultural mainstream. An entire generation of early eighteenth-century intellectuals rejected enthusiasm, shunned the French prophets, eschewed social radicalism, and yet found themselves immersed in millenarian expectation. Among the most remembered are George Berkeley (1685–1735), William Whiston (1667–1752), George Cheyne (1671–1743), and David Hartley (1705–1757).

Their expectations developed directly from well-established apocalyptic traditions of the previous century and still more emphatically possessed a pan-British, pan-Anglophone character. Berkeley, philosopher and sometime bishop in the Church of Ireland, became obsessed with founding of a college in Bermuda dedicated to converting the American Indians to Anglican Christianity. Berkeley and his associates, among them fellow bishop Robert Clayton (1695–1758), saw their project within an eschatological framework. Indian conversion was prerequisite to the coming of the millennium, and especially so as America promised to be the theater of the historical redemption, the focus of the millennial era. Berkeley's enduringly famous *Verses on America* (1726) describes the succession of empires portrayed in Daniel.

> Westward the Course of Empire takes its Way;
> The four first Acts already past,
> A fifth shall close the Drama with the Day;
> Time's noblest Offspring is the last.[29]

The expectation that the true faith would be achieved in America in contrast with declining Europe—and there initiate the millennium (and

Second Coming)—had a very long pedigree. Berkeley's lines find early seventeenth-century anticipation in George Herbert ("Religion stands on tip-toe in our land, / Ready to pass to the *American* strand, / . . . Then shall religion to *America* flee: / They have their times Gospel; ev'n as we") and, earlier still, in William Alexander ("*America* to *Europe* may succeed, / God may of stones raise up to *Abram* seed").[30] Berkeley's Indian obsession may have derived from his having embraced the theory that the Americans were the Ten Lost Hebrew Tribes who needed to be recovered before the millennial era. Again, we encounter continuity with thought from the seventeenth century.

Whiston, for a time Newton's successor in the Lucasian Chair of Mathematics at Trinity, was a major authority on the millennium (at one point expecting it in the 1730s). Cheyne, a significant medical theorist and practitioner in London, developed a rather mystical, medical millenarianism. All three enjoyed international reputations and developed powerful trans-Atlantic connections—Berkeley even residing for a while in Rhode Island. If all three had also eccentricities that startled contemporaries—Whiston's open Unitarianism cost him his professorship; Cheyne's odd rejection of Newtonianism limited his stature as a scientist; Berkeley's strategy for the Bermuda college seemed both brutal and wildly unrealistic—their eschatology was never at issue.

By far the most significant for the long-term was Cheyne's friend and fellow physician, Lockean psychologist David Hartley. Although Hartley drew directly on writers like Mede, Whiston, and Burnet, his major opus, *Observations on Man, his Frame, his Duty, and his Expectations* (1749), developed an apocalyptic vision that seemed to share much with the aspirations of the mid-seventeenth-century revolutionaries. All church government would collapse in the lead-up to the millennium. The triumph of Christianity meant the end of the "dogmatizing spirit" and the persecution that followed from it. Hartley completely endorsed the Protestant apocalyptic vision, but pressed it to drastic conclusions. "It is very true that the church of *Rome* is *Babylon the great, and the mother of harlots, and of the abominations of the earth*. But all the rest have copied her example more or less." "They have all left the true, pure, simple religion; and teach for doctrines the commandments of men." The denominational distinctions—"Papist, Protestant, Lutheran, Calvinist, Trinitarian, Unitarian,

Mystic, Methodist, &c."—would be swept away "like the chaff of the summer threshing-floors." "The corrupt governors of the several churches will ever oppose the true gospel, and in so doing bring ruin upon themselves."[31] This last age promised a world of apostles and saints, a world without organized religion.

The dissolution of clerical authority would be accompanied by the collapse of all civil authority—the state fell with the church. Both were equally and irredeemably irreligious and incompatible with the core Christian message. "All the known governments of the world have the evident principles of corruption in themselves." Like the churches, they were "composed of jarring elements," vain self-absorption competing with otherworldly Christian concerns. "The splendour, luxury, self-interest, martial glory &c. which pass for essentials in Christian governments, are totally opposite to the meek, humble, self-denying spirit of Christianity." The triumph of either side would overturn government. Reform along Christian principles might delay collapse, but could not prevent it. This same "jarring" would prove equally true of Islamic and pagan governments, once Christianity began to be propagated in these lands. To be sure, in previous ages the dissolution of political orders had given rise to new ones. But this would not be the case with the present governments in the final age: "The Prophecies do not admit of this; and it may be easily seen that the situation of things in the great world is very different from what it has ever been before." "The present circumstances of the world are extraordinary and critical, beyond what has ever yet happened." What would the universal "fifth monarchy, or kingdom of the saints, which is to be set up" actually look like? Dr. Hartley declined to say. "It seems as romantic ... for anyone to project the scheme of a perfect government in this imperfect state, as to be in pursuit of an universal remedy, a remedy that should cure all distempers, and prolong life beyond limit." Hartley's resolute empiricism could allow no more.[32]

What manifestly needed to occur was the conversion of the Jews and, apparently concomitantly, the creation of a Jewish state in the Middle East. Such a migration to Palestine struck Hartley as relatively straightforward—not least because the liquidity of Jewish assets facilitated relocation. The Jews particularly exercised Hartley's thinking as they had so many Calvinists and post-Calvinists. The Jewish experience of election, fall, redemption, he insisted, provided a "type" for the human salvation generally, foreshadowing both the first and second resurrections. Further, if the downfall of the Jewish state under Titus in antiquity provided "the occasion of the publication of the gospel to us Gentiles, so our downfall [in the present age] may contribute to the restoration of the Jews." Together latter-day Jews and Christians might then produce the final publication of the true religion—"the first fruit and the lump [being] made holy together." For all these reasons Hartley stood firmly by the recovery of the Lost Tribes. Those who claimed that the Tribes had long since been absorbed into other peoples, thereby losing their identity and their relevance, simply showed a woeful lack of faith. As he reminded his readers, "It was one of the great sins of the Jews to call God's promises in question, on account of apparent difficulties and impossibilities." The Jews were integral to the human future, part of a great common undertaking that would realize the destiny of mankind.[33]

It was no less imperative to apocalyptic purpose that the gospel, the authentic gospel, be propagated throughout the world. Herein lay the real meaning of progress. The Reformation, the advent of the printing press, the restoration of learning, the rise of global commerce, the growing achievements of natural science all served to spread the Christian faith and thereby to hasten the millennial era. "The great increase of knowledge, literary and philosophical, which has been made in the two last centuries, and continues to be made, must contribute to promote every great truth, and particularly those of revealed religion." Science and technology ("the useful manual arts") could only undergird the Christian message and encourage "progress amongst the yet heathen nations." Hartley's discussion breathes the spirit of Daniel 12:4, and the doctor is much more a Baconian than his contemporary Diderot.

Where the apostles healed through miracles, the modern world had medicine that "is improving every day." Where the apostles miraculously acquired the capacity to speak in tongues, moderns had developed language acquisition through an improved understanding grammar, logic, and the operations of the human mind. If the apostles and patriarchs had the gift of prophecy, moderns grasped the meaning of prophecy through improving textual and historical analysis. Even the new apostasy, presumably deism, sharpened Christian argument necessary for the conversion of heathens, and on that basis Hartley supported freedom of the press. The emergence of new sects—Hartley seems to have had Methodism in mind—promised to help purify religion.[34]

If human progress comprised a soteriological process, salvation itself was also at once universal and natural. Like Bacon, and perhaps even more like Winstanley, Hartley rejected any severe mind-body dualism. The redemption of mankind might well entail the revitalization of nature. Hartley could hope for the resurrection of every person along with "the whole creation, which groans and travails in pain together [with mankind], waiting for the adoption and glorious liberty of the children of God"—language reminiscent of the Digger leader.[35] We know that Cheyne had introduced him to Boehme. One startling consequence of Hartley's unblinking naturalism was the fundamental importance of physical resurrection. "The resurrection will be effected by means strictly natural." What happened to the soul in the meantime was uncertain. It might sleep, it might be conscious, or, splitting the difference, it might exist in a dreaming state. Such "conjectures" were of minor importance because only the restoration of the body could guarantee personal immortality.[36]

Hartley's Lockean epistemology did more than imagine the mind as a receptor of stimuli which it then associated in ever more complex configurations. That configuring process, the "vibrations" within the nervous system, created the personality, the self—in a sense, the "soul." What made us who we are was built into our cognitive processes. Consciousness became contingent rather than possessing a priori coherence. Thus our intuitive sense of ourselves as unified mental structures might well prove an illusion, and Hartley would reflect upon "the annihilation of that self." "The unity of consciousness seems to me an inconclusive argument."[37] Radical eschatology underwrote Hartleian psychology.

A number of consequences followed from Hartley's spiritualized naturalism. The millennial era would be a period of great joy, but, as a distinctly natural phenomenon, it could not be one of complete or perfect happiness. Further, once the human self became naturalized, the difference between people and animals inherently lessened—and the treatment of animals, not at all Descartes' clockwork automata, might need to improve. If salvation was a natural process, then it should also be a universal one. "As we now live in a more adult age of the world, more will be expected from our natural powers." Besides, there existed compelling scriptural and moral reasons for thinking so.

All humans, even the most wicked, Hartley came to believe, would eventually be redeemed and find happiness at the end of time. Scripture had spoken of "eternal" punishment in several senses, none truly meaning endless. Further, the fires of hell were rather purifying than punishing, and damnation itself, if the term could be used at all, became a spiritual exercise.[38]

At the most basic level Hartley's revaluation of mind and rejection of the mind-body dualism struck dramatically at one of the most reflexive assumptions of the Great Chain of Being: as mind needed to guide and shape matter in nature, so the clerical and aristocratic elites needed to guide and shape the inferior orders within society. That analogy, that axiom, had now collapsed. Here lay explosive stuff. Yet Hartley's *Observations* created no stir, and in fact prompted little reaction at all. That was because he adopted an emphatically quietist approach to the great events he described. Christ would come like a thief in the night. Again and again, right after each radical claim, Hartley insisted that his readers wait patiently for that time, meekly accepting civil and church authority. Millenarianism did not mean activism. In his remarkably conservative, even reactionary conclusion to the second volume, Hartley backed off his claims for the mechanist foundations of the self—running counter to the entire thrust of his argument.[39] Only some two decades later would the radical chemist Joseph Priestley (1733–1804) discover and detonate the highly charged materials in Hartley. Certainly, the republican and democratic thought of the British Revolution had not disappeared, any more than did the radical religion that was so often associated with it. Republicanism would persist as a vital force in British political life right through the 1840s. Nor did all British radicals accept Hartley. Priestley's friend and collaborator, Dr. Richard Price (1723–1791), firmly rejected any thought that the soul might possess an organic basis. Jeremy Bentham (1748–1832) and James Mill (1773–1836), on the other hand, systematically foreclosed the idea that values existed in nature, and certainly any apocalyptic scheme that accompanied them. Nevertheless, Hartley's eschatology and psychology, promoted and developed through Priestley, became cornerstones for the British left in the Age of the Democratic Revolutions.

Following Hartley, Priestley strongly denied that a significant distinction existed between mind and matter, spirit and body. All matter, he insisted, was enveloped with vitalist force-fields that continuously interacted with one another. Further minimizing the ancient dualism, he came to believe that the amount of genuinely impenetrable matter in the universe might prove infinitesimally small. This spirito-materialist perception of nature provided the basis for his study of physics, light, and, above all, chemistry. His work with the "airs" within the atmosphere led to the discovery (if not full comprehension) of oxygen and of the carbon dioxide–oxygen interdependence of plants and animals. All of these processes, for Priestley, manifested the presence of God, and the study of them possessed a redemptive, indeed eschatological character. In every respect—from his understanding of nature's structure and chemical bonding, to his experimentalism, to his perception of scientific inquiry as part of public culture, to the soteriological and prophesied purpose of science—Priestley is the direct heir of Francis Bacon, arguably the culmination of the Baconian tradition. Precisely this apocalyptic spiritualism, which suffused the whole of Priestley's thought and life, decisively separates him from his French contemporary and counterpart, Antoine Lavoisier (1743–1794).

Priestley further followed Hartley by extending this view of nature to cognition and the personality. The last arose as a neurological, organic creation, the product of association and "vibration," and consequently the self was, manifestly, self-made. This "materialist" psychology opened the prospect of unbounded human improvement. It enjoined civic society, where people constructed both themselves and their social world. It concomitantly provided the route to the millennium and the historical redemption of mankind. Republished in the 1770s by Priestley, Hartley's writing now for the first time burst upon politics and the intellectual scene with enormous effect. His influence seems to have extended to the young William Wordsworth. Samuel Taylor Coleridge named his first child David Hartley—embracing these views during his years before the 1797 onset of reaction, "higher" consciousness, and drugs. The American revolutionary and millenarian Dr. Benjamin Rush became a life-long enthusiast. Hartley's presence was felt "everywhere." Of course, the newly discovered Hartley did not go unchallenged. The "northern theorists," notably Thomas Reid at Aberdeen (1710–1796), posited an autonomous Common Sense that existed beyond mere physiology. At its most reflective, the choice—the clash—lay between Hartley and Reid.

This choice between association and intuition did not necessarily mean a choice between left and right. Dr. Price could reject Hartley, embrace mortalism, and still become a close associate of Priestley's, sharing his politics, his Unitarianism, his eschatology. Both saw the civic superimposed upon the soteriological. The genuinely political society inherently embodied the godly company, the community of the elect, because the exercise of virtue and the achievement of salvation comprised the same undertaking. The identification of the decision-taking citizen and the illumined saint was now a politico-spiritual tradition more than two centuries old. As in the British Revolution, so in the eighteenth century this identification demanded personal independence: the end of place, patronage, standing armies, the recognition of children's rights, law reform, and the abolition of that most dependent and degrading of all social relationships, chattel slavery.

Initially, however, Priestley and Price envisioned progress to the millennium as largely a slow, incremental process, no doubt enjoined on them by Hanoverian England's suffocating Gothic traditionalism. The Democratic Revolutions refocused their apocalyptic trajectory. The American republic possessed manifest apocalyptic significance. "Next to the introduction of Christianity among mankind," Price averred, "the American Revolution may prove the most important step in the progressive cause of human improvement." Subsequently, the French Revolution convinced them that the millennium was indeed imminent. The next generation, Priestley observed in a Matthew-like tone, would likely see the return of Christ. The emergence of the republic caused them to depart, increasingly, from *l'extase gothique* and to adopt a more thoroughgoing republicanism. Revolutions and other such cataclysmic upheavals had indeed been prophesied and described a fundamentally meliorist arc. The fall of the French monarchy, one of the ten horns of the Beast, would prove the pattern for Europe. The millennium would be realized through a world of democratic republics, perhaps federally linked, in a final era of peace and virtue. By the late 1790s the republican armies—that is, citizen-soldiers—had reached Rome and seized the papacy. Antichrist was visibly falling. In Rome, not just in the French civil church, clerics now became citizens.

In the British Isles, throughout all three kingdoms, arose vocal radicalism both secular and religious. It met with a massive and relentless reaction. Perhaps most remembered today are the clergy-inspired church and king riots of 1791 that destroyed Priestley's home, library, and laboratory. As early as 1792 the government sponsored the publication of prophecies designed to counter radical eschatology. For the first time the location and persona of the prophesied Antichrist began to shift. There had long been conservative Protestants who doubted whether the papacy should be identified with this scriptural figure or figures. Individual conservatives during the British Revolution occasionally had made half-hearted attempts to portray Cromwell as the little horn of the Beast, but here was something new. Works with titles like *Antichrist in the French Convention* began to circulate. A growing number of English clerics began to link atheist France with the papacy and the Turk. All three sought to overthrow Christian values. All three were the declared enemies of Britain. Bishop Samuel Horsley (1733–1806) went still further, finding Antichrist to exist exclusively in the French republic, and making his career by promoting this refocused vision. Horsley first achieved prominence through his tirades against Methodism and Jacobin conspiracies. He rejected out of hand the idea that France was any prophesied scourge of Rome. "I cannot discern any immediate signs of the fall of AntiChrist. I fear, I see too clearly the rise, instead of the fall, of the AntiChrist in the West."[40] The French subverted family values with the creation of secular, civil marriage, making it "nothing more than a temporary contract during the good pleasure of both parties." Here indeed was the mark of the Beast. The decline of the faith in the time of Antichrist, he insisted, will lead to "a professed indifference to any particular form of Christianity, under the pretense of Universal toleration." "Governments will pretend to an indifference to all, and will give preference to none. All establishments will be set aside."[41] Horsley, a reactionary's reactionary, had developed a millenarian political vision that completely diverted the entire thrust of Reformation eschatology. The apocalypse now turned against the very ideas it had done so much to create. With Horsley, the apocalypse became the enemy of modernity rather than either its crucial catalyst or its powerful ally.

Horsley's thought anticipates that of John Henry Newman (1801–1890) and the Anglophone Catholic right. Newman's initial view of the pope as Antichrist shifted to seeing modernity as the great prophesied challenge to Christianity and Christian society: Gog and Magog were democracy and atheism, the mark of the Beast nothing less than the French tricolor. The appeal of authoritarian Catholicism, firmly defined doctrinally and resolutely atemporal, proved hugely attractive to nineteenth-century reaction. It is the greatest irony that such a structure might be imagined as meeting an apocalyptic crisis.

THE LAST WORLD EMPIRE REDIVIVUS?

For Price, Priestley, and other religious radicals of the revolutionary period, no prophetic doctrine was more central than the restoration of a great Jewish state in the Middle East, accompanied by the Jews' acceptance of Christianity. The philo-Semitic tradition reached back to the 1590s, achieved prominence with the British Revolution, and became, once again, a flash point between left and right in the later eighteenth century. A 1790 government broadside print, accordingly, linked the Cromwellian soldier with the Jew, black-faced and bearded, in spoilage of the established church. In part the impetus for the issue arose from the career of the unstable religious agitator Lord George Gordon (1751–1793). Gordon converted to militant Scottish Presbyterianism at the end of the 1770s and then departed his apocalyptic Calvinism for Judaism in the middle of the next decade. But the real issue for British conservatives, then as earlier, was the radicalism historically associated with the philo-Semitic tradition, rather than Gordon's odd enactment of it.

Perhaps no one embodied that tradition more than did Joseph Priestley, who was in some ways its culmination. Priestley's philo-Semitism arose with his Calvinist origins—much as did Isaac La Peyrère's, Oliver Cromwell's, and that of so many others. These views deepened with his adopting radical Unitarianism. Jesus was simply a man, albeit a man with a messianic mission. If it was idolatrous to worship him, then the differences between Judaism and true Christianity might seem relatively marginal. Priestley was concerned to integrate the eschatologies of the two faiths, and modern scholars have repeatedly claimed that, more than anything else, he sought "a genuine convergence between purified Christianity and enlightened Judaism."[42] If Priestley's writings about Judaism remained conversionist and if he, somewhat reluctantly, accepted that the Jews were responsible for Jesus' death, he was acutely conscious of the great crimes committed against the Jewish people, from which not even England could be exculpated. He was prepared to believe that the Jews might return to their homeland in Palestine as Jews before any conversion. Further, he was at some pains to defend the Jews against contemporary detractors such as Voltaire. Contrary to Voltaire, to Diderot, to Hume, to Spinoza, they were not ignorant, superstitious, avaricious, or barbarous. Just the opposite. Pagan philosophers and their medieval successors were the true barbarians. The antique thinkers had refused to condemn heathen idolatry and appalling superstition. Many had even conformed to it. Hebrew wisdom made sense; Greek speculation and, still worse, the Greek theology that derived from it did not. "Are not their minds ... darkened, who can prefer the absurd conceits of these philosophers, to the rational doctrines of revelation?"[43] History bore witness to the manifest reasonableness of the apocalypse.

Precisely this characteristic was reformed Christianity's great strength. It was a time-soaked faith, and as such, like society itself, always remained in some ways a work in progress, as even relatively conservative Protestants could agree. The final truth, surely like the early Jewish churches that predated Greek corruptions (such as the trinity), might lie just over the horizon. Priestley became ever more persuaded that this final truth would prove to be a heavily Jewish one, not least in that the Jewish state and its people would be the dominant element in the millennial age. Light and authority would flow from the new Jews of Palestine.

Judaism too was a highly temporalized faith, and new dispensations too might well be imagined within it. Its incorporation of Christian ideas and culture was far from unusual, especially during the early modern period. In the event, however, Priestley's writing would be challenged by the London Jew David Levi (1742–1801), a man who certainly did not look to new dispensations. A remarkable autodidact, Levi was primarily concerned to translate Jewish religious texts and guides into English. He was exercised to preserve orthodoxy and to define the boundaries of the faith. Prophecy validated the rabbinic tradition against both secular deist aspersions and Christian apologetics. He had no knowledge of Enlightenment biblical criticism or any interest in further revelation. Christians ought first to agree on their faith—and what Jesus' status was within it—before they undertook to urge it on others. In addition to defending at length the authenticity of Mosaic authority and the implausibility of Jesus, Levi dismissed the

Unitarians at various points with such comments as "your sect (which are but a handful)."[44] Stung and personally hurt, Priestley continued writing on the subject, though he declined to address Levi directly (which did not stop Levi from continuing to reply). As a debate, the exchange is of limited interest. Yet the "reasonableness" of prophecy and the extraordinary political events of the age eventually moved even Levi. The fall of Rome and Napoleon's Egyptian campaign recalled Jewish prophecy from the end of the fifteenth century and seemed "to give some countenance to Abrabanel."

> When we see so many nations engaged in a war, carried on with almost unparalleled violence, desolating so many countries, and producing such extraordinary Revolutions, as have scarcely ever been witnessed ... I can not but consider all those occurrences, as indications of the near approach of the redemption of the nation.[45]

Levi might reject out of hand any further revelation or final synthesis of spiritual truth, and especially any prospect of a Judeo-Christianity. Still, by century's end the eschatological tug proved irresistible, and the two foes turn out to have become far closer than either fully recognized. Priestley had a point.

If the French seizure of Rome spoke to both Protestant and Jewish eschatologies, so too did the republic's activities in the eastern Mediterranean. Napoleon's Egyptian campaign of 1798 and his expedition to Palestine in the following year inevitably stimulated enormous apocalyptic interest. The prospective overthrow of the Turkish Empire and the founding of a Jewish state in its wake addressed some of the deepest hopes of Protestantism, Judaism, and even certain strains within Catholicism. And it all now seemed to be happening. Priestley is said to have followed news from the Middle East with a Bible open to Daniel upon the table beside him. The downfall of the Turks "will be a glorious event indeed." Whether Napoleon proved successful or not, he was launching developments of the greatest moment. "Something is promised in Egypt in the latter days, which I think are at hand, but I do not presume to say that Bonaparte is the deliverer ... promised them [the Jews]. He may be cut off; but what is promised will no doubt be fulfilled."[46] There are indications that the French government sought to manipulate such expectations. A "Letter of a

Jew to His Brethren" appeared in one of the pro-government news-papers in 1798 that purported to be an expression of Jewish hope for restoration in Palestine. Its provenance is unclear, but the effect on English millenarians was predictably dramatic. Still other French papers subsequently ascribed the most extraordinary statements to Napoleon at the time of his expedition to Palestine and Syria: "Bona-parte has published a proclamation in which he invites all the Jews of Asia and Africa to gather under his flag in order to re-establish the ancient Jerusalem. He has already given arms to a great number, and their battalions threaten Aleppo." All sorts of even more outlandish reports, claims, and exhortations circulated in France.[47]

Surely the most spectacular manipulation of prophetic promise occurred in 1806 when Napoleon convened the Grand Jewish Sanhe-drin, the first such since antiquity. Here indeed was the calling of the Jews, and not least because it had long been thought that such an as-sembly would occur as the prelude to the messianic age. The event made itself felt from Lithuania to the American frontier. If the effects of the great convocation were minor and largely repressive, its sym-bolic potential was loaded to the breaking point. Was not the new French ruler that long prophesied latter-day Cyrus, the messianic restorer of the Jews? Might he not prove to be the Last World Em-peror, reordering the political landscape, humbling the papacy, synthe-sizing freedom with order, fulfilling the great promises to Israel? A medal commemorating the occasion portrays an enthroned Napoleon giving the law to Moses who kneels before him. At one level its mes-sage was simple enough: the Sanhedrin had been called to fit the Jews and thus Jewish law into the laws of the French Empire. At another, Napoleonic claims could hardly have been more august or more unmistakable. After all, who else had given the law to Moses?

Or was its meaning unmistakable? An entirely contrary reading was also available—and altogether necessary, for it might otherwise appear that apocalyptic portents were speaking loudly against Britain and con-servatism. That radical reading of the portents made itself evident. In 1806 the editor of an Anglican journal, William Reid, abandoned his post, took up Unitarianism, and in the following year published *The New Sanhedrin*, a lengthy defense of the Jews and Napoleon's philo-Semitism. Conservative Britain palpably needed counter-prophecy, and the Oxford divines Geoffrey Faber (1773–1854) and Henry Kett

(1761–1825) labored to provide it. Bishop Horsley appears to have reached the conclusion that not just France but specifically Napoleon himself was the prophesied Antichrist. Initially, he had been emphatic that revolutionary France would not restore the Jews: "there is no reason to believe that the atheistical democracy of France is destined to so high an office." But the Sanhedrin seems to have shifted his view; he wrote his brother shortly before his death in October 1806, that he expected Bonaparte to settle many Jews in Palestine and "then set himself up as the Messiah." Furious persecution would follow, but he would eventually be overthrown and destroyed.[48] These remarks sound oddly medieval. Not only has the Antichrist become an individual once again, he is also the leader of the Jews and a deceiving prophet. Sixty years later Leo Tolstoy had a character in *War and Peace* try to calculate Revelation's 666 from Napoleon's name, and such numerical manipulations occurred in contemporaneous London and Moscow. Priestley and Horsley had clashed early on in their careers, and the range of their disagreement covered just about every possible topic, including the identity of the Beast. Still, that in itself is telling. Although far left and far right, the two remained at one in having an apocalyptic reading of the world. The struggle for and against democracy, for and against Napoleonic Europe, would be conducted within the apocalyptic idiom no less than within the emergent secular vocabularies—exercising decision-makers and their publicists in Whitehall, the Louvre, the Hermitage.

Revolution and Reaction

Priestley spent the last decade of his life as an exile in Pennsylvania. Throughout this time he continued to be intimate with the American revolutionary elite. He would tell John Adams that he thought the millennium imminent. He remained close to the millenarian revolutionary Dr. Benjamin Rush. He supported Thomas Jefferson and welcomed his victory in 1800. Earlier, in 1794, he had endorsed Maximillien Robespierre and celebrated his "admirable Report . . . on the subject of *morals* and *religion*, and I rejoice to find by it, that so great and happy a change has taken place in the leading men of France."[49] The *Report* is an extraordinary document that makes powerful reading even today. Contrasting "the grandeur of man" with "the littleness of the great," it declared the options facing humanity in the most stark and compelling terms.

"Two contrary spirits [genii]" were now struggling to determine irrevocably the future of mankind, the destiny of the world.[50] Although the language sounds much like Priestley, in important ways, its assumptions are actually far from his. Robespierre's "supreme being" occupies a different universe from the God of Priestley's Christian Unitarianism. The French leader most certainly did not anticipate the appearance of Christ, incarnate or otherwise. Similarly, Jefferson's deism left no room for Priestley's "rational" revelation. Despite overlapping agendas, despite the great common cause, despite Priestley's manifestly greater social radicalism, beneath it all lay an unbridgeable chasm separating him from Jefferson and Robespierre.

Priestley kept faith with radical democracy and the revolutionary movement throughout his life. This apocalyptic radicalism is part of a tradition that would run from the Levellers to Priestley to Martin Luther King Jr., one that did much to underwrite American achievement and Anglophone triumph at century's end. Yet in the later years of his life we encounter an eschatological reformulation. Priestley indicated in 1774 and long continued to believe that Christ would not appear and personally reign in the millennial era; nor would the martyrs then rise from the dead to live with him. "The figurative language of prophecy" suggested that during this (indefinite) period, their "cause" would triumph. At that point they would be realized through their truth, their aspirations, their social world, rather than personally. During that last era before the end of time, history and politics alone would redeem them. Doubts about this view arose for Priestley after encountering the theology of R. E. Garnham in the late 1780s. This thinking apparently gestated for some time. Jesus, not John the Baptist, would prove the second Elias foretold by the prophet Malachi, and Priestley became increasingly convinced that the Nazarene would appear physically at the culmination of history. By his last years Priestley had become quite explicit that Jesus would inaugurate the millennium by appearing "in the clouds, so as to be seen by all." He would then return to earth where he would "govern the people of Israel, and the world, as the Hebrew nation were directed by the *Shekinah*."[51] Priestley never abandoned the revolutionary cause. He never deserted politics or radical reform. The reconfiguring of his eschatology does not point to any new religiosity, but, instead, to an increasingly transcendent formulation of religion.

Priestley's changed vision might seem to anticipate the broader religious transition that occurred in America and Europe after 1800. Jefferson's election in that year brought to power the first (and only) non-Christian president. Significant numbers of religious revolutionaries found the prospect of his presidency profoundly troubling. The democratic republic had led not to the triumph of the spirit, but to infidelity. Just as in France, civil religion was dissolving into secular disbelief. If Priestley did not desert Jefferson, other revolutionaries did. Elias Boudinot (1740–1821) had served as president of the Continental Congress during the Revolution, signed the peace treaty with Britain, was elected to the first United States Congress, and subsequently became the first director of the Mint. However, in 1805 he broke with Jefferson, explaining that he could not be a part of a deist government. Boudinot had already foreshadowed his departure in 1801 when he published a riposte to Thomas Paine with the revealing title, *The Age of Revelation, or, The Age of Reason shewn to be an age of infidelity*. The volume concluded: "the evidence in favour of the great truths of revelation are daily increasing and will so continue till the second coming of our Lord Jesus, as he has promised." Boudinot remained a reformer, opposing slavery, seeking gender equality, along with Jewish liberation (and, of course, conversion), all precisely because he looked to the millennium. He even insisted upon the long-antiquated Jewish Indian theory. As a radical democrat Boudinot comprised the complete opposite of the reactionary English divines Faber, Kett, and Horsley. Nevertheless, on one point all four agreed. As Boudinot put it, "That the Antichrist foretold, as coming on the earth after the Man of Sin, had literally appeared in the new government of France, having Napoleon Buenaparte for her head, can scarcely be denied by any observing mind."[52]

A still deeper and more ominous fissure was opening within American political life. "Infidelity" prompted an explosive popular reaction: massive back country revivals, known today as the Second Great Awakening (c. 1800–1840). Altogether unprecedented eschatologies subsequently emerged to accompany the new preoccupation with a transcendent God, who, for many, replaced the immanent deity of revolutionary republicanism. A "new order of the ages" was variously proclaimed that came to have very little connection with the American democracy. Religion would exact its revenge on politics.

CHAPTER 9

Novus Ordo Saeculorum: The Rise of the Redeemer Republic

Kevin Phillips has identified three crucial moments in the rise of Anglo-America: the 1640s, the 1770s, and the 1860s. All three involved civil war and resulted in revolution. Each of these upheavals engaged the entire English-speaking world, and their enormous consequences made themselves immediately felt throughout it. Each of them witnessed the triumph of radicalism over traditionalism: citizens defeated subjects, civic society overcame hierarchy, public culture supplanted the Great Chain of Being. Each of these events so empowered the Anglophone societies as to lead to their domination of the late nineteenth and twentieth centuries. Moreover, Phillips argues, all three entailed an ongoing, if increasingly complex, religious confrontation. Even if the 1770s and, still more, the 1860s had available powerful secular ideologies, long-standing religious vocabularies with their roots in the Reformation continued to be decisive. At each of these junctures, the laicization and relative equality inherent in the priesthood of all believers successfully subverted clericalism, sacerdotalism, and traditional piety that supported old regime, corporate power structures.[1] The 1640s, 1770s, and 1860s emerge unmistakably as Protestant revolutions.

Phillips's thesis had proven unassailable. What he has not pointed out, however, is that each of these turning points was suffused with apocalyptic expectations that were uniquely widespread and embraced with unparalleled intensity. Such expectations, we have seen, formed part of the cultural bedrock of sixteenth-century Protestantism and comprised common property within the British Isles. There were English royalists who, almost desperately, wanted to see Charles I or his son as a latter-day Constantine, colonial Loyalists who pondered prophecies, and Southerners who visualized the Confederacy as the new dispensation Israel. Nevertheless, in each case these voices remained muted. Instead, eschatology gave voice and energy to revolution, not counter-revolution, serving as the driving force of progressive values. The apocalypse is historically allied with modern attitudes, rather than with reaction. Still more, it is the central motor of modernity.

The defining importance of this series of events for the Anglophone future is difficult to overstate. Comparable moments of reform emerged elsewhere in Europe, and almost without exception met with defeat. By the 1570s the French Reformation had developed a highly articulated civic culture and created the neologism "patriot" a full decade before the term entered English; as Henri Hauser observed long ago, "Le patriote de 1580 a déjà quelques traits du patriote de 1789."[2] But by 1598 public values had been dashed. The Last World Empire, not the civil millennium, lay ahead. At least by 1615 "patriot" had entered the vernaculars of central Europe, but radical reform proved a "false dawn," and the prospects for a civic world collapsed precipitously in the wake of the Bohemian catastrophe at White Mountain in 1620. Only in the northern Netherlands did a republican culture emerge to contend against traditional Europe.

COLONIAL NORTH AMERICA

Puritan strongholds in southeast England, radical pockets in the midlands, the covenanting southwest in Scotland, and the Presbyterian Scots-Irish in northern Ireland continued to retain many of the ideas of the mid-century revolution into the eighteenth century. So too, did New England (which would prove the most determined bastion of the American Revolution and, later, of the Civil War)—followed by the Presbyterians of western Pennsylvania, the exceptionally low Anglicans of Virginia and, to a lesser extent, of the fragmented society further south. The uprisings of Nathaniel Bacon (c. 1647–1676) and Jacob Leisler (c. 1635–1691) against the authoritarianism of the Stuart Restoration, as well as the subsequent agitations of John Wise (1652–1725) variously manifested the earlier revolutionary experience. Wise, although a minister, found himself particularly exercised by clerical claims and insisted that the "democratic" congregational church polity made it a lay institution. His argument was deeply informed by a radical reading of the Reformation apocalyptic, visibly founded on Foxe, and, still more, by an urgent sense of eschatological struggle. At one point he wanted to settle his congregation near to Spanish strongholds in North America as part of the effort to bring about the downfall of the great empire, an event that appeared to be imminent. Not surprisingly, Wise's writing would be reprinted during the revolutionary crisis.

The colonial communities were far from simply being the backwater successors to mid-seventeenth-century thinking. Wise sought to base his view of politics (and the mixed government of the British Empire), quite improbably, on the thought of Samuel Pufendorf (1632–1694). Wise's conservative opponent and nemesis, Cotton Mather (1663–1728), was no less immersed in the Protestant apocalypse, though he gave it a far less optimistic reading. He too became engaged in contemporary European thought, specifically the higher biblical criticism derived from Baruch Spinoza and Thomas Hobbes. His efforts to preserve a plausibly authentic Old Testament text were by no means obscurantist, but rational and seriously analytical, if not altogether successful. Mather's apocalyptic vision, like that of many American commentators, drew on current geology, and the eschatology of Burnet, Newton, and Whiston—emphasizing their naturalistic reading of the prophetic images as describing vulcanism. For the conservative Mather, again like his English contemporaries, such naturalism foreclosed human endeavor. Politics could not precipitate a new heaven, new earth. The most arresting feature about North America, however, was less the varied reading of the apocalypse than the widespread interest in the subject.

That interest rose dramatically with the extraordinary religious revival known as the First Great Awakening (primarily 1739–1743, but anticipated 1734–1735). No individual proved more central to these events than did the New England minister Jonathan Edwards (1703–1758). Until relatively recently Edwards has been treated as a negative figure in the American experience. His most famous writing, the sermon "Sinners in the Hands of an Angry God" (1741), has served as an iconic counterpoint to the previous century's seemingly more humane Roger Williams: fire and brimstone versus religious toleration. That both clergymen perceived their world through the Reformation apocalypse has appeared less striking than their theological differences. Certainly Edwards provided ferocious pronouncements: "There is the dreadful pit of the glowing flames of the wrath of God; there is hell's wide gaping mouth open; and you have nothing to stand upon, nor anything to take hold of; there is nothing between you and hell but the air; it is only the power and mere pleasure of God that holds you up."[3] Fearsome stuff, yet not in the least obscurantist. Edwards's uncompromising insistence on divine sovereignty led him directly to Newtonian gravity. So too, it necessarily enjoined Lockean empiricism. Like the great English scientist, Edwards utterly believed in the Lord God of Dominion. This neo-Calvinist God could not be coerced and still less understood through logical systems like Ramism, however reformist their intentions may have originally been. Harvard College's Protestant "scholasticism"—its "technologia," as it had come to be called—now fell before the awesome majesty of an ultimately unknowable God. Edwards's deity manifested himself, at least initially, through power, will, and history, rather than by means of timeless underlying structure.

Accordingly, the apocalypse always held a central place in his thinking, and from at least the age of twenty Edwards "read the public newletters" to grasp prophecy's course and meaning.[4] Edwards's apocalypse is therefore very much in the Reformation tradition, the unfolding of history leading to the eschaton, in fact to the millennium. Because the apocalyptic program was knowable through political history, it was optimistic, quite unlike Cotton Mather's much darker and ultimately unpredictable time scheme. It was optimistic in still further ways. Edwards's vision is unmistakably meliorist; things were patently getting better. Whatever crises and trials lay ahead, he simply could not believe that the Reformation might be undone and medieval darkness return. Further, Edwards found himself much exercised by the "discouragements" believers might feel if the millennium lay in a far distant future and the immediate prospects could only be horrific and bleak. How could such a view be other "than a great damp to their hope, courage and activity, in praying for, and reaching after the speedy introduction of those glorious promised times." Hope was well-founded. That did not mean that the millennium would happen "at one stroke," but would result from an incremental, historical process—"brought to pass by a gradual progress of religion."[5] Whatever the talk of burning brimstone, whatever "man's absolute dependence on the operations of the God's Holy Spirit," vitalist, "enthusiastic" faith and the prospect of conversion pointed away from terror rather than toward it. The "progress of religion" entailed the progress of conversion, and that could only be powerfully encouraging. History showed every indication of being on humanity's side, both personally and corporately. At the heart of the sacred narrative lay the conversion of mankind rather than the triumph of a particular church discipline, events crucial to the overthrow of the Antichrist. And conversion happened aplenty during the Great Awakening. Perhaps for that reason Joseph Bellamy (1719–1790), one of Edwards's closest disciples, came to believe that, eventually, barely one in 17,476 would confront damnation, while the millennium itself could last as long as 360,000 years. Hell might gape, but it threatened to become distinctly underpopulated.

The religious experience of the 1730s and early 1740s led Edwards to believe that the millennial era might be in the immediate offing. In a passage that has frequently attracted modern historians, Edwards declared that the last times might be initiated by these extraordinary events now taking place in New England. Britain lay too near the European mainland. Less bloodshed on behalf of religion had occurred in America. Its discovery shortly before the Reformation surely connected it to the most momentous events within the divine scheme.[6] This circumstance in no way detached America from Britain or Europe. Edwards sought to explicate the dramatic significance of the revival rather than imagine any form of American national "identity." American mission was a British project—and thereafter a universal one. Exactly one century earlier the great Scottish divine Samuel Rutherford adopted a range of prophecies to proclaim a similar mission for Scotland. "Now, O Scotland, God be thanked, thy name is in the Bible." Rutherford's purposes, just like Edwards's, were entirely British, and, again, thereafter universal.[7] Ethnic preoccupations barely touched Edwards, who could speak of taking "the Liberty of an Englishman (that speaks his Mind freely, concerning publick Affairs)." If Edwards all but reflexively assumed himself a part of a greater Britain, Rutherford had the much more concrete political aim of constructing just such a Britain.

Perhaps nothing better illustrates the nonnational character of the Edwardian millennium than its epicenters. On the one hand, as the revival intensified, Edwards came to believe that his own congregation in Northampton might prove the latter-day launching-pad. On the other, once established, the center of the millennial age would not be America or greater Britain, but restored and enlarged Israel. "Religion and learning will be there at the highest; more excellent books will be there written, etc." The Christian era would not segregate Jews from Gentiles, and people would be free to move to Judea and to settle in Jerusalem. Jews would regard Gentiles as their brethren, "much as the Christians in Boston and the Christians in other parts of New England look upon each other as brethren."[8] A Jewish restoration in the Middle East had been a part of Anglophone eschatology for well over a century. But we now encounter more confident, almost reflexive anticipations of latter-day Israel. If Edwards's hopes had proven true, we might easily imagine him departing Northampton and removing with his family to Jerusalem where he could settle with the great intellects.

Even so, learning in the millennial age will flourish everywhere: "excellent books will be published in Africa, in Ethiopia, in Turkey—and not only very learned men, but others that are more ordinary men, shall then be very knowing in religion." This uncompromising racial equality carried important implications for Edwards's other close disciple, Samuel Hopkins (1721–1803), the Congregationalist minister from Rhode Island, who became a fervent abolitionist. Ever improving technology (not static "technologia"), the stuff of Enlightenment progress, drove the apocalyptic program by improving communications, advancing knowledge, and thereby facilitating conversion. At the same time, much as Newton had anticipated, the work of science would reduce life's burdens, ease the curse of labor, the terror of famine, the weight of sickness. That in turn could only lead to a more harmonious, integrated world. Anticipating Condorcet, though without the mathematician's sophistication, Hopkins believed that growing international communication would lead to a single world language. These processes for Edwards and his followers were emphatically naturalistic. So too was the conversion experience itself: "this new spiritual sense is not a new faculty of understanding," but "a new kind of exercises of the same faculty of understanding."[9] Grace merely completed nature rather than abolishing it. That, in Edwards's hands, made the kingdom of Christ benign but far from republican, non-coercive, though far from fully civic. As the regenerative work of the spirit entailed a relatively modest step, so entry into the new age would not involve total transformation. Natural hierarchy would continue, and the Great Chain of Being persisted in modified form. But with massively improved agricultural productivity ("20, 30, and perhaps 100 fold more") class tensions would fade and disappear.[10] Even if the millennium grew out of human endeavor, that circumstance did not imply political reordering. There would be no "levelling behavior." Naturalism led to racial equality but no less to social conservatism.

Edwards was very far from an apolitical naif. He followed the news closely, took a close interest in Russian successes against the Ottoman Empire, and, hugely more, in the contemporary struggle at home which formed a major part of the titanic, global conflict against the French during the Seven Years' War (1756–1763). The Great Awakening had unexpectedly shifted the cultural landscape in profound ways. Although none intended it, the revival proved at once politicizing, democratizing, and integrative of all British North America. Richard Hofstadter has described the Awakening as eighteenth-century America's "first major intercolonial crisis of the mind and spirit."[11] It shattered and then reshattered the churches and, thereby, clerical power. The notion of the public good simply could not be identified with any specific doctrine, any particular creed, any exclusive religious claims. The millennium, it seemed, might only be achieved outside of any clerical framework, through political agency, through direct action. At the same time the new preoccupation with religion, and especially vital, "enthusiastic" religion that linked the individual directly with the spirit of God, promoted individual responsibility and civic capability: political values that reached back to the late sixteenth century and became increasingly sophisticated right through the eighteenth—what modern historians have sometimes termed the Atlantic Republican Tradition. The Awakening was a pan-British phenomenon, but crucially it spanned Anglophone America, integrating the patchwork of legal jurisdictions together with the widely varied social and religious communities that populated the Atlantic coastal basin. Religious revival generated revitalized politics. For many, surely most, the new politics retained a sacralized character. The saint and the citizen found themselves conjoined once again, but now they ceased to be identified with any particular church, or indeed any church at all.

Clerical authority inherently declined, supplanted by an increasingly public culture. No one discovered this more directly than did Jonathan Edwards himself. In 1750 the Northampton church rejected his claim to control admission to communion and deposed him. Edwards fell victim to the spiritual forces that he had done so much to encourage and that neither he nor anyone else could direct or control.

REVOLUTION IN AMERICA

From the middle 1740s to the late 1790s growing numbers of North Americans, even English-speakers generally, came to see the apocalypse as driven by political institutions and public action. An ever more artic-ulate "civil millennialism" developed where prayer meetings without denominational boundaries dissolved into public meetings without social boundaries. The spectacular victory of colonial citizen-soldiers over professional French troops at Louisburg in the summer of 1745 and the capture of that reputedly impregnable fortress, the greatest on the conti-nent, mandated an eschatological reading. The final defeat of counter-revolution at Culloden in the following year only confirmed this percep-tion. The great war against France of 1754/1756–1763 that finally and totally crushed the Last World Empire could have no other meaning. Civil millennialism reached crescendo proportions in the 1770s crisis. It went on to promote a still more radical republicanism in the 1790s. Eschatological civil religion offered an outlook more than a program, a historical vision rather than developed policies or intricate constitutions. Millennial expectations framed events rather than announcing them. There existed no prophetically prescribed checks and balances. Never-theless, civil religion enjoined public life and thereby underwrote revolu-tion. Civil millennialism proved crucial to a mental environment where rights were self-generated and only sustained through politics, rather than simply anchored in prior juridical authority.

During the Cold War, Western rhetoric constantly disparaged the Soviet claim to be creating "new men." But the Soviets were far less original than their critics made out. All revolutions since the eigh-teenth century have sought to achieve just that, "new men," and not least the America Revolution. Changing traditional people into politi-cal people, subjects bound by custom, ritual, authority into citizens who defined the public good—or as they sometimes said in France, peasants into Frenchmen—has lain at the heart of every major revolution and even many with modest objectives and limited impact. In colonial America where the apocalypse and Reformation piety shaped the outlook of so many, the new self might easily find expression in the language of conversion. Here was a transition all the more easily imaginable where there existed no massive gulf between grace and nature. With faculties simply drawn together more effectively, with vision simply sharpened, with the distance between all men no more than marginal, the spirit might just as readily lead to republican radicalism as to Edwardian hierarchy. Once again but more powerfully than ever, the civic became the soteriological.

Similarly, we would be unwise to distinguish sharply in the eighteenth century between apocalyptic upheaval and incremental secular progress. One modern commentator has spoken of Edwards's eschatological vision as "the afflictive model of progress." This conception of human history, it is claimed, contrasted with the steady improvement that characterized the concept of progress held by Edwards's secular contemporaries. The distinction is severely misleading, a bright red herring. Violence, cataclysm, crisis, setback, trials, and of course revolution might punctuate the trajectory of secular progress every bit as easily as in the apocalyptic program. As Condorcet noted, in the age of Francis Bacon "events had not yet determined whether the inevitable fall to which kings had been condemned by reason would be the peaceful work of enlightenment or the rapid effect of the indignation of peoples free from deception."[12] The apocalypse and progress differed profoundly from one another. But they embraced overlapping vocabularies and could appear to carry a common agenda—and, in Patricia Bonomi's words, "flowed in one stream toward the crisis of the 1776."[13] They would do so again in the 1790s and the 1860s. In the approach to revolution John Adams's apocalyptic *Dissertation on the Canon and Feudal Law* (1765) and Thomas Paine's secular *Common Sense* (1776) spoke simultaneously in multiple registers. The struggle against medieval legal structures was simultaneously a struggle against Antichrist, but the story need not obligate a spiritual dimension. For many clergy Paine's title sounded like Francis Hutcheson's and Thomas Reid's epistemologies with their theistic versions of "common sense."

Shared cause and joint purposes arose in response to Tory counter-revolution, led by perhaps the greatest Tory of all, George III. All of the issues that precipitated the crisis and for which the war was fought concerned the integrity of civic society: concerns regarding public decision-taking, public discourse, public dissemination of information. Personal autonomy was central not in itself, but because it enabled the sacred exercise of civic virtue. Some of the threats here were long-standing and commonplace. Place, patronage, standing armies, the court, all forms of paternalist authority, sometimes subsumed under the general term "robinocracy," comprised institutional practices that precluded just this civic capability. Herein lay anti-Christian corruption. Personal dependence, clientage, corporate coercion made moral decision-taking and public policy impossible. That was serious enough. But developments yet more sinister and threatening to public culture began to appear with the accession of George III.

The decision to establish a North American episcopate, strongly promoted by the king, immediately precipitated a major crisis (1767–1770). Here was nothing less than the introduction of an Old Regime hierarchy, completely at odds with the kind of political culture that had now emerged more or less uniformly throughout much of British North America. Talk about the projected Episcopal order tolerating dissent—regarded (rightly) as disingenuous—was simply beside the point. Unlike the earlier Hanoverians, who were distant, undistinguished, Europe-oriented, the third George actively sought an authoritarian, clericalized, and integrated empire. Integration had indeed occurred on a grand scale, but the commonalities that had emerged pointed to a shared public culture, and altogether away from his aspirations. The monarch's intentions resembled those of seventeenth-century Stuart kings and, to his opponents, made the millenarian language of liberation seem resoundingly apposite. Memories of the British Revolution surfaced quickly. The High Church Loyalist Joseph Galloway revealingly denounced "republican sectaries" as the fomenters of the Revolution, whose Congregational and Presbyterian "principles of religion and polity were equally adverse to those of the established Church and Government." George himself was quick to label the Revolution a "Presbyterian war."[14]

Arguably no issue galvanized the revolution more than the Quebec Act (1774). Most notably, the enactment re-established the Catholic hierarchy in defeated Quebec with all of its previous power and privileges, together with traditional society generally that included the

French system of seigneurial land tenures. The immediate, "volcanic" reaction in the colonies resulted less from anti-Romanism than from hostility to the Old Regime. Authoritarian government rather than Catholic belief was the issue. George had institutionalized the Counter-Reformation at its purest, and that really meant counter-revolution and reaction at their purest. We do not encounter mindless bigotry, but coherent political observation. At issue was not personal faith, but social institutions. Mistaken religion, many Americans believed, might lead to positive conclusions, "a possibly useful exploration of the nature of God." Mistaken politics could not, for the Old Regime could only defeat human purpose.[15] No one saw George as a papal agent or a Catholic dupe. With both the royal and papal crowns now subsumed under the rubric "arbitrary government," the danger became political repression, not formal theology. While the conflict for a great many was also a spiritual matter, it hardly touched dogmatics. Private belief fell before the securing of public right. For this reason, in 1776 the Reverend Samuel Sherwood declared that the great Beast in Revelation 13 applied to British tyranny rather than the Vatican: the prophecy could not intend "so narrow a circle as Papal Rome." Thereafter, the struggle against Antichrist focused entirely on Whitehall and the British monarchy, while the Vatican dropped out of the equation entirely and simply disappeared.[16] For this reason too, the fall of Rome before French republican armies in the late 1790s went relatively unnoticed. The new language now (briefly) in the city if not at the curia—"citizen bishop," "citizen monsignor"—appeared almost commonplace. The great aim of the Reformation became relatively marginal before larger concerns. Again for this reason, Irish Protestants and Catholics might hope to collaborate in 1798. It is seriously distorting—and in some respects plainly wrong—to describe the American Revolution as "the last religious war."

Civil millennialism would be rejected in the 1770s by several small millenarian movements that also rejected politics and public life. All of them proved extremely authoritarian, found meaning only within familial relations, and comprised living denials of the core values of the revolution. The most notable were the Shakers, founded by Ann Lee, who had immigrated to New York in 1774. Lee was jailed briefly as a counter-revolutionary, though even she expected the millennium to begin in America. Still other millenarians, such as Edwards's young confidant Samuel Hopkins, were reluctant to connect contemporary politics with the eschatological narrative. Hopkins discussed the millennial age in considerable, naturalistic detail, but he did not pay much attention to its social structure, beyond intimating that it would be stratified and undemocratic. Unlike his mentor, he did not look in the newspapers for clues to the future, and never went further than suggesting obliquely that the determined pursuit of liberty was undermining the Beast. Hopkins did not abjure politics. But both his highly formulated final age and his belief that an outpouring of the spirit into men would achieve it thoroughly discouraged an apocalyptic reading of the rise of republican democracy. The abolition of slavery and the repatriation of freed Blacks to Africa did carry eschatological significance in part because they were seen as crucial elements in evangelizing the world. In all these respects Hopkins anticipated the spinoff from the massive reaction against secularism, the Second Great Awakening (c. 1800–1840). But in the later eighteenth century Hopkins's voice was largely isolated.

Hopkins spoke remotely about preposterous "enthusiasts" discrediting millenarianism both in the patristic age and then in the wake of the Reformation. The Sabbatarian Baptist Henry Clarke agreed: it was "absurd" to think that the millennium and events associated with it could be brought about by "some revolution in the political transactions of the nations of the world."[17] This protestation and others like it served simply to confirm the prominence of the political millennium rather than confuting it.

The Revolution faced many enemies beyond simply the British government and Loyalists at home: High Anglicans, Irish Catholics, Jacobites, Highlanders, and a majority of Scots. George Buchanan, Samuel Rutherford, and other radical Scots from earlier periods had contributed directly to American revolutionary thought, but that largely ceased to be the case in the eighteenth century. Then many of them held important administrative and commercial "places" with the newly expanded empire, in addition to serving as government "placemen" in Parliament.

By far the most formidable intellectual opposition to revolution, whether secular or millenarian, arose from elements within the Scottish Enlightenment. Scottish philosophical skepticism, associated outstandingly with David Hume of Ninewells (1711–1776), promoted an ironic detachment that struck at civic capacity and political activism. In the words of a modern commentator Scotland's Enlightenment developed a skeptical sociology that "deconstructed ... the whole phenomenon of patriotism" and validated the authority and historical claims of the great empire.[18] Only the Secession Churches and the Relief Church, which retained the covenanting tradition, together with parts of the evangelical popular party in the established church, supported the American cause in significant numbers. As in the sixteenth century, skepticism was the ally of conservatism and reaction. "Le bon David" charmed Enlightenment France because his thought and intellectual acuity appeared to subvert clerical authority and inherited dogma. But no less, if less dramatically, did it subvert social activism. Hume altogether lacked the crusading energy of his Pyrrhonist forebears. Quite unlike Maldonat and his associates, he certainly did not believe in witches. His skepticism, however, was completely compatible with a thoroughgoing philosophical racism, a line of thought that could only justify slavery. The evangelical abolitionist Charles Crawford later challenged Hume, not about skepticism, but racial equality. Skepticism would more often prove debilitating than liberating. Its role in the creation of modernity has been oblique, and at times negative.

All of these conflicting claims, hopes, and ideological commitments occurred within what we might call an Anglophone *oikoumene*. The North Americans were passionately invested in the parliamentary cause championed by John Wilkes (1727–1797) and English reform; they "looked to the radical opposition movement in London" as the logical center of their political action and as having common goals. The American republic resulted not from "nationalist" aspirations (there were none), but from the failure of British public life, from the failure to redeem greater Britain. As John Murrin has observed, the American crusade was undertaken on behalf of the English-speaking world; it was also conducted through common vocabularies and widely shared modes of direct action.[19] Similarly, the struggle itself was by a variety of standards a civil war. Greater Britain as a whole found itself divided, and divided along patterns recognizably similar to the seventeenth-century British Revolution. The London government sponsored and publicized petitions in support of its coercive policies; historic centers of radicalism and dissent organized petition drives on behalf of reconciliation. The extent of Loyalism in America has long been recognized as greater than traditional mythologies ever wanted to admit. Yet sympathy for the America cause within Britain was also more widespread than commonly realized. Phillips has indicated that even elements within the English officer corps had doubts about the legitimacy of the war. Although violence and repression only occurred in America, conflict engulfed greater Britain.

When America's mission within greater Britain failed and the republic emerged from the bitter war against tyranny and Antichrist, American eschatological purposes not only remained very much a part of politics, but had actually deepened as a result of success. Claims made during the conflict that identified America with Daniel's little stone in Nebuchadnezzar's dream that overthrew tyranny and then grew into a mountain (Dan. 1–4), now became normative. Joel Barlow's poem, declaimed at the 1778 Yale commencement, spoke directly:

> From this fair Mount th'excinded stone shall roll,
> Reach the far East and spread from pole to pole; ...
> *That* signal spoke of a Savior's humble birth,
> *This* speaks his long and glorious reign on earth!
> Then Love shall rule, and Innocence adore,
> Discord shall cease, and Tyrants be no more;
> Till yon bright orb, and those celestial spheres,
> In radiant circles, mark a thousand years.

These claims echoed within American political rhetoric for the next two centuries, surfacing memorably in the 1960s and beyond. Similarly, Cyprian Strong's assertion in 1777 that America was latter-day Israel became commonplace. "There is no one (I trust) whose mind is not at once struck with the description of Israel, as being a most perfect resemblance of these American Colonies: almost ... as if spoken with a primary reference to them."[20]

In themselves such statements had been around for a very long time indeed, throughout the English-speaking world and at every point on the compass. The language reached back to Luther and Savonarola. It had informed the imperial visions of the Hapsburgs and the Bourbons. Yet America was different. European societies needed to read eschatological meanings into their historical pasts. Quite different readings were inevitably and readily at hand. Even Scotland's Covenanters had reinstituted long-standing political structures; only the church broke decisively with the past and became the focus of Scottish radicalism as a result. In contrast, the American past actually had been suffused with prophetic expectations from the outset. The prophetic therefore reached much more deeply into the textures of American politics than elsewhere. In some ways America was more the heir of the British Revolution than Britain itself. The language of world redemption became American English.

American apocalyptic discourse, like its secular counterpart, made emphatically universal statements, and remains far from modern nationalism. We do not encounter Edmund Burke's proto-Romantic "genius of the nation philosophically considered" or Johann Herder's "Volkseele." There existed no transcendent "spirit" that identified Americans and separated them from all other people. America had no "soul," and that proved its great strength. At the same time in American political thought, again both in its apocalyptic and secular forms, the commitment is to public values, not family values—not Burke's "dearest domestic ties" and "family affections." Redemption required civic action, not private retirement, "passionate" public engagement, not "warm" personal intimacy.

Few events illustrate the universalist character of American politics more clearly than its reaction to the French Revolution. It was one thing for a society of four million at the edge of civilization to see its achievements as a harbinger to the millennium. It was quite another for much the same upheaval to occur in a country of twenty-six million, the greatest power on the planet for over a century and the undisputed center of culture. These events became all the more dramatic because they completely reversed France's place in the sacred drama. No longer the signal crusader for anti-Christian oppression, the new France and especially the revolutionary republic became the agent of world liberation. The brave hopes of 1776 became the plausible future of 1789 and, still more, 1793. Joseph Priestley was far from alone in seeing the French Revolution as initiating the millennial era. The notion swept much of America, not least because it so validated American understanding of the world. The French civil church seemed to resemble the early steps toward reformation, as indeed it did. Religious toleration, much expanded under the republic, opened the way for Protestantism for the first time in over a century. Above all, the passionate civic ideal and large-scale public participation in politics spoke to American values. Robespierre's famous *Report*, much admired by Priestley, immediately appeared in translation at Philadelphia. Although more appealing to Republicans than Federalists, and especially to Republican Presbyterian and Baptist millenarians in Philadelphia and New York, the French Revolution initially found support just about everywhere. The end of tyranny in all its forms (most notably the increasingly reactionary British government) and a Christian world of democratic republics might lie just ahead. Perhaps predictably, Americans duly decoded "Louis XVI" into the Revelation's 666.

The future held the greatest promise. Or so it seemed. French irreligion was troubling. So too was anticlerical violence and the Terror generally. But that would only prove temporary, a waystation from Babylonish darkness en route to sincere faith. As disappointment and then disenchantment with the Directory grew during the course of the decade, it increasingly appeared that the French Revolution was leading not to the millennium but to infidelity. New England's Congregationalist clergy were among the earliest to rethink events in France. Although they had resolutely supported the American Revolution, they nevertheless emerged among the revolution's greatest losers: their power eroded, and their status declined through disestablishment in Connecticut, New Hampshire, and Massachusetts. Anticlericalism and disbelief seemed to strike directly at them. Both French and American radicalism—the latter much more visible in the 1790s than the 1770s—also challenged their social conservatism. By the end of the decade Timothy Dwight (1752–1817), the president of Yale College, and other clergy had come to view the French state not as a great step toward the historical redemption, but as the agent of Antichrist: "The liberty of Infidels was not the liberty of New England." David Humphreys (1752–1818), General Washington's aide-de-camp and later a senior government official, agreed that the new "monster-pow'r" did not serve the providential cause of righteousness. Atheism, deism, the rejection of faith—all promoted by radical Republicans, Jacobin Clubs, Masonic Lodges, and, still more ominous for being secret, Bavarian Illuminati—comprised the great crisis of the latter days. The New England clergy were not alone in their spiritual disquiet: figures such as Samuel Coleridge and William Wordsworth also broke with the revolution at this time for religious reasons. American attitudes need to be seen as part of a general reaction against democracy and secularism. Similarly, religious revivalism in early nineteenth-century America forms part of a broader cultural shift that transformed the whole of Europe. But nothing more convulsed the American sensibility than infidelity's seizure of the White House in 1800.

THE SECOND GREAT AWAKENING: BIPOLAR REACTION

Thomas Jefferson is the only avowed non-Christian ever elected president. The reaction to that event in the early decades of the nineteenth century, intensified by a context of deepening conservatism, transformed American politics and American apocalyptic thought. In New England there emerged secessionist agitation that lasted until 1815. Although the New England clergy based their eschatological reading of the French state on the "new tyranny" of infidelity and did not normally abjure republican principles, they certainly read the great reactionary exegetes, Horsley, Faber, and the other Oxford divines. Thomas Paine found himself socially ostracized for being an "atheist." "Reason Street" in New York City, named after his great work, became corrupted into "Raison," and then changed altogether.

Major revolutionary figures such as Elias Boudinot, Benjamin Rush (1746–1813), and David Humphreys found it difficult to countenance formal politics that now dismissed the spiritual underpinnings of the revolution. They looked away from government and instead focused on voluntary moral associations that would evangelize America (and world), bring about reform, and usher in the millennial kingdom. Such associations proliferated throughout the republic and often developed powerful links abroad. Their causes were extraordinarily wide-ranging: missions, prison reform, temperance, Lord's Day observance, Indian protection, Jewish conversion, scientific societies seeking to validate prophecy and determine its time scale, a near-infinity of Bible societies, and, especially after 1830, a crusade against slavery. Some of these activities will strike us as quite odd. At the end of the 1790s the Reverend David Austin (1759–1831) built dwellings in New Haven where the Jews would assemble just before the restoration of Israel. In a similar vein Mordecai Noah (*fl.* 1800–1820) attempted to set up a temporary Jewish state, Ararat, on Grand Island off Buffalo, New

York, in 1818. Noah had the enthusiastic backing of the city, and the project was inaugurated with a parade, bands, and the most extraordinary ceremony—only Jews were lacking. However extreme, both these events illustrate the extent to which eschatological expectations informed attitudes in the early republic and the kind of voluntarism through which they were expressed.

All of these events, from the reaction against France to the Hebrew waystations, were fueled by the Second Great Awakening, a nationwide series of religious revivals. It radically energized religion as a dynamic independent of electoral politics. Like its eighteenth-century predecessor, it brought unintended consequences of the first magnitude. Organized religion became increasingly fragmented, while a generalized religiosity, suffused with apocalyptic images, eschatological expectation, and shifting millenarian hopes, spread widely—migrating westward with American expansion particularly in the north. As in contemporary Europe, religion experienced powerful revival, but more often in the United States it could possess progressive and even radical implications. Friedrich Schleiermacher's insistence that religion comprised feeling rather than doctrine or François Chateaubriand's discovery of the transcendent in primitive and traditional religion, did not share in America's uninstitutionalized, disestablished spirituality. At the same time American revival bore no more than limited connection, at most, with the emerging romantic nationalism. Only with elements of British spirituality did American religious revivalism develop close, collaborative connections through linked voluntary associations. As in the age of the American Revolution, there existed a genuinely greater Britain, now concerned with moral issues rather than formal politics, millenarian missions rather than the civil millennium. Britain too experienced a direct but independent analogue to the Second Great Awakening revivalism. Nonconformity grew from 300 to 400 percent during the first four decades of the nineteenth century. By 1820 nonconformists had risen to a third of the population. During that decade, concomitantly with America, urgent millennial expectations achieved dramatic prominence. Where contemporaneous revivalism on the continent reinforced established churches and fired new readings of tradition, it energized spirituality against the Erastian establishment in Britain or, in America, transformed denominations and created new ones.

Out of the Second Great Awakening arose a theological reconfiguration that would hold enormous consequences for the future. Now for the first time appeared a serious, eventually defining divide between "premillennialism" and "postmillennialism." The former maintained that Christ would return personally to launch the millennium and thereafter actively direct events during this period. The latter claimed that Christ would only return physically at the end of the millennial era and conclude human history. In theory the first would devalue politics and discount the physical world, for it would all suddenly end—and end independently of either human activity or natural processes. The second, again in theory, envisioned the final age as resulting from history and as integral to the visible apocalyptic program. Seemingly, the emphasis on history would then root postmillennialism in the Reformation and, at least potentially, in human endeavor. Christ's spirit reigned through men during the Last Age. His physical presence arrived once the community of the saved (or humanity) had achieved its potential and the great Sabbath had worked its completion.

This dichotomy needs to be handled with care. Not only did these terms arise in the nineteenth century, so too did the thinking behind them. Historians will project them back into the early modern period only at their peril. Such categories simply cannot apply to the sixteenth century (Luther, Calvin, and virtually all the reformers emerge as both post- and premillennialists). Further, these theological differences were by no means defining—neither matters of central dispute, nor at all polarizing. There might need to be urgent and highly political activity in preparation for the premillennial advent. At the same time, activities leading to a postmillennial pouring out of the spirit might be limited to prayer, and possess no political dimension. Moreover, for a number of thinkers—ranging from wild Fifth Monarchy Men to cautious John Wesley—the millennial period would have a "morning" and an "afternoon." Rather than come either at the beginning or the end, Jesus might make his appearance once the party had gotten well under way. The earliest signs of a pre-versus-post polarity will not predate the end of the 1780s. Even so, this bifurcated configuration only gradually took shape during the course of the Awakening.

Both postmillennialism, the dominant American eschatology for most of the nineteenth century, and premillennialism became detached from electoral politics and secular "infidelity." Neither eschewed social agendas or activism, at least initially. But postmillennialism developed an ever deeper sense of time and development. It had much in common with the nineteenth-century notion of progress and needs to be seen as part of the second great temporalization of Western culture that occurred after 1800. History, development, process provided meaning within nearly every aspect of nineteenth-century thought. This would prove equally true right across the political spectrum: from the left with Marxism and the rise of the bourgeoisie, followed by the proletariat; to liberalism's rise of parliamentary institutions, democracy, and civil liberties; to the authoritarian Auguste Comte (1798–1857) who looked to the division of labor and the rise of corporate power; to the nationalists and the unfolding of the spirit of the nation. History held a no less decisive place for comprehending the individual. The self could only be of its moment, who you were depended on when you were, and modern autobiography like that of John Stuart Mill now became possible. The great sciences of the nineteenth century—geology, thermodynamics, and biology—examined nature through the lenses of linear time. Aesthetics could locate the universal only by focusing exclusively on the unique, the particular, the thing in its radical individuality, and thus in its time. Music labored to hear the past, Bach the way he sounded in the baroque age. Philosophy became preoccupied with temporal categories, and even God now had a history, a being, like so much else, now seeking self-actualization and, eventually, fulfillment. In this time-suffused cultural context postmillennialism was not in the least aberrant, but just the reverse. The apocalypse survived the secular world it did so much to create rather than being superceded by it, and it did so, in part, because its postmillennial form appeared to share so much in common with the new secularism.

Postmillennialism was not only immersed in time, the direct product of Reformation and Enlightenment Age apocalyptic, but it continued to develop and deepen its temporalized vision. Death itself became transformed, not only in theology but also in everyday physical culture. By the 1830s, James Moorhead has observed, there emerged a rural cemetery movement that turned frightening graveyards into attractive parks. Finality and mortality became further marginalized after the Civil War, with the advent of the "lawn cemetery" containing minimal markers and without images of skulls and crossbones, or statements discounting this life. Death, no longer the massive divide between the present and eternity, became less a chilling terminus than a step within a larger process. The self would strive and achieve its purposes beyond the grave, and so even eternity became temporalized.[21] If time transformed heaven, in the same process it moved hell to the margins—a long-term development that began at least as early as the later seventeenth century and would not be reversed, for the mainstream, until the late twentieth. Precisely this preoccupation with time enabled many postmillennial theologians to accept German higher biblical criticism at the end of the century: if, in the best traditions of the Reformation, text and time anchored truth and faith, then uncovering the historical truth—as it really happened (*wie es eigentlich gewesen*)—could only be positive.

There was nothing about postmillennialism in the least morally tepid or socially bland. It fired the engine of the most radical moment in nineteenth-century America: the Civil War. It remained a formidable force for reform well into recent times. But postmillennialism did have an intellectual competitor that eventually overtook it. Premillennialism offered a far more somber, even wrenching view of the future. Yet however unsettling, premillennialism nevertheless also possessed an urgency, drama, and exhilaration that drew people out of humdrum "illusions" and into cosmic reality. More easily visualized because it conformed more literally to texts that everyone knew, it utterly qualified all authority, both secular and clerical.

This type of spirituality received enormous impetus though the new revivalism during the 1820s. One enduring manifestation occurred with Joseph Smith (1805–1844) and what became the Church of the Latter Day Saints. Smith's apocalyptic narrative—elaborate, original, quixotic—enjoined an intensive missionary fervor combined with the imperative of withdrawal. Anyone with eyes could see and announce that time was drawing to a close. But only a true prophet was capable of directing people to sacred shelter before the imminent days of wrath. The Jews long knew their need to return to Jerusalem. Christians, however, had to locate Zion, Jerusalem's gentile counterpart, and that required an inspired emissary, an individual truly sent by God.

The most spectacular moment of premillennialism occurred under the leadership of the lay Baptist preacher William Miller (1782–1849). In 1816 Miller broke with secularism, with the Enlightenment, with Paine and Voltaire, and with politics generally. Through an elaborate calculation of biblical numbers, Miller became persuaded that Jesus would appear in the clouds with his angels sometime by the end of 1843. Although initially diffident about his findings, the excited revivalist context pressured him into public announcement in 1831. Enormous interest ensued, as the doctrine was proclaimed at conferences, camp meetings, and in the press. The movement had wide impact well beyond its growing body of followers, attracting comment from a surprising range of contemporary American authors. Large numbers of people abandoned their work and homes for the world to come and waited with Miller for the great events, slated to occur between 21 March 1843 and 21 March 1844. When nothing happened, a recalculation focused on 22 October 1844. Again, nothing. The result was the convulsive "Great Disappointment": significant disillusionment combined with public ridicule. Postmillennialism became strengthened, as did the traditional churches.

In themselves "disappointments" were nothing new. One occurred within a few years of Luther's Reformation; the last significant "disappointment" in America had taken place in 1796. In the supercharged environment of early nineteenth-century America, involving large numbers of people, the consequences could only be explosive. The most striking development from the 1843–1844 fiasco was not the repudiation of eschatological schemes, but their reformulation. Two new movements subsequently emerged from the prophetic failure: the Jehovah's Witnesses and the Seventh-day Adventists. What distinguished these two quite different movements was not their refusal to date the advent (the Witnesses felt no reluctance), but their far more radical rejection of the secular world. Both not only rejected political processes. They went on to develop a determined anti-politics that dismissed American mission, social reform, and voluntarism. Only conversion could matter. The people that gathered about William Miller included ardent abolitionists and individuals who anticipated still other varieties of reform. "Pre" and "Post" would truly separate not over the doctrine of the advent, but from an undergirding new theology that totally and resoundingly replaced the linear-time eschatologies of the Reformation.

Such a reconceived eschatology reached the American shores in just these years from the British Isles. Probably no figure provided premillennialism a more complete theological basis than did John Nelson

Darby (1800–1882), whose thinking shaped Anglophone Protestantism throughout the world, especially in America where his views are still felt today. Darby was raised a member of the Protestant Church of Ireland, but early on he rejected the church's sacramental formalism, hierarchy, and concern with tradition, and subsequently repudiated it altogether. In its place he turned to British millenarianism which had become heavily premillennial: civil millenarianism and republicanism, the world of Price, Priestley, and William Blake, had gone into decline by the 1830s and disappeared with the collapse of Chartism in the next decade. Darby insisted that biblical prophecy did not comprise a linear process underlying the human experience, but only obtained at discrete moments or epochs, "dispensations" as they came to be known. The last apocalyptic period had run from the rebuilding of the temple in Jerusalem after the Babylonian captivity to the coming of the messiah, Jesus. His rejection by the Jews brought prophetic time to a halt. Since then, for some 1800 years, human events bore no relation to biblical prophecy. This hiatus, the "great parenthesis," comprised the era of "the Church."

Now the "parenthesis" would soon reach its closure. The apocalyptic program will recommence, and prophecy will once again guide events. Those events would be the final acts of the sacred drama. Dramatic indeed. Drawing on Paul's first letter to the Thessalonians (4:16–17), Darby declared that the Lord would appear in the sky, raise the redeemed dead, and then "rapture" the saved among those still living on Earth up into the clouds to join him and the heavenly congregation. Events would move quickly. During the next three and a half years (1260 days; the prophetic day/year did not apply in this instance), a cataclysmic purification of the earth would take place through the greatest tribulations, which included natural catastrophes and, above all, the reign of Antichrist. At the end of that period, the Lord and the gathered host would descend to the new earth, and the final period, the era of "the Kingdom," would commence.

The sources for Darby's new apocalyptic have received much discussion. Parallels at certain points with the eschatology of Increase Mather (1639–1723) have been noted. Similarities with early modern Catholic efforts to discredit the Reformation apocalypse have also been observed. Counter-Reformers such as Cardinal Bellarmine (1542–1621) had argued that biblical prophecy described events that had already occurred during antiquity; others such as the Spanish Jesuit Francisco Ribeira (1537–1591) had claimed that most of the prophesied events in scripture would only occur in the remote future and bore no connection to the current confessional conflict. Recently it has been suggested that Darby drew on the apocalyptic of France's austere Catholic Jansenism. Comparisons have even been made with Patristic writings like the *Didache* (early second century). None have proven conclusive. Whatever his sources, Darby broke decisively with the Reformation, with the Enlightenment, and with the central assumptions of the earlier nineteenth century. For, in a word, history was bunk. Most of the past possessed no prophetic meaning whatever—and consequently not much meaning at all. Premillennialism now truly parted company with its postmillennial rival. The issues between them went beyond radically conflicting theology to the understanding of time and the vision of the world. It would be hard to imagine a more comprehensive rejection of the new secular culture.

THE AMERICAN CIVIL WAR

The American Civil War comprises the last major act of the Reformation and the culmination of the British Revolution. The earlier wars of the republic, against Britain in 1812 and against Mexico in 1846, had been ambivalent affairs. Although elements within the clergy had blessed these undertakings and pronounced them providential, important sections of the population regarded them with grave misgiving. In complete contrast, the American Civil War became for the North almost immediately an eschatological crusade, a struggle to realize the national mission and thereby bring about the prophesied millennium: global freedom through the creation of civic societies. Julia Ward Howe's "Battle Hymn of the Republic" (1862)—the gravest and most stirring of American patriotic songs—offers a verse rendering of the Revelation presented through a civil millennial reading. The "glory of the coming of the Lord" in the day of wrath will bring the triumph of righteousness and social justice. The interweaving of redemption and political liberation, conversion and political agency, that long-standing Anglophone commonplace, is famously explicit: "In the beauty of the lilies Christ was born across the sea, / With a glory in his bosom that transfigures you and me. / As he died to make men holy, let us die to make men free." The Army of the Potomac offered "a fiery gospel writ in burnished rows of steel." Mobilization often involved prayer meetings, revivalism, conversions, and E. L. Tuveson may well be right in commenting that "no army since Cromwell's ever had been endowed with such a sense of personal calling."[22] Very much the same sense of the providential, the universal, and, implicitly, the redemptive appears in Abraham Lincoln's address at Gettysburg a year later where he portrayed the war as a decisive test not only for this nation but "*any* nation so conceived and so dedicated." The republic bore the ensign for mankind, and thus American failure meant human failure.

Lincoln's Republican Party had arisen in the previous decade as an antiparty, integrating voluntary moral associations, among much else, into a political reform movement. The talk was of "Fusion Politics" or "Independent Politics." The electoral process acquired a prominent eschatological dimension such as had not been seen since the eighteenth century. Christ's kingdom became, once more, a political act, as the millennium reconverged with public life, and the developing struggle emerged as the postmillennial apogee, its greatest achievement.

The 1850s had been characterized by sectional crisis, by the social crisis of slavery, and by deepening religious tensions largely in response to the enormous influx of Irish Catholics fleeing the famine. Theirs was a traditional Catholicism, one bolstered by a hierarchy that soon became more open and powerful than had existed anywhere in the Anglophone world since the reign of Mary Tudor during the sixteenth century. Their politics too would be traditional and increasingly organized. Activist, proselytizing, with funding, it was claimed, from no less than Hapsburg Austria (and today no longer simply dismissed as Protestant paranoia), Catholic-Protestant tension provided a powerful socioreligious dimension to the great war. Raw bigotry abounded from every direction. Nevertheless, as in earlier centuries, though far more than before, simple religious animus was neither decisive nor absolute. Larger cultural cleavages—messianic republicanism confronting Counter-Reformed hierarchy—proved defining. The Republican Party was not nativist or xenophobic, and attracted large numbers of recent immigrants from Britain, Scandinavia, Germany, and the Netherlands. But its appeal was distinctly Protestant.

Radical reform, signally the crusade against slavery, in great measure grew out of radical religion. Support for the North, for the Union, for the prospect of a new egalitarian order accordingly took shape along broadly long-standing patterns. Both at home and abroad, high Anglicans and Catholics favored the South, evangelicals the North. If Irish Catholics fought on both sides during the Civil War, Irish sentiments were decidedly anti-Black and pro-slavery. Northern evangelicals as well as secular radicals identified their struggle with the contemporary movement in Italy led by Giuseppe Garibaldi (1807–1882), who in just these years was attacking Rome, and also that of Camillio Cavour (1810–1861): both threatened clerical power and seemed to promise a democratic era—"the Sabbath of Liberty, the Jubilee of Humanity." For some Americans all this presaged world revolution against old regime aristocracies and privileged churches everywhere. Conversely, it is surely no accident that the Vatican alone, unlike any other power, so strongly endorsed the South (and criticized the North) that its statement was taken to comprise formal recognition of the Confederate government. Nor is it incidental that John Wilkes Booth became a Catholic convert. Putative Jesuit conspiracies will tell us far less than do larger social patterns. Small wonder the *Philadelphia Inquirer* proclaimed Grant's victory with the headline, "Richmond! Babylon Is Fallen!"[23]

Both the United Kingdom and Second Empire France considered recognizing the Confederacy. Neither did, and in the United Kingdom the prospect became a highly divisive public debate. The Tory elites, the aristocracy and High Anglicans, along with the conservative press like the *Times* of London, were staunchly pro-Confederate. Victoria herself was actively interventionist; Britain and France would mediate the dispute, thereby recognizing the secession as a fait accompli and fundamentally legitimate. The Queen's declaration of British neutrality at the outset of hostilities (that implicitly accepted southern belligerence) met with Senator Charles Sumner's angry and telling comment: "the most hateful act of English history since the time of Charles 2nd." By 1862 Irish opinion was vociferously pro-Confederate. At the same time greater visibility of slavery as the war's underlying issue increasingly mobilized liberal opinion, the dissenting churches, and workingmen's organizations on behalf of the North.[24] Democratic reform came to appear in Britain too as a common cause, even a global aspiration.

The postwar United States emerged as a major military power for the first time in its history. It had fought what in retrospect would be recognized as the first modern war. It had mobilized massive resources, built an unprecedented infrastructure, and laid the foundations for industrialization. The Ladies' Christian Commission spoke more prophetically in 1865 than even they could have anticipated, when they declared: "The arbitrament of the world's destiny, the fate of the liberty of mankind, depends upon the American army and navy." Expansiveness, military, migratory, and especially missionary, promised to "bring the latter glory down upon the earth."[25] The new America's circumstances and aspirations, and the vocabulary through which they were articulated, found their sources in the republic's seventeenth-century British predecessor. Its ideology derived earlier still, from the Reformation's historical apocalyptic.

Like revolutionary America and revolutionary Britain, Civil War America became a more egalitarian society. However, unlike the settlements in 1650s Britain and 1780s America, the American Reconstruction, eventually, proved more reluctant to expropriate and redistribute the property and power of counterrevolution. By the 1890s that failure led to long-term social catastrophe. But a transformation of the most fundamental sort had occurred, and that transformation found its driving force in Protestant eschatology. The Union victory marked the final triumph of the Anglophone reform tradition, the postmillennial moment.

Beginning in the 1890s a shift in Western assumptions of seismic proportions began to take place. It resulted in new cultural patterns—often called "Modernism"—that reached beyond the deeply embittered push-pull of reform and reaction: Progressivism and Jim Crow, Dreyfusards and Anti-Dreyfusards, Georges Clemenceau and Charles Maurras, Herbert Asquith and Herbert Spencer, or Sergei Witte and Constantine Pobedonostev. Modernism challenged the significance, even the plausibility, of linear time. In so doing it confronted and refracted, if it did not reverse, the thrust of the Western experience since the sixteenth century. Modernism manifested itself in all aspects of the late nineteenth- and early twentieth-century intellect: politics, philosophy, natural science, literature, the fine arts, social science. Religion could not remain unaffected. Far more, an atemporal, anti-linear eschatology inherently fit the new sensibility. Premillennialism did not achieve dominance as a response to the trauma of the First World War and the shattering of confidence that accompanied it. Premillennial dominance occurred earlier as part of the shifting cultural tectonic that gave rise to Modernism.

CHAPTER 10

ANTICHRIST IN THE POSTAPOCALYPTIC AGE

The most striking feature of Anglophone Protestantism following the American Civil War is the erosion of postmillennial thought. In part its reformist, developmental vocabulary became increasingly difficult to distinguish from nineteenth-century notions of secular progress. Even Darwinian evolution did not necessarily trouble so time-oriented a faith as historical Protestantism. Quite the reverse. Process, development, incremental improvement had lain at its heart, and so it also seemed to do with evolution. Natural selection, however, did pose a massive and indeed insurmountable problem. Random mutation as the driving force in biology inherently foreclosed a providential universe, and thereby the central feature in any conception of the Judeo-Christian God. Nevertheless, the outward form of the new biology might appear to reinforce the faith rather than undermine it. Sanitized Darwin could prove to be Christianity's best friend.

No less significant for the postmillennial decline was the conversion of two generations of clergy to Darby's dispensational premillennialism, among the more notable Dwight L. Moody (1837–1899), Arthur Tappan Pierson (1837–1911), and Cyrus Scofield (1843–1921). All of them adopted the exhilarating, if bleak vision of a basically unchanging world hopelessly mired in sin whose future was expected to be short. They rejected any prospect of reform, any hope of amelioration, any version of progress. "Gigantic as it [American civilization] is in invention, discovery, enterprise, achievement," Pierson declared, "it is gigantically worldly ... monstrously God-denying and God-defying." "I don't find any place where God says the world is to grow better and better," Moody agreed. "I find that the earth is to grow worse and worse." Accordingly, Scofield concluded: "The true mission of the church is not to reform society." "What Christ did not do, the Apostles did not do. Not one of them was a reformer." Darwin was wrong not only because his theory dissented from the literal statements in scripture, but because of the progressivist vision it seemed to imply.[1] Progress might be an illusion, but premillennial views did not in the least lead to quietism or withdrawal. Just the opposite. They stimulated the greatest activism. Now in the closing moments before the advent, it became urgently necessary to spread the faith. Such was the precondition for that event. In the strongest possible terms, the times mandated missions at home and abroad. Quite unlike the hopes of Samuel Hopkins and his successors, premillennialists were too "realistic" to expect that their evangelizing efforts would actually convert the world. The point was to make the gospel globally available, to spread it to the nations. That alone comprised the fulfillment of prophecy. That alone would precipitate the advent and the millennium. The biblical basis for all this constituted the "fundamentals," and only in the last decades of the nineteenth century can we perceive the beginnings of what later came to be known as fundamentalism.

Premillennialism did not become official doctrine in any denomination; it did not become normative even in Utah. But these doctrines and the spiritual sensibility associated with them reached widely across America and well beyond. Pierson's writings addressed audiences in French and Dutch. His missionary activities spearheaded a movement in the Far East: "China for Christ in the Twentieth Century." In America, through national conferences, extensive publications, and church-based missions especially in the cities, dispensational premillennialism unquestionably became by the turn of the century the dominant Protestant eschatology. Postmillennialism did not face extinction and in later circumstances turned out to possess remarkable vitality and an important future. But the early twentieth-century cultural context pointed in an altogether different direction.

Surprisingly, Catholic thinking during the late nineteenth and early twentieth centuries in some ways paralleled Protestant premillennialism. In retrospect, this development might be seen as the first steps toward the subsequent Catholicization of Protestant tradition that took place in the late twentieth century. To be sure, the apocalypse never played well with the bishops of Rome. The atemporal and antitemporal Roman perspective and the medieval culture that grew up with the rise of the papal theocracy consistently regarded apocalyptic expectations with distrust, if not as outright heresy. This attitude became defining with the Tridentine decrees. It was one thing to adopt imperial insignia to support claims for the universal papal monarchy, quite another to give them an eschatological reading. Even the Hapsburg and Bourbon Last World Empires, so vital to Catholic survival, did not receive unreserved endorsement; the struggle between Louis XIV and Innocent IX had far-reaching political consequences for both Protestants and Catholics. Catholic eschatology from Campanella to Vieira, from the Jansenists in the 1730s to Emanuel Lacunza in the 1790s, continually ran afoul of clerical authority. The French Revolution attracted the enthusiastic support of a great many priests, but only the remarkable abbé Henri Gregoire (1750–1831) located it within an articulated apocalyptic vision of world salvation, the closest Catholic counterpart to the thought of figures such as Price, Priestley, Rush, and Humphreys. Catholic reactionaries like Joseph de Maistre (1754–1821) saw the revolution as God's scourge, but restoring the "organic" thirteenth-century theocracy did not enjoin eschatology. Only with the later nineteenth century and after did Marian visitations at Lourdes in France (1858), Fatima in Portugal (1917), Eskogia in Spain (1931), and elsewhere proffer prophetic expectations to large numbers of people—or, in the case of Lourdes, acquire them. Each of these manifested a powerful reaction against an emerging secular, democratic society. Each was premillennial: the kingdom of Christ lay in the offing with his imminent return. Each of them proclaimed the urgent need for traditional piety. In some instances the Virgin had revealed a number of "secrets" which intimated events that would precede the advent. Far more than Protestantism, Catholic eschatologies stressed the tribulations— indeed the extraordinary physical torment—that lay ahead. Mary experienced vast suffering in holding off the wrath of her son, and an unredeemed world would certainly come to know it. Like Protestant premillennialists, the Catholic visionaries discounted time and history, and focused on impending crisis, cataclysm, and unspeakable violence.

THE MODERNIST CHALLENGE: CYRUS SCOFIELD, DWIGHT MOODY ... AND FRIEDRICH NIETZSCHE?

The year 1909 witnessed the publication of two works that at a glance could hardly have been more different: the *Scofield Reference*

Bible and "Foundation and Declaration of Futurism," the first of two manifestoes issued by F. T. Marinetti (1876–1944) and his associates that announced the Futurist art movement. Scofield's Bible provided a detailed, Darby-based, premillennial reading of scripture. Utterly religious and militantly anti-secular, the book, published by no less than Oxford University Press, sold in the millions. The Futurist manifestoes, stridently irreligious, saw only an extremely limited distribution. If the Futurist movement proved surprisingly influential, its violent rhetoric could appear no more than metaphorically "apocalyptic." Scofield might actually have welcomed Marinetti's "demand" that all pictures of the Madonna should be thrown into the Tiber. But it is hard to think that the two could have had anything substantive in common.

And yet, on reflection, Scofield and Marinetti formed integral elements with a powerful cultural vector of Western and even global significance. Both were truly "futurist" and drastically anti-historical. Both bristled with expectations of cataclysmic change. Both rejected long familiar continuities. Both discounted linear time: "Time and space died yesterday," announced Marinetti. Both separated themselves from the confident, optimistic assumptions that seemed to characterize the era they inhabited.

They shared far more than simple functional similarities. Scofield and Marinetti—Darbyists and Futurists—self-consciously and emphatically rejected the Enlightenment and the Renaissance, and with them the temporality that had arisen with the Reformation. Futurists and premillennialists were obsessed with the decadence of the present. They felt a great longing for the rebirth of the spirit, experienced a deep aesthetic sense for the beauty of the new dawn, looked to the purifying effects of violence, whether as prophesied tribulations or Nietzsche-inflected destruction. They angrily dismissed liberalism, socialism, democracy, for an elitist world of transcendent authority. Moreover, despite their profound sense of discontinuity, they anticipated a surprisingly traditionalist order: whether in terms of gender relations, family structure, or the collapsing of public space. Arch-conservative premillennialists and proto-Fascist Futurists founded their entire undertaking upon an avowed irrationality.

The Enlightenment surely never encountered a more devastating critic than Friedrich Nietzsche (1844–1900). What made him so devastating was not his "irrationalism." The Enlightenment fully recognized that truth was a social construction. The quest for first principles, ultimate rationality, final answers, metaphysics could only lead to the poisonous "esprit de système." Nietzsche did much more. He rejected, totally and wittily, the possibility of consensus. There could be no "common sense." The dynamic of progress immediately collapsed. Authority became normative, and art supplanted science as the model of cognition. Was Giotto a poorer painter than Rembrandt? Aeschylus inferior to Shakespeare? "Historical men," Nietzsche observed, "believe that the meaning of existence will become ever clearer in the course of its evolution." That was patently untrue. What resulted was "not a real culture but a kind of knowledge about culture, a complex of various thoughts and feelings about it." Nietzsche looked to the rare, creative genius to invent the myths, images, and deep-seated mental structures that everyone else thought *with*—but not *about*. Culture needed "individuals who form a sort of bridge over the wan stream of becoming." "One giant calls to the other across the waste space of time, and the high spirit-talk goes on, undisturbed by the wanton, noisy dwarfs who creep among them."[2] One consequence of Nietzsche's thought, almost certainly unintended, was to make all significant truth claims untestable and thereby equally valid. It is no small irony that the self-proclaimed Antichrist should have validated authoritarian religion and, notable among others, Christian fundamentalism. Nor is it any accident that premillennialism achieved unprecedented prominence during the 1890s, just as Nietzsche's thought achieved recognition as a major philosophical force. Moody and Pierson did not read Nietzsche, and Nietzsche, who stopped writing in 1889, certainly did not read them. Yet they are all manifestations of a growing unease with "cold ineffectual knowledge" and its putative progress.

That unease did not simply fire a radical conservatism. The critique of time, both sacred and secular, extended well beyond the right to embrace the full range of politics, and, much more, forms part of a broad cultural shift of the greatest consequence. In literature the Victorian novel with its intricate, interwoven plot and character development came to be replaced by modernist poetry and novels that rejected narrative for the "mythic method" and drastically compressed time in densely layered, simultaneous ways. In social science the rise of complex organization from simple hunter-gathers to the intricacies of industrial modernity became displaced by atemporal analyses of social structures: interpreting symbol systems rather than assessing historical development. The life sciences now focused on microbiology rather than Darwinism, while Sigmund Freud looked away from evolution, the panorama of the rise and fall of species, to the largely timeless engines that powered evolution, the "drives." The physical sciences reveal a similar pattern. Newton had maintained that "absolute, true, and mathematical time, of itself, and from its own nature, flows equally without relation to any external thing." Albert Einstein's theories of special and general relativity (1905, 1910) changed time from an absolute to a local and diminished phenomenon, defined contextually. Fine art—whether Romantic, Realist, or Impressionist—had sought to capture a moment in time. Modernist art, like Cubism, collapsed many moments into a single, layered space that defied the linear. Pablo Picasso did not see ancient artifacts and contemporary African masks as objects that illustrated a particular moment or manifested a particular kind of society, but as immediate aesthetic structures that spoke across time and development. Even the two great leaders who emerged in the final years of the first world war, Woodrow Wilson (1856–1924) and V. I. Lenin (1870–1924), although both firmly anchored in the Enlightenment tradition, spoke the language of cataclysm. For Wilson, this would be the war to end all wars, the war to make the world safe for democracy. For Lenin, the war had precipitated the world proletarian revolution, the great leap into the future.

The intellectual thrust of the early twentieth century, even at its most sophisticated, melded surprisingly well with premillennial expectations and spirituality. Fundamentalism was not simply the product of backwater obscurantists, altogether isolated from the larger issues of the age, but a manifestation of its central preoccupations. Remarkably, Friedrich Nietzsche proved its intellectual godfather. He would do so again at century's end.

BOLSHEVIK REVOLUTION: THE ENLIGHTENMENT MOVES EAST

In common with Jefferson and Robespierre before him, Lenin saw secularization as one of the crucial objectives of political revolution. "Man's intelligence," he declared, "may be only a feeble rush-light in the darkness of night, but I am not going to let that flickering flame be blown out by mystics and metaphysicians."[3] Fellow Bolsheviks such as Alexander Bogdanov (1873–1928) who seemed to spiritualize Marxist theory, Lenin memorably insisted, were fishing "in polluted waters." Jefferson and Robespierre also were immediately relevant. The Russian Revolution could only become intelligible, not least to the Bolsheviks themselves, when placed within the European revolutionary tradition. It grew out of these earlier struggles, identified with secular radicalism and sought to fulfill it. Lenin's challenge to Wilson, just like the later Soviet challenge to the United States, involved competing secularisms.

Not everyone saw the revolution or the Bolshevik victory in 1921 in these terms. One of the earliest intellectuals to rally to the Bolshevik cause was the writer Alexander Blok (1880–1921). Blok inhabited an environment suffused with eschatological expectations, and regarded the revolution as inaugurating the triumph of the Christian spirit. It would "*remake* everything" and "organize things so that everything would be new," literally new heaven, new earth. Within barely two months of Lenin's seizure of power Blok had composed a remarkable poem, "The Twelve." Twelve soldiers of the Red Guard set out at night during a ferocious snowstorm to secure an unidentified city (clearly Petrograd) on behalf of the revolution. Without realizing it, they are the apostles following Christ, who turns out to be carrying their blood-red banner. They alone have a "revolutionary step" and keep their footing in the storm, an elemental force that blows down all aspects of traditional society. Their justifiable anticlericalism, their proletarian anger, working-class coarseness, even their anti-Christian blasphemies serve to remake the world. Just as the coming of Christ had brought down the Roman Empire, so his return would bring down the Russian Empire and the false church that was associated with it. Since the sixteenth century it had been a commonplace that Moscow was the third Rome: the emperor Constantine translated the seat of Christianity to Constantinople in the fourth century, and Moscow succeeded Constantinople after the Ottoman Turks conquered the Bosporus in 1453. No subsequent translation would occur; thereafter in Russia stood the final order before the eschaton. That order now rapidly approaches its end. "The Twelve" is replete with apocalyptic imagery, the whore of Babylon (and her fate), Judas, the end of Daniel's fourth monarchy, and the poem concluding with the apocalyptically charged, violently anti-state Old Believer spelling of "Jesus." The end of empire is the eschatological event that will "light a fire through all the world."[4] However secular the intentions of the revolution, its early admirers and, later, its bitter detractors would often portray it within a religious vocabulary and in specifically eschatological terms.

At a popular level the early years of the Soviet republic also stimulated apocalyptic visions. During the 1920s the Russian Orthodox Church declined, while apocalyptic sectarians grew dramatically. Notably among them were the Skropsy and, more surprising, evangelical Protestantism. The latter encouraged a Bolshevik-style discipline of sobriety, literacy, and fraternity, while looking to an imminent, premillennial Second Coming. The former added a violent, self-destructive anti-sexuality to such values. All these phenomena have little to do with social "disorientation" or the psychological effects of "upheaval," but rather with the intellectual structures that now became prominent. Whether they supported the revolution or not, the sects in their primitive way shared common attitudes about "new worlds." Nor should it be surprising that a range of Bolshevik-Christian syncretisms also should have arisen: images of Lenin and Bolsheviks sympathetic to the peasantry such as Mikhail Kalinin (1875–1946) turn up on icon corners; the "Octobering" of infants in some regions supplanted baptism.[5] In this environment Soviet science necessarily carried multiple meanings, and the line between the rational and the occult, between the most advanced and the most preposterous, might not prove indelible.

Radical Bolsheviks such as Anatoly Lunacharsky (1875–1933), Maxim Gorky (1868–1936), and the former Bolshevik Bogdanov were entirely secular in outlook and aspiration. Yet their language easily encouraged apocalyptic vistas. They spoke of "god-building" and looked to the power of Soviet science to prolong life, perhaps indefinitely. Might it be technically possibly, as some intellectuals had hoped, actually to raise the dead? Even so, the living might find themselves empowered through integrated information systems that transformed both the structure and accessibility of knowledge. Such expectations were "millenarian" only in a metaphorical sense. They found their origins in the Enlightenment rather than Bacon and Campanella. But they did give voice to radical spirituality. They also departed from Lenin's increasingly practical preoccupations: the New Economic Policy, a mixed economy, reconstruction, and normalized relations with the capitalist world. Electrification rather than the promise of "proletarian culture" shaped the early years. Like many American liberals and Progressives, Lenin looked to greatly increased productivity and new levels of efficiency—the "cult of efficiency," to its critics—to transform society.

The Bolsheviks, Blok, and popular Russian religious culture reveal the extraordinary densities, power, and persistence of apocalyptic imagery in the modern world. For some they continued to serve as the prism through which events became intelligible and change meaningful. Here lay the dynamic of history and redemption. For others they simply provided uniquely compelling metaphors. In 1498 at the cusp of modernity Albrecht Dürer did an engraving of the whore of Babylon and accompanying prophecies to visualize and comprehend a world on the verge of drastic transformation. More than four centuries later Fritz Lang adopted the same image as a metaphor on film to confront severe class tension (Figures 10.1 and 10.1a). Between these two poles lay an intermediate area inhabited by people like Blok, both spiritualizing and secularizing—sweeping away old faith and suffocating forms for new worlds at once human and divine. If radical enough Bolshevism could negotiate mysticism and rationalism with astonishing creativity.

The Stalinist "revolution from above" resynthesized Bolshevik ideals and changed the Communist world. Starting in 1928 the regime forcibly collectivized most peasant land, and the brutal struggle that accompanied it was intended to transform the traditional peasant countryside into a form of urban and secular modernity. The new policies encountered widespread resistance, often cast within apocalyptic terms, which apparently comprised the "dominant idiom of protest." The Communist regime now emerged as the prophesied Antichrist, just the reverse of some earlier readings of it. Joining a collective farm—all dens of total iniquity, atheism, depravity, and immorality—stamped one with the mark of the Beast. Salvation would come only to those who refused.

Missing from the peasant apocalypse was a projected future millennium. So, too, no inspired prophet or latter-day witnesses seem ever to have to turned up. Peasant resistance inverted the Communist order, but did not look to a new earth beyond the NEP. Christ inhabited the peasant commune, Antichrist the collective farm, an eschatology that did not proceed further than inversion. The tractor more than

Figure 10.1 The whore of Babylon being worshiped by the princes of the earth as portrayed in Fritz Lang's *Metropolis* (1927). In this case the "princes" have become the privileged capitalist elite. Apocalyptic imagery was popular during the 1920s as a result of the 1916–1926 wave of revolution and counterrevolution. Like Katie in Blok's poem, "The Twelve," Lang's character Maria is at once the corrupting whore and the true church, the woman in the wilderness. The former persona is forced upon her by the evil inventor-magician C. A. Rotwang, who imposes Maria's form over his robot, the "New Man." The false Maria not only seduces the industrialists, who will continue to party and merrily watch "the world go to hell." She also seduces the hugely exploited workers, leading them to seize (and destroy) the machines. This action initiates the apocalypse, literally opening the floodgates and threatening the entire city. The apocalypse is ultimately avoided by a "mediator"—the son of the leading capitalist—who reconnects head and hand by serving as the heart that will rehumanize Metropolis. The false Maria is burnt at the stake (her true identity emerging in the process). Rotwang (red cheek; a play on "rotweg," the red way?) gets thrown off the cathedral roof by the "mediator."

No "New Man" is sought; no inventors need apply. Revolution will only lead to the apocalypse and catastrophe. There can exist but one solution: reconciliation. We are far from the Soviet view and also far from Blok's—for whom the revolution was an event of genuinely eschatological importance. For Lang the apocalypse, along with other biblical and medieval Christian anything else became the emblem of modernity and appeared in almost every poster celebrating or promoting the collectives. The Stalin regime was introducing the "second serfdom," and peasant resisters would invert that image just as their predecessors had inverted the image of the tsar. "The tractor plows deeply, / The land dries up. / Soon all the collective farmers / Will die of starvation." The tractor did not symbolize triumph, but death.[6] The apocalypse has often served conflicting causes, but arguably never more so than in the Russian Revolution.

COLD WAR CONFRONTATION AND THE IRONY OF APOCALYPTIC SHIBBOLETH

Winston Churchill predicted that the Grand Alliance between the Soviet Union, Great Britain, and the United States would last a generation, after which troubles would arise. In the event the alliance survived the war by barely two years. Churchill's surprise is understandable. Utterly unlike their Axis enemies, the Allied powers subscribed to universal human equality, to democracy as a norm (even though the Soviet Union was never a democracy), and to secular culture. It is hard to visualize a British, American, or Soviet "soul." In each case the roots of these societies lay with the Enlightenment. The slogan of the pre-war American Communist Party may have contained a pinch of truth, and perhaps more, when it claimed that Communism was "Twentieth-Century Americanism."

←—————————————————————————————

references, simply serve as metaphors. His prime concern is not to have the "apocalypse" occur, but to ensure that it does not.

Metropolis almost seems to be a counterpiece to an earlier Soviet film, Yakov Protazanov's *Aelita, Queen of Mars* (1924). Mars, the red star whose name seemed a variant of "Marx," would long be a favorite location for radical science fiction in the late Russian empire and the USSR. *Aelita* posits a society on the planet that closely anticipates the structure of *Metropolis*, but one that is overthrown when Russians turn up. However, the apocalypse forms no part of these events. At the end of the film *Aelita* turns relatively conservative. The Marian revolution—universal revolution—is revealed to be a daydream, and the point is to get down to work in the practical world of the New Economic Policy. By the later 1920s eschatology increasingly served counterrevolution—and, as it turned out, nowhere more so than in the Soviet Union.

Figure 10.1a Albrecht Dürer's image of the whore of Babylon and the princes of the earth (1498), like Lang's, is part of this evocative image's long tradition. As we have seen, such images lost power with the Reformation's
heavily historical reading of the Revelation's symbols. Modernist antitempor-
alism once again encouraged the identification of these symbols with individuals, and it may not be accidental that the medieval seven deadly sins prop
up Lang's beast and whore. Midway on the right side of Dürer's engraving, we
see the destruction of the metropolis, Babylon/Rome.

The first decade of the Cold War, 1948–1958, was characterized
especially in the West by a quest for the "vital center" and the proclamations of "the end of ideology." Literature became "disengaged";
decision-taking involved technical competence rather than judgments

of value or larger visions. In this context idealism, or even political conviction, invited caricature as mindless fanaticism, simply a form of religion. A torrent of Cold War volumes was directed against the Communist movement, often by former Communist intellectuals, which portrayed it as "the god that failed."[7] No writing was more prominent or more persuasive among these efforts to discredit the Soviet experiment than those that labeled it specifically as "apocalyptic." The outstanding work of this sort was Norman Cohn's *Pursuit of the Millennium: Revolutionary messianism in medieval and Reformation Europe and its bearing on modern totalitarian movements* (1957). One of the few studies of the Middle Ages to achieve bestseller status, Cohn's history has had an enormous impact. French, German, and Italian editions appeared within five years of its initial publication. Cohn argued that apocalypticism had consistently arisen among the dispossessed in moments of utter hopelessness, drawing on the ancient prophecies and their medieval elaborations to perpetrate massive explosions of mindless violence.

Further, Cohn went on to claim that Marxism, the Soviet Union, National Socialism, and the Third Reich were all manifestations of these traditions. Indeed, there were all one and the same. These ideologies and the societies founded on them shared "the structure of the basic phantasies" that seemed to "have changed scarcely at all." "Such was the [medieval] tradition of apocalyptic fanaticism which—secularized and revivified—was inherited by Lenin and Hitler." "For what Marx passed on to present-day Communism was not the fruit of his long years of study in the fields of economics and sociology but a quasi-apocalyptic phantasy which as a young man, unquestioningly and almost unconsciously, he had assimilated from a crowd of obscure writers and journalists."[8] Cohn conceded that to develop the common Nazi-Communist identity "in detail" would require another volume, and that volume never appeared. But it did not need to; the simple intimation proved far more effective (and was far less vulnerable) than any elaborate study. Its consequences were profound and hugely serviceable to the Cold War. The Soviet vast war effort became marginalized. The conflict amounted to a struggle between two twins with the same purposes. No less important, Cohn's analysis held a chilling prospect for any hope of significant social change. Radicalism was simply another form of apocalypse and invited the Third Reich. Cohn spoke frequently of "paranoia," "delusion," "phantasies," which suggested that radical ideology was less rooted in social reality than in psychological disorientation. Programs for change and agitation promoting them were at best socially dangerous if not an indication of mental unbalance—an attitude adopted increasingly both in the Soviet Union and the United States.

There existed no small irony in all this. Although the Soviet Union stood charged as "the god that failed" and as an apocalypse-based state, it would be the West and signally the United States that embraced eschatology as one of its main lines of Cold War attack. An extraordinary range of mainstream Western polemic, Protestant and Catholic, identified the Soviet Union specifically as the central figure in the latter-day scenario, the prophesied Antichrist. If both sides of the Cold War actually comprised secular societies, the United States was in truth vastly more open to the charge of being "apocalyptic." The Soviets never capitalized on that fact, most probably because they simply found it too alien for their vocabularies. Secularism almost always finds itself ill-equipped in a context of religious aggression.

Our Lady of Fatima, more than any other Catholic "miracle," led the Roman church's anti-Communist charge. Originally directed against the new Portuguese republic, the Virgin revealed a further "secret" that was described in 1929 by one of the original visionaries, Lucia dos Santos (1907–2005). God had asked that the pope "in union with all the bishops of the world to make the consecration of Russia to my [the Virgin's] Immaculate Heart, promising to save it by this means." By 1941 this instruction had become an apocalyptic imperative. The conversion of Russia and the overthrow of Communism would lead to world peace. Failure to achieve this would lead to war and persecution, although in the end the conversion had to occur and "a period of peace" would ensue. The Virgin's announcements became hugely popular during the 1940s and 1950s, and a Cold War commonplace.[9]

Protestant anti-Communism in the United States possessed longer roots. At least since the eighteenth-century revolution Americans had often found themselves hostile to the Russian autocracy, Abraham Lincoln not least among them. Darby, Scofield, and the premillennial movement identified the Russian monarchy and its growing empire with Gog and "the prince of Rosh" described in Ezekiel 38–39. Darby had made this identification as early as 1840, and by the end of the century it had become standard premillenniarian doctrine. In addition, the premillennialists inherited the philo-Semitism that had been so central to Anglophone Protestantism (doctrines they continued to share with their postmillennial competitors). There would be a restored Israel before the great tribulations, and Russian anti-Semitism—the pogroms began in the 1870s and often enough had official sanction and encouragement—supported this view of Russia as the great northern power that would attack Israel at the end of days. Further, official hostility to the substantial conversion of Russians to premillennial Protestantism during the late nineteenth century could only clinch this perception. If still more proof was needed, the coming of Communism and secularism certainly supplied it. Ronald Reagan's famous comments on the matter in 1971 articulated a well-established truism. "Ezekiel tells us that Gog, the nation that will lead all the other powers of darkness against Israel, will come out of the north. Biblical scholars have been saying for generations that Gog must be Russia." And "now that Russia has set itself against God ... it fits the description of Gog perfectly."[10] Reagan joined the drumbeat of decades.

THE 1960s: THE FINAL FLOWERING OF THE ENLIGHTENMENT AND THE POSTMILLENNIAL MOMENT

Between 1958 and 1968 the public culture that had emerged with the eighteenth-century Enlightenment resurfaced with remarkable power and extraordinary reach. Resurfacing too were the apocalyptic traditions, now called postmillennial, that had made the Enlightenment possible, and, more, proven integral to its creation. The last occurred primarily in the United States where these traditions had the most enduring historical foundations, and, with Martin Luther King, it issued in some of the most evocative political statements of the entire postwar period. They spoke compellingly to the nation and inspired people across Europe, even if their layered meanings were not fully understood in either. King seemed to have captured and articulated the aspirations of all people.

In a mental and social world that stressed people's similarities and common interests, there occurred as well an enormous expansion of personal liberty and public right, going well beyond anything that had ever previously existed. The American civil rights movement formed part of a much broader Western upheaval (what some historians have called a "rights revolution") that greatly extended boundaries of public life. The popular 1960s slogan—"the personal is the political"—obtained where the self became closely identified with civic capacity and social activism, and this could only be founded on the broadest understanding of universal right.

The politicization of the private went still further. In religion, saving grace appeared to derive through the immanent workings of the political process. One's own redemption became integral with the historical redemption of mankind. Whether Catholic, Protestant, or Jewish, religion tended to become civil religion, and personal salvation required social action. A focus on ethics rather than dogma softened ancient demarcations between people and between religions: whether through Vatican II, Reform Judaism, or liberal Protestantism. This environment necessarily validated the postmillennial vision, and that eschatology found expression in King's neo-orthodox writings. At the same time the environment drastically discounted its premillennial rival.

The dream King presented in 1963 bore no connection whatever to the commonplace American dream of self-absorbed, personal social mobility—a myth that succeeds only in devaluing the country's industrial base. His address instead embraced the Enlightenment in its American expression as a creed and ideal that urgently needed to be realized. But it also went further and spoke from the historical sources of those values. The dream was Nebuchadnezzar's from Daniel 2. It was the little stone that grew into the great mountain of righteousness that filled the whole earth at the end of days. "With this faith we will be able to hew out of the mountain of despair a stone of hope. With this faith we will be able to transform the jangling discords of our nation into a beautiful symphony of brotherhood."[11] King's words moved the nation, inspired the world. Nevertheless, most of his listeners missed his scriptural reference, which he then linked to mountains everywhere in America—and its eschatological meaning. That would not have happened a hundred years before. His voice was that of an earlier America, at once radical and yet comfortingly familiar, of the Anglophone apocalypse, and of the European Reformation. It was the voice of the crusade against slavery, the voice of radical abolition. We can hear in it Joel Barlow, Joseph Priestley, and William Blake.

Despite what would have seemed odd syntax and bewildering geography, the Levellers and the Diggers, Oliver Cromwell, Rembrandt van Rijn, and Menasseh ben Israel, could have caught King's meaning far more quickly than did some of his contemporaries. It may well be that precisely King's archaism made him so compellingly effective, so universally attractive. He enjoined modern ideals, secular values, but at the same time he appealed to the eschatological imperatives that had underwritten them and made them so powerful. It was the moment of postmillennial triumph and climax.

THE GREAT REACTION: PREMILLENNIAL AND POSTMODERN

Between 1968 and 1973 there occurred a series of crises—political, economic, cultural—that sapped confidence in politics and precipitated a rapid weakening of public culture throughout the West. The two great rivals, Communism and liberalism, went into decline together because, increasingly, their core values no longer carried conviction. The year 1968 stimulated the greatest hopes and brought the most searing disappointments. It was a tale of three cities: Prague (where radical Communism failed), Paris (where radical socialism failed), Chicago (where radical liberalism failed). At the end point of these critical years, the 1973 Arab oil embargo induced a crisis in economies already vulnerable and pointed away from public solutions. Indeed privatization became normative in almost every aspect of life, from economic policy to the conception of the self, from gated communities to the creation of corporate armies, from the images projected by popular culture to the questions that engaged the most sophisticated intellects.

In this far less optimistic environment people everywhere became much more inward-looking. Images of blood—race, nation, kindred, family, gender—became defining. The language was "roots," "soul," "heritage"; the preoccupation was with a priori essence rather than social achievement. Diversity supplanted humanity, identity supplanted public purpose, the intuitions of "blood" supplanted common sense. The world came to be seen as one we inherited, not one we created, and the slogan of the 1960s would be inverted, for the political was now the personal. Another cultural shift of tectonic proportions was occurring, and by 1974 its effects had become apparent in

Moscow and Belgrade, London and Washington. King never used the word "soul" in his 1963 address. By 1970 the word cropped up everywhere. Even British Prime Minister Harold Wilson could claim in 1970 that the Labour Party somehow had "soul."

The new sensibility received considerable impetus from the extensive revival of interest in Friedrich Nietzsche, and took shape in a tissue of formulations that came to be known as postmodernism. As Nietzsche had rejected the claims of the Enlightenment, so too his late twentieth-century successors rejected them most notably in their 1960s manifestations. There existed no universal reason, no common sense; assertions to the contrary comprised power mechanisms intended to coerce and enslave. Nothing could more powerfully reinforce the claims of blood exclusivity and the perception of being victimized by outsiders. Public life declined before what Richard Wolin has called "the anti-politics of cultural self-affirmation."[12] Nation, race, ethnicity, gender, however conceived, each entailed a grammar, logic, and reasoning system of its own, structures at once precious and constantly threatened. People no longer differed in style but in mind, a structure at once defining and unbridgeable.

Radicalism itself became privatized as a result. As Michel Foucault (1926–1984) put it, the real struggle concerned "the status of the individual" and the quotidian encounter with power in "immediate everyday life." People rightly did not look to solutions in "liberations, revolution, end of class struggle."[13] Foucault and the many others who promoted "identity" in this way departed from Nietzsche in that they did not seek to seize power but to resist it. They did not look to Nietzsche's "great politics," vague as that was, but to no politics at all. Nor could they, for there existed no shared reasoning mechanisms, but, instead, radically disjoined and conflicted "rationalities." Competing identities supplanted the public good, the common weal. Still, the differences between modernism and postmodernism should not be overdrawn. Neither Nietzsche nor his late twentieth-century successors saw significance in historical development. Quite the contrary, postmodernists such as Foucault took considerable pain to show that there had been no achievements in the past, merely reformulations and trade-offs. If anything the world today was severely more repressive than that of the Great Chain of Being, more insidious, more calculating, more totalizing. Foucault described himself as a historian of the present, and posed the question, "where are we now?"[14] But with the possibility of coherent political action foreclosed, there was little to do but await some sort of anarchic explosion. This mentality shared much with the premillennial.

Civil religion declined before traditional forms of piety whether Catholic, Protestant, or Jewish. Catholic eschatology, inherently premillennial, flourished widely, reaching unprecedented audiences. Jewish sectarian messianism took dramatic form with Menachem Schneerson (1902–1994), the Lubavitcher Rebbe in New York City. Undoubtedly the most visible shift occurred within American Protestant eschatology. King's postmillennialism withered before a resurgent dispensationalism. If the assassinated civil-rights leader achieved iconic status in American politics, his neo-orthodox theology did not. In 1970 Hal Lindsey (b. 1929) published *The Late Great Planet Earth*, which presented a detailed description of the contemporary moment completely cast within Darby's apocalyptic framework. Lindsey's was far from the only publication of this sort to appear at this time, but the book's simple language, lack of intricate theology (Darby is not mentioned), and sharp focus on current events made it readily accessible. In 1974, that bellwether year, Lindsey's book became a bestseller.

The projected future was both terrifying and thrilling. The saved would experience the rapture. Those who were left behind would endure seven years of tribulation, which included the rule of Antichrist (probably a leader of the European Community) who would rebuild the Temple in Jerusalem, and a Soviet attack on Israel, which would lead to thermonuclear war in the Middle East. Most would perish. Only those Jews who accepted Christ in the face of these calamities would survive and find redemption. They would then be joined by the raptured, who would descend with Christ to live with them on a now purged and purified world. A diagram of the rapture timeline (Figure 10.2)—described as a "tribulation map" by one of its distributors—lays out the story in simplest clarity. The implications were unmistakable: politics had nothing to offer. Social justice, however conceived, could only be irrelevant. Human agency had little meaning beyond conversion and the encouragement of conversion by proclaiming the Christian truth. In almost every way the rapture message reversed the hopes of 1963.

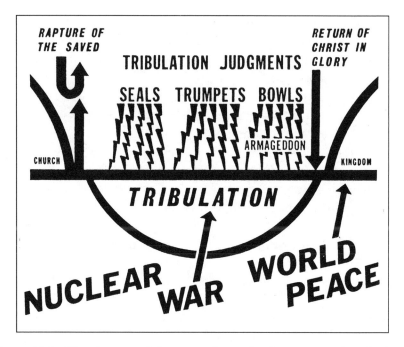

Figure 10.2 This drawing of the time scheme for the rapture—described as a "tribulation map" by one of its current distributors—dramatically illustrates the impulse to escape politics, where reform and public life are neither meaningful nor possible. Although the premillennial "tribulations" are now thermonuclear, the thinking behind it is firmly rooted in the nineteenth and early twentieth-century eschatology of Cyrus Scofield and John Nelson Darby.

The origins of the drawing are uncertain, but the attitudes it represents are characteristic of the 1970s and 1980s. As at the turn of the nineteenth century, these ideas again achieved prominence as part of a much broader cultural transformation. The drawing provides a history of the present. The period of the Church, on the left, does not involve sacred time and is largely irrelevant from an apocalyptic perspective—indeed, comprising a *longue durée*. The drawing asks, as Foucault was asking contemporaneously, "what's going on just now? What's happening to us? What is the world, this period, this precise moment in which we are living?" (Foucault, 1982; see n. 59).

In addition, the period of the "tribulations" is intense, but brief, a mere seven years. This view breaks sharply with the Reformation tradition, but it shares much both with contemporaneous Catholic apocalyptic and with earlier Catholic "futurist" apologetic.

Perhaps unwittingly the "map" may imply a level of human agency ultimately incompatible with the premillennial insistence on divine intervention and transcendent direction. Presumably humanity, not God, will ignite the

Perhaps no greater rejection of earlier expectations could occur than it did from the apocalypse of the Nation of Islam. The eschatology promoted by Elijah Muhammad (Elijah Poole, 1897–1975) and his militant successor Louis Farrakhan (Louis Wolcott, b. 1933) is distinctly premillennial, and, despite its putative Islamic sources, bears much in common with the rapture, Darby in blackface. It differs from King (and in this respect from Darby) in that it proclaims racism as its central eschatological tenet: God is a racialized being who provides Black identity (as is his opposite, the white devil), and the present dispensation will shortly end, leading to Black redemption and the destruction of the white world.

The contrast between the civil rights march in 1963 and Farrakhan's "Million Man March" in 1995 is a stark one. The 1963 march was a highly political event. Organized under the aegis of A. Philip Randolph's Brotherhood of Pullman Porters, it, like King, struck a strong universalistic note entirely in keeping with its labor movement traditions. It urged the passage of specific legislation with far-reaching social implications. The march sought to overcome racial divisions within America, for what seemed to be the higher ends that everyone shared. The march was inclusive both in its claims and in its participants. The 1995 march was blood-based, exclusivist in terms of both race and gender. The march challenges us to identify any political objective, for its central and explicit aim was atonement. Farrakhan spoke at moments of an "agenda" and of the need to register and vote for it, but that agenda was "the revival of the houses of God." Centrally, the march called upon its participants to look inward and find their identity.[15] In keeping with the postmodernist moment Farrakhan appealed to higher wisdom, special insight, race-based intuition that "transcended" the intellectual poverty of rationalist whites. Foucault might well have applauded.

Probably nothing separates King from Farrakhan more completely than their attitude toward Jews. King's religious tradition is historically

---

nuclear holocaust. Hal Lindsey hedged on the issue in the *Late Great Planet Earth*. Ezekiel's spectacular imagery could describe "a direct judgment of God, or God could allow the various countries to launch a nuclear exchange of ballistic missiles on each other."

philo-Semitic, views reinforced with Enlightenment universalism. Further, Darby, Scofield, and Lindsey were also philo-Semitic in the sense that they expected the Jews to play a significant and positive role at the end of days; many, they believed, would survive the tribulations and reach the millennial age. The Nation of Islam, by contrast, is violently anti-Semitic. The cause derives directly from the new preoccupation with identity and is of a piece with the anti-Semitism that characterizes most European nationalism since the later nineteenth century. The Jews as the motor of secularization emerge thereby the motor driving forces that have prevented Blacks from realizing who and what they truly are. Mythic claims about the role of Jews in the early modern slave trade become an unassailable metaphor of Black spiritual and cultural bondage. As with most premillennialisms, as in significant ways also with Foucault, the historical past is of far less importance than the eschatological present. Observers have noted the striking similarities between Nation of Islam's eschatology and that of Adventist and other premillennial groups. But the closest analogue to the Nation of Islam lies in its mirror image, literally, the Christian Identity Movement that is racist, supremacist, separatist, violently anti-Semitic—and premillennial. Both came to prominence in the 1970s.

The rise of sectarian religions during this period—often called "cults" by their critics—has long attracted attention because of their apocalyptic expectations and the accompanying bizarre, even horrific behavior. More significant than their idiosyncrasies, however, is their commonality with more respectable religion and participation in larger cultural patterns. From the People's Temple Christian Church of James Warren Jones (1913–1978) to the Heaven's Gate group of Marshall Applewhite (1932–1997), the consistent theme has been a rejection of politics in this world in favor of transcendent spirituality and eschatological escape.

The Rise of Dominion: From Transcendent Escape to Transcendent Theocracy

Lindsey had stated directly that "the sad prediction in the Bible is that mankind will not accept God's diagnosis or His cure. Therefore, they will seek to solve the problem [of war] themselves."[16] That will fail, inevitably, and the prospect could only be the rapture followed by the tribulations, outstandingly World War III. This cataclysmic event will be a massive face-off between the latter-day Roman Empire of United Europe (led by a fuehrer/Antichrist, an empire whose core comprised the prophetic ten countries, the long-familiar horns of the Beast) and the Communist Chinese. The Soviet Union would have already been destroyed just before by its attack on Israel; the United States will have declined and succumbed to the Roman-European order. The message seemed crystalline: find Christ, await the rapture. The future lay in escape.

Or was there a wrinkle? Lindsey conceded that American decline might be delayed. "The only chance" of slowing it up lay in "a widespread spiritual awakening." For all of its evident escapism, Lindsey's book contained a subtext that went beyond a simple rejection of this world: American leadership of the Western world required the acceptance of Christ.[17] If this possibility did not obviate the cascading catastrophes that lay ahead, it opened the door to human volition in ways that were not immediately obvious. The world might be changed by human activity after all. In the late twentieth century Darby's premillennialism might bleed into something that increasingly looked like postmillennialism. The rebuilding of the Jerusalem Temple, large-scale conversions, religious "awakening" might increasingly lengthen the foreground events before the recommencing of prophetic time. Pre- and postmillennialism always remained far from stable categories, despite even Darby's theology. A more salient test of people's outlook is their attitude toward the Enlightenment, rather than their "pre" or "post" formulations.

A kind of postmillennialism appeared in the later century that bore no connection whatever to Joel Barlow and the American revolutionaries, or the abolitionists, or Julia Ward Howe and the crusade against slavery, or to Martin Luther King and civil rights. With the quite obscure figure, Rousas J. Rushdoony (1916–2001), there emerged in America, again in the 1970s, a systematic call for Christian theocracy that was postmillennial in the sense that its achievement was a necessary prelude to the return of Jesus. Despite their ostensible doctrinal difference, Lindsey and Rushdoony shared much in common. They saw secular society as a spiritual catastrophe. They believed—and Foucault agreed—that the modern dilemma had arisen with the Enlightenment. They had found the 1960s a searing experience (as had

Foucault). Most of all, both shared an apocalyptic sense of the urgent need to sacralize society and culture. The elision from "pre" to "post"—from Christianizing America in preparation for the rapture to the imposition of Christian morality on America in advance of the Second Advent—was an easy one. Both sprang from a common eschatological mentality and from the fierce rejection of politics that so characterized the period. Both fervently sought the "reconstruction" of society—in ways that contrasted completely with the postmillennial Reconstruction a century earlier.

Michelle Goldberg has observed that premillennialists increasingly embraced Rushdoony's notion of "Christian Dominion" and formed alliances with the "Reconstructionists," perhaps most notably in 1984. It has proved easy for followers to move from one to the other, and even disputes between them suggest commonality. Efforts to create a compromise doctrine have taken place.[18]

But nearly all these individuals were quite marginal figures—even Lindsey, despite the sales of his book. Their immediate followings were limited, their influence abroad more limited still. Their apparent impact owed much to a general receptivity to things transcendent and "spiritual" that could adopt or invent modified forms of these doctrines. Their prominence also owed much to their connection with the far better organized Catholic right. Above all, it resulted from the absence of coherent secular opposition. In the end, postmodernism not only legitimated the rise of authoritarian religion—and was a manifestation of the same underlying impulse—but it also devastated the political left on a global scale. "Identity" subverted the meaning of political radicalism, and nothing did more to put the rapture on hold than electoral success.

The Collapse of the Left

Since the mid-eighteenth century and arguably since 1650 or even earlier, the political left has made universal claims, imagined an emergent world as the result of social activism, and found civic ideals to be at once ends and means. This commitment to the civic—public values as sharply distinguished from family values—has remained the case whether articulated through religious (and apocalyptic) vocabularies or through secular (and progressive) ones. The political right has no less consistently maintained just the opposite: the status of blood, whether family and lineage or, after Romanticism, of nation, race, and gender. Such was the language of the great critics of the Enlightenment. The latter triumphed in the 1970s throughout the West, and, increasingly, on a global scale. What made the Great Reaction different—and so devastating—was that these values were embraced, promoted, and ultimately realized through the efforts of the left. What had defined the left, historically with fair consistency for two centuries and more, now largely broke down, and the distinction between right and left no longer possessed its earlier clarity. The quest for transcendence, along with the varied rejection of Enlightenment, Reformation, and Renaissance temporality, linked earlier conservatism with the current sensibility. Integral to this transformation was the concomitant rejection of the temporalizing dynamic, crucially linked to all three, the historical apocalypse.

Political progressives found themselves ill-equipped to confront the religious right because so many of their "spiritual" assumptions, the preoccupation with "blood" and "soul," were now shared on the left. The driving force behind this shift arose from "family values" and traditional authority, but that simply meant the rejection of "public values" that, historically, had defined Protestantism. Protestants became co-opted by authoritarian Catholicism because they ceased to know their own tradition and its guiding principles. It is no accident at all that Rushdoony began his career as an advocate of homeschooling and a severe critic of the "secular" public schools. Nor was it any accident for him to insist on theocratic ecumenism. If Christians' reading of the gospels was warped or partial, it did not matter, God could still use it because the real issue was secularism. Conservative Protestants admired John Paul II, the most authoritarian pope since the 1950s, and even a liberal and ostensibly secular filmmaker celebrated him for seeking to make people more "spiritual." Evangelicals applauded the election of the hard-line Cardinal Joseph Ratzinger (b. 1927) as his successor. The phenomenal success among Protestants of so deeply a Catholic film as *The Passion of the Christ* (2004) provides a telling measure of the extent to which Protestantism has lost its moorings.[19] That detachment found its origins in the shifting eschatologies of the nineteenth century.

Jeffrey Rosen was surely right when he claimed that the ending of the division between church and state had less to do with prominent conservative evangelists such as Pat Robertson (b. 1930) than with the triumph of identity politics. The decline of public culture and the collapse of the left had opened the way for the sacralization of society. The intellectual landscape that accompanied all these developments encouraged ahistorical apocalyptic perspectives, and, for those promoting religion, the project at hand softened the distinctions between pre- and postmillennial. An apocalyptic framework, normally lacking any highly articulated theology, shaped the thinking of a remarkable range of extremely successful political figures in the United States. Outstanding among them was Ronald Reagan, whose interest in eschatology—and admiration for Lindsey and other commentators— is well known. Such members of his cabinet as the Secretary of Defense Caspar Weinberger (1917–2006) and Interior Secretary James Watt (b. 1938) shared these interests. So too, more recently, do George W. Bush and his former attorney general, John Ashcroft. A president who apparently believes that he speaks directly with God on policy matters has excited remarkably little comment in the still more spiritualized world that developed after the 9/11 attacks. Important elements within the Texas Republican Party have drawn inspiration directly from Reconstruction doctrine.[20]

The larger intellectual context, however, will prove considerably more telling than does the fact that Reagan read *The Late Great Planet Earth* and liked it, or than do the shifting contacts between individual religious leaders and powerful politicians. The central issue is, as it has continued to be for more than two centuries, the meaning and persuasiveness of public life. The debate about policies concerning such disparate matters as private schools and contract soldiers directly engages not only public culture but the core religious values from which the secular mentality arose. If the apocalypse proved a crucial catalyst in the creation of secular politics, the apocalypse, especially in its nineteenth-century "futurist" formulations, has proven no less crucial in their subsequent decline. In a still larger sense the historic fissure remains much as it was in the sixteenth century: time and its meanings.

One of the key objectives of Foucault's anti-temporal critique of the Enlightenment was personal toleration. It became impossible on his telling to enter the mind of a person whose outlook was significantly different or to grasp the logic of a group that was significantly different. If one could not comprehend the "other," then one could not judge him (or them). There could only be toleration in the sense of co-existence. In the event, just the opposite has been the case. Nothing is more censorious than identity. John Milton, not Michel Foucault, got it right. Toleration, like social equality, requires a under-lying sense of common purpose that can only be realized, if never finalized, through time.

The World Perspective

There may exist no greater historical mistake than the claims often made for American exceptionalism. If the Protestant apocalypse proved decisive to the rise of America and then to its later undoing, precisely the same issues of public culture and its precipitous decline have been occurring in contemporaneous Europe. Religious revival has accompanied the decline of more secular-oriented faiths. The spectacular success of John Paul II's 1997 World Youth Day in Paris that attracted well over a million young people caught all observers by surprise. No less surprising has been the discovery in France of widespread interest in the paranormal. This phenomenon obtains throughout the West. Protestantism in Britain, France, and Germany has declined before authoritarian revival or, far more commonly, Catholic conversion. European intellectuals have found themselves increasingly attracted to spiritualized modes of thought, from "Radical Orthodoxy" that insists on a close connection between faith and post-modernism (and will "reclaim" the world through them), to the conversion of leading atheist intellectuals such as Antony Flew, to the attention given the annual Templeton Prize "for progress in religion." Often these developments have entailed eschatological expectations. Martin Lings, a student and life-long friend of the Anglo-Catholic writer C. S. Lewis, eventually converted to Islam, became immersed in Islamic eschatology, and argued in his *The Eleventh Hour: The Spiritual Crisis in the Modern World in the Light of Tradition and Prophecy* (1987) that the world neared its end. Lings's vision embodied a violent attack on secularism, the Enlightenment, science, and especially Darwinian evolution. At its heart lay an antitemporal premillennialism that paralleled contemporaneous evangelicals. Again like the premillennial evangelicals, the problem with Darwin did not arise so much from Darwin's conflict with scripture, but in his apparent progressivism.

Politics was not the solution, but the problem; transcendent finality was the answer. Despite their evident learning—despite their anti-Semitism and corporatist commitments—Lings and such similar apocalyptic spiritualists as Frithjof Schuon and René Guénon turn out to share much with Hal Lindsey.[21] Through such widely-regarded writers, apocalyptic expectations have acquired a respectability in Western Europe that would have been inconceivable twenty-five years ago.

The collapse of Communism between 1970 and 1990 has proven more dramatic than the decline of liberalism, but remains basically the same phenomenon. Identity politics destroyed Eastern public culture, in large part under the banner "Russia First." By far the most explosive encounter between the Enlightenment and its enemies occurred with the Afghan war (1978–1991) that, in the most direct terms, entailed a conflict between secularism and revivalist, apocalyptic Islam. It was perhaps only appropriate that the Reagan government should have funded the religious insurgents, for, in its way, Washington was undertaking the same project. Both were heavily engaged in what Kevin Phillips has recently called "Disenlightenment."[22] There may exist heavy irony here: American apocalypticism helped secure the success of the Islamic apocalypticism that then launched a war against its sponsor—and an ever-deepening spiral tragedy. Warnings abounded at the time. Seyyed Hosseim Nasr declared in 1987 that "the manipulation of these so-called 'fundamentalist' Islamic forces by external powers"—whether to combat Communism or for economic reasons—was "particularly dangerous."[23] It is widely claimed that a sense of failure within the Islamic world—in confrontation with the West or with unsuccessful local secular governments—has given rise to militant religious traditionalism, the imperative to impose the sharīʿia. Simultaneously, analogous perceptions of failure have enjoined for many the imperative of authoritarian Christian renewal, the legislation of traditional attitudes, the "Reconstruction" of theocracy. At the heart of resurgent religion has lain resurgent eschatology. What emerges unmistakably is that there exists no "clash of civilizations"—and, arguably, there may never have been such at any point—but a clash across civilizations.

The values that triumphed in 1945 were everywhere in retreat by 1985. Perhaps Communism really was a form of twentieth-century Americanism. Still, the greatest irony lies elsewhere. The apocalypse has turned on the world it did so much to create—including its most signal achievements—and now threatens to destroy them all.

NOTES

CHAPTER 1

1. Most notoriously, Norman Cohn, *The Pursuit of the Millennium: Revolutionary Messianism in Medieval and Reformation Europe and Its Bearing on Modern Totalitarian Movements* (New York, 1957).

2. Jonathan Z. Smith, "Wisdom and Apocalyptic," in Smith, *Map Is Not Territory: Studies in the History of Religion* (Chicago, 1993), pp. 74, 81, 86; originally in *Syncretism in Antiquity*, ed. B. A. Pearson (Missoula, MT, 1975); Bernard McGinn, "Early Apocalypticism," in *The Apocalypse in English Renaissance Thought and Literature*, ed. C. A. Patrides et al. (Ithaca, NY, 1984), pp. 5, 14–16.

3. Moshe Idel, *Messianic Mystics* (New Haven, CT, 1998), pp. 6–8; R. R. Wilson, "The Biblical Roots of Apocalyptic," in *Imagining the End: Visions of Apocalypse from the Ancient Middle East to Modern America*, ed. Ahbas Amanat and Magnus Bernhardsson (New York, 2002), pp. 58–60; Bernard McGinn, ed., *Visions of the End: Apocalyptic Traditions in the Middle Ages* (New York, 1979), pp. 29–32.

4. Josephus, *Antiquities* 10:26; Josephus, *The Complete Works*, trans. W. Whiston (Nashville, TN, 1998), p. 341.

5. D. C. Allison, "Eschatology of Jesus," in *Encyclopedia of Apocalypticism*, ed. B. McGinn et al., 3 vols. (New York, 1999), 1:267–301.

6. The shifting attitude toward the empire can be seen as early as Luke-Acts, compiled sometime after 70 CE.

7. John of Salisbury, *Policraticus*, V.2.

8. Bernard McGinn, *Antichrist: Two Thousand Years of the Human Fascination with Evil* (New York, 1996), p. 121.

9. McGinn, *Visions of the End*, p. 31; R. B. Barnes, *Prophecy and Gnosis: Apocalypticism in the Wake of the Lutheran Reformation* (Stanford, CA, 1988), p. 17; L. A. Smaller, "Of Earthquakes, Hail, Frogs, and Geography: Plague

and the Investigation of the Apocalypse in the Later Middle Ages," and "Introduction," in *Last Things: Death and the Apocalypse in the Middle Ages,* ed. C. B. Bynum and P. Freedman (Philadelphia, 2000), pp. 10, 156–87.

10. M. Reeves, "Medieval Attitudes," in *The Apocalypse in English Renaissance Thought and Literature,* pp. 45, 49.

11. B. McGinn, ed. and trans., *Apocalyptic Spirituality* (New York, 1979), p. 111; B. McGinn, *The Calabrian Abbot: Joachim of Fiore in the History of Western Thought* (New York, 1985), pp. 112–13; B. McGinn, "Angel Pope and Papal Antichrist," *Church History* 47 (1978): 155–73, at 158–59. Translations of the key passages from Joachim's letters, "Book of Figures," "Book of Concordances," "Treatise on the Four Gospels," and "Exposition of the Apocalypse" appear in McGinn, *Apocalyptic Spirituality,* pp. 113–46; McGinn, *Visions of the End,* pp. 130–41.

12. Petrus Alphonsi / Moses Sephardi (1062–1110). M. Reeves and B. Hirsch-Reich, *Figurae of Joachim* (Oxford, 1972), pp. 40–46; McGinn, *The Calabrian Abbot,* pp. 27, 33, 35, 108, 155, 171.

13. Bernard McGinn, "The Abbot and the Doctors: Scholastic Reaction to the Radical Eschatology of Joachim of Fiore," *Church History* 40 (1971): 30–47, at 34–35; repeated in McGinn, *Visions of the End,* p. 129.

14. "Tercets on Fortune," in *Machiavelli: The Chief Works and Others,* ed. and trans. A. Gilbert, 3 vols. (Durham, NC, 1965), 2:747.

15. Dante Alighieri, *De monarchia* (On World Government), trans. W. H. Schneider (Indianapolis, 1949), p. 78. I have slightly altered Schneider's translation in order to make Dante's meaning more accessible.

16. R. G. Musto, *Apocalypse in Rome: Cola di Rienzo and the Politics of the New Age* (Berkeley, CA, 2003), pp. 3, 57, 135, 232, 290, 310, 346, and passim.

17. Hans Baron, *The Crisis of Liberty in the Early Italian Renaissance: Civic Humanism and Republican Liberty in an Age of Classicism and Tyranny* (1955; rev. ed., Princeton, NJ, 1966).

18. David Wooton, "The True Origins of Republicanism, or *de vera respublica,*" published at Wooton's website, University of York, pp. 12–13.

19. M. Reeves, *Influence of Prophecy in the Later Middle Ages: A Study in Joachism* (Oxford, 1969), pp. 354–58; McGinn, ed., *Apocalyptic Spirituality,* pp. 268–71; Donald Weinstein, *Savonarola and Florence: Prophecy and Patriotism in the Renaissance* (Princeton, NJ, 1970), pp. 166–68.

20. Wooton, "The True Origins of Republicanism," p. 14.

21. Weinstein, *Savonarola,* p. 146.

22. R. H. Popkin *The History of Skepticism: From Savonarola to Bayle,* 3rd ed. (Oxford, 2003), pp. 20–27.

23. Wooton, "The True Origins of Republicanism," pp. 14–15; Lorenzo Polizzotto, *The Elect Nation: The Savonarolan Movement in Florence, 1494–1545* (Oxford, 1994); J. H. Whitfield, "Savonarola and the Purpose of *The*

Prince," in ed. J. H. Whitfield, *Discourses on Machiavelli* (Cambridge, 1969), pp. 87–110, esp., 88, 94, 96, 102; V. B. Sullivan, *Machiavelli's Three Romes: Religion, Human Liberty, and Politics Reformed* (DeKalb, IL, 1996), p. 135.

24. Sandro Botticelli (1444–1510). Weinstein, *Savonarola*, pp. 334–37.

25. Luca Signorelli (*c.* 1441–1523). E.g., André Chastel, "L'Apocalypse en 1500. La fresque de l'Antéchrist à la chapelle Saint-Brice d'Orvieto," *Bibliothèque d'humanisme et renaissance* 14 (1952): 124–40; S. Meltzoff, *Botticelli, Signorelli, and Savonarola* (Florence, 1987), esp. pp. 342–56.

CHAPTER 2

1. John Fortescue (*c.* 1394–*c.* 1476), *De laudibus legum Anglie* (In Praise of the Laws of England), ed. and trans. S. B. Chrimes (Cambridge, 1949), pp. 38–41.

2. E.g., the appeal *To the Christian Nobility of the German Nation* (Wittenberg, 1520), *Martin Luther Selections from His Writings*, ed. and trans. John Dillenberger (New York, 1961), pp. 412, 417. As early as 1518 Luther had begun to think privately that the papacy was the prophesied Antichrist.

3. David Calderwood, *History of the Kirk of Scotland*, ed. Thomas Thomson (Edinburgh, 1842–49), 1:136 (Alexander Cunningham, fifth earl of Glencairn, d. 1574).

4. Luther, cited in R. B. Barnes, *Prophecy and Gnosis*, p. 46.

5. Pont (1524–1606), *A Newe Treatise of the Right Reckoning of Years and Ages of the World* (Edinburgh, 1599), a brief, vernacular popularization, followed posthumously by his *De sabbaticorum annorum periodis chronologica ...* (London, 1619).

6. John Jewel (1522–71), a leading apologist for the English reformation, "Exposition upon the Second Epistle to the Thessalonians" (2:4), in *Works of John Jewel*, ed. John Ayre, 4 vols. (Cambridge, 1840–50), 2:902.

7. Gerald Strauss's translation captures Luther's engaging conversational style, in "The Mental World of a Saxon Pastor," in *Reformation Principle and Practice: Essays in Honor of Arthur Geoffrey Dickens*, ed. P. N. Brooks (London, 1980), p. 169. Cited by Barnes, *Prophecy and Gnosis*, p. 41.

8. McGinn, *Antichrist*, p. 209; Barnes, *Prophecy and Gnosis*, pp. 188–94.

9. John Bale (1495–1563), *Selected Works* (Cambridge, 1849), 341, repeated 401.

10. Ibid., pp. 370, 491, 582.

11. Ibid., pp. 322–23, 253.

12. Ibid., p. 252.

13. John Foxe (1516–87), *Acts and Monuments*, ed. S. R. Cattley (London, 1837–41), 8 vols. 1:249–92, esp. 250, 256; 2:727.

14. A. H. Williamson, *Scottish National Consciousness in the Age of James VI* (Edinburgh, 1979), p. 44.

15. P. J. McGinnis and A. H. Williamson (eds.), *George Buchanan: The Political Poetry* (Edinburgh, 1995), pp. 84–85.

16. Desiderius Erasmus (*c.*1467–1536), "Paraclesis" to the Greek New Testament (*Novum instrumentum omne*, 1516), in *The Oxford Reformers*, ed. and trans. F. Seebohm (London, 1896), pp. 326–31.

17. Foxe, *Acts and Monuments*, 3:719–21.

18. Pierre Eskrich (Cruche), *Histoire de la mappa-monde nouvelle papistique* ... (detail), (Geneva, 1567), reprinted in N. Z. Davis, "The Sacred and the Body Social in Lyonis," *Humanities in Review* 1 (1982): 66.

19. The fullest analysis of these images is provided by R. W. Scribner, *For the Sake of Simple Folk: Popular Propaganda for the German Reformation* (Cambridge, 1981), pp. 142–43, 169–74.

20. E.g., Paul Boyer, *When Time Shall Be No More: Prophecy Belief in Modern American Culture* (Cambridge, MA, 1992).

21. Schrott, *On the Terrible Destruction and Fall of the Papacy* (1550?), cited by Scribner, *For the Sake of the Simple Folk*, p. 172.

22. Discussed by Scribner, *For the Sake of the Simple Folk*, pp. 170, 174, 185–89.

23. Guibert of Nogent (1064–1124), *On Sermons*, in Karl Morrison et al. eds., *History of Western Civilization: Selected Readings* V (Chicago, 1976), p. 92.

24. Seebohm, ed. and trans., *The Oxford Reformers*, pp. 326–31.

25. G. N. Conklin, *Biblical Criticism and Heresy in Milton* (New York, 1949), pp. 1–2.

26. Aquinas's words are startling: "it is obvious to our senses that, after the consecration, all the accidents [physical appearances] of the bread and wine remain. Divine providence very widely arranged for this. First of all, men have not the custom of eating human flesh and drinking human blood; indeed, the thought revolts them. And so the flesh and blood of Christ are given to us to be taken under the appearances of things in common use, namely bread and wine. Secondly, lest this sacrament should be an object of contempt for unbelievers, if we were to eat our Lord under his human appearances. Thirdly, in taking the body and blood of our Lord in their invisible presence, we increase the merit of our faith."

27. Aquinas, *Summa Theologiae*, pas III, quaes. 73–78.

28. Funkenstein, "The Body of God in Seventeenth-Century Theology and Science," in *Millenarianism and Messianism in English Literature and Thought, 1650–1800*, ed. R. H. Popkin (Leiden, 1988), pp. 149–92.

CHAPTER 3

1. Marie Tanner, *The Last Descendant of Aeneas: The Hapsburgs and the Mythic Image of the Emperor* (New Haven, CT, 1993), pp. 223–25, 234–36.

2. The *"impresa"* and Edmund Spenser's inversion of it is described by René Graziani, "Philip II's *Impresa* and Spenser's Souldan," *Journal of the Warburg and Courtauld Institutes* 27 (1964): 322–24.

3. E. William Monter, "The Death of Coexistence: Jews and Moslems in Christian Spain," in *The Expulsion of the Jews: 1492 and After*, ed. R. B. Waddington and A. H. Williamson, pp. 5–17.

4. Earl Rosenthal, *"Plus Ultra, Non Plus Ultra*, and the Columnar Device of Emperor Charles V," *Journal of the Warburg and Courtauld Institute* 34 (1971): 216.

5. McGinnis and Williamson, *Buchanan*, p. 74.

6. Ibid., pp. 84–91.

7. George Buchanan, *History of Scotland*, ed. and trans. James Aikman, 4 vols. (Edinburgh, 1827–30), 1:236.

8. In J. A. H. Murray, ed., *The Complaynt of Scotlande* (London, 1872), p. 241, appendix 3.

9. R. A. Mason, ed., *John Knox, on Rebellion* (Cambridge, 1994), pp. 41, 40.

10. Michel de l'Hôpital, *Oeuvres complètes*, ed. P. J. S. Dufféy, 5 vols. (Paris, 1824–26; Geneva, 1968), p. 336; C. Wells, "The Language of Citizenship in the French Religious Wars," *Sixteenth Century Journal* 30 (1999): 441–56.

11. David Read, *Temperate Conquests: Spenser and the Spanish New World* (Detroit, 2000).

12. Nowell Smith, ed., *The Life of the Renowned Sir Philip Sidney* (Oxford, 1907), pp. 87, 88, 97, 98, 99, 107, 117–19, 111, 114, 204.

13. McGinnis and Williamson, *Buchanan*, pp. 33–35, 276–81.

14. Ibid., pp. 278–80.

15. D. S. Katz, *Philo-Semitism and the Readmission of the Jews to England, 1603–1655* (Oxford, 1982), p. 200; Roy Strong, *Henry Prince of Wales and England's Lost Renaissance* (London, 1986), p. 8.

16. Andrew Willet, *Ecclesia Triumphans* (Cambridge, 1603), sig. 7^v.

17. Strong, *Henry*, p. 72; Malcolm Smuts, *Court Culture and the Origins of a Royalist Tradition in Early Stuart England* (Philadelphia, 1987), p. 29.

18. *Valerius Terminus* in *The Works of Francis Bacon*, ed. James Spedding et al., 14 vols. (London, 1857–74), 3:222, 220–21; *The New Organon*, in *Works*, 1:200/4:92; *Advancement of Learning*, in *Works*, 3:340; *Redagutio Philosophiarum*, in *Works*, 3:584.

19. R. Tuck, *Philosophy and Government, 1572–1651* (Cambridge, 1993), p. 110; Michael Kiernan, ed., *Sir Francis Bacon: The Essayes or Counsels, Civill and Morall* (Cambridge, MA, 1985), p. 106.

20. *Encouragements. For such as shall have intention to be under-takers in the new plantation of Cape Briton, now New Galloway in America* ... (Edinburgh, 1625), B3ʳ.

21. *Scotlands Welcome* (Edinburgh, 1633), sigs. A3ᵛ, F1ʳ⁻ᵛ, D1ʳ; *The Totall Discourse of the rare adventures* ... [of William Lithgow] (Edinburgh 1632, rpt. 1906), pp. 11, 18, 69, 133–34; *The Gushing Teares of Godly Sorrow* (Edinburgh, 1640), sigs. L2ᵛ–L3ʳ.

22. Laura Knoppers, *Constructing Cromwell: Ceremony, Portrait, and Print, 1645–1661* (Cambridge, 2000), esp. pp. 106, 108.

23. A. H. Williamson, "Union with England ... Sir James Hope and the Mid-Seventeenth-Century British State," *English Historical Review* 110, no. 2 (1995): 319 n. 3.

24. Vieira, *Esperança de Portugal. Quinto Império do Mundo* (1659). Quite unlike Cromwell, Vieira promoted African slavery as a means of protecting the Amerindians. Again quite unlike Cromwell, Vieira's thought was heavily invested into numerological prophecy.

25. *A Declaration of the Parliament of the Commonwealth of England, concerning the Settlement of Scotland* (28 October 1651).

26. J. G. A. Pocock, ed., *The Political Works of James Harrington* (Cambridge, 1977), pp. 332–33, 337–38.

27. J. G. A. Pocock, ed., *James Harrington: The Commonwealth of Oceana and A System of Politics* (Cambridge, 1992), p. xxiv.

28. Most prominently, Steven Pincus, "Neither Machiavellian Moment nor Possessive Individualism: Commercial Society and the Defenders of the English Commonwealth," *American Historical Review* 103 (1998): 705–36.

29. Charles Webster, *The Great Instauration: Science, Medicine, and Reform, 1626–1660* (New York, 1975), p. 355.

30. A. H. Williamson, "Latter-Day Judah, Latter-Day Israel: The Millennium, the Jews, and the British Future," in *Pietismus und Neuzeit: Chiliasmus in Deutschland und England im 17. Jahrhundert*, ed. Klaus Depperman et al., vol. 14 (Göttingen, 1988), pp. 160–61.

31. E.g., Richard Overton, *A Remonstrance of Many Thousand Citizens* (1646), reprinted in *Leveller Manifestoes*, ed. D. M. Wolfe, 2nd ed. (New York, 1967), pp. 120, 123, 125, 129.

32. Overton, *An Appeale from the Degenerate Representative Body ... to ... the Free People ... of England* (July 1647), reprinted in *The Levellers in the English Revolution*, ed. G. E. Aylmer (Ithaca, 1975), p. 86.

33. Wolfe, *Leveller Manifestoes*, pp. 123, 129.

34. A. H. Williamson, "James Hope," in new *DNB*.

35. Campanella, *La Monarchia di Spagna*, trans. Edmund Chilmead, 2nd ed. (London, 1660), p. 155.

36. Ibid., p. 9.

37. Jean-Frédéric Schaub, *La France espangol: Les racines hispaniques de l'absolutisme français* (Paris, 2003), p. 192.

CHAPTER 4

1. Joseph Mede, *Clavis apocalyptica* (Cambridge, 1627); Johan Heinrich Alsted, *Diatribe de mille annis apaclypticis* (Frankfurt am Main, 1627).

2. Campanella, *La Città del Sole: Dialogo Poetico/The City of the Sun: A Poetical Dialogue*, trans. D. J. Donno (Berkeley, CA, 1981), pp. 106, 107 (all subsequent references are to this edition); Campanella, *La Monarchia di Spagna*, p. 9.

3. Bacon, *The Great Instauration*, 1:127/4:14–15; *The Advancement of Learning*, 289–90; *Valerius Terminus*, 222; *Cogitava et Visa*, in *Works of Francis Bacon*, 3:612 (omnium enim consensu *veritatem Temporis filiam esse*).

4. Bacon, *Advancement of Learning*, 328–29; *The New Organon*, 1:217/4:109; *The Great Instauration*, 1:127/4:15.

5. E.g., *The Great Instauration*, 1:141/4:29.

6. John Donne, "The Extasie," in *The Complete English Poems of John Donne*, ed. C. A. Patrides (London, 1985), p. 101 (ll. 60–68).

7. Bacon, *The New Organon*, 1:310/4:195.

8. Bacon, *The Advancement of Learning*, 421; *The Great Instauration*, 1:132/4:21, 1:136/4:24.

9. Bacon, *New Atlantis*, in *Works*, 3:136.

10. Ibid., 3:147, 151.

11. 2 Samuel 11, 12.

12. D. P. Walker, *Spiritual and Demonic Magic: From Ficino to Campanella* (London, 1958; 3rd ed., 1975), p. 199.

13. 1 Kings 4:33.

14. Walker, *Spiritual and Demonic Magic*, p. 200.

15. Campanella, *La Città del Sole*, pp. 43, 45.

16. Ibid., p. 45.

17. Ibid., p. 103.

18. Ibid., p. 123.

19. Ibid., pp. 55, 59, 61.

20. Ibid., pp. 61, 63, 85.

21. Ibid., pp. 53, 57, 41; cf. 97.

22. Ibid., p. 105.

23. Ibid., pp. 55, 59.

24. Ibid., p. 59.

25. D. M. Frame, ed., *Complete Essays of Montaigne* (Stanford, 1958), p. 155; Maurice Rat, ed., *Essais de Montaigne,* vol. 1 (Paris, 1962), 239.

26. "Le sage doit au dedans retirer son ame de la presse." "La société publique n'a que faire de nos pensées." Rat, *Essais de Montaigne,* 1:125 ("De la coustume et de ne changer aisément une loy receüe," 1:23); Frame, *Complete Essays*, p. 86.

27. Cited by D. Allan, *Philosophy and Politics in the Later Stuart World* (East Linton, Scotland, 2000), pp. 13–14.

28. Guicciardini, *Ricordi,* C.23, trans. Mario Domandi, *Maxims and Reflections of a Renaissance Statesman (Ricordi)* (New York, 1965), p. 47.

29. Frame, *Complete Essays*, pp. 150, 151, 152 (I.31; "Of Cannibals"); Rat, *Essais de Montaigne,* 1:154 ("De pedantisme"; 1.25; Frame, *Complete Essays,* p. 106).

30. Bacon, *Advancement of Learning,* 420–21.

31. Frame, *Complete Essays*, pp. 430–31; Rat, *Essais de Montaigne,* 1:642 ("Apologie de Raimond Sebond"; II.12).

32. J. L. Pearl, *The Crime of Crimes: Demonology and Politics in France, 1560–1620* (Waterloo, Canada, 1999), pp. 62–63, 67, 73, and passim.

33. Pearl, *The Crime of Crimes*, pp. 43–46; cf. Andrew Keitt, "The Miraculous Body of Evidence: Visionary Experience, Medical Discourse, and the Inquisition in Seventeenth-Century Spain," *Sixteenth Century Journal* 36 (2005): 77–96.

34. William Bradford Smith, "Friedrich Förner, the Catholic Reformation, and Witch-Hunting in Bamberg," *Sixteenth Century Journal* 36 (2005): 115–28.

35. Michael Roberts, *Gustavus Adolphus: A History of Sweden, 1611–1632,* vol. 1 (London, 1953), 379.

36. Michael Wasser, "The Privy Council and the Witches: The Curtailment of Witchcraft Prosecutions in Scotland, 1697–1628," *Scottish Historical Review* 82 (2003): 24–25, 29, 42. Erskine of Dun (c.1508–91): Gordon Donaldson, *The Scottish Reformation* (London, 1960), pp. 127, 161–62, 214 and n. 1.

37. John Knox, *The Works of John Knox,* ed. D. Laing, 6 vols. (Edinburgh, 1846–52), 3:289.

38. Wasser, "The Privy Council and Witches," pp. 21 n. 5, 31. Hume, *History of the House of Douglas* (Edinburgh, 1644), pp. 418–19, 261.

39. King James, *Daemonologie* (Edinburgh, 1597), pp. 53–54.

40. Ibid., p. 81, citing Revelation 12.

41. Ibid., pp. 22, 53, 62, 65, 75, and passim.

42. Ibid., pp. 22–23, 55.

43. A. H. Williamson, "Number and National Consciousness: The Edinburgh Mathematicians and Scottish Political Culture at the Union of Crowns" in *Scots and Britons: Scottish Political Thought and the Union of 1603*, ed. R. A. Mason (Cambridge, 1994), pp. 193–97, 200–203, 210–12; David Hume of Godscroft, *The British Union: A Critical Edition and Translation of David Hume of Godcroft's De Unione Insular Britannicae*, ed. P. J. McGinnis and A. H. Williamson (Aldershot, 2002), Introduction; James Maxwell, *Admirable and Notable Prophecies* (London, 1615), p. 14.

CHAPTER 5

1. M. Y. Hughes, ed., *John Milton, Complete Poems and Major Prose* (Indianapolis, 1957), pp. 720, 739, 743.

2. Ibid., pp. 741, 742, 743.

3. Ibid., p. 743.

4. Ibid., p. 744.

5. John Saltmarsh, *Smoke in the Temple* (1646), in A. S. P. Woodhouse, ed., *Puritanism and Liberty* (London, 1938; Chicago, 1974) pp. 181–82.

6. Woodhouse, *Puritanism and Liberty*, pp. 270, 272.

7. Ibid., p. 182.

8. Thomas Edwards, *Gangraena; Or a Catalogue and Discovery of many of the Errours, Heresies, Blasphemies and pernicious Practices of the Sectaries of this time* (1646), cited by N. McDowell, "Latin Drama and Leveller Ideas: Pedagogy and Power in the Writings of Richard Overton," *The Seventeenth Century* 28 (2003): 230.

9. Richard Overton, *Mans Mortalitie: or, A Treatise wherein 'tis proved ... that whole Man (as a rational is a Compound wholly mortall ...*, ed. Harold Fisch (Liverpool, 1968), pp. 48–49.

10. Richard Overton, *The Araignement of Mr. Persecution: Presented to the Consideration of the House of Commons and to all the Common People of England* (1645), pp. 22, 24–25.

11. Ibid., pp. 5, 28, 29, 30, 35, 47, and passim.

12. Ibid., pp. 22, 25, 38, 43, 46.

13. Ibid., pp. 12–14, 38, 46.

14. Ibid., pp. 30, 47.

15. Ibid., pp. 22–23, 26–27.

16. Ibid., p. 23.

17. Roger Williams, *The Hireling Ministry None of Christs, or a Discourse touching the Propagating of the Gospel ...* (1652), reprinted in *Roger Williams: His Contribution to the American Tradition*, ed. Perry Miller (1953; New York, 1974), p. 201.

18. A. H. Williamson, "The Jewish Dimension of the Scottish Apocalypse: Climate, Covenant, and World Renewal," in *Menasseh ben Israel and His World*, ed. Y. Kaplan et al. (Leiden, 1989), pp. 7–30.

19. Gerrard Winstanley, *The Law of Freedom in a Platform* (1652), ed. R. W. Kenny (New York, 1973), p. 116.

20. Ibid., p. 70.

21. Ibid., pp. 111–12.

22. Ibid., pp. 49–62, 72.

23. Frontispiece to *Law of Freedom*, reprinted in ibid., p. 48.

24. William Walwyn, *The Power of Love* (1643), in *The Writings of William Walwyn*, ed. J. R. McMichael and B. Taft (Athens, GA, 1989), pp. 87, 88.

25. Walwyn, *A New Petition of the Papists* (1641), reissued later that year under the title *The Humble Petition of the Brownists*, in *Writings of William Walwyn*, pp. 55–61; yet a close reading of *The Power of Love* indicates the great limitation to Walwyn's toleration; *Writings of William Walwyn*, p. 94, also see p. 91.

26. Walwyn, *Walwyn's Just Defence (1949)*, in ed. W. Haller and G. Davies. *The Leveller Tracts, 1647–1653* (Glouster, MA, 1964), pp. 362, 365; R. H. Popkin, *The History of Skepticism from Erasmus to Spinoza* (Berkeley, 1979).

27. Walwyn, *Defence*, in *Leveller Tracts*, p. 364.

28. Walwyn, *Petition of the Papists*, p. 60.

29. James Harrington, *The Political Works of James Harrington*, ed. J. G. A. Pocock (Cambridge, 1977), p. 332; Mark Goldie, "The Civil Religion of James Harrington," in *The Languages of Political Theory in Early-Modern Europe*, ed. A. Pagden (Cambridge, 1987), pp. 197–222, esp. 203–6.

30. *Leviathan*, pp. 18–19 (I.2). Thomas Hobbes, *Leviathan*, ed. R. Tuck (Cambridge, 1999).

31. Ibid., p. 257 (III.32).

32. Ibid., pp. 22–23 (I.3).

33. Ibid., p. 150 (II.21).

34. Thomas Carlyle, ed., *Oliver Cromwell's Letters and Speeches*, 4 vols. (London, 1850), 1:273, 283, 290.

35. Ibid., 290, 291.

36. W. C. Abbott, ed., *The Writings and Speeches of Oliver Cromwell*, 4 vols. (Cambridge, MA, 1937–47), 3:434.

37. D. S. Katz, *The Jews in the History of England, 1485–1850* (Oxford, 1994), p. 107.

38. Carlyle, ed., *Letters and Speeches*, p. 230.

39. William Medley, *A Standard Set Up* (1657), pp. 12–22, excerpted and reprinted in *Seventeenth-Century England: A Changing Culture*, ed. Ann Hughes, 2 vols. (London, 1980), 1:223–24.

40. B. S. Capp, *The Fifth Monarchy Men: A Study in Seventeenth-Century Millanarianism* (Totowa, NJ, 1972), pp. 137, 192; Hughes, ed., *Seventeenth-Century England*, 1:224–25.

CHAPTER 6

1. J. G. A. Pocock, "Time, History, and Eschatology in the Thought of Hobbes," in *Politics, Language, and Time* (New York, 1973), p. 161.

2. Dryden, *Absalom and Achitophel* (1681), ll. 179–83, 965–69, in *The Poems and Fables of John Dryden*, ed. J. Kinsley (Oxford, 1958), pp. 194, 214.

3. Ibid., ll. 1000–1004, p. 215.

4. Ibid., ll. 985–88, p. 215.

5. Ronald Knowles, "The 'All-Attoning Name': The Word *Patriot* in Seventeenth-Century England," *Modern Language Review* 96 (2001): 624–43, esp. 634–43.

6. Dryden, *Absalom and Achitophel*, ll.1, 522, pp. 190, 203.

7. Ibid., ll. 1021–24, p. 216.

8. Cited by J. E. Force, "Jewish Monotheism, Christian Heresy, and Sir Isaac Newton," in *The Expulsion of the Jews*, ed. Waddington and Williamson, pp. 259–80, at 264.

9. Cited by J. R. Jacob and M. C. Jacob, "The Anglican Origins of Modern Science: The Metaphysical Foundations of the Whig Constitution," *Isis* 71 (1980): 251–67, at 265.

10. Cited and described by Force, "Jewish Monotheism, Christian Heresy, and Sir Isaac Newton," pp. 268–70.

11. Thomas Burnet, *Sacred Theory of the Earth* (Carbondale, 1965), IV.4, 6, pp. 334, 352.

12. Ibid., I.8, p. 89; III.8, p. 281.

13. Ibid., I.8, p. 84.

14. Ibid., IV.5, p. 345.

15. Ibid., III.7, pp. 270–77.

16. Ibid., III.8, p. 282.

17. Ibid., III.10, pp. 288–91.

18. Ibid., IV.3, 8, pp. 327–29, 365–73, and at 369 where Burnet notes the prospect of "that happy state to come, where Prophets, Apostles, and Angels, will meet in conversation together."

19. Ibid., IV.9, 10, pp. 371, 374–75.

20. Ibid., IV.10, pp. 376–77.

21. Ibid., I.12, pp. 128–29.

22. Ibid., IV.9, p. 368.

23. J. I. Israel, *Radical Enlightenment: Philosophy and the Making of Modernity, 1650–1750* (Oxford, 2001), pp. 126, 605.

24. Cited in J. E. Force, *William Whiston: Honest Newtonian* (Cambridge, 1985), p. 39.

25. Burnet, *Sacred Theory*, p. 411, 358–59, 364, and passim.

26. Ibid., IV.7, p. 355.

CHAPTER 7

1. I. L. Ingle, *First among Friends: George Fox and the Creation of Quakerism* (New York, 1994), pp. 110, 168, 178–80, 184, 235–26, 331, n. 73.

2. Voltaire, *Philosophical Letters* (1733), trans. E. Dilworth (New York, 1961), p. 19.

3. Rufus M. Jones, ed., *The Journal of George Fox* (New York, 1963), p. 77.

4. Fisher, *Rusticus ad academicos ... The Rusticks ALARM to the Rabbies* (1660; reprinted 1679), Second Exercitation, p. 152.

5. Cited by G. Scholem, *Sabbatai Şevi: The Mystical Messiah, 1626–1676*, trans. R. J. Z. Werblowski (Princeton, 1973), pp. 12–13; Scholem, "Toward an Understanding of the Messianic Idea," in Scholem, *The Messianic Idea in Judaism and Other Essays on Jewish Spirituality* (New York, 1971), p. 29.

6. Cited by M. Idel, "Jewish Apocalypticism: 670–1670," in *The Continuum History of Apocalypticism*, ed. B. McGinn et al., 3 vols. (New York, 1999), 2:229; Scholem, "The Crisis of Tradition in Jewish Messianism," in *The Messianic Idea*, pp. 54–5.

7. Idel, *Messianic Mystics*, pp. 61, 97–8; Idel, "Jewish Apocalypticism," p. 213; G. Scholem, Major Trends in Jewish Mysticism (Jerusalem, 1941; third revised edition, New York, 1961), p. 128.

8. Cited by Idel, "Jewish Apocalypticism," p. 218.

9. J. I. Israel, *European Jewry in the Age of Mercantilism, 1550–1750* (Oxford, 1989), p. 31.

10. Idel, *Messianic Mystics*, pp. 160–61; Idel, "Jewish Apocalypticism," p. 219.

11. Robert Sacks, "Abravanel, Commentary on the Bible," in *Medieval Political Philosophy*, ed. R. Lerner et al. (Ithaca, NY, 1963), p. 167.

12. Abbott, ed., *The Writings and Speeches of Oliver Cromwell* 1:677.

13. Menasseh ben Israel, *The Hope of Israel*, ed. H. Méchoulan and G. Nahon (Oxford, 1987), pp. 102, 146–48, 158.

14. Ibid., p. 100.

15. Cited in *Philo-Semitism and the Readmission of the Jews to England*, p. 198.

16. R. H. Popkin, "Jewish Messianism and Christian Millenarianism," in *Culture and Politics from Puritanism to the Enlightenment*, ed. P. Zagorin (Berkeley, 1980), p. 76–77.

17. S. Schama, *Rembrandt's Eyes* (New York, 1999), pp. 359, 609; Van de Waal, *Steps Towards Rembrandt*, Henri van de Waal, *Steps towards Rembrandt, Collected Articles, 1937–1971*, ed. R. H. Fuchs (Amsterdam, 1974), pp. 113–24 (from whom Schama borrows heavily).

18. Menasseh, *Hope of Israel*, p. 99.

19. Williamson, "Sir James Hope and the Mid-Seventeenth-Century British State," p. 321; R. H. Popkin, "A Note on Moses Wall," appended to the modern edition of ben Israel, *The Hope of Israel*, p. 167.

20. William Prynne, *A Short Demurrer to the Jews*, 2nd ed. (London, 1656), "To Christian Reader," and pp. 65, 83–84, 89–90, 91, 93.

21. British Library: Harley 7003, fol. 179, cited in J. R. Jacob, *Robert Boyle and the English Revolution* (New York, 1977), p. 97.

22. Menasseh, *Hope of Israel*, pp. 51, 56–57, 59; E[dward] S[pencer], *A Breife Epistle to the Learned Manasseh Ben Israel* (London, 1650), dedication to William Lenthall.

23. Scholem, *Sabbatai Şevi*, pp. 262, 272–73, 394, 427, 431, 443.

24. Ibid., p. 262, 532, 615, 617, 630–32; Scholem, *The Messianic Idea in Judaism*, p. 143.

25. Ibid., pp. 63, 94, 403–4, 671, 692.

26. Paul Rycaut, *History of the Turkish Empire from the Year 1623 to the Year 1677* (London, 1680), p. 201, cited by R. H. Popkin, "Three English Tellings of the Sabbatai Zevi Story," *Jewish History* 8 (1994): 46.

27. Anonymous, *The Devil of Delphos, or, The Prophets of Baal* ... (London, 1708), p. 56, cited by Popkin, "Three English Tellings of the Sabbatai Zevi Story," p. 49.

28. Scholem, *Major Trends in Jewish Mysticism*, pp. 330, 334. Scholem, "The Naturalization of the Messianic Element in Early Hasidism," in *Messianic Idea in Judaism*, pp. 176–202.

29. Fisher, *Rusticus ad academicos*, Exercitation II, p. 118.

30. E. G. E. van der Wall, "The Amsterdam Millenarian Petrus Serrarius (1600–1669) and the Anglo-Dutch Circle of Philo-Judaists," in *Jewish-Christian Relations in the Seventeenth Century*, ed. J. van den Berg et al. (Dordrecht, 1988), p. 88.

31. La Peyrère, *Prae-Adamitae* ([Amsterdam], 1655), English ed. *Men before Adam* (London, 1656), p. 47; also pp. 6–11, 32–33, 41–46.

32. La Peyrère, *Men before Adam*, p. 25; Book IV, pp. 204–8, and passim.

33. Fisher, *Rusticus ad academicos*, Exercitation II, p. 152.

34. La Peyrère, *Men before Adam*, p. 20.

35. Cited by R. H. Popkin, *Isaac La Peyrère (1596–1676)* (Leiden, 1987), p. 82.

36. Spinoza, *Tractatus Theologico-Politicus*, in *Spinoza Complete Works*, trans. Samuel Shirley (Indianapolis, 2002), chap. 2, pp. 425–26.

37. R. H. Popkin, "Spinoza and Samuel Fisher," in *Philosophia* 3 (1985): 219–36, at 231; Fisher, *Rusticus ad academicos*, reprinted in *The Testimony of Truth* ... (n.p., 1679), p. 546.

CHAPTER 8

1. K. M. Baker, *Condorcet: From Natural Philosophy to Social Mathematics* (Chicago, 1975), p. 343; Louis Gabriel Ambroise, viscomte de Bonald (1754–1840), "Observations sur un ouvrage posthume de Condorcet ...," in *Oeuvres complètes de M. Bonald*, ed. J. P. Migne, 3 vols. (Paris, 1859), 1:722; Cohn, *Pursuit of the Millennium*, p. xv, also 311–12.

2. Denis Diderot, "The Encyclopedia," in *Rameau's Nephew and Other Works*, trans. Jacques Barzun and R. H. Bowen (New York, 1956; reprinted, Indianapolis, 1964), pp. 277–78, 282, 283.

3. Denis Diderot, "Art," in *Encyclopédie or dictionnaire raisonné des sciences, des arts, et des métiers*, 17 vols. (Paris, 1751–65), 1:717; cited and trans. W. H. Sewell, *Work and Revolution in France* (Cambridge, 1980), p. 65.

4. Diderot, "Encyclopedia," pp. 298–99, 302–3.

5. Ibid., p. 306.

6. Ibid., pp. 292–93.

7. Ibid., p. 293; Baker, *Condorcet*, pp. 92–93.

8. Voltaire, *Philosophical Letters*, p. 66.

9. Ibid., pp. 52–55.

10. Ibid., pp. 72–74.

11. Voltaire, "Dialogue Between the Philosopher and Nature," in *The Philosophical Dictionary*, ed. B. R. Redman for *The Portable Voltaire* (New York, 1949; reprinted 1961), pp. 171–72.

12. David Hume, *History of England*, 6 vols. (New York, 1879), 6:344; Baker, *Condorcet*, pp. 90–91, 111–12, and part 1 passim. All analyses of Condorcet, including this one, are indebted to the pioneering work of Keith Baker.

13. Colin MacLauren, *An Account of Sir Isaac Newton's Philosophical Discoveries* (Edinburgh, 1750), p. 9; cited by James Buchan, *Crowded with Genius—The Scottish Enlightenment: Edinburgh's Moment of the Mind* (New York, 2004).

14. Voltaire, "Micromegas," in *Portable Voltaire*, p. 435.

15. Bonald, "Observations sur un ouvrage posthume de Condorcet ...," in Migne, ed., *Oeuvres completes de M. Bonald*, 1:722.

16. Condorcet, "Sketch," in *Condorcet: Selected Writings*, ed. K. M. Baker (Indianapolis, 1976), pp. 210, 242–43, 268, 272.

17. Ibid., pp. 211, 214, 261, 267.

18. Ibid., p. 216; Baker, *Condorcet*, p. 359.

19. Bruce Brown, "The French Revolution and the Rise of Social Theory," *Science and Society* 30, no. 4 (1966): 385–432; Baker, *Condorcet*, pp. 363ff; G. G. Iggers, *The Doctrine of Saint-Simon* (New York, 1958; 2nd ed., 1972), p. vi.

20. Condorcet, "Fragment on the *New Atlantis*," in *Condorcet: Selected Works*, ed. Baker, p. 284.

21. Henry More, *A Modest Inquiry into the Mystery of Iniquity* (London, 1664), cited by C. Hill, *Antichrist in Seventeenth-Century England* (London, 1971), p. 149.

22. Henry More, *The Immortality of the Soule* (London, 1659), III.9.1–8, pp. 414–27.

23. Henry More, *Divine Dialogues* (London, 1668), p. 402.

24. Ibid., pp. 280, 326 (also 249, 289, 294, 326, 327, 329); 255 (also 200, 201, 236, 240, 251, 253, and passim).

25. Ibid., pp. 224, 351.

26. Ibid., pp. 403–4.

27. William Craig Diamond, "Public Identity in Restoration England: From Prophetic to Economic," diss., Johns Hopkins University, Baltimore, 1982, pp. 79–154, esp. pp. 83, 92, 104, 114, 145. My discussion is indebted to this important, if flawed thesis.

28. Voltaire, *Philosophical Letters*, p. 26.

29. George Berkeley, "America, or the Muses's Refuge: A Prophecy," in *Works*, ed. A. A. Luce et al., 9 vols. (Edinburgh, 1948–57), 7:373. A variant final appeared in Berkeley's *Miscellany* (1752) as: "The world's great Effort is the last" (370).

30. George Herbert (1593–1633), "The Church Militant," in *Works*, ed. F. E. Hutchinson (Oxford, 1941), pp. 196–97; Alexander (1567?–1640), "Doomes-day, or the day of the Lords judgement," in *Poetical Works*, ed. L. E. Kastner and H. B. Charlton, 2 vols. (Edinburgh, 1921–2): 2:50.

31. Hartley, *Observations on Man, His Frame, His Duty, and His Expectations*, 2 vols. (London, 1749), 2:356, 370–71, 399–400.

32. Ibid., 2:366–67, 369, 379.

33. Ibid., 2:373–75, 434.

34. Ibid., 2:376–80, 355; cf. 2:452–53.

35. Ibid., 2:375.

36. Ibid., 2:403.

37. Ibid., e.g., 1:509, 2:419; 1:512; R. C. Allen, *David Hartley on Human Nature* (Albany, NY, 1999), pp. 331–53, 380–81.

38. Hartley, *Observations*, 2:380–81, 401, 437.

39. Ibid., 2:368–69, 372, 437–54, 455, and passim.

40. Andrew Robinson, "Identifying the Beast: Samuel Horsley and the Problem of Papal AntiChrist," *Journal of Ecclesiastical History* 43 (1992): 592–607, citation at 599.

41. Ibid., pp. 602, 603.

42. Iain McCalman, "New Jerusalems: Prophecy, Dissent, and Radical Culture in England, 1786–1830," in *Enlightenment and Religion,* ed. K. Haakonssen (Cambridge, 1996), pp. 315–16; repeated verbatim by R. E. Schofield, *The Enlightened Joseph Priestley* (University Park, PA, 2004), p. 210.

43. C. Garrett, *Respectable Folly: Millenarians and the French Revolution in France and England* (Baltimore, 1975), p. 132; Schofield, *Enlightened Joseph Priestley,* p. 380.

44. J. Van den Berg, "Priestley, the Jews, and the Millennium," in *Sceptics, Millenarians, and Jews,* ed. D. S. Katz et al. (Leiden, 1990), p. 268.

45. David Levi, *Dissertations on Prophecies* ..., 3 vols. (London, 1793–1800), 3:138.

46. McCalman, "New Jerusalems," pp. 330–31.

47. J. Popkin, "Zionism and the Enlightenment: The 'Letter of a Jew to His Brethren'" *Jewish Social Studies* 43 (1981): 113–20; Simon Schwartzfuchs, *Napoleon, the Jews, and the Sanhedrin* (London, 1979), pp. 24–27.

48. McCalman, "New Jerusalems," pp. 330, 331; Robinson, "Identifying the Beast," pp. 597, 603; Garrett, *Respectable Folly,* p. 212; Schwartzfuchs, *Napoleon, the Jews, and the Sanhedrin,* p. 65.

49. Joseph Priestley, *A Continuation of Letters to the Philosophers and Politicians of France on the Subject of Religion,* 21:113–14; cited by Garrett, *Respectable Folly,* p. 139.

50. Robespierre, *Report on the Principles of Political Morality* (5 February 1794), in *Old Regime and the French Revolution,* ed. K. Baker (Chicago, 1987), p. 374.

51. Garrett, *Respectable Folly,* pp. 131–32; Van den Berg, "Priestley, the Jews, and the Millennium," p. 272.

52. R. H. Popkin, "Newton and the Origins of Fundamentalism," in *The Scientific Enterprise,* ed. E. Ullmann-Margalit (Dordrecht, 1992), pp. 246–47.

CHAPTER 9

1. Kevin Phillips, *The Cousins' Wars: Religion, Politics, and the Rise of Anglo-America* (New York, 1999).

2. Henri Hauser, *Le Principe des Nationalités* (Paris, 1916), p. 18.

3. Jonathan Edwards, "Sinners in the Hands of an Angry God," in *Colonial American Writing,* ed. R. H. Pearce (New York, 1950), pp. 368–69, 371.

4. Jonathan Edwards, "Personal Narrative," in ibid., p. 354.

5. Jonathan Edwards, *An Humble Attempt to Promote Explicit Agreement and Visible Union of God's People in Extraordinary Prayer* (Boston, 1747), in *The Works of Jonathan Edwards: Apocalyptic Writings,* ed. S. J. Stein, 6 vols. (New Haven, 1977), 5:378–80, 410.

6. Edwards, "Personal Narrative," p. 358; Edwards, *Some Thoughts Concerning the Revival* (Boston, 1742), in The *Works of Jonathan Edwards: The Great Awakening*, ed. C. C. Goen (New Haven, 1972), 4:353–57.

7. Samuel Rutherford, *A Sermon Preached Before the House of Commons ...* (London, 1644); A. A. Bonar, ed., *Fourteen Communion Sermons*, 2nd ed. (Glasgow, 1877), p. 116.

8. Jonathan Edwards, "Letter to William McCulloch" (1744), *Works*, 4:560; Edwards, "Notes on the Apocalypse," *Works*, 5:134–35, 197 n. 1

9. Jonathan Edwards, *Religious Affections*, cited by J. W. Davidson, *Logic of Millennial Thought in Eighteenth-Century New England* (New Haven, CT, 1977), p. 218.

10. Davidson, *Logic of Millennial Thought*, pp. 219–20.

11. Richard Hofstadter, *American at 1750: A Social Portrait* (New York, 1971), p. 216; cited by P. Bonomi, *Under the Cope of Heaven: Religion, Society, and Politics in Colonial America* (Oxford, 1986), p. 160.

12. Davidson, *Logic of Millennial Thought*, pp. 161, 175, and passim; Condorcet, "Fragment on the *New Atlantis*," p. 284.

13. Bonomi, *Cope of Heaven*, p. 188.

14. C. Birdenbaugh, *Mitre and Scepter: Transatlantic Faiths, Ideas, Personalities, and Politics, 1689–1775* (Oxford, 1962); Bonomi, *Cope of Heaven*, p. 187; Phillips, *Cousins' Wars*, pp. 92, 244.

15. N. O. Hatch, *The Sacred Cause of Liberty: Republican Thought and the Millennium in Revolutionary New England* (New Haven, CT, 1977) pp. 1, 75–76.

16. Hatch, *The Sacred Cause of Liberty*, p. 17, 86–87; R. Bloch, *Visionary Republic: Millennial Themes in American Thought, 1756–1800* (Cambridge, 1985), p. 77; cf. M. A. Noll, *America's God: From Jonathan Edwards to Abraham Lincoln* (Oxford, 2002), pp. 71–72.

17. Henry Clarke, *A History of the Sabbatarian or Seventh Day Baptists in America* (Utica, NY, 1811), p. 165, cited by Hatch, *Sacred Cause of Liberty*, p. 150 n. 26.

18. C. Kidd, "North Britishness and the Nature of Eighteenth-Century Patriotisms," *The Historical Journal* 39 (1996): 361–82, at 374, 377.

19. John Murrin, "A Roof without Walls: The Dilemma of American National Identity," in *Beyond Confederation: Origins of the Constitution and American National Identity*, ed. R. Beeman et al. (Chapel Hill, 1987), pp. 333–48, at 340.

20. Joel Barlow, "The Prospect of Peace," in *The Works of Joel Barlow*, ed. W. K. Bottorff and A. L. Ford, 2 vols., facs. ed. (Gainesville, 1970), 2:10, 11; Cyprian Strong, *God's Care of the New England Colonies* (Hartford, 1777), p. 5; cited by Hatch, *Sacred Cause of Liberty*, p. 60.

21. James Moorhead, "Apocalypticism in Mainstream Protestantism, 1800 to the Present," pp. 92–93; James Moorhead, "The Erosion of Post-millennialism," *Church History* 53 (1984): 72.

22. James Moorhead, *American Apocalypse*, pp. x, 69, 79–80; E. L. Tuveson, *Redeemer Nation* (Chicago, 1968), pp. 189–202, at 202.

23. Cited by H. S. Stout, *Upon the Altar of the Nation: A Moral History of the American Civil War* (New York, 2006), p. 438. Stout's effort to disconnect the British Revolution and the American Revolution from the Civil War discounts eschatological continuities and continuing universalist aspirations.

24. H. Jones, *Union in Peril: The Crisis over the British Intervention in the Civil War* (Chapel Hill, NC, 1992) pp. 27, 164–65, 201, 258 n. 23; Phillips, *Cousins' Wars*, pp. 501, 518; P. S. Foner, *British Labor and the American Civil War* (New York, 1981).

25. *Christ in the Army: A Selection of Sketches of the Work of the U.S. Christian Commission* (Philadelphia, 1865), p. 140; R. R. Booth, "The Relation of the Work of Mission to Christianity," *American Presbyterian and Theological Review*, n.s. 5 (1867): 457, cited by Moorhead, *American Apocalypse*, pp. 77, 199.

CHAPTER 10

1. Pierson, cited by D. L. Robert, *Occupy Until I Come: A. T. Pierson and the Evangelizing of the World* (Grand Rapids, 2003), p. 108; Moody and Scofield, cited by Boyer, *When Time Shall Be No More*, pp. 94, 298. In much the same way Black religious leaders in the post-Reconstruction era grew disillusioned with politics and adopted a Darby-like premillennialism. Notable among them were J. T. Holly (1829–1911), T. G. Stewart (1843–1924), and eventually Elijah Poole (later Elijah Muhammad, 1897–1975).

2. Nietzsche, *Use and Abuse of History* (Vom Nutzen und Nachteil der Historie für das Leben), trans. Adrian Collins (Indianapolis, 1949), pp. 10, 23, 59.

3. Cited by B. D. Wolfe, *Three Who Made a Revolution* (New York, 1964), p. 512.

4. Alexander Blok, "The Twelve," in *"The Twelve" and Other Poems*, trans. J. Stallworthy and P. France (New York, 1970); S. Hackel, *The Poet and the Revolution: Aleksandr Blok's "The Twelve"* (Oxford, 1975), 64–76, 84–88.

5. Lynne Viola, *Peasant Rebels under Stalin: Collectivization and the Culture of Peasant Resistance* (New York, 1996), pp. 51, 52.

6. Ibid., pp. 3, 10, 45, 46, 56, 60, 63, 64, 66.

7. Arthur Koestler et al., *The God That Failed*, ed. Richard Crossman (New York, 1949; London, 1950).

8. Cohn, *Pursuit of the Millennium*, pp. xiv, 310, 311. The "writers and journalists" were not identified.

9. S. H. Zimdars-Swartz and P. E. Zimdars-Swartz, "Apocalypticism in Modern Western Europe," pp. 280–82; S. J. Stein, ""Apocalypticism Outside the Mainstream in the United States," *Encyclopedia of Apocalypticism*, ed. B. McGinn et al. 3 vols. (New York, 1999) 3:130.

10. Boyer, *When Time Shall Be No More*, pp. 154–57, 162; also described in R. H. Popkin and D. S. Katz, *Messianic Revolution: Radical Religious Politics to the End of the Second Millennium* (New York, 1998), p. 213.

11. Martin Luther King Jr., "I Have a Dream," in *I Have a Dream: Writings and Speeches That Changed the World*, ed. J. M. Washington (New York, 1992), p. 105.

12. Richard Wolin, *The Seduction of Unreason: The Intellectual Romance with Fascism from Nietzsche to Post-Modernism* (Princeton, NJ, 2004), p. xiii.

13. Michel Foucault, *The Subject and Power* (1982), reprinted in *Twentieth-Century Europe*, ed. J. Boyer and J. Goldstein (Chicago, 1987), pp. 587, 588. Bruce Brown's *Marx, Freud, and the Critique of Everyday Life* (New York, 1973) provides an early indication of the directions in which radicalism would move.

14. Foucault, *The Subject and Power*, pp. 586, 591–92.

15. A. H. Williamson, "Lapses of Reason," *In These Times* 20 (1996): 16–18.

16. Hal Lindsey, *The Late Great Planet Earth* (Grand Rapids, 1970), p. 150.

17. Ibid., p. 184; Popkin and Katz, *Messianic Revolution*, p. 209.

18. Michelle Goldberg, *Kingdom Coming: The Rise of Christian Nationalism* (New York, 2006), p. 39. The elision from dispensationalism and dominion theology is well illustrated by Steve Schissel and David Brown, *Hal Lindsey and the Restoration of the Jews* (Edmonton, 1990).

19. Jeffrey Rosen, "Is Nothing Secular?," *New York Times Magazine*, January 30, 2000; Helen Whitney, "John Paul II: The Millennial Pope" (Frontline, PBS, 1999); Goldberg, *Kingdom Coming*, p. 70.

20. Popkin and Katz, *Messianic Revolution*, pp. 211–17; K. Phillips, *American Theocracy: The Peril and Politics of Radical Religion, Oil, and Borrowed Money* (New York, 2006), pp. 232–33.

21. Martin Lings, *The Eleventh Hour: The Spiritual Crisis in the Modern World in the Light of Tradition and Prophecy* (Cambridge, 1987), pp. 2, 7, 13, 15, 19–23, 33–34, and passim.

22. Phillips, *American Theocracy*, p. 232.

23. Seyyed Hosseim Nasr, *Traditional Islam in the Modern World* (London, 1987), p. 85.

INDEX

About the Author

ARTHUR H. WILLIAMSON is professor of history at Cal State Sacramento and is the author of six books, including *The Expulsion of the Jews*, *The British Union*, and *Shaping the Stuart World*.